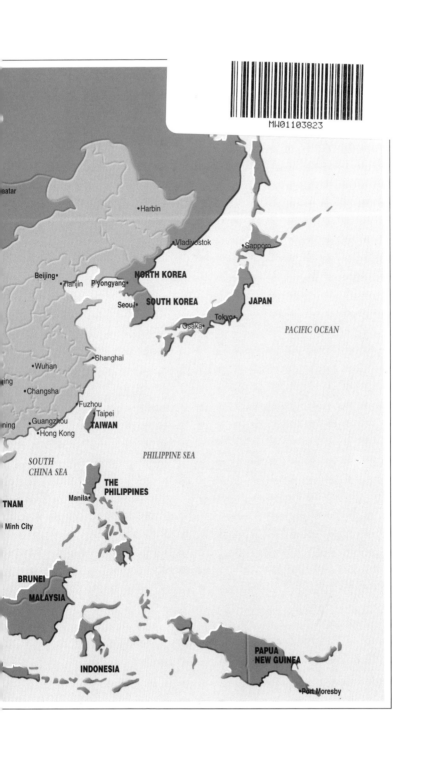

MW01103823

·aatar

·Harbin

·Vladivostok   ·Sapporo

Beijing·   NORTH KOREA
·Tianjin   P'yongyang·
                    Seoul·   SOUTH KOREA   JAPAN
                              ·Osaka   Tokyo·
                                                    PACIFIC OCEAN

·Shanghai

·Wuhan
ing
·Changsha
                    Fuzhou
                      ·Taipei
ning ·Guangzhou   TAIWAN
      ·Hong Kong

                    PHILIPPINE SEA
SOUTH
CHINA SEA
                         THE
                         PHILIPPINES
TNAM   Manila·

Minh City

BRUNEI
MALAYSIA

                                             PAPUA
                                             NEW GUINEA
      INDONESIA
                                        ·Port Moresby

INTERPRETING CHINESE FOREIGN POLICY

INTERPRETING CHINESE FOREIGN POLICY

The Micro-Macro Linkage Approach

Quansheng Zhao

HONG KONG
OXFORD UNIVERSITY PRESS
OXFORD   NEW YORK
1996

Oxford University Press

Oxford New York
Athens Auckland Bangkok Bogota Bombay
Buenos Aires Calcutta Cape Town Dar es Salaam
Delhi Florence Hong Kong Istanbul Karachi
Kuala Lumpur Madras Madrid Melbourne
Mexico City Nairobi Paris Singapore
Taipei Tokyo Toronto

and associated companies in
Berlin Ibadan

Oxford is a trade mark of Oxford University Press

First published 1996

This impression (lowest digit)
1 3 5 7 9 10 8 6 4 2

Published in the United States
by Oxford University Press, New York

British Library Cataloguing in Publication Data
available

Library of Congress Cataloging-in-Publication Data
Zhao, Quansheng.
Interpreting Chinese foreign policy : the micro-macro linkage
approach / Quansheng Zhao.
p. cm.
Includes bibliographical references and index.
ISBN 0–19–587429–3 (alk. paper)
ISBN 0–19–587430–7 (pbk. : alk. paper)
1. China—Foreign relations—1949– 2. International relations.
3. China—Politics and government—1976– I. Title.
DS777.8.Z43 1996
327.51—dc20 96–8219
CIP

Printed in Hong Kong
Published by Oxford University Press (China) Ltd
18/F Warwick House, Taikoo Place, 979 King's Road,
Quarry Bay, Hong Kong

For Robert A. Scalapino

Acknowledgements

This book is dedicated to Professor Robert A. Scalapino, who, since 1981, has remained a *liangshi yiyou* for me, a thoughtful teacher and a trusted friend; I have always appreciated his guidance and friendship. Deep gratitude also goes to Harry Harding, Allen Whiting, and Tang Tsou, who read the early version of the entire manuscript and provided constructive advice and encouragement.

I also appreciate valuable comments on parts of the book at various stages from two different groups of scholars. The first group includes China specialists: Doak Barnett, Tom Bernstein, Tom Christensen, Deborah Davis, Thomas Fingar, Carol Hamrin, Gaochao He, Alastair Johnston, Samuel Kim, Kenneth Lieberthal, Gerard Mare, Peter Moody, Michel Oksenberg, Lucian Pye, Stanley Rosen, Lynn White, Brantly Womack, and David Zweig. The second group consists of micro-macro linkage theorists or international relations theorists: Alexander George, John Montgomery, Richard Munch, Mancur Olson, George Ritzer, James Rosenau, and Neil Smelser. I would like to pay special thanks to Jing Mei, with whom several extensive discussions about the micro-macro linkage approach were conducted during my post-doctoral research appointment at Harvard University. I also thank Mary Child and Nigel Quinney for their excellent and professional editing, and Elaine Dowson, Shaozhou Ma, Paula Smith, and Tin Sang Yip for research or technical assistance.

The early versions of several chapters benefited from comments at the following institutions where I made presentations over the past few years: the American Political Science Association annual meetings (1990–5), the Association of Asian Studies annual meeting (1995), the American Society for Public Administration annual meeting (1992), Harvard University, the University of California at Berkeley, Yale University, Simmons College, St. John's University, College of William and Mary, Old Dominion University, University of Hawaii, University of Arizona, the University of Massachusetts at Amherst, the American University, the University of Kansas, the United States Naval Postgraduate School, the East-West Center, the United States Institute of Peace, the Atlantic Council of the United States, the Chinese Academy of Social Sciences, the Chinese Academy of Military Science, Soka University/the University of Macau, Seoul National University, Korea University, Hanyang University, the Korea Development Institute, the Institute of East Asian Political Economy (Singapore), the *Straits Times*, the Institute of International Relations (Taipei), the National Sun Yat-sen University (Kaohsiung), the Hong Kong University of Science and Technology, the University of Hong Kong, and the Chinese University of Hong Kong.

The manuscript's initial draft and substantial revisions were completed during my two separate one-year fellowships: Peace Fellow at the United States Institute of Peace in 1991, and Pacific Basin Research Fellow at Harvard University between 1993 and 1994. The intellectual environment and research support at these two institutions were most rewarding. I am grateful to Old Dominion University, the Fletcher School of Law and Diplomacy at Tufts University, the East–West Center, the Hong Kong University of Science and Technology, the Pacific Cultural Foundation, the United Daily Cultural Foundation, and the Ohira Memorial Foundation either for institutional support or for research and publication grants at different stages. I would like to thank also the PRC's Taiwan Affairs Office and Taiwan's Mainland Affairs Council for providing me with opportunities to conduct field research on both sides of the Taiwan Straits in the summer of 1992 in China, and the summer of 1993 in Taiwan.

Several chapters in this book are based on previously published articles of mine. I have substantially revised and enlarged these articles, along the theoretical framework developed in this book. I thank the following publishers for permission to use these materials for this book: Sage Publications for 'Domestic Factors of Chinese Foreign Policy: From Vertical to Horizontal Authoritarianism,' *The Annals of the American Academy of Political and Social Science*, vol. 519 (January 1992); *The American Asian Review* for 'Achieving Maximum Advantage: Rigidity and Flexibility in Chinese Foreign Policy,' vol. 13, no. 1 (Spring 1995); Walter de Gruyter & Co. for 'The Political Economy of Japan's Relations with China,' *Business and the Contemporary World*, vol. 8, no. 2 (1996); The Chinese University Press for 'China's Foreign Relations in the Asia-Pacific Region: Modernization, Nationalism, and Regionalism,' in *China Review 1995*, ed. by Lo Chi Kin, Suzanne Pepper, and Tsui Kai Yuen, 1995; and Heldref Publications for 'Patterns and Choices of Chinese Foreign Policy,' *Asian Affairs*, vol. 20, no. 1 (Spring 1993).

Finally, my warmest appreciation goes to my wife Jiujiu, son Justin Xu, and daughter Jennifer Xiaolu, without whose enduring support and understanding this book would never have been completed.

QUANSHENG ZHAO
March 1996

Foreword

Chinese foreign policy is a fascinating, but frustrating subject. It has existed for more than four millennia, yet lacks a comprehensive history in English. It projects the world's largest population onto the world scene, yet the relatively few Chinese scholars on Chinese foreign policy are outnumbered by their foreign counterparts. Its records are enshrined in meticulously preserved archives, ancient and modern, yet access to them requires mastering a difficult language as well as political permission in Beijing or Taipei.

As if these were not enough obstacles, post-war Sino-American relations added political hurdles that effectively precluded objective analysis at home as well as abroad. In China, Communist Party control straitjacketed all writing on foreign policy in general, and Chinese foreign policy in particular. After Mao's death, constraints loosened up with respect to wider international relations, but they did not disappear entirely. Moreover, they remained firmly in place with respect to serious analysis of the People's Republic of China's (PRC) foreign policy.

In the United States, the 'Who lost China?' furore that followed the Communist victory on the Mainland sharply inhibited American scholars from studying Chinese foreign policy as a lifetime enquiry; less than a handful of fully trained specialists emerged in the 1950s. Chinese scholars in the United States felt even more leery of addressing Beijing's foreign policy in anything but standard anti-communist terms, lest they suffer political opprobrium. Last, but not least limiting was the total absence of Chinese from the PRC who could share their knowledge and insight with foreign audiences and scholars. The result was a scarcity of genuine scholarship on Chinese foreign policy during the first twenty years of the PRC.

Fortunately, the situation has basically improved since the full restoration of US–PRC relations in 1979. American and Chinese scholars, here and in China, both separately and jointly are laying the foundation for richer and more rigorous analysis by exploiting newly released archival materials, oral history, interviews, and other sources. Professor Zhao exemplifies this new generation of scholars.

However, another set of obstacles continue to confront both teachers and students in this field. Formidable challenges lie in mastering the language, the history, and what might be called the 'political culture', of China. Once having entered the field of Sinology, the political scientist must then master the theories, models, concepts, and methods of both comparative politics and international relations. In 1976 I co-chaired a workshop addressing these problems and proposed ways to bridge the gap between general international relations specialists and Chinese foreign policy scholars. In 1995 a second such workshop addressed the same problems in virtually identical language. After twenty years the epistemological and intellectual gap remained intact, in part because of the conflicting demands on time, energy, and financial resources, both at the collective and the individual levels, in the field of Chinese foreign policy.

Professor Zhao's book is especially welcome under these circumstances. His life in the PRC sensitized him to the patterns of politics and policy-making, while his academic maturation in the United States equipped him with American disciplinary tools for research and analysis. His adaptation and application of a social science theory concept — micro-macro linkage — to the study of Chinese foreign policy is to be appreciated as an early attempt to bring theoretical rigour to the field of China studies. His illuminating use of this model and its concepts enrich case-studies drawn on valuable interviews, Japanese and Chinese sources, and his keen sense of strategy and tactics. This study also opens a door onto a new direction for future Chinese foreign policy studies and identifies a range of areas and topics for new research.

Professor Zhao's contribution is also to be appreciated for addressing the diverse audiences of peers and students. Since 1979, a wealth of articles and books have begun to fill the virtual vacuum of the previous two decades. To a certain extent, however, these fall short of what is needed by the non-specialist teacher and undergraduate student. Some studies lack any conceptual framework, emerging either as contemporary history or current events analysis. Other works are tenure-driven, written primarily for peer review and difficult to use in the classroom.

This is not to disparage the growing library of Chinese, British, Australian, Japanese, American, Canadian, and more recently Russian, writings in English on Chinese foreign policy. The subject has spawned a burgeoning literature in journals, doctoral dissertations, monographs, and conference symposia. However, the dearth of single-volume studies that combine the sophistication of disciplined scholarship with the intelligibility of a high-grade textbook makes Professor Zhao's study a genuine contribution to students and teachers alike.

An extra contribution is provided by the focus on Sino-Japanese relations as a case-study demonstrating the utility of the micro-macro linkage approach which Professor Zhao has adopted. This relationship is central to the nature of East Asian international relations in the next century. These two neighbours have grossly disparate power in population, economic growth, and military potential. Yet they must overcome the historical heritage of conflict so as to manage peacefully their territorial conflict in the East China Sea and their political rivalry in the region. How they cope with this challenge will depend largely on their mutual perceptions and decision-making processes, insightfully illuminated by Professor Zhao's research.

After the collapse of the Soviet Union, foreign observers speculated on how the PRC would survive the multitude of social, economic, and political problems attending the transition from communist rule to a market economy. The gradual fading of Deng Xiaoping from political leadership spurred worst-case forecasts of regime collapse either through a succession struggle or from massive public opposition to corruption, inflation, and unemployment, or by both contingencies interacting.

Under such uncertain circumstances, it might seem better to wait until the dust settles before making Chinese foreign policy under the PRC a serious subject for political science. But the PRC is not the Soviet Union; the nation-state will not end with the regime. China will remain China, whether under the same title or another one. Professor Zhao's analysis provides a sense of the enduring qualities that characterize *Chinese* foreign policy, before, during, and almost certainly after communist rule. The foreign policy agenda may change but the policy process will not, at least not in any fundamental way. Therefore, *Interpreting Chinese Foreign Policy* will have a long shelf life, regardless of what happens in Beijing.

ALLEN WHITING
Washington D.C.
January 1996

Contents

Abbreviations

ADB	Asian Development Bank
APEC	Asia-Pacific Economic Cooperation
ASEAN	Association of South East Asian Nations
CCP	Chinese Communist Party
COCOM	Coordinating Committee of the Consultative Group (established by Western powers to control the trade of strategic goods with the Communist bloc)
DPP	Democratic Progressive Party
GATT	General Agreement on Tariffs and Trade
IEOs	International economic organizations
KMT	Kuomintang (Nationalist Party)
MFA	Ministry of Foreign Affairs
MFN	Most-favoured-nation (treatment)
NPC	National People's Congress
ODA	Official Development Assistance
PLA	People's Liberation Army
PRC	People's Republic of China
UN	United Nations
WTO	World Trade Organization

Chinese Terms

gaige	reform
kaifang	opening (to the outside world)
linghuoxing	flexibility
sanhe yishao	three reconciliations and one reduction
taidu	independence of Taiwan
yibiandao	'leaning to one side' (Beijing's policy of leaning towards the Soviet Union in the 1950s)
yuanzexing	strict adherence to principle

Note: Following common practice in the West, Chinese names and Korean names in this book are given in the Asian manner, surname first, such as Deng Xiaoping and Kim Il-sung; whereas Japanese names are placed in the Western order, given name first and surname second, such as Toshiki Kaifu.

Tables

Figures

Figures

Part I

INTRODUCTION

1 The Study of Chinese Foreign Policy

This book has two objectives. First, to offer a 'bird's eye view', or overview of Chinese foreign policy since the establishment of the People's Republic of China (PRC) in 1949. In particular, it analyses the process by which China gradually evolved from a revolutionary power into a post-revolutionary power, while adjusting itself to the world nation–state system. At the same time, it provides a means of grasping the essential character of Chinese foreign policy behaviour and the shift in that character since the beginning of China's 'opening and reform' (*kaifang he gaige*) in 1978. In this sense, it may be most valuable to those who are interested in discovering the broad outlines of, and the key factors that shape Chinese foreign policy.

The second objective is to call to the attention of Chinese foreign policy specialists the *micro-macro linkage approach*, to further bridge the gap between China studies and social science theory. The micro-macro linkage approach, as the name suggests, examines Chinese foreign policy at both the *micro* and *macro* levels (these categories will be defined in the following chapter). Instead of concentrating on a single level of analysis (such as the domestic determinants or the international determinants of Chinese foreign policy), this book will examine the cross-influences of influential elements at various levels. The model adopted in this book focuses on the processes, situations, and structures of Chinese foreign policy, analysing the interaction of such key factors as the international environment, domestic constraints, and individual decision-makers, which have a combined impact on Chinese foreign policy. This approach provides a better understanding of Chinese foreign policy behaviour patterns, the sources of these patterns, and policy choices.

The micro-macro linkage approach, when applied to Chinese foreign policy concentrates on three dimensions. First, it analyses the changes over time in: Beijing's interpretation of the external environment and China's internal developments; the impact on foreign policy of learning and adaptation; and the leadership's changing priorities in foreign policy. Second, it illuminates the societal and institutional inputs to Chinese foreign policy, changes in the rules, norms, and mechanisms in the policy-making process, and the scope and degree of participation in the formulation of foreign policy. Third, it studies: the sources of Chinese power politics and authority; regime legitimacy; individual leaders' policy preferences; and Chinese foreign policy strategies, tactics, and behaviour patterns. This approach makes it possible to offer a comprehensive interpretation of Chinese foreign policy without falling into the traps of 'historicism' or, what Andrew Nathan (1993: 935) termed, a 'culturally particularist' view (that is, a view of Chinese foreign policy that is limited by culturally inbred assumptions). Before further elaborating on the micro-macro linkage approach (the focus of the next chapter) and reviewing the various established approaches to foreign policy studies, it is necessary to discuss briefly China's international role since 1949 and the study of Chinese foreign policy in general.

China's International Role

Interpreting Chinese foreign policy is an important key to understanding the tides of global affairs in the 1990s, not only because China, with the world's largest population, wields demographic (and now growing economic) clout, but also because it is arguably the most dynamic country in the second half of this century. Its dynamism bears watching for its immediate, practical relevance to policy-makers, and its longer-term interest to scholars as part of China's long continuum toward modernity.

China's transformation from a revolutionary power to a post-revolutionary state, and the effect of this change on China's external behaviour, has drawn broad attention.[1] This profound change is reflected in the apparent shift in national priorities between the two major periods in PRC history — the era of Mao Zedong (1949–76) and the era of Deng Xiaoping (since 1978).[2] From the first era to the latter, China's national priorities for domestic and foreign policies changed dramatically; while for Mao the enchanted word was 'revolution', the key utterance for Deng was 'modernization'.[3] One needs to comprehend this change to interpret the development of Chinese foreign policy.

It is also important, of course, to view China within the context of world politics. Three geographical areas of conflict have decisively shaped world politics and the global balance of power since World War II: Europe, the very centre of the Cold War waged by the United States

and the Soviet Union; the Middle East, where enduring hostility between Israel and the Arab countries has frequently erupted in open
warfare; and East Asia, home to numerous disputes, most notably the
Korean War, the Vietnam War and the Sino-Vietnam War, and the
confrontation between Taiwan and the PRC. In each of the East Asian
disputes, China has been a major player, confronting not only other
regional players but also the two superpowers. Chinese foreign policy
has thus acquired both regional and global significance, a significance
that is certain to grow further throughout the 1990s and into the twenty-
first century.

In the post-Cold War era, every major power, as well as every state
within East Asia, must factor China as a key element into its foreign
policy considerations. This state of affairs was reflected in *The Far
Eastern Economic Review*'s 1994 'Year in Review', the China section
of which began, 'China continued to play its now-familiar role as a
leading magnet for investment and diplomatic attention.'[4] James Baker,
Secretary of State under President George Bush, described China's
important international role as ranging from 'missile and nuclear proliferation, to cooperation in the Gulf crisis, to resolving regional conflicts', which he said, 'underscores the need for sustained engagement
with China on issues of common concern' (Baker, 1991/92: 16). For
scholars too, the study of Beijing's role in East Asia and in the international community has become a key area within the field of international relations and foreign policy studies.

The most apparent evidence of China's rising importance is its rapidly
growing economic power. According to a widely publicized International
Monetary Fund report (*World Economy Outlook*, 1993) and other similar
reports, China's economy could overtake that of Japan in absolute size
and, if its growth continues at the very high rates of the late 1980s and
early 1990s, the Chinese economy would become larger than the current economy of the United States 'shortly after the turn of the century'
(N. Lardy 1994: 106–110). A report to the Trilateral Commission
(Y. Funabashi, M. Oksenberg, and H. Weiss, 1994: 32) entitled *An
Emerging China in a World of Interdependence*, made the following
statement:

The development of a vigorous market economy in China, a country of 1.2
billion people, is surely one of the most significant events in recent history.
Whether measured using current exchange rates or on a purchasing-power-
parity basis, China's GNP is rising at an unprecedented pace, outstripping even
the miraculous growth of the 'East Asia Tigers' . . .

Two *New York Times* reporters, who covered China from 1988 to 1994, were inspired by these reports to speculate further about the future of Greater China (the PRC, Taiwan, Hong Kong, and Macau):

The global economy is sometimes said to be tripolar, revolving around the United States, Japan and the European Community. But Greater China is rapidly becoming a fourth pole, a new pillar of the international economy.[5]

They continued, to posit optimistically that China has 'a chance to grow and prosper and become a major international power, perhaps eventually a superpower such as the world has never known'. Such reports and speculation reflect China's concentration on its national priority since the late 1970s — economic growth.

On the other hand, there are also a number of far less optimistic predictions about China's future, particularly in the forthcoming post-Deng era. In a study released in early 1995 commissioned by the US Defense Department, half of the panel of China experts argued that China would experience a 'Soviet-style break-up' within seven years of Deng's death.[6]

On the economic front, there are also more gloomy reports. In terms of energy production, which is key to Beijing's modernization drive, China became a net importer in 1994, after several decades as a large exporter. China's population of 1.2 billion amounts to 21 per cent of the world's population. But it has only 2.4 per cent of proven global oil reserves and 1 per cent of gas reserves. Unless new fields can be brought into production, the country will have to import about 50 million metric tons (373.1 million barrels) of oil by the end of the decade, and 100 million tons by the year 2010.[7] Whether the future of China's economy is bleak or bright, there is no doubt that it will continue to be of global interest and impact as the world enters the twenty-first century.

In addition to the growing attractions of the Chinese market, China's strategic importance has been increasingly recognized since the world entered the 1990s. US Senator Sam Nunn highlighted this point when he forcefully advocated awarding most-favoured-nation status to China in 1994, simply because the strategic relationship between the two countries is 'too important to sacrifice'.[8] Strategic and economic factors were certainly the main considerations behind US President Bill Clinton's decision in May 1994 to renew China's Most-favoured-nation (MFN) status and to de-link the issue from human rights.[9]

Throughout its history, the PRC's ability to promote or to undermine peace and stability has been an important concern of China's neighbours, and of other nations in the global community.

On many occasions, the PRC has been willing to resolve external conflicts through peaceful means. Its border disputes with Nepal, Mongolia, and Afghanistan, for example, were settled peacefully by bilateral border treaties in 1961, 1962, and 1963 respectively. However, China has not hesitated to use military force to resolve external conflicts whenever the Beijing leadership deemed that there was no other alternative. In order to understand better the importance of China's strategic position, let us briefly review the recent history of China's use of military force with the United States and the Soviet Union or their allies. China fought, directly or indirectly, with the United States four times:

- once, directly, in Korea, during the Korean War in the early 1950s;
- twice through conflicts in Vietnam (once supporting North Vietnam against the US in the 1960s; and once fighting against US-backed South Vietnam over disputed islands in the South China Sea in 1974); and
- during the 1950s with the US-protected Taiwan regime over its off-shore islands.

At the same time, China fought against the former Soviet Union or Soviet-backed regimes three times:

- a direct border clash with the Soviet Union in 1969;
- the border war with India (morally supported by the Soviet Union) in 1962; and
- a punitive war of invasion in Vietnam, which had a military alliance with the Soviet Union, in 1979.

Chapter 3 will present more discussion of China's military conflicts in the context of China's foreign policy, although this study will not provide a detailed analysis of these military actions.[10] It will, however, seek to provide a useful conceptual framework and to answer such questions as why the Chinese resort to military measures on some occasions, while on others they are able to resolve conflicts peacefully. Before getting into a detailed discussion of the need for a new Chinese foreign policy research agenda along more theoretical lines, let us first briefly review developments in the study of Chinese foreign policy over the past two decades.

Chinese Foreign Policy Studies in Review

The study of China's foreign policy has long received less scholarly attention than the study of China's domestic politics. This point was ·

forcefully raised in a report in 1977 by the Steering Group on Chinese Foreign Policy and International Relations, jointly sponsored by the Social Science Research Council and the American Council of Learned Societies. The committee, headed by Allen Whiting, a leading scholar of Chinese foreign policy, conducted a survey of the field and concluded that the study of Chinese foreign policy was much less common and less supported in the China field than the study of domestic policy (Whiting, 1977). Since that time there has been significant progress in the study of Chinese foreign policy; both the quantity and quality of the published books and journal articles have been raised to a new level.[11]

The most notable reason for this progress is the growing recognition of the importance of studying Chinese foreign policy; political scientists and policy-makers increasingly identify China, along with the Asia-Pacific area, as one of the most important countries to study and research. In the early history of the PRC, the sheer size and power potential of the country alone were impetus to attempt to understand Chinese foreign policy. But by the 1990s, China has also become such an important and active player in the theatre of contemporary world politics and economic development, that the very sustenance of a stable and peaceful world requires a genuine comprehension, on the part of Beijing and other capitals, of the factors that influence Chinese external policy.

Given China's growing economic and military might and its regional as well as global influence, the study of Chinese foreign policy naturally has become a very real interest for its neighbours in the Asia-Pacific area, as well as for specialists of international relations and Asian studies. This heightened attention has brought an increase in research and educational institutions for the study of Chinese foreign policy; this, in turn, has improved the quality and quantity of research on the subject.

Having discussed the above progress in the field, however, one should not ignore problems in the study of Chinese foreign policy. Harry Harding, a top sinologist, has identified 'weakness' as a major problem and one of the 'unique characteristics' of this field. According to Harding, three factors have caused this deficiency: first, 'the uncertain role of comparative foreign policy in political science in general'; second, 'the resulting fact that, until recently, most of the scholars writing on Chinese foreign policy . . . have been trained primarily as students of domestic Chinese affairs'; and third, 'the parallel fact that many of those have also been engaged in other lines of research, as well as in drawing the implications for US policy toward China'.[12]

One other conspicuous problem is a lack of imaginative and theoretical approaches that could lead to comprehensive and conceptual ways

to interpret Chinese foreign policy. A number of leading China specialists have noted this problem. Kenneth Lieberthal, for example, has
suggested that 'the study of Chinese diplomatic history has become
fairly well developed, the study of Chinese foreign policy decision-
making remains very undeveloped, and the study of China's foreign
relations is barely on the radar scope.' He attributed this underdevelop-
ment, in part, to the 'paucity of theoretical rigor'.[13] Samuel Kim (1994a:
10–11), a well-known scholar of Chinese foreign policy, has also asserted that 'although the 1980s witnessed a dramatic increase in Chinese
and Western scholarly monographs, there is as yet no widely accepted
metatheory that explains the wellsprings of Chinese behaviour in any
succinct and persuasive fashion.' He further calls for more 'integrated
and synthetic theoretical approaches' that will 'cross-fertilize and in-
vigorate' the study of Chinese foreign policy. With these critical assessments in mind, let us look at various approaches in the field that may
be called *single-level analysis*.

Single-Level Approaches to Analysis

Students of international relations have long been concerned with the
question of what constitutes the appropriate level and unit of analysis
for the study of a country's foreign policy. Kenneth Waltz, for example,
in his classic study of international relations theory (Waltz, 1959),
explicitly distinguishes three different levels: the individual, the state,
and the international system. The various approaches scholars have
taken can, in fact, be divided into two groups: *single-level analysis* and
multi-level analysis.

Let us first look at some of the basic single-level approaches that are
popular in the field. For years international relations theorists and foreign policy specialists have debated the relative weight of internal and
external factors, as well as individual decision-making, in determining
a country's foreign policy and international behaviour. Some advocates
of the school of *realism*, for example, define the primary goal of foreign
policy as survival in the international system. From the realist's perspective, the issues that have the most influence on international behaviour are security, military capability, political alliances among states,
and the pursuit and balance of power (Morgenthau and Thompson,
1985; Waltz, 1979). This 'billiard-ball' model, as Christopher Hill and
Margot Light (1985: 157) have termed it, sees foreign policy positions
as determined primarily by the interplay of international forces.

Interdependency theorists, on the other hand, analyse the multiple channels and actors in the interaction of world politics, the impact of non-military instruments of state craft, and the role of economic variables in the international system that make the world more complicated and interdependent (Keohane and Nye, 1989). In terms of foreign policy issues, many believers of interdependency emphasize the importance of international political economy, and pay more attention to the influence of domestic politics and the ways in which its fluctuations shape perceptions of national interest and the formulation of diplomatic strategies. Specific foreign-policy decisions, as Alexander George (1980: 114) points out, 'may be more responsive to the internal dynamics of such a policy-making process than to the requirements of the foreign-policy problem itself'.

Social-psychologists (or *political psychologists*) take individual decision-makers as their unit of analysis and the behaviour of these individuals as the object of systematic observation. According to this school of thought, although the state is the basic actor in international politics, state actions can be analysed most effectively by focusing on the behaviour of 'those individuals whose responsibility is to act for the state' (Herbert Kelman, 1965: 586). The role of decision-makers in the formulation of foreign policy, therefore, is elevated to the predominant determinant of foreign policy.

All these schools of thought — realist, interdependency, or social psychological — when applied to the study of foreign policy, can be more or less regarded as representing single-level analysis. As illustrated in Table 1.1, each attributes the primary inputs to the formulation of foreign policy to one main factor. To discuss the policy-making process further, we first need to define two important concepts — *input* and *output*. According to Karl Deutsch (1966: 88), output means 'any change produced in the surroundings by the object'; whereas input

Table 1.1: Single-Level Analysis Approaches

	Input	Output
Type A	International Constraints (Structure and System)	Foreign Policy
Type B	Domestic Determinants (Society and Institutions)	Foreign Policy
Type C	Decision-makers' Influence (Psychological and Ideological Factors)	Foreign Policy

means 'any event external to the object that modifies this object in any manner'. David Easton (1965: 37–39) also stresses, 'demands as the inputs of a system'.[14] That is to say, the policy-making process is affected by *demands* from various directions and sources. Type A views the international environment as the principal source of policy inputs. Type B sees domestic determinants as the major factor; whereas Type C believes that individual decision-makers hold the key.[15] Understandably, the following areas are more useful sources of data for fleshing out the above theoretical models respectively: the interactions among states in the international arena to the first approach, the study of the domestic roots of foreign policy to the second approach; the psychological and ideological motivations of decision-makers to the third approach.

The differences among various schools of thought in the study of Chinese foreign policy correspond with the development of approaches in international relations theory as a whole. In practice, however, one should notice that people writing at one level may well be aware of the multi-faceted, multi-layered reality of international relations and may simply want to elucidate one part, without necessarily believing in the overall primacy or exclusiveness of that argument or level.[16] In some cases, with edited, collective volumes in particular, scholars may be assigned to concentrate on one level to analyse Chinese foreign policy.

A number of studies concentrate on the international constraints of Chinese foreign policy (the Type A approach) with specific purposes. Several works, for example, have examined China's position in the world system and the international community (Barnett, 1977; Yahuda, 1983a; Chan, 1989; Dreyer and Kim, 1989; Jacobson and Oksenberg, 1990), or the Sino-US–USSR strategic triangle (Kim, 1987; Chang, 1990; Ross, 1993). From these studies, we may learn a great deal about the international environment that Beijing has faced since 1949, and about China's relations with the major players in world political economy.

Approaches of Types B and C have also been applied to the analysis of specific aspects of Chinese foreign policy. On the institutional and societal level of analysis, a number of scholars have examined Chinese foreign policy behaviour by focusing on the decision-making process (Garver, 1982; Barnett, 1985; Zhao, 1992). Along the same line, the perceptions of the Chinese elites toward the outside world have also become a focus of research. Studies on Chinese perceptions of the major powers, such as the Soviet Union (Rozman, 1987), Japan (Whiting, 1989), and the United States (Shambaugh, 1991), are works of this kind, and have attracted attention in the field. Others have attempted to study decision-makers' strategies (Bobrow, Chan, and Kringen, 1979) or coalition politics (Pollack, 1984a).

Another group of studies deals with China's bilateral relations with other countries without necessarily concentrating on one particular level. These include studies of China's relations with the United States (Tow, 1991; Harding, 1992; Foot, 1995; Ross, 1995), Japan (C. Lee, 1976 and 1984; Bedeski, 1983), the Soviet Union (Dittmer, 1992), and Vietnam (Ross, 1988). Some focus on the making of China policy in other countries, such as in the United States (Sutter, 1983; Tan, 1992), the former Soviet Union (Rozman, 1985), and Japan (Zhao, 1993a). These analyses generally concentrate on the ongoing bilateral relationships, starting with neither the international nor the domestic elements, but rather somewhere in the middle — that is, choosing not to emphasize any one particular element.

Nevertheless, it is noteworthy that there are indeed preferences among scholars who consider one particular level of elements to be the primary source of Chinese foreign policy. Scholars, for example, who subscribe to the Type A approach have emphasized the importance of international constraints to the formulation of Chinese foreign policy (Levine, 1980; Ng-Quinn, 1983; Pollack, 1984b; Ross, 1986; Cumings, 1989; Tow, 1994). They especially stress the extent to which the international environment, and superpower bipolarity in particular, frames Chinese foreign policy options. William Tow (1994: 120) for example, contends that, 'Since the PRC's inception, its foreign policy has been most influenced by the balance-of-power, state-centric approach to international politics and security.' According to this group of scholars, the internal elements of Chinese politics are less important to Chinese foreign policy, or as Jonathan Pollack (1984a) puts it, they are 'not the critical determinant'. Robert Ross (1986: 286) has argued along this line that, 'the relative importance of domestic politics has been a function of the range of choice allowed by the pattern of triangular (i.e. Soviet–US–China) politics.'

According to this analytical line, Chinese foreign policy issues and external actions are seen as responsive to the changing dynamics of the international environment. 'The external sources of Chinese policies', Bruce Cumings (1989: 220) argues, can be viewed as 'a matter of conditioning and shaping' Chinese options. One well-known example is China's *yibiandao* (leaning to one side) policy, meaning to favour the Soviet Union (*vis-à-vis* the United States). This policy was begun by Mao Zedong in June 1949 and it lasted until the late 1950s. The 'leaning toward the Soviets' policy has been viewed as a direct result of the bipolar structure of world politics in the Cold War era.[17]

Those who favour the Type B analysis focus on the domestic determinants of Chinese foreign policy (Gottlieb, 1977; Lieberthal, 1984;
Mancall, 1984; Bachman, 1989). Both scholars and policy-makers have
increasingly recognized the influence of domestic politics on foreign
policy, and a number of commentators have gone so far as to claim, as
David Bachman (1989: 31) does, that domestic factors 'have had a
greater impact than international factors in shaping Chinese foreign
policy'. Each of China's domestic political campaigns (such as the
Anti-Rightist Campaign of 1957, the Great Leap Forward of 1958, and
the peak of the Cultural Revolution of 1966 to 1969), Kenneth Lieberthal
(1984: 43) asserts, 'has had clear and direct implications for its posture
toward the rest of the world'. This school of thought has emphasized
that domestic factors are important to every country's foreign policy,
but they are perhaps more important to the PRC's external behaviour
than to that of most other countries. The constant challenge which
Taiwan presents in both the domestic and international arenas has made
Beijing supersensitive to such issues as regime legitimacy, territorial
sovereignty, and national survival.

Adherents of the Type C approach believe that foreign policy is
determined, ultimately, at the level of individual decision-making, and
take this as the primary level for analysing Chinese foreign policy.
Cultural (political) psychology, and group theory are the preferred
perspectives of this school of thought, which argues for the decisive
impact of the political leaders and their ideologies, strategies, tactics,
and personal styles, on the direction of Chinese foreign policy (see Van
Ness, 1970; Hinton, 1972; Armstrong, 1977; O'Leary, 1980; Shih, 1990;
Hunt, 1996). A factor related to this psycho-cultural and ideological-
based perspective is that internal power struggles among political leaders
profoundly affect the directions of Chinese politics, which, in turn,
influence Beijing's foreign policy orientations.

The most notable example of this Type C approach is the *Mao-in-
command model* (Tsou and M. Halperin, 1965; B. Schwartz, 1967;
Teiwes, 1974; Pye, 1976; M. Meisner, 1977).[18] This analytical approach,
which was especially popular during the 1960s and 1970s when Mao
was still the dominant figure on China's political scene, assumes that
Chinese domestic and foreign policies 'reflected the changing attitudes
of a Party Chairman who remained very much in control of his country's
affairs' (Harding, 1984: 296). In a comprehensive study of Mao Zedong's
major policy commitments over half a century (1921–76) (six out of
twenty policy commitments during this period were foreign policy
issues). Michel Oksenberg (1976: 23) concludes that Mao 'achieved the
least success in the foreign policy and economic realms'. This is a

typical example of foreign policy analysis which takes as its key causal factors an individual leader's personal commitment and preferences.

While each of these three approaches is valuable in explaining some aspects of Chinese external behaviour, all have inherent shortcomings. Advocates of the importance of international constraints have often overemphasized the role played by the international system in the formulation of Chinese foreign policy. According to the *world structural view*, for example, the bipolar nature of the post-war international structure has severely limited Chinese foreign policy options. These limitations have made Chinese foreign policy 'largely consistent since the end of World War II' and 'even in the post-Mao era', because Beijing has been forced to lean toward either the United States or the Soviet Union (Ng-Quinn, 1983: 204, 211). China's strategic and economic policies throughout the 1970s are seen as 'shaped' by the United States, as China adopted the policies that 'the United States wanted it to have' (Cumings, 1989: 220). By overemphasizing the impact from outside, the influences of Chinese domestic politics and Beijing's ability to maintain a 'neutral position' or an independent foreign policy have been underplayed or altogether neglected.

Conversely, but equally mistakenly, scholars who focus on domestic constraints have often paid too much attention to factors such as the policy-making process and political institutions, as well as to political culture and ideology, and have overlooked the influence of the changing international structure. For example, as Samuel Kim (1989: 24) points out, if all Chinese political factions in the post-Mao era were committed to Mao's vision of an evil 'revisionist' Soviet Union as some of these scholars believed, 'any immediate prospect of Sino-Soviet rapprochement 'would have been impossible'.[19] Yet that is exactly what happened when the two communist giants gradually normalized their relations from the middle to late 1980s.

As for those studies that concentrate on the part played by individual decision-makers, these analyses also tend toward over-simplification. By applying a psycho-cultural perspective, for example, Chih-yu Shih (1990) has attributed Chinese foreign policy behaviour patterns over the past century — from Li Hongzhang of the Qing Dynasty, to Yuan Shikai and Chiang Kai-shek of the Republic of China, to Mao Zedong and Zhou Enlai of socialist China, and finally to Deng Xiaoping of the present, reform-oriented China — to a single factor, namely, 'face-saving'. Although this approach may be helpful in explaining the backgrounds against which foreign policy issues are framed, it usually falls into a predetermined mould, and becomes irrelevant to the task of explaining concrete international events, diplomatic and negotiation processes, and, in particular, situations where policy choices and preferences are involved.

One of the main reasons for what Kenneth Lieberthal called the 'paucity of theoretical rigor',[20] is the gap between the field of China studies and the development of social science theories. The importance of conceptual guidance for area specialists has perhaps best been described by Lucian Pye, a leading China scholar and former president of the American Political Science Association. Pye (1975: 21) argues that, 'as the division of labour between general theorists and area specialists eroded, normative and larger conceptual questions have become more important.' The micro-macro linkage approach, which will be elaborated in next chapter, can be considered one of the efforts to bridge this gap. While the theoretical model developed in this study may not necessarily achieve the optimal 'succinct and persuasive fashion' (called for by Samuel Kim) it nevertheless attempts to integrate some aspects of social science theory with the study of Chinese foreign policy.

Notes

1 A number of scholars have studied the changes in communist systems. A well-known author is Richard Loewenthal, who has published 'Development vs. Utopia in Communist Policy' (1970), and 'The Post-Revolutionary Phase in China and Russia' (1983). Please see 'References' at the end of this book for the detailed citations corresponding to the references within the endnotes.

2 Between the Mao and Deng eras, there was a two-year (1976–8) transitional period under the leadership of Hua Guofeng, Mao's hand-picked successor.

3 The words 'revolution' and 'modernization' are referred to here as slogans used by Mao and Deng. Although they can symbolize the different national priorities in the eras of Mao and Deng, they are not used here as concepts of social science theory.

4 'Year in Review: Free Trade: Key Asian Value', *Far Eastern Economic Review* (29 December 1994 and 5 January 1995): 27.

5 Nicholas Kristof and Sheryl WuDunn, 'China's Rush to Riches', *The New York Times Magazine* (4 September 1994): 54.

6 For details see, Nigel Holloway, 'For Whom the Bell Tolls', *Far Eastern Economic Review* (2 February 1995): 14–15.

7 Michael Richardson, 'China Scrambles for Oil', *International Herald Tribune*, 3–4 June 1995, p. 9.

8 See Carl Goldstein, 'Jerky Movements: US-China Ties See-Saw on Human Rights', *Far Eastern Economic Review* (17 February 1994): 20.

9 Susumu Awanohara and Lincoln Kaye, 'Full Circle', *Far Eastern Economic Review* (9 June 1994): 14–15. For a detailed account of the Clinton Administration's considerations on China's MFN status, see D. Lampton (1994), 'America's China Policy in the Age of the Finance Minister: Clinton Ends Linkage'.

10. For detailed studies of the Chinese use of military force, see, among others, Allen Whiting (1972); Jonathan Adelman and Chih-yu Shih (1993); and Paul Godwin (1994).

11 It should be made clear here that the brief review of the studies of foreign policy in general and Chinese foreign policy in particular in this and the following chapters is far from a complete one (and is not intended to be). The studies identified are only those that are relevant to the theoretical model developed in this book and to the discussions of various approaches. For more detailed information about the study of Chinese foreign policy, one may wish to read the bibliography section of Samuel Kim (1994b), and David Shambaugh (1994).

12 Harry Harding, from his 'Talking Points' at a round-table discussion on Chinese foreign policy organized by Quansheng Zhao, annual meeting of the Association for Asian Studies, Washington, DC, 6 April 1995.

13 Kenneth Lieberthal, in his correspondence with the author, 22 November 1993.

14 According to David Easton (1965: 37–39), a demand may be defined as 'an expression of opinion that an authoritative allocation with regard to a particular subject matter should or should not be made by those responsible for doing so'.

15 Some social-psychologists and political culture specialists also emphasize that their analyses operate not only at the individual level, but also at the societal level.

16 This point was raised by Gerard Mare in his correspondence with the author, 30 November 1994.

17 One may criticize this point of view by arguing that it was actually Mao's decision to 'lean' for his ideological reasons which contributed to the bipolarality of the world

balance of power. Which was the cause and which was the effect? This point was raised by Lucian Pye in his correspondence with the author, 21 November 1994.

18 Efforts have also been made to concentrate on Zhou Enlai; see, for example, Ronald Keith (1989).

19 See Lucian Pye (1981: 35–37). Also, Kim (1992: 22) in a review article further criticizes the tendency of what he calls 'overemphasizing on domestic factors' in shaping Chinese foreign policy by arguing that, 'China as an international actor is subject to the same economic, technological, and normative dynamics and controls inherent in the capitalist world system.'

20 Kenneth Lieberthal, in his correspondence with the author, 22 November 1993.

2 The Micro-Macro Linkage Approach

As discussed in the previous chapter, one may adopt a variety of notions, approaches and perspectives to study foreign policy. In a 1981 article entitled (like this book) 'Interpreting Chinese Foreign Policy', Arthur Huck observes how scholars have tended, naturally, to focus on those approaches favoured within their own fields of study: 'Historians have been inclined to stress the historical legacy and the similarities with past behaviour; political scientists have been inclined to stress factional politics and its outcome; economists have stressed the problems of resources and dependency; strategists have emphasized the military balance; ideologists have underlined ideology.'[1]

In order to help bridge the gap between China studies and social science theory, an important objective stated earlier, this study adopts an interdisciplinary perspective, calling to the attention of Chinese foreign policy specialists the development of the social science concept of *micro-macro integration*. As a relatively new theoretical development in the study of international relations (which we will discuss later), the micro-macro linkage approach has never previously been applied to the study of Chinese foreign policy.

The tradition of interpretive theory, or *hermeneutics*, in social science is to 'uncover the internal coherence amongst ideas, beliefs, intentions, actions and practices, to show how the understanding of participants makes sense in terms of the institutions and relationships within which they are located' (Gibbons, 1987: 3–4). '[I]nterpretive social science', as Paul Rabinow and William Sullivan (1979: 5) state, 'can be called a return to the objective world, seeing that world as in the first instance the circle of meaning within which we find ourselves and which we can never fully surpass.' Following this theoretical line, this study attempts to develop an interdisciplinary and interpretive approach — *micro-macro linkage* — to examine Chinese foreign policy.[2]

Recognizing the deficiencies in the interpretive power of the single-level analyses discussed in the previous chapter, specialists in international

Table 2.1: The International-Domestic Linkage Approach

Input	Output
International Constraints *Plus* Domestic Determinants	Foreign Policy

relations theory and foreign policy studies have increasingly seen the need to integrate the various elements of policy input to analyse and explain foreign policy issues. One of the earlier efforts in this direction was to combine the analysis of foreign policy at both the international and domestic levels.

The International–Domestic Linkage Approach

As early as 1969, James Rosenau (1969: 1–16), in his edited volume *Linkage Politics: Essays on the Convergence of National and International Systems*, strongly expressed the need for a *linkage approach* to analysis. He advocated a new method that would combine the shaping influence of international constraints and domestic determinants as policy inputs to explain a country's foreign policy. Henry Kissinger (1969: 263) also has stated that a systematic assessment of the impact of domestic elements on foreign policy 'would have to treat such factors as historical traditions, social values, and the economic system'. This approach, illustrated in Table 2.1, can be labelled the *international–domestic linkage approach*.

The emphasis of the international–domestic linkage approach is on the *interdependence* and *overlap* of national and international systems.[3] The development of this approach represented a significant effort to situate and advance the study of foreign policy issues in the field of international relations. The connection between internal and external elements has been advanced by the political scientist Robert Putnam (1993), who states that the foreign policy-making process can best be understood as a 'two-level game', in which policy-makers play at the politics of both the international arena and the domestic environment. Following Rosenau's lead, many scholars have since asserted the need to integrate domestic and international analyses to illuminate a country's foreign policy (McKeown, 1986; Haggard and Simmons, 1987; Rohrlich, 1987; Odell, 1990).

One of the earliest efforts to adopt the international-domestic linkage approach in the study of Chinese foreign policy was made in 1979 by Samuel Kim in his book *China, the United Nations, and the World Order*, which examines domestic and international sources of China's external behaviour in the international community and Beijing's relations with the United Nations. In his later studies, Kim (1989a: 21–23) has subsequently advocated the formulation of 'a variety of domestic/external linkage hypotheses for both qualitative and quantitative analyses', in which either domestic sources or the international environment are viewed 'in a relative and probabilistic, rather than an absolute and deterministic manner'.

Similar efforts have been made by a number of other scholars. Kuang-sheng Liao (1984), for example, has analysed the linkage between domestic politics and foreign policy throughout his book *Antiforeignism and Modernization in China*. Carol Hamrin (1986: 50–51) also has stated that in order to understand Chinese international behaviour at any given time, one must look at, 'both the international situation to which China must respond and the attitude toward the outside world prevailing within the Chinese leadership'. Several comprehensive studies on Chinese foreign policy such as those of Thomas Fingar (1980), Harry Harding (1984), Lillian Harris and Robert Worden (1986), Allen Whiting (1992), Thomas Robinson and David Shambaugh (1994), and Robert Ross (1995) have given welcome attention to both international and domestic analysis.

One may then argue along this line that the drastic change of domestic politics in the post-Mao era has redirected China's foreign policy goals by replacing Mao's 'closed-door' policy with Deng's 'open-door' policy. Furthermore, this linkage approach helps to frame the argument that China's further integration into the world economic system and its reform policies have caused Chinese foreign policy to become more pragmatic and flexible.

Nevertheless, the international–domestic linkage approach also has its limitations. Although the international system and domestic constraints must be distinguished from each other, they both in fact focus on the macro level (as defined later in this chapter); what is missing in the linkage politics model is an examination of the *interaction* of these factors with individual decision-makers at the micro level. As Rosenau himself has observed 21 years after the publication of his linkage model: 'Most theories of world politics tend to underestimate, even ignore, the interplay of macro and micro dynamics.' The fact is that these theories, including the international-domestic linkage approach, have not gone 'micro' enough. The 'micro level' in the context of these theories is only 'identified with nation-states' *vis-à-vis* the international environment and the macro-level factor (Rosenau, 1990: 25). Some domestic factors, such as interest groups and the foreign policy-making community, have occasionally been treated as micro-level units, 'but rarely does the level of analysis go lower than that' (Rosenau, 1990: 152).

The advantage of the macro-oriented theories, as represented by the international-domestic linkage approach, is that they can provide the overall historical, structural, and societal backgrounds of the major foreign policy issues. They may, however, lead to *structural determinism* (the idea that foreign policy is shaped only by the international and domestic *structures*) and neglect the dynamics of individual decision-makers' choices and preferences at the micro level.

The need for foreign policy analysis to connect to the micro-level factors has also been raised by Alexander George, who advocates the 'actor-specific' theory. In an effort to 'bridge the gap' between the worlds of academia and policy-making, George (1993: 9) argues:

Practitioners find it difficult to make use of academic approaches such as structural realist theory and game theory, which assume that all state actors are alike and can be expected to behave in the same way in given situations, and which rest on the simple, uncomplicated assumption that states can be regarded as rational unitary actors. On the contrary, practitioners believe they need to work with actor-specific models that grasp the different internal structures and behavioural patterns of each state and leaders with which they must deal.

This theoretical effort represented by the actor-specific models has, as Valeria Hudson and Christopher Vore (1995: 229) state, 'enormous theoretical, methodological, and policy potential: a potential that is only starting to be recognized as researchers work to develop theories that facilitate our understanding of why certain foreign policy decisions are made, at particular points in time, by individual decision makers and collectivities of decision makers.'

There is, therefore, a need to go beyond the argument that both international and domestic elements are important and to link these macro-level elements to the micro level in order to provide a framework that can answer such questions as: How have such elements as the international environment, domestic institutions, and social conditions converged on the policy-making process? By what mechanisms are these elements converged as policy inputs? How do the elements interact among themselves, ultimately influence policy-makers, and alter policy outcomes?

The Micro-Macro Linkage Model

Recent research efforts in social theory have tried to integrate macro and micro analyses.[4] It has been said that micro-macro linkage 'emerged as the central problematic' in the 1980s, and it continues to be of focal concern in the 1990s (Ritzer, 1992: 224). The issue of levels of analyses has become closely connected to what is called *micro-macro dichotomy and integration*. As Heinz Eulau (1986: 67) argues, 'linking different levels of analysis, the levels of individual or small-group behaviour and the global levels of institution, community, or nation, constitutes a major unsolved item on the methodological agenda of the behavioural persuasion, and a challenging one.' The micro-macro problem is believed to be 'one of determining how to represent the relationship between levels of analysis' (Cook, O'Brien, and Kollock, 1990: 175).

A further challenge is that it is not just a matter of 'linking' (or establishing cause and effect between) elements at the macro and micro levels. One may also regard this task as, what Jeffrey Alexander (1987: 299) termed, an 'hermeneutical reconstruction of the micro-macro link', which can be regarded as a reconceptualization of the legacies of social science theorists Max Weber, Vilfredo Pareto, and Talcott Parsons.[5] Alexander's theoretical framework rejects tendencies either toward *macro-determinism* or *micro-determinism*, or an excessive reliance upon either macro or micro levels as prime determinants; it emphasizes instead the movement and mutual influence between the two levels. Macro-determinism and micro-determinism are represented by *structural functionalism/conflict theory* and *symbolic interactionism/exchange theory*[6] respectively (Ritzer, 1992: 592). Each school of thought has its own analytical focus: while the former emphasizes elements at the macro level, the latter concentrates on the micro level (Ritzer, 1991: 592). In short, it combines the analytical advantages of, for example, structural functionalism and symbolic interactionism; at the same time this theoretical framework avoids the shortcoming of one-sidedness that exists with these two approaches.

The micro-macro linkage issue has also become a focal point in various sub-fields of social science theory, such as conflict theory (Collins, 1990) and rational choice theory (Friedman and Hechter, 1990). Those who are concerned with the micro-macro links claim that the confrontation between micro and macro theory belongs 'to the past' (Eisenstadt and Helle, 1985: 3). Richard Munch and Neil Smelser (1987: 385) believe that 'those who have argued polemically that one level is more fundamental than the other ... must be regarded as in error.' Micro-

Table 2.2: The Micro-Macro Linkage Approach

Input	Output
Macro-Level:	
International Constraints ⟷ Domestic Determinants	Foreign Policy
(Structure and System) (Society and Institutions)	
Micro-Level:	
Decision-Makers	

macro integration is regarded as critical to the study of international relations and foreign policy; the study of Chinese foreign policy is no exception.

One needs first to define the terms 'micro level' and 'macro level' in the context of a specific subject such as foreign-policy analysis. In general, the micro-macro dichotomy is understood to convey a sense of relativism. Drawing an analogy from the history of the life sciences (physiology, biochemistry, and molecular biology), Jeffrey Alexander (1987: 290–291) points out that 'the terms "micro" and "macro" are completely relativistic. What is macro at one level will be micro at another.' This is a useful point to keep in mind when trying to under-stand the evolutionary process of variables at different levels. One may, for example, regard this analysis as an examination of multiple levels of activity and/or causation. 'Multiple levels' refers to international structure, domestic institutions (national bureaucratic, provincial, re-gional, societal, etc.),[7] as well as to individual leaders.

But for the sake of lucidity and consistency, we still need a more precise definition when applying the terms to the analysis of a specific subject. For general social science purposes, the micro level is defined as 'the empirical reality of the individual in everyday life', and the macro level refers to 'social reality or the social world' (Ritzer, 1990: 348). This is also because most social scientists 'use these terms em-pirically' (Ritzer, 1992: 542), as manifested in this book. In this study, the *micro level* refers to decision-makers (whether individuals or small groups), whereas the *macro* analysis focuses on the international ele-ments (relating to system and structure) and domestic elements (aspects of society and internal institutions).

Table 2.2 depicts a three-way interaction: while international con-straints and domestic determinants are involved in a dynamic relationship

Table 2.3: Bernhard Giesen's Evolution Theoretical Model

	Process	Situation	Structure
Symbolic Reality	Rational interpretation of the situation	Symbolic core structure, relevant pattern of conceiving	Worldviews, morals
Practical Reality	Action	Practical core structure, valid rules and norms, interests induced by social positions	Valid institutions and structures of differentiation
Material Reality	Organic behaviour	Material core structure, material resources, and techniques available in a situation	Material resources, size of collectivity, technostructure

See Giesen (1987, 349)

at the macro level, they also converge on, and receive feedback from, individual decision-makers. Rather than simply describing the importance of both international and domestic elements, the challenge with the micro-macro linkage approach lies in analysing:

- the channels and mechanisms through which demands from the international and domestic environments converge on the policy-making process;
- how the changing dynamics of domestic and international environments affect each other in shaping a country's external behaviour; and
- how they influence individual decision-makers in the formulation of foreign policy.

To meet this challenge, we need to introduce new concepts that can help to clarify and advance our understanding of the ways in which and the mechanisms by which movements from macro to micro and vice versa occur. In pursuit of this objective, we may first divide social reality into different dimensions, and then examine their interactions with micro-level actors. In an excellent study on micro-macro interplay, Bernhard Giesen (1987) has introduced the *evolution-theoretical model*.[8] This model divides social reality (*macro-structure*) into three dimensions: *symbolic*, *practical*, and *material* (see Table 2.3).

Table 2.4: The Micro-Macro Linkage Model of Chinese Foreign Policy (1949–present)

Macro-Structures	Macrostructural Change (key analytical concepts)	Micro Processes in Beijing
Symbolic Macrostructure	From *Revolution* to *Modernization*	Orientational change in the interpretation of the internal and external environments; learning and adaptation; the changing priorities of foreign policy
Institutional Macrostructure	From *Vertical Authoritarianism* to *Horizontal Authoritarianism*	Increased scope and degree of participation in foreign policy-making; changes of rules, norms, and mechanisms in policy-making process
Power/Regime Macrostructure	From *Rigidity* towards *Flexibility*	Dynamics of individual leaders' power and authority; regime legitimacy; decision-makers' preference and choices; foreign policy strategies and tactics

Giesen's contribution to macro-micro linkage is not only his division of social realities into three distinct dimensions; he also has differentiated each category in terms of *process*, *situation*, and *structure*, demonstrating how the macrostructure is manifest at the micro level (Giesen, 1987: 348).

The Micro-Macro Linkage Model of Chinese Foreign Policy

Applying Giesen's evolution theory allows us further to develop the micro-macro linkage model of Chinese foreign policy (as shown in Table 2.4).

Table 2.4 offers a comprehensive picture of the micro-macro linkage approach as it can be applied to the study of Chinese foreign policy. In this model there are three dimensions of the macrostructure — *symbolic*, *institutional*, and *power/regime* — and corresponding to each macrostructure is a different set of individual and group processes. (Please note that the *power/regime* dimension in this model corresponds to the *material dimension* in Giesen's model).

The first dimension of macro-micro linkage concentrates on how fundamental changes in the *symbolic macrostructure* have affected Beijing's interpretation of the international and domestic environments. Since ideological concepts and beliefs are part of the interpretive lens through which leaders have viewed China and its role in the world, following the shifts in these factors is crucial to understanding the changing priorities of Chinese foreign policy. The second dimension deals with the impact on China's foreign policy of changes in the *institutional macrostructure* — which refers, for our purposes, to the established systems through which policy-makers must operate, and includes such factors as the rules and norms of political actions, the mechanisms of the policy-making process, and the scope and degree of participation within a given political structure. The last dimension of micro-macro linkage, the *power/regime macrostructure*, sheds light on the importance to the policy-making process of the realm of power, its possessors, and their means of controlling and wielding it. In particular, this dimension is concerned with such issues as how different sources of power are allocated within China's foreign policy community, and how they are mobilized by different groups in a struggle for the control over policy-making; it ultimately deals with the issue of regime legitimacy and foreign policy strategies, tactics, and behaviour patterns.

What makes this model different from others, therefore, is that it not only 'links' the micro and macro levels, it also analyses the three dimensions of the Chinese foreign policy macrostructure, thereby taking into account both elements of the 'levels' (in a vertical way) and the 'stuctures' (in a horizontal way). The different macrostructures featured under the three categories each involve various influences and exigencies, leaving room for decision-makers at the micro level to react. Thus, the choices and preferences of individual decision-makers may play an active role in the formulation of foreign policy. The micro-macro linkage model, argues that neither the macrostructure, nor the decision-makers at the micro level has absolute control over a country's foreign policy. Their influences are all considered in a relative sense. To understand the dynamics of foreign policy-making one has to look at the mutual influences and the channels and mechanisms between and among the elements at the micro and macro levels.

One may wish to push this model further to illuminate precisely the interactions between the micro and macro levels. It should be made

clear, here, that the channels, mechanisms, and patterns of these interactions are situational and case contingent. They may differ over such
variables as time, space, and the particular issue. As Jon Elster (1993:
1–7) points out, in the real world, 'the number of possible permutations
of conditions is too great for us to be able to establish the characteristic
mechanism operating in each of them'; and 'a mechanism is a specific
causal pattern that can be recognized after the event but rarely fore-
seen.' We may reach two points from here. First, this model is not
intended to construct a 'general' or 'grant' theory to cover every aspect
of human activity; this 'is and will always remain an illusory dream'
(Elster, 1993: 2). Rather, as Allen Whiting (1994: 507) has put it, 'Theory
aims at explanation of a category of behaviour over a prolonged period
of time.' The mico-macro linkage approach only lays out an analytical
framework as a starting point to study foreign policy issues. Second,
the micro-macro linkage model is essentially an approach to interpreting causal relationships among various factors at the micro and macro
levels, and is not intended to be a tool for predicting future events.

This model is, however, intended to interpret the trends and directions of Chinese foreign policy over time. It features three pairs of key,
guiding analytical concepts as a promising way to apply the linkage
approach under each macrostructure:

- from *revolution* to *modernization* (describing the shift in the symbolic
  structure);
- from *vertical authoritarianism* to *horizontal authoritarianism* (characterizing the changing institutional structure); and
- *rigidity* versus *flexibility* (describing the fluctuating nature of power/
  regime structure).

These concepts are employed to highlight the changing dynamics of
Chinese foreign policy as the PRC has shifted from being a revolutionary power to becoming a member of the world nation–state system.
They are the tools with which this model will interpret Chinese foreign
policy patterns and policy choices.

Although both the international-domestic linkage approach and the
micro-macro linkage approach can be regarded as linkage theories, the
two approaches have quite different understandings of the concept of
linkage. The former deals with two different units — international structure and domestic institutions — without covering the dynamics of
individual actors and their interactions with these two units. From the
micro-macro link perspective, the challenge of linkage 'is how to create
theoretical concepts that translate or map variables at the individual level

into variables characterizing social systems, and vice versa' (Gerstein, 1987: 86). Therefore, despite the fact that the international-domestic linkage approach has greatly advanced our analytical ability in the study of foreign policy, it can be criticized as an incomplete, and thus misleading approach which only operates at the macro level of analysis.

The Application of the Micro-Macro Linkage Model

One major obstacle to applying this linkage model to the study of Chinese foreign policy is, as Kenneth Lieberthal has suggested, 'a lack of necessary data', particularly at the micro level.[9] As Valerie Hudson and Christopher Vore (1995: 221) point out:

> If the research is not part of the group or bureaucracy in question, detailed accounts of what transpired, preferably from a variety of primary sources and viewpoints, are necessary. Because of security considerations, such information is usually not available for many years (when it is declassified or the archives are opened to historians).

The fact that China has not yet established a policy or system for declassifying government documents makes the task of Chinese foreign policy scholars all the more difficult.

Inevitably, one encounters many 'black boxes' when conducting a comprehensive study of any country's foreign policy and its formulation. Indeed, this problem is likely to be particularly daunting in studies that apply the micro-macro linkage approach, which emphasizes the channels and mechanisms connecting a wide variety of factors at different levels. Micro-level analysis, or the actor-specific theory mentioned earlier, involves what Herbert Simon (1985: 303) called 'specification of the situation' which is 'data intensive', 'time consuming', and 'often requires country or regional expertise' (Hudson and Vore, 1995: 211).

This study, it must be made clear, is not intended to open every 'black box' in Chinese foreign policy. Its purpose is more modest, but none the less valuable — namely, to provide a starting framework within which to examine the combined impact of international and domestic environments on individual decision-makers, while allowing us to analyse the choices and preferences of decision-makers when faced with concrete foreign policy issues.

Having recognized the difficulties in terms of data collection, however, on a more hopeful note, sources from China have increased tremendously and become more accessible to academic researchers since the inception of China's Open Door policy toward the outside world.

With a much relaxed atmosphere, a number of high-ranking diplomats (now retired) have published their memoirs, contributing important new insights into Chinese foreign policy decision-making. Examples include Ambassador Wang Bingnan (1985), who was the major negotiator with the US in the famous Warsaw talks before the normalization of relationship between the two countries; Ambassador Liu Xiao (1986), who was ambassador to the Soviet Union from 1955 to 1962, when Beijing was shifting from a 'honeymoon period' to open confrontation with Moscow; and former vice-minister of foreign affairs Wu Xiuquan (1991), who participated in negotiations with the United States during the Korean War, and was China's first ambassador to Yugoslavia (between 1955 and 1958) when Belgrade was a focal point of tension in the international Communist movement.

There is even a collective volume entitled *Nü Waijiaoguan* (Women Diplomats) (Cheng, 1995) which features the recollections or records of Chinese female diplomats. Most of them are foreign ministers' or ambassadors' wives (though they, themselves, are not appointed to official posts, they also serve as diplomats).[10] A few of them, are well known appointed diplomats, themselves, such as Gong Peng (bureau chief of the News Department of the Foreign Affairs Ministry and wife of Qiao Guanghua); Ding Xuesong (ambassador to the Netherlands and Denmark); and Gong Pusheng (ambassador to Ireland and wife of Zhang Hanfu). Some top diplomats' wives have also written their own, single volumes. For example, Zhu Lin (1991), the wife of Ambassador Huang Zhen (the first envoy from the PRC to the United States, from 1973 to 77), has published her recollections, offering detailed description of Huang's more than twenty years of diplomatic service in various countries, including Hungary (1950–4), Indonesia (1954–61), France (1964–73), and the United States (1973–7).

These accounts, though sometimes restrained and unbalanced, are welcome additions to the body literature in the field, for they have provided first-hand insights into the internal workings of the Chinese foreign affairs establishment. They are particularly instructive for the study of Chinese foreign policy in terms of its formulation and implementation, and are helpful sources for the study of the domestic roots of Chinese foreign policy.

Furthermore, there have been some very interesting, unprecedented memoirs published outside of the Mainland by those who have moved abroad. Those memoirs are largely from two groups of people: ex-high-ranking officials or personal associates of top Chinese leaders. The memoirs of Xu Jiatun (1993), the former head of the Chinese Xinhua News Agency in Hong Kong (the PRC's shadow head in Hong Kong), is a typical example of the former group; Mao Zedong's personal physician Li Zhisui's (1994) *The Private Life of Chairman Mao* represents the latter.[11]

These works are normally far less restrained by political conditions prevailing within China, and therefore often provide much more detailed pictures of the inner workings of Chinese politics. These first-hand materials help to open some of the 'black boxes' at the micro level in terms of the top leaders' personal thinking and perceptions of major foreign (as well as domestic) policy issues.

An equally important development is that Beijing has begun to publish its own reference book on China's foreign relations and foreign policy. The most important example is *Dangdai Zhongguo Waijiao* (Diplomacy of Contemporary China), produced by the ministry of foreign affairs, with former vice minister Han Nianlong (1987) as editor-in-chief. There are also publications (books and journal articles) about China's major external actions and foreign relations, such as the Korean War and the Vietnam War. The increase of English analyses on China's foreign affairs by scholars in mainland China is also noteworthy. Although most works concentrate on China's relations with the United States (either as a history of bilateral relations, or analysis of US policy toward China), a few scholars in China have begun to pay attention to the internal dynamics of Chinese foreign policy. Wang Jisi (1994), for example, has written a fine summary about the evolution and characteristics of Chinese theories of international relations. He also has analysed Chinese attitudes toward Western theories, stressing 'the uniqueness of Chinese thinking on world affairs'. Another example is Chen Xiaolu, son of former foreign minister Marshal Chen Yi. Chen (1989) published an article in English on the evolution of Chinese foreign policy toward the United States from 1949 to 1955. Chen, using the example of the Korean War, emphasized the differences between socialist China and the Soviet Union in global strategic thinking as early as the 1950s. These new publications have provided not only detailed accounts of the internal workings of Chinese foreign policy-making, but also give us Chinese perspectives on international affairs, which are important contributions to the field as a whole, and are particularly valuable to the model of micro-macro linkage.[12] Despite the above-mentioned progress, the available materials are still inadequate for capturing and reflecting the full and complicated picture of Chinese foreign policy. There is a great need for more empirical studies to continue this research direction. (For further discussion about a future research agenda, see Chapter 8.)

Introduction to the Other Chapters

Part II of this book (Chapters 3 to 6) applies the micro-macro linkage model of Chinese foreign policy presented in this chapter to China's external affairs from 1949 to the present. It analyses the fundamental changes in Chinese foreign policy at the macro and micro levels. In so doing, it examines such issues as the paramount importance of regime survival (in the face of both external and internal threats) to the Chinese leadership; China's gradual shift from security issues to economic concerns, which 'has further increased the relative weight' of domestic structures on foreign policy (Katzenstein, 1978: 10); and the distinctive combination of rigidity and flexibility in Chinese foreign policy behaviour.

Chapter 3 concentrates on the symbolic macrostructure and the changing priorities of Chinese foreign policy. It analyses the major shift in Beijing's interpretations of international and domestic environments, examining the concomitant changing perceptions and priorities in the PRC's external policies. It pays special attention to the critical changes between the era of Mao Zedong and the era of Deng Xiaoping. Examining Beijing's shifting interpretations of the outside world through learning and adaptation can help us better to understand the changing priorities of Chinese foreign policy. These changing priorities are more often than not regarded as responses to the changing dynamics of the international and internal environments rather than to the individual leaders' preferences.

Chapter 4 studies the institutional macrostructure and policy-making process. It examines China's societal and institutional inputs, namely the scope and degree of participation in the foreign policy-making process, as well as China's general political and economic conditions. It analyses the changes in rules, norms, and mechanisms in the policy-making process, and investigates the interactions between decision-makers and societal and institutional elements.

The power/regime macrostructure is the focus of Chapter 5, which looks more closely at this dimension and its impact on decision-makers' policy preferences and choices. China's foreign affairs have been profoundly shaped by internal politicals, as well as traditional and ideological considerations, and this chapter seeks to develop this connection further by studying Beijing's concerns about regime legitimacy and its characteristic strategies and tactics in dealing with external affairs. The analyses of the distinctive combination of rigidity and flexibility in Chinese foreign policy behaviour attempt to answer such questions as:

How should one conceptualize Beijing's policy choices when examining its changing dynamics and behaviour patterns? Under what circumstances might Chinese foreign policy become more flexible or more rigid? Why has the PRC sometimes acted in different ways when facing seemingly similar conditions?

No model can be deemed truly valid or useful without testing its congruity and pertinence to real life events and circumstances. Towards that end Chapter 6 offers an empirical summary of the micro-macro linkage model of Chinese foreign policy. It utilizes case studies, to illuminate the theoretical approach and to demonstrate its applicability to the 'real world'. This chapter applies the model to Japan's official development assistance (ODA) to China to highlight the internal and external workings of Chinese foreign policy, and to compare it with the policy-making process in Japan.

Following the theoretical and empirical analyses of the changes in Chinese foreign policy at the macro and micro levels, Part III (Chapters 7 and 8) concludes the book, calling attention to the behaviour patterns and policy choices of Chinese foreign policy in the post-revolutionary era. From these patterns and choices it is possible to conclude that China is more than likely to enlarge the degree and range of its participation in international activities and that its pursuit of economic modernization and regional stability will incline China toward greater cooperation on security matters and increasing economic and cultural exchanges. Chapter 7 identifies modernization, nationalism, and regionalism as important trends in Chinese foreign policy in the post-Cold War era. This chapter provides analyses of the PRC's role in the Asia-Pacific region, its policies toward Tokyo, Seoul-Pyongyang, Washington, Moscow, and South-East Asia, as well as Beijing's Taiwan policy. It also points to the future trends and direction of Chinese foreign policy in these bilateral relationships.

The final chapter also discusses the future direction of the study of Chinese foreign policy itself. The micro-macro linkage approach calls for a re-examination of the long-established Chinese foreign policy issues and more diversified research on both old and new questions for the latter half of the 1990s. The micro-macro linkage approach, as Alexander and Giesen (1987: 37) state, establishes 'a radically different starting point' in order to make 'a genuinely inclusive micro-macro link', thereby creating new research agendas for the study of Chinese foreign policy.

Interpreting Chinese Foreign Policy is different from most previous studies of Chinese foreign policy, which have either dealt with concrete events or have analysed policies toward specific countries. By design, the book does not seek to cover every foreign policy issue that China has faced. The focus here is on such factors as:

- the changes in interpretations of China's internal and external environments;
- foreign policy priorities;
- the policy-making process;
- societal and institutional inputs; and
- the power politics among political elites in Beijing that lie behind the strategies and tactics used to implement foreign policy.

Political, security, and economic issues receive more attention than some other concerns, such as cultural issues.

In essence, this book is intended to give readers a broad understanding of:

- why there have been profound changes in Beijing's interpretation of its internal and external environments;
- what are basic outlines of Chinese foreign policy and its behaviour patterns;
- how Chinese foreign policy is made and implemented; and
- how the decision-makers' consideration for regime legitimacy and power politics affects foreign policy choices.

While this model of analysis mainly focuses on the change between the policies of the Mao era and the Deng era, it draws on the entire history of the PRC and looks also toward the post-Deng future. As such, *Interpreting Chinese Foreign Policy* may prove useful not only to established scholars but also to new students of China, and to policy-makers in such capitals as Washington, Moscow, Tokyo, Seoul, London, and elsewhere who might benefit from a guide to the essential character and direction of Chinese foreign policy.

Two years after the Tiananmen Incident, veteran China-watcher Doak Barnett (1991: 22–23) conducted a thorough analysis of China's directions and concluded that, 'China will continue to undergo profound changes, but at its own pace and in its own distinctive way.' *Interpreting Chinese Foreign Policy* attempts to define these 'profound changes' and to determine the nature of China's 'own pace' and 'own distinctive way' in not only its foreign policy behaviour but also in its domestic behaviour, insofar as it influences foreign policy.

Notes

1   See Arthur Huck, 'Interpreting Chinese Foreign Policy', *Australian Journal of Chinese Affairs*, 6 (1981): 217; quoted from Michael Yahuda (1983b: 534).

2   This study is not intended, however, to participate in the theoretical debate between the hermeneutic approach and the positivistic notion, as Andrew Nathan (1993) did in his *Journal of Asian Studies* article.

3   James Rosenau (1969: 46) presented three basic linkage processes — *penetrative, reactive*, and *emulative* — to elaborate his linkage theory:

    a) A penetrative process occurs when members of one polity serve as participants in the political processes of another. That is, they share with those in the penetrated polity the authority to allocate its values. Example: occupying army.

    b) A reactive process is the contrary of a penetrative one: It is brought into being by recurrent and similar boundary-crossing reactions rather than by the sharing of authority. Example: foreign aid.

    c) An emulative process is established when the input is not only a response to the output but takes essentially the same form as the output. Example: nationalism and democratization.

4   For a detailed discussion, see the excellent theoretical summary by George Ritzer (1990).

5   For further references, please see Guenther Roth and Wolfgang Schluchter (1979); Vilfredo Pareto (1980); and Talcott Parsons (1937).

    In the case of Max Weber, for example, his 'enlarged framework' is worth special attention. Within this framework, Weber analyses the relationship between religion and economy in a world-historical perspective: 'the relation of the dominant religious ideas to the economic ideas, the relation of these economic ideas to the economic systems, and the changing primacy of the religious and economic ideas themselves' (Rath and Schluchter, 1979: 18).

6   Due to space limitations, only brief definitions will be provided here without further elaboration:

    Structural functionalism — It identifies society as a 'unit of analysis independent of individual action. This approach seeks to explain certain structures and institutions in a society by identifying the functions they fulfill in maintaining the working of society as a whole' (Munch and Smelser, 1987: 371).

    Conflict theory — Its basic themes are the following: '1) The central feature of social organization is stratification, the kind and degree of inequality among groups and individuals and their domination over one another; 2) The causes of what happens in society are to be sought in the interests of groups and individuals; aboveall, their interests in maintaining their positions of domination or evading domination by others; 3) Who wins what in these struggles depends on the resources controlled by the different factions, including material resources for violence and for economic exchange, but also resources for social organization and for shaping emotions and ideas; 4) Social change is driven especially by conflict; hence, long periods of relatively stable domination are punctuated by intense and dramatic episodes of group mobilization' (Collins, 1990: 68).

    Symbolic interactionism — It has three premises: 1) 'Human beings act toward things on the basis of the meanings that the things have for them; 2) The meanings of such things are derived from, or arise out of the social interaction that one has with one's fellows; 3) These meanings are handled in, and modified through an interpretative process used by the person in dealing with the things he encounters' (Blumer, 1969: 2).

    Exchange Theory — It 'focuses attention on the relationships between interconnected actors, be they individuals, corporations, or nation-states, rather than represent actors as isolated entities — processes like the exercise of power and influence, the potential for coalition formation and other power-gaining strategies, the normative aspects of exchange, especially conceptions of fairness and unfairness, inequalities in the distribution of resources and perceptions of the legitimacy of power' (Cook, O'Brien, and Kollock, 1990: 159).

7   This point was raised by Carol Hamrin in her correspondence with the author, 22 November 1993.

8   Giesen has also discussed other linkage models such as: the coordination model — individual actions and macrosocial effects; the categorical-analytic model — language and speech act; and the antagonism model — social repression and individual autonomy. See Giesen (1987).

9   Kenneth Lieberthal, in his correspondence with the author, 22 November 1993.

10 These women diplomats include the wives of Qiao Guanhua (foreign minister), Huang Hua (foreign minister), Wang Jiaxiang (ambassador to the Soviet Union and deputy foreign minister), Zhang Hanfu (deputy foreign minister), Chai Zemin (ambassador to the United States), Fu Hao (ambassador to Japan and deputy foreign minister), Han Xu (ambassador to the United States and deputy foreign minister), Wang Shu (ambassador to West Germany), Yang Shouzheng (ambassador to the Soviet Union and several African countries), Zhang Wenjin (ambassador to the United States and deputy foreign minister), Yang Zhenya (ambassador to Japan), Lin Ping (ambassador to Chile), Hu Dingyi (ambassador to England), Hu Gang (ambassador to Malaysia), and Chen Shuliang (ambassador to Cambodia).

11 The books by Xu and Li have not been received without controversy. To dispute Li Zhisui's recollections about Mao, for example, a new book entitled *Lishi de zhenshi* (The Truth of History) was published in Hong Kong in October 1995. This book was authored by three long-time staff members working for Mao before his death in 1976: Lin Ke — Mao's secretary and English teacher; Wu Xujun — another of Mao's personal physicians; and Xu Tao — Mao's head nurse. See *Yazhou Zhoukan* [The International Chinese Newsweekly] (19 November 1995): 75–78.

12 For further information on newly available Chinese materials, one may wish to read Hunt and Westad (1990) and David Shambaugh (1994).

Part II

MICRO-MACRO ANALYSES:
THE EVOLUTION OF A REVOLUTIONARY
POWER

3 China's Symbolic Macrostructure and Changing Priorities: From Revolution to Modernization

A key and challenging objective of the micro-macro linkage theory is to establish a causal connection between factors at the macro and micro levels. In his *Foundation of Social Theory*, James Coleman (1990: 21) has taken the relationship between the advent of Calvinistic religious doctrine and the rise of a capitalist economy in the West as an example to illustrate this 'causal connection'; he questions 'not only how the doctrine gets transmitted to individuals and then has an effect on their behaviour, but also how that behaviour comes to be combined, that is, how social organization which constitutes capitalist enterprise takes place'. Attention is paid here to the transitional avenues among various elements at the micro and macro levels.

The symbolic macrostructure is one dimension of the macrostructure, or basic social reality, examined in this chapter to develop the micro-macro model for interpreting Chinese foreign policy. Abner Cohen, a social anthropologist, has emphasized the importance of two domains — *symbolic action* and *power relationships* — in modern, complex society. Cohen (1976: 23–24) defines symbols as 'objects, acts, relationships or linguistic formations that stand ambiguously for a multiplicity of meanings, evoke emotions, and impel men to action'. Furthermore, symbols 'tend to be grouped together within the frameworks of dynamic ideologies, or world-views, that are developed and carried by specific groupings'. Although Cohen is concerned with social activities in general terms, we may utilize this concept to indicate the 'dominant mood' of the society, which, in general, reflects the ruling elites' interpretations of internal developments and the external environment. These interpretations can also be called 'world views', which are, as Judith Goldstein and Robert Keohane (1993: 8) defined them, 'embedded in the symbolism of a culture and deeply affect modes of thought and discourse', and are 'entwined with people's conceptions of their identities, evoking deep emotions and loyalties'.[1]

This symbolic macrostructure often has critical influence in deciding the priorities of foreign policy agendas. Behaviour patterns at the micro level often evolve in the process of learning and adaptation. In a study on the changes of Soviet foreign policy, Charles Ziegler (1993) has applied the concept of learning and adaptation, with the following definitions:

Adaptation: 'a process of utilizing new knowledge for adjustments within existing structures, to achieve a closer approximation to regime goals.'

Learning: 'a process of building consensus, through new knowledge, on the seriousness of existing problems, on the inadequacy of current problem-solving strategies, and on the need for fundamental changes to realign methods with goals' (Ziegler, 1993: 12–13).

Changes in foreign policy priorities may be caused by both adaptation and learning. But a genuine learning process is more likely to lead to 'fundamental changes in the ideology, governing structures, or basic goals' (Ziegler, 1993: 13).

Therefore, it is only natural to ask such questions as:

• How does the international environment impact domestic factors to cause a 'learning process' at the level of individual decision-makers?;
• What are the Chinese policy-makers' new interpretations and perceptions of, and attitudes toward the outside world?; and
• What is the effect of Beijing's changing perceptions on China's foreign policy priorities?

In addressing these, one may pay equal attention to both the micro and macro levels, and more importantly, to the ongoing relationships and transitional avenues among various factors at different levels.

Changing Priorities

The death of Mao Zedong in 1976 brought the ten-year Cultural Revolution to an end. After a one-year transitional period under the leadership of Mao's hand-picked successor Hua Guofeng, Deng Xiaoping overcame political disgrace and returned to power in 1977, achieving the status of China's permanent leader in 1978.[2] (He had been purged twice by Mao in 1966 and 1976 during the Cultural Revolution, but was rehabilitated in 1973.) This change of leadership marked the beginning of a new period in contemporary Chinese history. (For a detailed picture of the changes in leadership from 1949, see Appendices I and II.) The Mao Zedong era, which lasted from 1949 to 1976, was a radical revolutionary period highlighted by the Cultural Revolution, which caused what the Chinese Communist Party (CCP) itself has described as 'the most severe setback and the heaviest losses . . . since the founding of the People's Republic'.[3] The Deng Xiaoping era (1978–present), a period of pragmatism, has led to 'a new situation in all fields of socialist modernization' (Deng, 1984: 395). In both the Mao and the Deng periods, as Kenneth Lieberthal (1984: 43) points out, 'each of China's principal domestic strategies — from the First Five Year Plan and the Great Leap Forward of the 1950s, through the Cultural Revolution of the 1960s and 1970s, to the Four Modernizations of the 1980s — has had clear and direct implications for its posture toward the rest of the world.'

The Deng era can be regarded as a post-revolutionary era, clearly different from the Mao era in its national priorities and behaviour toward the rest of the world community. A revolutionary state conducts a 'continuous revolution' internally and externally, whereas a post-revolutionary state sets economic development as its first priority, thereby introducing 'a more mass-regarding political climate' (Womack, 1987: 507). A revolutionary state regards itself as an outsider trying to change the status quo within the international community, whereas a post-revolutionary state acts like an insider seeking maximum opportunities for its development from within the existing order. And a revolutionary state emphasizes ideological considerations, whereas a post-revolutionary state believes that pragmatism better serves its national interests.

It is necessary to examine the evolution since 1949 of the Chinese leadership's interpretations and perceptions of China's internal and external environments; the transition has brought considerable changes in Beijing's foreign policy priorities. Many studies have analysed the importance to Chinese foreign policy of the changing international environment, yet few have examined shifts in priorities in light of the leadership's changing interpretations of the outside world. Yet, as mentioned earlier, such world views frequently form the basis for determining priorities, or at least for determining how such enduring priorities as regime survival and the promotion of national interests can be best advanced. This chapter analyses the symbolic macrostructure dimension of our theoretical model, in this case, the transformation of the Chinese leadership's interpretation of the internal conditions and external environment, and the effects of this transformation on the priorities of Chinese foreign policy. It also will discuss the changes and continuities in China's foreign policy since the establishment of the People's Republic in 1949.

China experienced a fundamental change from the era of revolution to the era of modernization. Under Mao, the regime emphasized revolutionary objectives: dramatic and sweeping social reform in the domestic arena and survival as a communist nation in the international environment. This period was characterized by an emphasis on revolutionary ideology, a lack of respect for the prevailing international norms and extreme sensitivity to outside threats. This perception of external threats to the new Communist regime often led the Beijing leadership under Mao to meet perceived threats to security with military means.[4]

In the post-revolutionary era, or the era of modernization, China has moved beyond a single-minded preoccupation with world revolution. As the world becomes increasingly interdependent, particularly in terms of economic integration, the Beijing leadership has gradually recognized that the concept of regime survival has broader meanings. National security today is not only related to political and strategic issues, but also to economic development. Beijing, of course, recognized the importance of the economic aspect previously, but felt that economic security and development could be achieved in a self-sufficient, classless, socialist fashion. Now the leadership has realized that economic development by necessity in this age also means 'economic interdependence' which requires less antagonistic world behaviour than Maoist ideology would prescribe. Deng Xiaoping has warned on several occasions that China may face the danger of losing its *qiuji* (global citizenship) if its economy fails to catch up with that of the rest of the world. The PRC leadership now has multiple goals for national development, and places particular emphasis on economic development and modernization. In order to understand better the change in Chinese foreign policy priorities, let us briefly review the recent history of China's external use of military force.

The Use of Military Force

Since 1949, Beijing has determined to use force seven times with external forces and twice with Taiwan.[5] These military actions have been quite different from each other in terms of scope and nature. Some, such as the Korean War in 1950 to 1953, were major wars; others, such as the Sino-Soviet border confrontation in 1969, are better described as military clashes. China in some conflicts was reactive (the Sino-Indian border war in 1962); and on other occasions appeared to have taken the initiative (the Sino-Vietnam border war in 1979). These external military conflicts all had one thing in common, however — they all drew broad attention in the international community.

In October 1950, the new Chinese Communist leadership made the momentous decision to cross the Yalu River and enter the Korean War, placing itself in direct military confrontation with the United States. This conflict was to end in a military stalemate three years later and left the Korean Peninsula with the long-term legacy of North–South division. The casualties for both sides, the estimations for which vary, were tremendous. According to Chinese statistics, US casualties reached 390,000, whereas the Chinese casualties were 366,000 with 115,000 dead and 221,000 wounded (Deng Lifeng, 1994: 312–313). One other account claimed that the number of dead on the Chinese side alone reached about 400,000 (Adelman and Shih, 1993: 189).[6] China's decision to enter the Korean War had other lasting consequences for the Asia-Pacific region as well. It prompted President Harry Truman to order the US Seventh Fleet into the Taiwan Straits to guarantee Taiwanese security, thereby internationalizing the issue of Taiwan and making it a focus of future conflict between Beijing and Washington.

In 1962, China and India became involved in several border disputes, one of which concerned the legitimacy of the MacMahon line, drawn by the British in 1914 when India was still under the rule of the British Empire. The MacMahon line was never recognized by the Chinese government, including the Nationalist (Kuomintang, or KMT) government before 1949. The Soviet Union, which had serious quarrels with Beijing over ideological issues, gave its moral support to New Delhi. The resulting military conflict lasted for about a month, from October to November of 1962. Chinese troops pushed the Indian troops back, and the war was ended with the voluntary withdrawal of Chinese troops. Total Indian losses were 4,897 dead and 3,968 prisoners of war, while China suffered far fewer casualties and no prisoners were taken by India (Xu, 1993: 185).[7] Since then, although there have been sporadic fights along the border, no major military engagements have been reported. Negotiations over the border disputes and other bilateral issues between China and India have resumed since 1981 and continued into the 1990s.[8]

China's next major external military conflict was centred in Vietnam, and lasted for more than two decades. Beijing's support for the North Vietnamese Communist regime of Ho Chi Minh ultimately led to a confrontation with the United States. The gradual US move into Vietnam to support the South, following the defeat of the French forces at the battle of Dien Bien Phu in 1954, was initially limited to military advisers. By early 1965, however, American ground troops were committed to the struggle. China, for its part, over the period from 1965 to 1973, sent North Vietnam, more than 20,000 military advisers and about 300,000 troops (Deng Lifeng, 1994: 330–352). The peak year was 1967, when 170,000 Chinese troops were present in Vietnam. Most of these troops were the so-called 'Chinese People's Volunteer Engineering Force' (CPVEF), carrying out the tasks of building and rebuilding railways and defence works and constructing air fields in Vietnam. Starting in 1965, seven divisions of CPVEF units entered Vietnam during different periods. All these CPVEF troops were accompanied by anti-aircraft artillery units (Chen, 1995: 371–380). Casualties on the Chinese side during this period reached more than 5,000, and more than 1,000 Chinese soldiers were buried in Vietnam. Although these troops were engaged primarily in construction and anti-air-raid fighting,[9] their presence posed a real danger of direct US–Chinese fighting, a danger that continued until the United States entered negotiations in 1968.

In conjunction with the Vietnam War, China also faced direct confrontation with US forces in Laos. From 1969 to 1973 China sent three anti-aircraft units to Laos to fight with American fighters and bombers. These units, totalling 21,000, fought 95 times. Thirty-five US planes were shot down in these skirmishes, and 24 soldiers were wounded. Among the Chinese casualties, 269 people were killed, of which 210 were buried in Laos (Deng Lifeng, 1994: 359–361).

The next military action between China and the Soviet Union actually took place directly along their border; the two countries clashed several times over Zhenbao island (or Damansky island to the Russians), located on the China side of the main channel in the Wusuli (Ussuri) River, which demarcated the Sino-Soviet border. There are various accounts of these clashes. According to one report, several thousand troops from each side were involved during this conflict, and China's People's Liberation Army (PLA) suffered at least 800 casualties, while the Russians suffered about 90 casualties (Robinson, 1970: 38–40). This serious military conflict was resolved within six months by a meeting at the Beijing airport between the two countries' premiers — Zhou Enlai and Aleksei Kosygin — followed by negotiations over the border issues at the deputy foreign minister level (Wich, 1980: Ch. 9; and Hinton, 1971: 53–60). Nevertheless, this confrontation, along with other disputes, ensured that a high level of tension between the two communist giants would prevail during the next two decades.[10] After the Sino-Soviet rapprochement in 1989, Moscow, under Gorbachev's leadership, finally recognized Zhenbao island as a territory of China.

China's external military conflicts in the 1970s and 1980s were all with Vietnam. The first one between the PRC and South Vietnam, which took place in January 1974, was a territorial dispute over the Xisha (Paracel) Islands, located in the mid-western part of the South China Sea. The clash was almost exclusively naval, involving six combat ships from China and four from South Vietnam. Although the South Vietnam navy, with support from the United States, was better equipped than the Chinese side, it was defeated — one ship sank into the sea and three were damaged, while one Chinese ship was wounded. The next day the People's Liberation Army, supported by the navy, launched an attack on the islands of Shanhu, Ganquan, and Jinyin, which had been occupied by the Vietnamese since 1956. Losses on the Chinese side included 18 dead and 67 wounded; whereas on the Vietnamese side more than one hundred died or were wounded and 48 were captured; an American liaison officer was also captured in this conflict (Deng Lifeng, 1994: 405–410; Fan, 1992: 77–79). The Chinese took over the Xisha (Paracel) Islands after the war was over. Since 1974, the Chinese navy have garrisoned the islands, keeping permanent stations at its capital, Yongxing Dao.[11]

From February to March of 1979, Beijing ordered Chinese troops into Vietnam to 'punish' the Vietnamese for invading Cambodia. This clash graphically revealed the depth of hostility existing between Vietnam, supported by the Soviet Union, and China. The Chinese mobilized about 225,000 troops, giving them a two to one superiority in terms of man-power over the 100,000 Vietnamese troops in the northern part of Vietnam. According to one estimation, each side suffered about 50,000 casualties (Adelman and Shih, 1993: 226–227).[12] The war lasted for less than a month, and was ended by the voluntary withdrawal of the Chinese troops back within the PRC border.[13]

A more recent, though minor, military engagement with Vietnam, took place in March 1988. This conflict was caused by the territorial dispute over the Nansha (Spratlys) Islands, 1,500 kilometres away from China's coast lines. China sent 15 naval ships with 1,000 soldiers. Chinese and Vietnamese naval vessels exchanged gunfire in the waters around the islands. Five Vietnamese war ships were either sunk or damaged, and permanent military stations were established by the Chinese navy (Fan, 1992: 80–81). The dispute still festers, however. Several of the Nansha (Spratlys) Islands, in the south part of the South China Sea, are still occupied by the Vietnamese and claimed by China. The military action alarmed Malaysia and the Philippines, who also have claims over the Nansha Islands. In 1990, China offered to hold the sovereignty question in abeyance while supporting joint economic development of the oil and gas resources.[14] (For details of later developments, see Chapter 7).

The PRC had two military crises with Taiwan (in 1954 to 1955, and again in 1958) in which Beijing and Taipei bombarded one another in clashes over the islands of Jinmen (Quemoy) and Mazu (Matsu), a few miles off the Mainland coast. This fighting was regarded by Beijing as a continuation of the Chinese Civil War (1946–9), and was initially regarded by both sides as an internal conflict. However, the United States, which at that time was committed to the preservation of the KMT regime led by Chiang Kai-shek, provided the Nationalist forces with the logistical support necessary to hold the islands when the Korean War broke out in 1950. This action created a barrier to Chinese–American rapprochement that lasted for more than 20 years — until President Richard Nixon's visit to China in 1972.[15]

The Revolutionary Era

After the Chinese Communist victory in 1949, the new leadership faced serious domestic and international problems, namely internal instability and external isolation by the West. The victory in the three-year civil war (1946–9) was regarded as a victory over the Communists' main rival, Chiang Kai-shek's Nationalist Party (the Kuomintang, or KMT). During the war, Chiang was supported by the United States with both military equipment and financial aid. This support was interpreted by the Chinese Communists as yet another Western imperialist invasion, not unlike that of the Opium War in the mid-nineteenth century. Those recent factors in 1949 were to colour Chinese perceptions and foreign policy, particularly toward the United States, for years to come.

In 1949, Mao Zedong established three principles on which Chinese foreign policy would be based:

- *Lingqi luzao* — literally 'to start up the fire in a new stove' — in this context meaning that the new China should initiate diplomatic relations with every country on a new basis;
- *Dasao ganjing wuzi zai qingke* — 'to clean house first and then invite guests' — meaning to consolidate the regime internally and then develop foreign relations;
- *Yibiandao* — 'leaning to one side' — meaning (under Mao) to favour the Soviet Union.[16]

Mao's principles for foreign policy after the establishment of the PRC in 1949 were clear, and answered three questions: how to establish

Beijing's new foreign policy, how to deal with the United States and other Western powers, and how to treat the Soviet Union and other socialist countries.[17]

The new Chinese leadership was confronted with the need to establish its legitimacy, an urgent task that was complicated by the rival leadership of Chiang Kai-shek in Taiwan. Domestically, the hostility between Taiwan and the Mainland was regarded as a continuation of the civil war. Internationally, it involved the issues of representation in the United Nations and regime recognition in the international community. Both Beijing and Taipei claimed that they were the sole legitimate representative of China. The issue of Taiwan became critical to the PRC's foreign policy, and for a long time was regarded by Beijing as a top priority in its external activities.

A second feature of Mao's new government was the importance assigned to communist ideology. As Andrew Janos (1964: 32–36) pointed out, the communists' theory of revolution is world revolution.[18] Although in the mid-1940s Mao had hoped to develop a smooth relationship with the United States,[19] the PRC chose a policy of leaning towards the Soviet Union. Beijing's decision to side with Moscow and against Washington was a predictable result of the US–Soviet Cold War, which had divided the world into two hostile camps: capitalist versus socialist. To show China's socialist colours, naturally, Beijing was compelled to join the socialist camp.

Driven by the perception of outside threats to the revolutionary regime, the Beijing leadership under Mao, as discussed earlier, often resorted to military means. It was with the goals of regime survival, national security, and the preservation and enhancement of ideology that China entered the Korean War and the Vietnam War.

Mao, until his death stuck to his belief that China must undertake 'continuous revolution'. Revolution has been defined as 'smashing the structure of authority, an action assuming charismatic leadership, mass mobilization, and structural vulnerability' (Dittmer, 1987: 43). Mao recognized that the establishment of a socialist society does not automatically lead to a genuine embracement of the new ideology by the masses. While seizure of political power and ownership from the exploiting classes could be completed within a relatively short period of time, it would take many generations before remnants of their old ideas and habits could be rooted out. From this Mao concluded that the struggle and the revolution 'must therefore continue'.[20]

Mao believed that any difficult problem could be overcome as long as the masses were mobilized. As he declared in 1949, 'Of all things in the world, people are the most precious. Under the leadership of the Communist Party, as long as there are people, every kind of miracle can be performed.'[21] Under this belief, Mao, through numerous political campaigns, challenged the structure of authority not only domestically, but also in the international arena. In 1962, Mao called for the preparation for a 'great era of the next 50 to 100 years that would undertake complete and profound changes in the world social systems' (Xie, 1993: 65–66). In an editorial of the *People's Daily* in early 1965, Beijing, for the first time, openly raised the slogan of 'world revolution' as a guide for Chinese foreign policy.[22] Such slogans as 'Down with imperialism', 'Down with revisionism', and 'Down with reactionists in the world', then became popular throughout much of the Cultural Revolution.

Mao's revolutionary ideas also derived from his beliefs in idealism and Utopianism in his youth (R. Li, 1992: 42–43). As Li Rui, Mao's secretary in the 1950s (R. Li, 1992: i) pointed out, Mao's radical ideas in his late age actually reflected his *huaijiu* ('cherish the old times') mentality.

Mao's idea that China was a revolutionary power and that it must support revolutionaries in other countries prevailed among the top leadership in Beijing. It is difficult to know just to what extent this belief was taken to heart, as those leaders who opposed Mao's ideas were severely criticized. But some did nevertheless speak out against it. In 1961 to 1962, Wang Jiaxiang, Secretary of the CCP Central Secretariat and General Director of the Party's International Liaison Department, argued that in order to concentrate on domestic economic development and to overcome the economic hardship that China faced at that time, China should be more moderate in its foreign policy. In an internally circulated letter of 1962, Wang further suggested that China should improve its relations with the United States, the Soviet Union, and India; at the same time, he felt, China should reduce its material support to the national liberation movements in Third World countries. Several top leaders, Liu Shaoqi and Deng Xiaoping included, expressed support for Wang. But Mao sharply criticized Wang and labelled his suggestions '*sanhe yishao*', meaning 'three reconciliations, and one reduction':

- reconciliation with imperialism headed by the United States;
- reconciliation with revisionism headed by the Soviet Union;
- reconciliation with reactionists represented by India; and
- a reduction of support to national liberation wars and revolutionary campaigns.

Wang Jiaxiang himself was later labelled a 'revisionist' and was removed from his leading positions (Wang, 1993: 20–25). Mao further pushed his revolutionary ideas in Chinese foreign policy to fight against 'imperialism' (the United States), 'revisionism' (the Soviet Union), and 'reactionism' (India), and to support revolutionaries around the world.

During this period, political-strategic considerations dominated Chinese foreign policy. In the early 1970s, Allen Whiting (1975: 202–203) conducted a study of China's external behaviour and found that, under Mao, Beijing's essential deterrence principles were as follows:

1. To justify active deterrence, China must perceive a threat to its border security or its national territorial integrity.
2. China's external situation mirrored its domestic situation, and was affected by the following axioms:
   • a superior power in proximity will seek to take advantage of China's domestic vulnerability;
   • two or more powers will combine against China if they can temporarily overcome their own conflicts of interest;
   • China must prepare for the worst while hoping for the best.
3. The best deterrent is belligerence:
   • to be credible, China will use military force; words will not suffice;
   • to be diplomatic, China will leave the enemy 'face' — a way out without humiliation;
   • if at first China does not succeed, it will try again.
4. Correct timing is essential:
   • warning must be given when a threat is perceived, not when it is imminent;
   • the rhythm of signals must permit the enemy to respond and China to confirm the situation;
   • China must control its own moves and not respond according to the enemy's choice.

These political-strategic considerations during the era of Mao often overshadowed other aspects of Chinese foreign policy, notably, China's foreign economic relations. Beijing was preoccupied domestically with political campaigns, and remained essentially an isolated country. For example, during the peak of the Cultural Revolution in 1967, the PRC went as far as to recall all (except one) of its ambassadors from abroad for the purpose of participating in the domestic political campaign. On 9 September 1966, Mao Zedong issued an instruction, known as the 'Nine-Nine Instruction' to the Foreign Affairs Ministry stating that all Chinese diplomats should disown their 'luxurious' clothes and automobiles. Consequently, all Chinese diplomats changed their clothes from brightly coloured Western-style suits and dresses to grey or black Chinese-style uniforms. Their luxury automobiles, such as Mercedes-Benz, were replaced with the domestic-made Hongqi (Red Flag) brand.[23] This simple style remained until more than a decade later, when Beijing began its policy of opening to the outside world.

Many of the earlier works on Chinese foreign policy which focus on the era of Mao have emphasized its revolutionary orientation with such titles as *Revolution and Foreign Policy* (Van Ness, 1970), or *Revolutionary Diplomacy* (Armstrong, 1977). This study emphasizes the long-term importance of this ideological era in the context of our theoretical model of analysis; this study will not, however, provide a systematic examination on the era of Mao and its policies.

The Trend Towards Modernization

By contrast to Mao's priority, Deng Xiaoping deemed modernization to be China's chief national goal. Zhou Enlai first raised the call for China's modernization at the first National People's Congress convention in 1954, calling for China's modernization in industry, agriculture, transportation, and defence. Ten years later, in 1964, the term Four Modernizations, referring to agriculture, industry, defence, and science and technology, was formally put forth to the Chinese people (P. Li, 1994: 276–286). The call for modernization was soon overshadowed by a series of political campaigns, such as the Anti-Rightist Campaign of 1957, and the advent of the Cultural Revolution in 1966. Toward the end of the Cultural Revolution in 1975, Zhou attempted to raise the issue again in a speech to the Fourth National People's Congress. As the First Deputy Premier at that time, Deng Xiaoping quickly picked up the theme of the Four Modernizations and called the 'entire Party and nation' to 'strive for the attainment of this great objective'.[24] Zhou and Deng's efforts could not resist Mao Zedong's determination to maintain 'continuous revolution' as China's top priority.[25] After Zhou's death in January 1976, Deng, himself, was again labelled 'a capitalist roader' by Mao and his associates, and was removed from all leading positions.

In 1977, one year after the death of Mao, Deng returned to power. From then on, he repeatedly emphasized the need to shift China's priority from revolution to modernization. This shift of national priority symbolizes the beginning of the post-revolutionary era in China. In a

1978 speech, Deng claimed that 'only if we make our country a modern, powerful socialist state can we more effectively consolidate the socialist system and cope with foreign aggression and subversion.'[26] Here, Deng clearly placed modernization as the priority for both domestic politics and foreign policy issues. Deng pushed further, calling the Chinese people to break down 'rigid thinking' (referring to blind or dogmatic thinking) and stated that 'the minds of cadres and of the masses' should be 'completely emancipated' (or freed from such thinking).[27] Beijing's change of attitude and policy toward foreign loans from the West serves as a good example in this regard (see Chapter 6).

In the beginning of 1980, Deng raised three tasks for China to work on for the decade ahead (the 1980s):

• to 'oppose hegemonism' and to 'preserve world peace';
• to work on 'China's reunification' with Taiwan; and
• to 'step up the drive for China's four modernizations'.

Deng singled out the third task as the most important one by stating that, 'modernization is at the core of all these three major tasks, because it is the essential condition for solving both our domestic and our external problems';[28] and 'nothing short of a world war could tear us away from this line.'[29] In his later years, one may notice, Deng often used the word development as a substitute for modernization.[30] In this sense, modernization and development are interchangeable for the purpose of examining China's priority goals under Deng.

Under Deng's leadership, China has undergone a series of profound domestic economic and political reforms that have pushed Beijing's foreign policy to become more open to the international community. Reform policies in the domestic economic area have been particularly important for the development of China's Open Door policy toward the outside world. Four reasons explain this dramatic change in policy.

First, as the domestic situation was gradually consolidated, so the Deng leadership acquired more self-confidence. This confidence was reinforced by the national consensus that China must concentrate on economic construction rather than the sort of all-consuming political campaigns that prevailed during the just-passed Cultural Revolution. The Chinese leadership now believes that emphasis should be given to economic modernization rather than to ideology. And this new priority inspired China's Open Door policy, because it required greater contacts with capitalist nations that were in a position to help China achieve its goal of economic modernization.

Table 3.1: Number of Countries Officially Recognizing the PRC (1949–1972)

Year	Number of Countries	Total
1949	10	10
1950	7	17
1951	1	18
1952	0	18
1953	0	18
1954	1	19
1955	3	22
1956	3	25
1957	1	26
1958	4	30
1959	2	32
1960	4	36
1961	2	38
1962	1	39
1963	2	41
1964	6	47
1965	1	48
1966	0	48
1967	0	48
1968	1	49
1969	0	49
1970	5	54
1971	15	69
1972	18	87

Source: Han Nianlong, (chief ed.), *Dang Dai Zhongguo Waijiao* [The Foreign Relations of Modern China] (Beijing: Zhongguo Shehuikexue Chubanshe, 1987)

Second, China's international status has changed since the early 1970s. In 1971, the United Nations voted to admit Beijing as the sole representative of China, as a result of which the PRC gained not only membership, but also a permanent seat on the UN Security Council. China's entrance into the international community was further accomplished by the 1971 to 1972 Kissinger–Nixon visit and by the establishment since 1972 of diplomatic relations with Japan and major European countries. In 1972, the Beijing government was officially recognized by 87 countries around the world, moving up from ten countries in 1949 (see Table 3.1).

Throughout the 1970s and most of the 1980s, China was regarded as one side of the 'strategic triangle' formed with the United States and the Soviet Union. Even after the collapse of the Soviet empire in the early 1990s brought an end to this triangle, the widespread recognition of China's strategic importance in East Asia has continued. Such vital global issues as 'international security, environmental protection, trade, development, and human and political rights', as Steven Levine (1992: 241) points out, 'cannot be addressed without full Chinese participation'. Thus, China has become a player rather than a challenger in the international community.

Third, the influence of ideology, particularly communist ideology, has declined, and pragmatism has correspondingly increased. China's early disputes with the United States (in the 1950s and 1960s) and the Soviet Union (in the 1960s) stemmed from considerations not only of national interest but also of ideology — namely, Maoist struggles against both capitalism/imperialism (the usual label for the United States) and revisionism (the typical label for the Soviet Union). Since the late 1970s, ideological considerations have largely given way to economic considerations.

Fourth, the countries surrounding China — Japan and the newly industrialized economies (NIEs) of South Korea, Taiwan, Hong Kong, and Singapore — have undergone rapid economic development. Three of these 'little dragons' are societies composed entirely or chiefly of Chinese people — Taiwan, Hong Kong, and Singapore. Recognition of this fact has stimulated fundamental changes in the Beijing leadership's interpretation of national survival on the world stage; economic competition, Beijing has come to appreciate, is no less important than political and military confrontation.

The new orientation of Chinese foreign policy in the era of Deng was further confirmed by what was called 'the 28-character strategy' which Deng raised in the wake of the Tiananmen Incident of 1989, when China was facing economic sanctions from the West, and dealing with the implications of the disintegration of the Soviet Union, and the collapse of communism in Eastern Europe. These strategies included the following seven phrases:

- *leng jing guan cha* — watch and analyse [developments] calmly;
- *wen zhu zhen jiao* — secure [our own] positions;
- *chen zhe ying fu* — deal [with changes] with confidence;
- *tao guang yang hui* — conceal [our] capacities;
- *shan yu shou zhuo* — be good at keeping a low profile;

- *jue bu dang tou* — never become the leader;
- *you suo zuo wei* — make some contributions.

In his talk with leading members of the CCP Central Committee in 1990, later published under the title 'Seize the Opportunity to Develop the Economy', Deng explained the strategy:

> Some developing countries would like China to become the leader of the Third World. But we absolutely cannot do that — this is one of our basic state policies. We can't afford to do it and besides, we aren't strong enough. There is nothing to be gained by playing that role; we would only lose most of our initiative.... We do not fear anyone, but we should not give offense to anyone either.[31]

This strategy has been summarized as the 'four *bu* and two *chao*' (Qu, 1994: 18–19), the key items of which are as follows:

- *bu kang qi* — do not carry the flag [of socialism], China should not seek to replace the role of the former Soviet Union, which was the leader for the socialist camp;
- *bu dang tou* — do not become the leader, China also should not become the leader for Third World countries;
- *chao yue yi shi xing tai yin su* — go beyond ideological considerations;
- *chao tuo* — detach from concrete events (or, try to avoid controversy).

That is to say, in order to concentrate on economic development (or modernization), China should keep a low profile in international affairs. Deng's idea is that 'by the middle of the next century', China should 'have basically realized modernization', and then it can be said that 'China has succeeded'.[32]

The remainder of this chapter examines five key characteristics that define the shift in the PRC's foreign policy from Mao to Deng:

- a change from the advocation of world revolution to the pursuit of a peaceful international environment;
- a change from hostility toward existing international norms to membership in the international order;
- a change from an emphasis on political and military build-up to a concentration on economic modernization;
- a change from dogmatic communism to growing pragmatism; and
- a change from the policy of 'liberation of Taiwan by force' to a policy of peaceful unification and the notion of *one country–two systems*.

From World Revolution to World Peace

As discussed in the beginning of the chapter, 'continuous revolution' was one of the main themes of the Mao era. Mao emphasized that 'our revolutions follow each other, one after another.'[33] Internally, class struggle and political campaigns were emphasized; and externally, China pursued radical policies to promote world revolution. Furthermore, according to the Maoist theory of revolution, domestic and international politics are equally relevant to the implementation of world revolution (Janos, 1964: 40).

These world revolutionary actions were reflected in two areas. The first was an effort to increase Chinese influence in the communist world, where an ideological debate was being waged concerning the nature of true Marxist–Leninist countries and adherence to Marxist–Leninist principles. This debate was waged particularly fiercely from the late 1950s to the mid-1970s, during which time the Soviet Union was under the leadership, first of Nikita Khrushchev and then Leonid Brezhnev. China asserted its independence within the communist camp, developing relations with Albania and later with Czechoslovakia and Rumania, which were on poor terms with Moscow. The PRC also attempted to play a leadership role in the communist movements of nearby countries, such as Burma, Cambodia, Japan, India, Indonesia, Korea, Laos, Malaya, the Philippines, Thailand, and Vietnam. At the same time, Beijing projected itself as a leading representative of Third World interests, and played an active role in the internal politics of Asian and African countries.

In 1965, China's defence minister Lin Biao elaborated on Beijing's strategy for world revolution. Lin (1965) believed that the Chinese Communist strategy of a people's war — the establishment of a revolutionary base in rural districts and the subsequent encirclement of the cities — could be applied equally well to world revolution: Europe and North America were the cities, the Third World countries were the countryside. Thus, world revolution hinged on the revolutionary struggles of the Asian, African, and Latin American people, who made up the overwhelming majority of the world's population. As the logic of this theory dictated, China gave strong support to the struggles of the Third World and vigorously opposed the two superpowers, a clear departure from the 'leaning to one side' policy of the 1950s.

China was the major supporter of communist armed movements in South-East Asia, including Burma, Indonesia, Laos, Malaya, the Philippines, Thailand, and Vietnam.[34] On some occasions in the 1950s and

1960s, Beijing sent military advisers to supervise local military activities. It is no secret that several well-known Chinese generals, such as Chen Geng and Wei Guoqing, directly advised the Vietnamese to fight against the French in the early 1950s. The Chinese support greatly aided the Vietnamese victory in 1954 at Dien Bien Phu, which led to the agreement of the Geneva Conference that temporarily settled the Indochina conflict.[35] From 1964 to 1967, a Chinese military 'working group', headed by General Duan Suquan, was sent to Laos to advise its Communist Party and to establish military bases (Quan and Du, 1990).

Since the late 1950s and throughout the 1960s, China accused the Soviet Union of 'revisionism', charging that under Khrushchev the Soviets were seeking 'peaceful coexistence' with 'the number one imperialist country', the United States, and therefore, were abandoning their 'revolutionary' responsibilities. Mao and his colleagues were also alarmed by what they perceived as Soviet attempts to control China, such as Khrushchev's proposal in 1958 to establish a joint Sino-Soviet fleet.[36]

At the same time in the 1960s, the United States was viewed with no less hostility. In East Asia, China supported North Korea and North Vietnam in their respective conflicts with the United States. Those countries that stood with the United States, such as Japan, South Korea, and South Vietnam, were labelled 'running dogs of American imperialism'. Mao's preoccupation with world revolution continued even into the era of rapprochement between the United States and China. It is true that Mao was the major architect of the reconciliation with the United States, but he never relinquished his revolutionary ideals. On the contrary, Mao continued to advocate struggle against the two 'hegemonic countries' — 'the American imperialists' and 'the Soviet social imperialists'.

Three explanations can be found for Chinese behaviour in this period. First, with national survival preoccupying the Beijing leadership, China was exceptionally sensitive to outside threats, particularly in the PRC's first two decades.

Second, the Chinese Communists regarded their revolution as a part of the world revolution. After defeating the US-backed forces of Chiang Kai-shek, the Beijing leadership saw no reason not to continue its successful pursuit of world revolution.

Third, the historical consciousness of 'China as the central kingdom of the world' remained in the minds of many Chinese leaders, especially Mao. For a long time, especially during the Cultural Revolution, the Chinese propaganda machine vigorously affirmed that China was the centre of world revolution and Mao its 'great leader and great helmsman'.

This radical position has been abandoned since the end of the Mao era and the start of the era of modernization. No longer does China regard itself as the centre of world revolution. Chen Qimao (1986: 26), director of the Shanghai Institute of International Studies, acknowledged in 1986 that human society is multicentric, not monocentric, and that 'this phenomenon has never been truer of the world than today'. Furthermore, Chinese leaders have repeatedly claimed that the maintenance of international peace is one of the major goals of Chinese foreign policy. On a number of occasions, Deng Xiaoping emphasized the importance of world peace to China. In 1984, for example, Deng stated, 'The aim of our foreign policy is world peace.' He further confirmed, 'we sincerely hope that no war will break out and that peace will be long-lasting, so that we can concentrate on the drive to modernize our country.'[37] This statement, compared with Lin's 1965 article mentioned earlier, typically reflects the changing priorities in Chinese foreign policy.

From Outsider to Insider

China's actions in the first two decades after the establishment of the PRC in 1949 demonstrated a strong dissatisfaction with the existing international order. China's bitter experience with the imperialist powers, dating back to the Opium War of 1839 to 1842, profoundly influenced the attitudes of the Chinese leadership and people toward the West. When, beginning in the mid-1950s, the Soviet Union began to conduct what Beijing perceived as 'a chauvinistic and expansionist' policy toward China, the Chinese became yet more suspicious of the established powers.

Beijing vigorously criticized existing international organizations, particularly the United Nations, from which it was excluded until 1971. Only once, in November 1950 when the General Assembly discussed the issue of a Korean war, was a Beijing representative permitted to address the United Nations.[38] Ever since the early 1950s, China emphasized its relationship with the Third World countries. In 1954, Chinese Premier Zhou Enlai and Indian Prime Minister Jawaharla Nehru jointly issued the well-known 'Five Principles of Peaceful Coexistence' (mutual respect for sovereignty and territorial integrity, mutual non-aggression, non-interference in each other's internal affairs, equality and mutual benefit, and peaceful coexistence), which became the official base of

Chinese foreign policy. A year later, China, Indonesia, India, and others initiated an Asian–African conference known as the Bandung Conference, held in Indonesia. In the early 1960s, Mao's China and Sukarno's Indonesia launched a dramatic — albeit eventually fruitless — initiative to create a new United Nations, the members of which would be the 'newly emerging forces'.[39] China also supported — this time with tangible results — the Jakarta 'International Games of Newly Emerging Forces', which were designed eventually to replace the Olympic Games.

Although the PRC joined the United Nations in October 1971, Chinese suspicion of the United Nations and other international organizations did not immediately disappear. In the early 1970s, China was still in the midst of the domestic turmoil caused by the Cultural Revolution, and the Chinese political stage was still dominated by Mao Zedong and his followers, known as the Gang of Four (Mao's wife, Jiang Qing, Zhang Chunqiao, Yao Wenyuan, and Wang Hongwen), who continued to criticize the United Nations for its vulnerability to manipulation by the two superpowers.

This outsider position, however, was destined to become a thing of the past when China instituted its far-reaching policy of reform and openness in 1978. China began to participate actively in international economic and cultural organizations, including the World Bank, the International Monetary Fund, and the Asian Development Bank. In 1984, the PRC sent teams to participate in the Olympic Games for the first time; and in 1990 China hosted the Asian Games in Beijing. In 1992 to 1993, China lobbied the international community (although ultimately unsuccessfully) to select Beijing as the host for the 2000 Olympic Games. Beijing has regularly participated in the UN voting activities.[40] China has also enhanced its working capacity in the United Nations; in addition to the regular members of its UN permanent delegation, the PRC greatly increased the number of its UN staff.[41] The number of Chinese staff members reached 171 in 1990, ranking third only after the United States (466) and France (235), and ahead of Britain (166), Germany (122), and Japan (96).[42]

Today, as Harry Harding (1988: 12) has pointed out, 'Beijing has secured the formal recognition of all major nations, occupies a permanent seat on the United Nations Security Council, is respected as a major regional power in East Asia, and is considered by some analysts to be a "candidate superpower" which will make an increasing mark on global issues as well.' Much to Beijing's satisfaction, the number of countries that have established diplomatic relations with the PRC has increased dramatically, rising from 54 in 1970 to 179 in 1992, while

Table 3.2: Number of Countries Recognizing the PRC and Taiwan (1969–1992)

Year	PRC	Taiwan	UN Membership
1969	49	67	126
1970	54	67	127
1971	69	54	132
1972	87	41	133
1973	89	37	135
1974	96	31	138
1975	105	27	144
1976	109	27	147
1977	111	23	149
1978	113	22	151
1979	117	22	152
1980	121	22	154
1981	121	23	157
1982	122	23	157
1983	125	24	158
1984	126	25	159
1985	127	23	159
1986	127	23	159
1987	127	23	159
1988	130	22	159
1989	132	23	159
1990	136	28	160
1991	140	29	167
1992	154	29	179

Source: Samuel Kim (1994a: 135) and Han Nianlong (1987)

over the same period, Taiwan's diplomatic ties have decreased from 67 to 29 (see Table 3.2).

As with global relations, in regional affairs China now, in general, plays a constructive rather than a disruptive role. Many Western observers recognize that 'sentiment in China itself favours continued integration internationally, not a return to isolation' (Polumbaum, 1990/91: 180–181). An example is China's attitude toward the Association of South East Asian Nations (ASEAN). Today China no longer considers ASEAN a threat to its security; rather, Beijing now believes that ASEAN is very important to regional stability, especially to the settlement of the

Indochina situation. China has significantly improved its relations with every ASEAN member state.[43] In July 1994, China, as an invited guest, actively participated in the first ASEAN Regional Forum in Bangkok, which was considered a significant first step at reducing opportunities for confrontation in a potentially volatile region.[44] At the meeting, Chinese Foreign Minister Qian Qichen provided a detailed explanation of China's military build-up and Chinese foreign policy towards this region.[45]

Beijing's new approach to arms control is that of an insider. China's long-standing policy in the era of Mao was to denounce arms control as a ploy by the United States and the Soviet Union to perpetuate their own nuclear superiority, and as an ineffective barrier to the arms race. In 1963 China sharply criticized the partial nuclear test ban agreement signed by the United States, the Soviet Union, and Great Britain. At that time, it may be noted, China did not possess nuclear weapons, and therefore felt compelled to protect their option to undertake nuclear tests. Successful tests in 1964 heralded the development of a Chinese nuclear arsenal over the next two decades, which removed China's previous rationale opposing nuclear non-proliferation efforts. In 1984, China joined the International Atomic Energy Agency and ratified the Outer Space Treaty, and began to participate in the UN disarmament meetings in Geneva (Joffe, 1987: 91–92). China's record of cooperation on nuclear arms control is not impressive from the standpoint of the Western nuclear club, and there is, doubtless, room for, and some hope for improvement in this sphere. As Zachary Davis (1995: 603) points out, however, the 'evolution of China's nuclear nonproliferation policy is not unlike that of other countries, including the United States.'[46]

On several occasions, Beijing, has at least indicated its interest in active participation in the nuclear non-proliferation treaty.[47] Beijing has made clear, however, that as long as the proposed test-ban treaty is not achieved by the signatories to the agreement, China will not discontinue its nuclear tests programme. This position was reiterated by China's president, Jiang Zemin, in August of 1995.[48] In May and August 1995, China conducted two underground nuclear tests at Lop Nor in Xinjiang. These tests have drawn protests from Japan, the United States, Australia, and New Zealand.[49]

China's position on UN peacekeeping forces in the Middle East has also changed over the years. Under Mao, Beijing consistently opposed the establishment and dispatch of UN peacekeeping forces to conflict-ridden areas. Even after it joined the United Nations, China continued its opposition, abstaining from voting — rather than vetoing outright —

to authorize peacekeeping missions. The beginning of the Deng era brought a significant change in this position. From 1978 onward, Beijing began to emphasize a greater role for the United Nations[50] and to support UN peacekeeping forces in the Middle East. In the General Assembly, for example, the Chinese voted for 258 of the 262 resolutions related to the Middle East that were adopted between 1982 and 1988, including 22 on the financing of Middle East peacekeeping forces. In 1985, Beijing began to explore the possibility of sending a group to join the UN peacekeeping forces in the Middle East.[51] And in 1992, Beijing sent a small contingent of troops (consisting of some 370 military men) to Cambodia to join the UN peacekeeping forces there. This is the first time the PRC ever sent troops to participated in UN peacekeeping activities.[52]

The PRC has appeared more flexible in other international disputes, notably the long-standing antagonism between Cambodia and Vietnam. In October 1991, China hosted a conference in Beijing (attended by Premier Li Peng, among others) in which the leaders of all four major Cambodian factions participated. China played a major role in the settlement of the Cambodia issue, which culminated in May 1993 elections that restored Prince Norodom Sihanouk to the position of head of state and marked the end of the Vietnamese-backed Hun Sen regime, which was installed after Vietnam invaded Cambodia in 1979 to oust the Khmer Rouge. In November 1991, Beijing and Hanoi normalized relations after a summit meeting in Beijing, claiming that 'a new era has begun in Sino-Vietnamese Relations.'[53] Despite the unsolved territorial disputes over islands in the South China Sea, Li Peng conducted an official visit to Vietnam in December 1992, signing four agreements guaranteeing foreign investment in each other's countries and encouraging economic, scientific, and cultural cooperation. China also provided Vietnam up to Rmb 80 million (US$14 million) worth of interest-free credit.[54]

From Political-Military Orientation to Economic Modernization

Under Mao Zedong, the goal of Chinese foreign policy was to secure maximum political influence and military strength. This ambition arose in part from a keen sense of vulnerability rooted in painful memories of successive invasions of China over the past century and enhanced by the regional wars following the 1949 revolution — the Korean War, the Vietnam War, and the border clashes with India and the Soviet Union. Convinced that World War III was inevitable, Mao Zedong, Lin Biao, and other radical leaders firmly believed that China must prepare for 'an early and total war'. They also sought to develop political and military power in order to further China's leadership of 'world revolution' and its support of other countries' revolutionary courses. In addition, when guiding domestic political campaigns, Mao Zedong constantly stressed the importance of continuous revolution and class struggle. When applying these principles to foreign policy, ideological, political, and strategic considerations retained the upper hand.

These beliefs were overshadowed by new thinking in the era of Deng Xiaoping. The new leadership painfully realized that China was not only far behind the developed countries, such as the United States and Japan, but also behind its small neighbours. Even Hong Kong and Taiwan, Chinese territories ruled by capitalist governments, were far more prosperous than the socialist Mainland. In an article entitled 'Deng Xiaoping's View about National Interests', Yan Xuetong (1994: 29–30) points out that 'the foremost national priority under Deng was China's economic interests'. For the first time in China's modern history, economic modernization became the primary goal for national development. Table 3.3 and Figure 3.1 show that China's national income increased less than three times in the last 15 years (from 1961's 99.6 billion yuan to 1976's 242.7 yuan) under Mao and more than eight times in the first 15 years (from 301.0 billion yuan in 1978 to 2,488.2 billion yuan in 1993) under Deng.

These changes have been reflected in Chinese foreign policy behaviour. Beijing's modernization drive has two chief components, *reform* and *openness,* both focused on economic development rather than on political campaigning. Furthermore, China has enlarged the range of its foreign-policy issues to include not only political-strategic elements, but also economic and cultural aspects. More recently, in December 1994, Chinese Foreign Minister Qian Qichen made clear that economic development is one of the most important goals in Chinese foreign policy.[55] China's foreign economic activities, including trade, investment, joint ventures, and the export of labour, have increased rapidly.

China's new direction in its foreign policy has long been recognized by the international community, and Western powers have adjusted their foreign policies to take account of this transition. As European Commissioner Leon Brittan points out, 'China is at a turning point in its relations with the outside world. . . . It is in Europe's interest to steer China into the world economic and political mainstream and away from isolation.' Based on this consideration, the European Union Commission in Brussels unveiled an ambitious new blueprint in July 1995 to

Table 3.3: Chinese National Income, 1952–1993

Year	National Income (billions of yuan)	Growth Rate (%)
1952	58.9	
1953	70.9	20
1954	74.8	6
1955	78.8	5
1956	88.2	12
1957	90.8	3
1958	111.8	23
1959	122.2	9
1960	122.0	0
1961	99.6	−18
1962	92.4	−7
1963	100.0	8
1964	116.6	17
1965	138.7	19
1966	158.6	14
1967	148.7	−6
1968	141.5	−5
1969	161.7	14
1970	192.6	19
1971	207.7	8
1972	213.6	3
1973	231.8	9
1974	234.8	1
1975	250.3	7
1976	242.7	−3
1977	264.4	9
1978	301.0	14
1979	335.0	11
1980	368.8	10
1981	394.1	7
1982	425.8	8
1983	473.6	11
1984	565.2	19
1985	702.0	24
1986	785.9	12
1987	931.3	19
1988	1173.8	26
1989	1317.6	12

Table 3.3: (cont.)

Year	National Income (billions of yuan)	Growth Rate (%)
1990	1438.4	9
1991	1611.7	12
1992	2022.3	25
1993	2488.2	23

Source: *Chinese Statistical Yearbook 1992* (Beijing: Statistical Bureau of the PRC, 1992); *Zhongguo Tongji Zhaiyao 1994* [Chinese Statistical Abstract 1994] (Beijing: Statistical Bureau of PRC, 1994)

further upgrade Europe's relations with China. One may notice that bilateral Euro-Chinese trade has been growing steadily over the past decade, rising from US$12 billion in 1985 to over US$40 billion in 1994.[56]

China's growing international involvement is also reflected in other areas. In terms of arms sales, China has become one of the largest arms suppliers in the world. While principally motivated by long-term political and strategic calculations, Beijing's military leaders also welcome arms sales as a means of financing the army's modernization (for further details about China's military policy and arms sales, see Chapter 4).

In practice, China's economic activities are often mixed with political goals. One such example can be found in the PRC's competition with Britain — ever since the early 1980s, when the two sides began negotiating over Hong Kong's future status after 1997 — to gain support from local Hong Kong people. Beijing, based its tactic on the theory that in a highly commercialized society such as Hong Kong, any businessperson's political attitude would be closely related to his or her commercial activities, and such a person would provide political support to those who could provide business benefits. Beijing therefore initiated — through its unofficial representative in Hong Kong, the Xinhua News Agency — a policy to cultivate a group of pro-China capitalists. On several occasions Beijing mobilized financial resources to support local capitalists by helping, mostly through loans, to make their businesses more prosperous or to overcome financial difficulties. This practice was described as *zhengzhi jiuhuodui* ['political fire brigade'] (Xu, 1993: 127–132).

Figure 3.1 Chinese National Income (1952–1993)

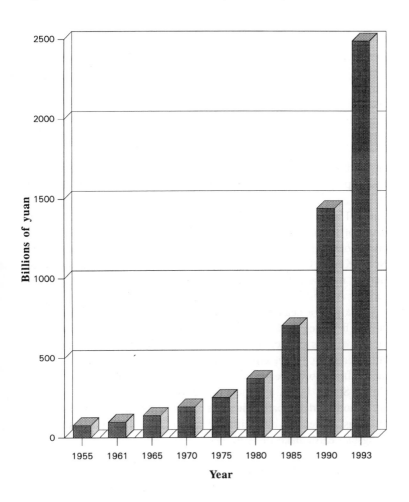

From Dogmatism to Pragmatism

During the peak of the Cultural Revolution, China conducted a radical foreign policy not only in word (its famous slogans), but also by its actions. Beijing isolated itself from the outside world as much as possible, leaving its population one of the least informed about international events in the world. As mentioned previously, China recalled all but one of its ambassadors in 1967, effectively shutting down its traditional foreign diplomatic channels. People were jailed if they were discovered to have listened to foreign radio broadcasts such as 'Voice of America' or 'Radio Moscow'. During this period, China was fighting against both superpowers: in border clashes with the Soviet Union in the north, and in an undeclared war with the United States in Vietnam to the south. There were major differences of opinion between China and many of its socialist 'brothers' and Third World friends. Among the many countries with which China was at odds were Indonesia, Burma, North Korea, Britain (over Hong Kong), Japan, Thailand, and India. Beijing maintained good relations with a handful of small countries, such as Albania and several African states.

China paid a heavy price for this dogmatic and isolationist foreign policy. It lagged far behind most other countries economically. Strategically, it was encircled by the two superpowers and hostile neighbours, creating a threatening environment. Although in the 1970s Mao made efforts to break the isolation by seeking rapprochement with the United States, Japan, and most of the Western powers, his revolutionary rhetoric and dogmatic principles remained fundamentally unchanged; this was evidenced by Beijing's actions following the catastrophic Tangshan earthquake in 1976.

Tangshan, a large coal manufacturing city in northern China, was struck by an earthquake that killed at least 250,000 people (by official account). Many governments, organizations, and individuals from throughout the world offered their help. The Beijing government, however, refused all such offers, believing that if they were accepted, China's principle of 'self-reliance' would be violated. In addition, the Gang of Four was still in power, and one of their most infamous slogans was 'we would rather have socialist grass [to eat] than capitalist grain'. How, then, could a socialist country accept support from capitalist nations?

It would be wrong, however, to assume that foreign policy was totally dominated by dogmatism during the Mao era; occasionally, Chinese foreign policy may appear pragmatic. Even on these pragmatic occasions, however, the Chinese leaders had to pay lip-service to dogmatic considerations. One typical example was Mao Zedong's decision to invite Henry Kissinger, US President Richard Nixon's national security adviser, to visit Beijing in October 1971. This decision was obviously based on the realistic and geopolitical considerations of world politics rather than any kind of ideology. But after Kissinger and his aides arrived in Beijing, they were shocked by the big eye-catching posters at the airport and the small pamphlets at their hotel rooms, all carrying such slogans as 'Down with the US imperialists and their running dogs'. Mao, himself, had to explain these away to his American guests as *fang kongpao* (meaning 'issuing empty statements for propaganda purposes'), a way to stick to China's projected revolutionary image in the world (Gong, 1992: 144–146).

This rigid policy had to change. Since 1978, Beijing has adopted reform-oriented and much more practical economic policies, both internally and externally. China has totally changed its attitudes towards such previously labelled 'capitalist practices' as joint ventures, foreign investment, and foreign loans (Chapter 6 will discuss the issue of foreign loans in detail). Throughout China, governments at the central, provincial, and district levels, all have worked hard to attract investment from abroad, one of the main avenues for obtaining foreign capital (such as foreign direct investment and loans), updated technology, and reaching international markets. The annual figure of foreign direct investment, for example, did not exceed one billion US dollars until 1984. It surged to new high levels in the early 1990s, exceeding US$4.5 billion in 1991, US$11 billion in 1992, and then almost US$26 billion in 1993 (Lardy, 1994: 63–64).

Since the early 1980s, Beijing has adopted an 'independent foreign policy', trying, on one hand, to maintain a friendly relationship with the United States, and, on the other hand, to improve its ties with the former Soviet Union. In practice, however, China has moved closer to the West, which is better able to meet the demands of China's modernization drive than was the Soviet bloc or today's Russia. Chinese foreign policy in the 1980s can be described as a 'tilted independent policy' — tilting toward the United States, Japan, and Western Europe. Clearly, this constituted a reversal from Mao's policy in the 1950s of leaning toward the Soviet, communist side, and a profound change from the policy in the 1970s of fighting against the two 'hegemonistic powers' — the Soviet Union and the United States.

China has also shown more flexibility regarding its policies towards Israel and South Africa. For many years, the PRC had refused to establish any official contact with Israel or South Africa, demonstrating Beijing's moral support of the Arabic states and China's disapproval of

South Africa's apartheid system. This situation began to change in the 1980s. China, while retaining its pro-Arabic stance, created unofficial ties with Israel by establishing academic exchanges in Tel Aviv and Beijing, and moved to full diplomatic relations in 1991. This flexibility has paid off for Beijing. China has since enjoyed good relations with Israel. There has been some form of military cooperation between the two countries. The Chinese military, for example, was able to acquire some advanced technology, such as that for air-refuelling, from Israel to upgrade its equipment.[57] More importantly, Tel Aviv has been closer to Beijing in the PRC–Taiwan rivalry. In 1994 Israel's exports to China reached more than US$1 billion, while its sales to Taiwan amounted to a mere US$70 million. In the spring of 1995, unlike neighbouring Jordan and the Gulf monarchies, Israel flatly refused to accept an 'unofficial' visit by Taiwan's president, Lee Teng-hui.[58]

A similar, although more gradual development has taken place between China and South Africa. In 1990, the two countries set up unofficial offices in one another's capitals — the 'Centre for Chinese Studies' in Beijing and 'Centre for South African Studies' in Pretoria. Most staff members in these two 'cultural centres' are diplomats. Since then, a few high-level visits have been made between the two countries. In October 1991, for example, South African Foreign Minister R. W. Botha paid a clandestine visit to Beijing to discuss bilateral relations.[59] This diplomatic manœuvre confirms that the Chinese leadership is much less concerned about ideological differences now than ever since 1949.

This new pragmatism also can be found in China's policy toward South Korea. The Beijing government has actively sought to expand economic relations with Seoul. China established indirect bilateral trade (via Hong Kong) and informal ties with Seoul in the early 1980s, and bilateral trade has since increased rapidly. In 1990, bilateral trade reached US$3.5 billion, far exceeding China's trade with North Korea of US$480 million; also in that year, Beijing and Seoul established permanent trading offices with each other. In November 1991, Foreign Minister Qian Qichen visited Seoul for the first time to attend the Asian Pacific Economic Cooperation (APEC) meeting. In September 1992, the two countries finally established diplomatic relations, marked by a visit to Beijing by President Roh Tae Woo. This relationship has satisfied the needs of both parties: China needs South Korea's capital and advanced technology, and South Korea needs China's vast markets and political recognition. (There will be a detailed discussion in Chapter 7 about Beijing's policies toward Seoul and Pyongyang.)

In a departure from previous practice, Beijing is now willing to accept all kinds of foreign aid, from World Bank loans to disaster relief funds. In 1991, China experienced devastating floods in both the north-eastern and south-eastern regions of the country. This natural disaster caused tremendous damage, including more than 2,000 deaths, and cost more than US$10 billion.[60] Beijing appealed to the international community and the people of Taiwan, Hong Kong, and Macau for support. By the end of 1991, China had received donations totalling 2.5 billion yuan (about US$500 million).[61] The Chinese government even agreed to allow the US Peace Corps to send volunteers to China.[62] And, of course, numerous forms of economic cooperation now exist between China and the West, including direct investment and joint ventures.[63]

In the strategic area, China's practices and policies have also become flexible. In 1986, several US naval vessels visited Qingdao, an important naval base in northern China. This was the first US military visit since the 1949 revolution. The United States was also allowed to place monitoring stations, aimed toward the Soviet Union (then the major rivalry of the United States), in the Xinjiang Minority Autonomous Region in the far western part of China.

China also showed flexibility in presenting new formulas for the peaceful settlements of the territory disputes with neighbouring countries, notably the formula of 'joint development'. Deng Xiaoping first raised the concept in 1978 during his visit to Japan, when he was asked about the Sino-Japanese dispute over Diaoyu Island (Senakaku to the Japanese). Deng answered that 'it should be set aside for the moment; probably the next generation will be cleverer than we and will find a practical solution.'[64] Deng's idea was that 'by having the countries concerned jointly develop the disputed areas before discussing the question of sovereignty' to resolve this kind of territorial dispute. This could also applied to the Nansha Islands (Spratlys).[65] There are two choices, according to Deng, 'one alternative is to take all these islands back by force; another is to set aside the question of sovereignty and develop them jointly.'[66] When compared with the first alternative, the 'joint development' idea seems more flexible. All these examples can be said to reflect increasing pragmatism in China's external activities.

From the 'Liberation of Taiwan' to 'One Country–Two Systems'

The fundamental shift in Chinese foreign policy from the era of Mao to the age of Deng is also evident in the PRC's Taiwan policy. The liberation of Taiwan by military force was a major objective during the Mao era. The slogan 'Liberate Taiwan' was the counterpart to the Taiwanese slogan 'Recover the Mainland'. In the late 1970s, Beijing made a significant change in its Taiwan policy by advocating a new catch phrase: 'Peaceful unification'. In the early 1980s, this policy developed into a new formula: 'one country–two systems'.

Mao proclaimed that, as a continuation of the civil war between the CCP and the KMT, the regime in Taiwan must be overthrown, and Taiwan must be integrated into the PRC as a province governed by socialist principles. During the 1950s and 1960s, Beijing was prepared to use military force to take over Taiwan, and sporadic military clashes occurred. Given the domestic and international atmosphere prevailing at that time — class struggle internally and the Cold War externally — little room existed for Beijing and Taipei to reach a compromise on the Taiwan issue. Hostility between the two sides was expressed in a propaganda war, in which each side offered huge cash incentives to lure defectors from the opposite side.

Since the start of the Deng era, Beijing has abandoned this hostile, uncompromising position. In 1978, Deng told a group of visiting US legislators that Beijing had given up the 'Liberate Taiwan' policy and had turned instead to a policy of peaceful unification. Since then, the PRC has made a series of overtures toward Taipei: Ye Jianying's Nine-Point Plan in January 1979, sent on behalf of the People's National Congress, emphasized peaceful unification with Taiwan; and in 1982, a personal letter to Taiwan's president, Chiang Ching-kuo, from CCP Politburo member Liao Chengzhi (both former classmates in the Soviet Union in the 1930s) stressing brotherhood. Deng Xiaoping's formula of 'one country-two systems', first expressed in 1983, has now become the foundation of Beijing's policy.

The proposal for 'one country-two systems' was formulated in recognition of the changing domestic and international situation. Freed from the Maoist ideological straight-jacket, Deng and his colleagues recognized that it was virtually impossible to incorporate Taiwan into the framework of socialism; differences in political, economic, and social life had become so great that neither the ruling elites nor the Taiwanese masses would accept a socialist system for the purpose of unification.

According to this proposal, after unification Taiwan would be allowed to maintain its foreign economic and cultural ties with other countries, as well as its own political, economic, and social system. Furthermore, it will maintain its own military forces and independent judicial power. Deng emphasized that 'The Party, governmental and military systems of Taiwan will be administered by the Taiwan authorities themselves.'[67] The KMT and opposition parties would participate in the leading bodies of the central government, such as the State Council, the Standing Committee of the National People's Congress, and the People's Supreme Court.

There are some other interpretations of 'one country-two systems'. Scholars have considered various possible impacts of the implementation of this proposal on China's political development.[68] In 1992, Yang Shangkun, then president of the PRC, suggested that once negotiations for unification begin, the issue of 'central-local' — that Beijing would represent the central government, whereas Taipei would function as a local one — would become moot, implying that the negotiations would be based on equal footing. For its part, Taipei has repeatedly expressed doubt about the promise of autonomous status under this formula.

Beijing's leadership has become aware that another possibility is that Taiwan may opt gradually to become independent. For this reason, Beijing steadfastly refuses to renounce the use of military force against Taiwan. Should Taiwan some day claim independence, it is believed that the PRC will use all means, including military force, to prevent independence. Beijing has no room to make any concessions to Taiwanese independence, having consistently insisted that it will prevent the creation of 'two Chinas' or a 'one China, one Taiwan' situation. Beijing has further demanded that Taipei should not be allowed to become an official member of any international political organization, such as the United Nations. After Taiwanese president Lee Teng-hui expressed what Beijing considered to be pro-independence opinions to the *Overseas Japanese Weekly* (in a rare exclusive interview published in May 1994), Beijing launched a series of open criticisms of Lee's 'independence tendency'.[69]

When Beijing perceives that China's sovereignty and regime legitimacy are being threatened, it will adopt an uncompromising stance, even to the point of using military force. Chinese Premier Li Peng, for example, sharply denounced the ideas of 'federation' or 'confederation', two widely discussed proposals for China's unification with Taiwan, as the same as creating 'two Chinas'.[70] Beijing's overtures for national unification have not so far been well received in Taipei. There is still considerable suspicion in Taiwan about the intentions of mainland China.[71] (A continued discussion of the Taiwan issue will be conducted in Chapter 7.)

However, if the basic principles are preserved, Beijing may show flexibility, thereby rendering some principles purely rhetorical. When the PRC deals with foreign countries over the issue of Taiwan, it may exhibit rigidity in official political relations, but flexibility in unofficial matters, such as economic, trade, and cultural ties (for further discussion see Chapter 5).

Beijing's flexibility can also be seen on some other issues. For example, beginning in the early 1980s, Beijing began to consent to Taipei's participation in some nonpolitical international organizations, such as the Olympic organizations and the Asian Development Bank (ADB). China consented to Taipei's membership in the ADB on the condition that Taipei use the name 'Chinese-Taipei.'

Continuities

Despite the many fundamental transformations in Chinese foreign policy since the end of the Mao era, it has remained consistent from 1949 to the 1990s in four important areas.[72] In the first place, China has continued to oppose any moves to establish regional hegemony, such as the military expansion of the former Soviet Union in the Asia-Pacific area. From the late 1970s to the late 1980s, prior to the normalization of relations between Beijing and Moscow, China stood firm on three conditions for normalizing relations with the USSR: a reduction of the number of Soviet troops on the Sino-Soviet and Sino-Mongolian borders; the withdrawal of Soviet troops from Afghanistan; and a halt to Soviet support of the Vietnamese-backed regime in Cambodia. China also strongly opposed Vietnam's attempt to establish regional hegemony in Indochina.

Second, China has maintained its support, albeit more in the sense of moral support since the late 1970s, for the countries of the Third World. The PRC leaders have frequently claimed that, economically, China, as a less developed country, is a part of the South in the great 'North–South dispute' and that China will defend the interests of less developed countries.

Third, the PRC remains sensitive to external threats, especially those that endanger national sovereignty or regime survival, such as support for Taiwanese independence. As under Mao, Beijing in the Deng era will take whatever steps are necessary, including the use of military force, to prevent the integrity of China's sovereignty and territory from being violated.

Fourth, the formation of foreign policy in China has always been highly centralized. The decision-making process in many other fields,

CHINA'S SYMBOLIC MACROSTRUCTURE

such as economic planning and cultural policy, has tended toward decentralization in recent years. Despite broader participation in the policy-making process (see Chapter 4), however, foreign policy continues to be controlled by a small group of top leaders.

Although economic modernization has become Beijing's major goal under the leadership of Deng Xiaoping, this does not mean that China is now unconcerned with other issues. National security and political-strategic considerations are also regarded as closely connected to modernization; even ideological considerations still exercise some influence; and regime survival remains, as it always has been, a top priority in Chinese foreign policy.

The Chinese leadership has shifted from single-minded concern with political-strategic considerations to a more encompassing approach to national interests. Beijing, under the leadership of Deng, no longer views the international system as invariably hostile. Because it has lost much international diplomatic recognition, Taiwan has become much less threatening to the legitimacy of the Beijing regime. The PRC has a solid standing in the United Nations, where it has played an increasingly active role. China, near the beginning of the twenty-first century, has border treaties with most of its neighbours and has maintained manageable and operational relations, although there have been ups and downs, with Europe and Japan, as well as with the United States.

In short, compared with the Mao era, the Beijing leadership in the Deng era perceives fewer external threats to its survival or to China's sovereignty, embraces a broader view of national interests, and recognizes the advantages of flexibility and cooperation, especially in economic matters.

Notes

1 According to Goldstein and Keohane (1993: 7–11), in addition to *world views*, there are two other types of beliefs. The first are *principled beliefs*, consisting of 'normative ideas that specify criteria for distinguishing right from wrong and just from unjust'. The second are *causal beliefs*, which are beliefs 'about cause-effect relationships which derive authority from the shared consensus of recognized elites'.

2 In July 1977, Deng Xiaoping attended the Tenth CCP Central Committee's Third Plenum, and was reinstated to all his offices: Party Vice-Chairman and member of the Politburo Standing Committee; Vice-Chairman of the Central Military Affairs Committee (CAC); Vice-Premier; and PLA Chief of Staff. He emerged as the CCP's third-ranking leader, after Hua Guofeng and Ye Jianying. A year later in December 1978 at the Third Plenum of the Eleventh Central Committee, Deng consolidated his power and achieved what Doak Barnett (1993: 10) called 'political primacy', although he never took the Party's top positions as did Mao Zedong. (By 1981, Hua Guofeng formally lost all three of his positions — Party chairmanship, to Hu Yaobang, premiership, to Zhao Ziyang, and the CAC chairmanship, to Deng Xiaoping.)

3 See Central Committee of the Communist Party of China (1981: 32).

4 For the theory of perception in international relations, see Robert Jervis (1976).

5 It should be emphasized that both Beijing and Taiwan regard Taiwan as a *domestic* issue with international implications. This will become clear later in this book, where the example of Taiwan is used to illustrate several points.

6 There are many studies analysing the Korean War. One may see, for example, Allen Whiting (1960); Dean Acheson (1971); Walter Zelman (1967); Robert Simmons (1975); Rosemary Foot (1985); Bevis Alexander (1986); Max Hastings (1987); Bruce Cumings (1981, 1990); Goncharov, Lewis, and Xue (1993); and Jian Chen (1994).

7 For detailed studies of the Sino-Indian border war, see Neville Maxwell (1970); Allen Whiting (1975); Nancy Jetly (1979); Yaacov Vertzberger (1984); and Xu Yan (1993).

8 Although there has been a significant improvement in bilateral relations between China and India, some observers believe that 'the two sides are poised for rivalry for regional dominance and influence in the multipolar world of the 21st Century'; see John Mohan Malik (1995).

9 See Han Nianlong (chief ed.) (1987: 280–283).

10 For detailed accounts of the Sino-Soviet border clashes in 1969, see Harrison Salisbury (1969); Thomas Robinson (1970); and Richard Wich (1980).

11 'Patriotism in the Paracels', *Eastern Express*, 25 October 1994, p. 8.

12 Another estimate of the PLA's casualties during the war is 26,000. See John Garver (1994: 315).

13 For more references to China's war with Vietnam, see Pao-min Chang (1986); Robert Ross (1988); Anne Gilks (1992); and Steven Hood (1992).

14 See Paul Godwin (1994: 180).

15 For detailed accounts of these cases, see Thomas Stolper (1985); Xu Yan (1992); and Morton Halperin; Warren Cohen (1990: 184); and He Di (1990: 222–245).

16 For a detailed elaboration of Chinese foreign policy during this period from Beijing's perspective, see Zhou Enlai's speech, 'Our Foreign Policy and Task', 30 April 1952 (Zhou, 1990: 48–57). Also see Han Nianlong (1987: 3–5); and John King Fairbank (1976: 386).

17 In his memoirs, Bo Yibo (1991: 35–45) explained the internal and external conditions for the *yibiandao* policy.
18 Quoted from Tsou (1965: 81).
19 Mao, himself, in 1944 even asked about the possibility of aid from the United States. See J. Reardon-Anderson (1980), particularly Chapters 3 and 4. According to Reardon-Anderson (1980: 44–45), 'Mao's target was Washington. The Central Committee directive prohibited requests for arms and ammunition, and Mao presented the idea to Service [Mr John Service was an American diplomatic to China at that time] only in an indirect fashion . . . In September a "qualified person in Yenan" [almost certainly Mao himself] issued an open call for aid on the front page of *Chieh Fang Jih Pao* [Jiefang Ribao].' Also see Michael Schaller (1979: 99–100); and Warren Cohen (1990: 162–163). For detailed accounts of the origins of the Cold War and the interactions among China, the Soviet Union, and the United States, see Odd Westad (1993); Rosemary Foot (1995); and Michael Hunt (1996).
20 This point has been elaborated by David Ho (1978: 393).
21 See Mao Zedong, 'The Bankruptcy of the Idealist Conception of History', originally published in 1949 (Mao, 1961: 454).
22 *Renmin Ribao* [People's Daily], 5 January 1965, p. 1.
23 For details, see Yuan (1995: 376).
24 See Deng Xiaoping, 'The Whole Party Should Take the Overall Interest into Account and Push the Economy Forward', 5 March 1975 (Deng, 1984: 14).
25 For a detailed account of Mao's continuous revolution, see Lowell Dittmer (1987).
26 See Deng Xiaoping, 'Speech at the Opening Ceremony of the National Conference on Science', 18 March 1978 (Deng, 1984: 102).
27 See Deng Xiaoping, 'Emancipate the Mind, Seek Truth from Facts and Unite as One in Looking to the Future', 13 December 1978 (Deng, 1984: 154).
28 See Deng Xiaoping, 'The Present Situation and the Tasks Before Us', 16 January 1980 (Deng, 1984: 224).
29 See Deng Xiaoping, 'Building A Socialism with A Specifically Chinese Character', 30 June 1984 (Deng Xiaoping, 1994: 73).
30 In 1985, for example, Deng stated that 'the two really great issues confronting the world today' are 'first, peace, and second, economic development'. See Deng Xiaoping, 'Peace and Development are the Two Outstanding Issues in the World Today', 4 March 1985 (Deng Xiaoping, 1994: 110).
31 See Deng Xiaoping, 'Seize the Opportunity to Develop the Economy', 24 December 1990 (Deng Xiaoping, 1994: 350–352).
32 See Deng Xiaoping, 'With Stable Policies of Reform and Opening to the Outside World, China Can Have Great Hopes for the Future', 4 September 1989 (Deng Xiaoping, 1994: 305–311).
33 Quoted from Robert Dernberger, et al. (1986: 184).
34 For details, see Robert C. North (1978: 106–107).
35 Regarding China's early support to Vietnam, see King Chen (1969); Han Nianlong (1989); Han Huaizhi (1989); and Zhai Qiang (1992).
36 For detailed accounts of discussions between Mao and Khrushchev, see Quan Yanchi (1989: 108–133).
37 See Deng Xiaoping, 'We must safeguard World Peace and Ensure Domestic Development', 29 May 1984 (Deng Xiaoping, 1994: 66–67).
38 See Wu Xiuquan (1991: 253–283).
39 For details, see Peter Van Ness (1971).
40 For an early record of China's voting behaviour on resolutions adopted by the UN Security Council, see Samuel Kim (1979: 518–521).
41 These staff members are officially recruited by the United Nations, but they have been approved by the Chinese government.
42 See Edward Lincoln (1993: 140).

43 For further details about China's relations with ASEAN countries, see Joyce K. Kallgren, et al. (1988); and Leo Suryadinata (1990: 682–696).
44 Rodney Tasker and Adam Schwarz, 'Preventive Measures', *Far Eastern Economic Review* (4 August 1994): 14–15.
45 Nayan Chanda, 'Gentle Giant: China Seeks to Calm Southeast Asia's Fears', *Far Eastern Economic Review* (4 August 1994): 15–16.
46 For detailed analysis, see Davis, Zachary (1995), 'China's Nonproliferation and Export Control'.
47 'Kaifu Visits Beijing to Refresh Ties', *Beijing Review*, 33, 34 (19–25 August 1991): 7.
48 *Far Eastern Economic Review* (24 August 1995): 15.
49 'Zhongguo zai jinxing dixia heshi' [China Conducts Underground Nuclear Test Again], *Yazhou Zhoukan* [The International Chinese Newsweekly] (27 August 1995): 41; Also see *Far Eastern Economic Review* (7 September 1995): 13.
50 See Li Luye, 'UN Role in Establishing a New World Order', *Beijing Review*, 34, 39, (30 September–6 October 1991): 12–16.
51 For a detailed account, see Yitzhak Shichor (1991: 255–269).
52 *World Journal*, 25 April 1992, p. 10.
53 Chen Jiabao, 'A New Era Begins in Sino-Vietnamese Relations', *Beijing Review*, 34, 46 (18–24 November 1991): 7–9; and Lincoln Kaye and Murray Hiebert, 'A Lesson in Ideology: China, Vietnam Sign Trade and Border Pacts at Summit', *Far Eastern Economic Review* (21 November 1991): 10–11.
54 Murray Hiebert, 'Comrades Apart', *Far Eastern Economic Review* (17 December 1992): 23.
55 *Renmin Ribao*, 15 December 1994, p. 6.
56 Shaha Islam, 'Softly, Softly: EU Wants Closer Ties with China', *Far Eastern Economic Review* (20 July 1995): 20.
57 Nayan Chanda, 'Fear of the Dragon', *Far Eastern Economic Review* (13 April 1995): 25.
58 Yarosiav Thofimov, 'Jilt and Tilt: Israel Stops Wooing Taiwan and Turns to China', *Far Eastern Economic Review* (25 May, 1995): 29.
59 'China Card', *Far Eastern Economic Review* (31 October 1991): 9.
60 There were many reports about the floods and donations from abroad in Chinese news media. See *Renmin Ribao*, 19 August 1991, p. 2.
61 *Renmin Ribao*, 10 February 1992, p. 1.
62 One should note, however, that the entry of the US Peace Corps was allowed with the proviso that the volunteers would only be allowed to teach English in a limited area and not to do their usual broader agenda, including development work and health education. Furthermore, they were not allowed to operate in China under the name 'Peace Corps', but as 'US-China Friendship Volunteers'.
63 For an excellent account of joint ventures in China, see Margaret Pearson (1991).
64 See Deng Xiaoping, 'Speech at the Third Plenary Session of the Central Advisory Commission of the Communist Party of China', 22 October 1984 (Deng, 1994: 94).
65 See Deng Xiaoping, 'A New Approach to Stabilizing the World Situation', 22 February 1984 (Deng, 1994: 59).
66 See Deng Xiaoping, 'Speech at the Third Plenary Session of the Central Advisory Commission of the Communist Party of China', 22 October 1984 (Deng, 1994: 94).
67 See Deng Xiaoping, 'An Idea for the Peaceful Reunification of the Chinese Mainland and Taiwan', 26 June 1983 (Deng, 1994: 40–42).
68 See Quansheng Zhao (1989), 'One Country Two Systems and One Country Two Parties: PRC-Taiwan Unification and Its Political Implication'.
69 Julian Baum, 'Dire Straits: Beijing Frets Over a More Independent Taiwan', *Far Eastern Economic Review* (21 July 1994): 19–20.
70 *Renmin Ribao*, 3 February 1992, p. 1.

71 For detailed accounts of the Taiwan issue and some other models of national uni-
    fication, see Quansheng Zhao and Robert Sutter (1991).
72 For detailed analyses of the changes and continuities in Chinese foreign policy, see,
    among others, Harry Harding (1983), 'Change and Continuity in Chinese Foreign
    Policy'; and Richard Walsh (1988).

4 Institutional Macrostructure and the Policy-making Process: From Vertical to Horizontal Authoritarianism

Institutional macrostructure refers to the practical social reality, the level at which foreign policy is made and implemented. The study of the *processes* and *mechanisms* of foreign policy is one of the most effective ways to comprehend and apply the micro-macro linkage approach. This chapter seeks to understand elements at the macro level such as societal-institutional inputs, examining the scope and degree of a society's participation in the policy-making process, and changes in the institutional structure, rules, and norms governing the formulation of foreign policy. The study is thus made more dynamic, or applicable to a variety of circumstances, rather than static.

The study of mechanisms and processes for the purposes of this exploration of the institutional macrostructure requires our research to become more specific. Efforts must be made to obtain enough new sources to enable us to establish links between the macro and micro spheres in terms of the policy-making process for Chinese foreign policy. More specifically, this research should ask such basic questions as during what time periods has the specific policy been made, toward what countries is a particular policy targeted, and what issues have influenced China's foreign relations. Now let us look at these specific institutional circumstances where Chinese foreign policy has been made.

Policy-making Structure

The primary interest of a state, according to Machiavelli, is to seek survival.[1] And for the PRC, state survival in the international arena is as important as regime survival domestically, as evidenced by the repression of pro-democracy forces in Tiananmen Square in June 1989. In every country, of course, foreign policy behaviour is affected by the domestic environment. In the case of China, though, the close connection between internal conditions — social, political, economic, and institutional — and external actions is worth special attention, for it often holds the key to understand Beijing's external behaviour. Indeed, for the leadership of the PRC, as Foreign Minister Qian Qichen noted, 'Diplomacy is the extension of internal affairs.'[2] To understand the institutional macrostructure and its impact on Chinese foreign policy, one must examine China's policy-making structure, and focus, in particular, on the changing process of political institutions, elite politics, and general political and economic conditions. This chapter also discusses the relationship between domestic politics and foreign policy, and attempts to explain how domestic politics affect Beijing's choices in external affairs and why Chinese foreign policy has not changed drastically in the post-Tiananmen period of the early 1990s. It concentrates on the interrelationship among social, economic, and political conditions and the changing process of foreign policy-making. In the course of this investigation, the following institutional and social elements will be discussed: policy-making mechanisms, policy-issue agendas, bureaucratic interests, the relationship between the central government and local authorities, general political and economic conditions, and the role of the people.

From One-Person Domination to Collective Authoritarianism

In the wake of the political and economic reforms following the Cultural Revolution, the Chinese political system and decision-making process has remained fundamentally authoritarian in nature. This is particularly noticeable in the formulation of foreign policy, which continues to be highly centralized and personalized and lacks institutionalization. That is to say, foreign policy is directed by and highly reflective of either one individual's or a certain set of individuals' perceptions, tendencies, and preferences. Nevertheless, a number of changes have occurred under Deng Xiaoping, changes significant enough to affect the process of foreign policy-making. A number of scholars have analysed this 'halfway change', which stops short of transforming the authoritarian nature of Chinese politics. Harry Harding (1987: 200) has called the post-Mao regime a 'consultative authoritarian' regime. He argues that China has experienced 'a significant departure from the totalitarianism of the recent past', but has not yet become a 'truly pluralistic, or even quasi-democratic, political system'. Here Harding referred not only to the foreign policy process, but also to the entire political system. Robert Scalapino (1989: 127) has pointed out that while 'keeping a rein on political rights yet enabling initiatives to operate in such areas as enterprise and religion, governments achieve a mix of stability and dynamism suitable to indigenous conditions'. Scalapino believes that the Asian Leninist states, primarily China, 'are now gravitating in this direction'. Kenneth Lieberthal and David Lampton (1992) have raised a 'fragmented authoritarianism model' to describe bureaucratic politics and decision-making in post-Mao China. This model argues that 'authority below the very peak of the Chinese political system is fragmented and disjointed. The fragmentation is structurally based and has been enhanced by reform policies regarding procedures' (Lieberthal, 1992: 8).[3] Some other scholars, emphasizing the decentralizing nature of China's economic reforms, have described China's development since the 1980s as 'federalism, Chinese style' (Montinola, Qian, and Weingast, 1995).

This trend has had an impact on the making of Chinese foreign policy: Beijing has moved away from the Mao era, when a single leader dominated foreign policy-making. This transformation has been described by Doak Barnett (1985: 16) as a move 'from individual to collective decision-making'.

The organization of the Chinese policy-making apparatus has shifted from *vertical authoritarianism* to *horizontal authoritarianism*, a notion developed in a 1992 article by this author, published in *The Annals of the American Academic of Political and Social Science* (Zhao, 1992). The terms used here refer primarily to the policy-making process rather than to the nature of the regime itself, although the two may have a close connection. To avoid confusion with regard to the terminology, it is necessary to note that *vertical* and *horizontal* when used here refer only to the scope, character, and nature of participation in the foreign policy-making process (for example, *collective decision-making versus one-person domination*), and not to the command channels of foreign policy. Indeed, foreign policy formulation and implementation in virtually every country, authoritarian or democratic, takes place within vertical command channels.

Vertical authoritarianism refers to a policy-making process in which a paramount leader dominates through a vertical command system. Vertical authoritarianism is often seen in communist countries, such as the Soviet Union under Stalin, Rumania under Ceausescu, North Korea under Kim Il-Sung, and China under Mao. The paramount leader makes virtually every strategically important decision regarding foreign policy issues. Under Mao, Premier Zhou Enlai, in consultation with members of the Politburo and a small group of foreign affairs specialists, was primarily 'in charge of the conduct of foreign affairs'.[4] Governmental bureaucracies, particularly the Ministry of Foreign Affairs, implemented foreign policy.

Vertical authoritarianism is characterized by one-person domination, a single, vertical, command system, and one fundamentally unified foreign policy. Political institutions and governmental bureaucracy participate in the policy-making process in a passive manner. Foreign audiences are permitted to hear only one voice on foreign policy issues.

Horizontal authoritarianism refers to a policy-making process that is essentially authoritarian and highly centralized, but in which several power centres at the top level represent and coordinate various interests and opinions. Multiple command channels, both institutional and *ad hoc*, exist. More players participate in the foreign policy-making process, and conflicting voices may occasionally represent different interests and policies. Horizontal authoritarianism is also called 'collective authoritarianism'.

In a comparison of the two, horizontal authoritarianism seems less personalized and more institutionalized than vertical authoritarianism and therefore may lead to a more pluralistic policy-making system. This possibility is discussed later in this chapter. The change that China has undergone has been driven by the lessons of recent history, particularly from the Cultural Revolution, the upheavals of which created an unprecedented challenge to regime legitimacy. This legitimacy crisis made the Chinese leaders realize the serious problem of 'internal security', prompting a consensus among the post-Mao leadership that to ensure the survival of the Communist regime, profound changes must occur in the basic interpretations of internal and external environments. This change at the symbolic macrostructure level of Chinese foreign policy was analysed in Chapter 3.

Other forces behind the transformation include economic development and modernization efforts, the emerging power and influence of technocratic bureaucrats at the top level, the passing away of the old revolutionary generation, China's opening up to the outside world, the enormous increase in the diversity and complexity of foreign policy decisions, and, finally, the political awakening of the Chinese people. Despite the setbacks of 1989, economic reforms and other developments of the Deng era have continued.[5] The continuing existence of these forces will maintain the momentum of transformation and will prevent China from returning to vertical authoritarianism.

An examination of the transformation from vertical authoritarianism to horizontal authoritarianism and the relationship between domestic and foreign policy requires an analysis of the following characteristics of this change:

- the existence of, and debates among power centres at the top levels;
- the representation of bureaucratic interests in political institutions;
- a broadening of the agenda of policy issues;
- the growing involvement of local interests in the central government;
- the increasing participation of intellectuals and think tanks;
- the influence of general political and economic conditions;
- an increased sensitivity to the power and opinions of the Chinese people.

This chapter focuses more on political institutions and elite politics than on mass politics. As Mancur Olson (1990: 26) suggests, in Soviet-type societies and autocratic environments, 'it is usually better to look at the regime and at the civil and military officials rather than only at the preferences of the people to understand what happens.'

However, this does not mean that the demands of the people are not important. China's domestic politics and its foreign policy have been influenced in recent years by the people's political demands and new forms of political participation, namely demonstrations and passive resistance.

Power Centres are Allowed a Voice

The existence of various factions at the top level of Chinese politics is widely known. Kenneth Lieberthal (1984: 44–45) identifies three prominent schools of thought within the Chinese foreign policy-making establishment: *nativists*, who encourage a closed-door foreign policy; *eclectic organizers*, who want to strengthen China by using foreign technology, while shielding the country from the cultural influences that accompany technological imports; and the *all-around modernizers*, who strive to alter the fundamental nature of Chinese culture in favour of rapid economic development to speed up the country's modernization process.[6]

Factional differences among the elite are not new. Mao Zedong and Zhou Enlai differed in their perceptions of the outside world and on foreign policy issues. Under vertical authoritarianism, however, the paramount leader was usually able to silence different opinions. According to 'some Chinese who were close to Zhou at that time', Mao's influence in the making of broad strategic decisions on foreign policy 'greatly overshadowed that of Zhou' (Doak Barnett, 1985: 7–8). One case in point was the famous 'ping-pong diplomacy', in which China invited an American ping-pong team to visit Beijing in April 1971; this became one of the first steps toward normalization between the two countries. Mao had initially agreed with Zhou's recommendation that American players should not be invited at that time, and relayed his decision back to Zhou. But several hours later, Mao changed his mind and asked his nurse to call Wang Hairong, chief of protocol at the Ministry of Foreign Affairs, to invite the American team to China right away. Mao, himself, changed this decision on a major foreign policy issue without any consultation with Zhou Enlai, and Zhou simply carried out Mao's instruction (Z. Li, 1994: 558).

Nevertheless, until his death in 1976 Zhou Enlai remained the second most influential figure (only after Mao) in China's foreign affairs, especially in the implementation of Chinese foreign policy. Even Mao Zedong himself once admitted to a foreign visitor in 1957 that, 'Comrade Zhou Enlai is better than me in broad international activities. He is good at dealing with various controversies, and is very smart and capable.' Chinese foreign minister Qian Qichen, who worked under Zhou for a long time, regarded Zhou as 'a founding father of the new China's diplomacy' (P. Li, 1994: 306–311). One important reason for Zhou's remarkable political survival throughout one campaign and purge after another, was his undisputed loyalty to Mao and his indispensable role as the chief administrator in the Chinese government.

The muffling of disagreement was often accomplished by severe measures. As discussed in the previous chapter, in the early 1960s Mao labelled Wang Jiaxiang's ideas for a more moderate foreign policy as '*sanhe yishao*' (three reconciliations and one reduction), and was criticized as revisionist. Wang himself was removed from his prominent position in the foreign policy apparatus, and was severely struggled against during the Cultural Revolution. Another example is the fate of Peng Dehuai, the former marshal and defence minister. When Peng voiced dissenting opinions on domestic and foreign policy issues at the Lushan Conference in 1959, he was immediately removed from the top military position. Later, during the Cultural Revolution he was placed under house arrest and was tortured to death in 1974.

Under horizontal authoritarianism, Deng Xiaoping has had less authority and power than did Mao. It is now relatively difficult to silence or eliminate political leaders who have different opinions but similar political power. (Leaders with a weaker power base, such as Hu Yaobang and Zhao Ziyang, however, may still be removed from leading positions.) Deng has had to tolerate different opinions at the top level.

Beijing's 'independent foreign policy' — independent, that is, from both superpowers[7] — reflects China's national interests, but it can also be regarded as a compromise between two schools of thought represented by different power centres. These power centres are not institutionalized; they are based on personal prestige and connections. But the very fact that more than one power centre exists, and that differences of opinion on policy issues are actually expressed, is a major change from the previous regime of one-person domination.

Deng Xiaoping and Chen Yun, a senior leader who, prior to the Cultural Revolution, ranked higher than Deng within the Party hierarchy (see Appendix I), shared many similar ideas on a broad range of domestic and foreign policy issues. Nevertheless, there were differences between the two over policy directions throughout the 1980s. Domestically, Chen favoured a more centrally planned economy than Deng. Internationally, Deng, who had experience in dealing with the Soviet Union and was deeply concerned about Soviet expansionist intentions, was in favour of a foreign policy that would draw China closer to the West. By contrast, Chen was virtually the only top Chinese leader who had never publicly criticized the Soviet Union. Long before the formal normalization of relations between China and the Soviet Union (marked by the Deng–Gorbachev summit in May 1989), Chen advocated a conciliatory policy toward Moscow.

By using the factionalism model to explain Chinese politics, Lowell Dittmer and Yu-shan Wu (1995: 493) have characterized the difference between Deng and Chen as a 'debate between economic growth and economic stability under reform: Deng's pro-growth group favoured "rapid growth, even at the expense of stability"; whereas Chen's pro-stability group considered "stability the paramount goal (*wending yadao yiqie*), even overriding considerations of growth'.[8]

Before Chen's death in 1995, one could still hear different voices from the two power centres. Beginning with the 1990s, the health conditions of both Deng and Chen declined noticeably when they approached or passed 90 years old (Deng and Chen were born in 1904 and 1905 respectively). In 1990, there was open support for 'Chen Yun thought', which called for studying and mastering 'Comrade Chen Yun's economic thinking about the correct relationship between planning and market'.[9] Chen's son Chen Yuan, a deputy governor of the Chinese People's Bank (a position equal to vice-minister) and widely regarded as the spokesman for Chen Yun's thinking, actively advocated his father's ideas on economic and political issues in Beijing's political circles.[10]

To advance his own reformist ideas and combat the voice of Chen Yun and Chen's proteges such as Li Peng, Yao Yilin, and Song Ping, Deng Xiaoping made a high-profile trip in January 1992 to Shenzhen and Zhuhai, China's most dynamic and prosperous Special Economic Zones. On this trip, Deng sharply criticized 'leftist ideas', which he felt had become the greatest obstacle to the modernization of China.[11] Deng's remarks were later circulated as a CCP Central Document and set the tone for the 14th Party Congress, held in October 1992. The leadership that emerged from that Party congress can be regarded as a compromise between Deng and Chen: while Li Peng survived his premiership, Yao Yilin and Song Ping were removed (and retired) from the standing committee and were replaced by two reformists, Zhu Rongji and Hu Jintao.

The apparent rivalry relationship between the two power houses did not end until Chen's death in April of 1995. As recently as the 1994 Spring Festival, both Deng and Chen made several appearances in Shanghai, again making different assessment of the current situation. Deng reportedly stressed a rosier assessment of the current economic situation, whereas Chen's emphasis was on 'difficulties and problems'. This enduring competition between the two power centres was called 'the death watch' by some observers.[12] Actually, in many ways Chen was not necessarily against Deng's reform policy. But people had been afraid prior to Chen's death that if Deng should happen to die first, then some left-wing officials would attempt to use Chen's name to alter reform-oriented policies.[13]

By the beginning of the mid-1990s, all factions in Beijing's Party/State leadership have begun to prepare for the arrival of the post-Deng era. Among them, the leading power centre has been Jiang Zemin, the general secretary of the Party and the president of the State. After the Tiananmen Incident of 1989, Deng Xiaoping designated Jiang as the 'core' of the CCP's 'third generation of collective leadership'.[14] Since then, Jiang has gradually built up his own power base.

From 1994 to early 1995, Jiang made significant manœuvres on several important fronts. At the top level, he promoted two of his allies — former Shanghai Party Secretary Wu Bangguo and former Shandong Party Secretary Jiang Chunyun — to become members of the CCP Central Secretariat. In March 1995, both Wu and Jiang were further promoted to vice-premier, in charge of state enterprises and agriculture respectively. Along the same line, Jiang Zemin's protege Zeng Peiyan, a vice-minister at the State Planning Commission, was promoted to secretary-general of the Central Committee's secretive Leading Group on Finance and Economics, the country's highest authority on economic policy. By this tactic, Jiang has further increased his influence on China's economic affairs, sharing control with China's economic tsar, Vice-Premier Zhu Rongji.[15]

As chairman of the Central Military Commission, Jiang also promoted more of his proteges into key positions in the PLA, the PAP (People's Armed Police), and the security apparatus. His close aide Zeng Qinghong, the head of both the Office of the Central Committee and the Office of the President (the office which administers presidential affairs) was also given new and expanded responsibility for intelligence and security. Jiang also made a move to consolidate his control over personnel matters by promoting another of his proteges, Zhang Quanjing, to become head of the powerful Central Organization Department of the CCP's Central Committee.

Jiang Zemin made his next strategic offensive in the field of propaganda. In December 1994, a major conference on the study of the third volume of Deng Xiaoping's Selected Works was held in Beijing. It was organized by such propaganda power houses as the Central Propaganda Department, the Central Party School, the Central Archives' Research Office, the State Education Commission, the Chinese Academy of Social Sciences, and the PLA's General Political Department. This conference was believed to be targeted at the Party's internal factions on both the left and right, and was designed to show these factions that 'Jiang and his followers had the support of various sectors, including the army'.[16]

The further consolidation of Jiang's power base does not mean that he will not be challenged by other power centres within the 'third generation of Chinese leadership'. There have been periodical speculations and reports about other potential power centres, including top leaders such as Li Peng, Qiao Shi, and Zhu Rongji. Yet, all these leaders kept low profiles prior to the passing away of the 'second generation of leadership' centred around paramount leader Deng Xiaoping.

When differences are openly voiced at the top level, consultation, coordination, and compromise are required to reconcile them. Because it takes time to gather consensus, the best temporary solution to many problems is to maintain the status quo. This is especially true in the field of foreign policy because foreign policy issues may appear less relevant to a top-level power struggle than domestic issues such as political and economic reform. Thus, it is not surprising that the Seventh Plenum of the CCP's Central Committee, held in December 1990, a year and a half after the Tiananmen Incident, produced nothing of substance in either domestic or foreign policy. A China watcher observed that 'this lack of substance underlines the present paralysis gripping the policy-making process.'[17] The inability to generate new initiatives due to the temporary tension between power centres partially explains why Chinese foreign policy after the 1989 Tiananmen Incident remained relatively unchanged, despite the turmoil in domestic politics.

The Growth of Bureaucratic Participation

In China, every political institution is led by the Communist Party. However, the Party and the government have separate agencies for dealing with foreign affairs, each with different functions. The International Liaison Department is in charge of the Party's international activities, while the State Council controls several ministries that have jurisdiction over foreign policy issues, most notably the Ministry of Foreign Affairs. Many other institutions also have organizations that deal with foreign affairs; for example, the National People's Congress (NPC) has a foreign affairs committee.

The administrative reforms of the 1980s brought a generation of technocrats into the ranks of the government bureaucracy. These technocratic bureaucrats are relatively young, well educated, and confident and assertive in their fields of specialization.[18] As David Bachman (1989: 37) argues, this younger generation of leaders, including the State president and the Party's general secretary, Jiang Zemin, and Premier Li Peng, has a smaller power base and less authority than the older generation, which includes Mao, Zhou, and Deng. If Bachman is correct, politics in the near future will probably be based more on persuasion and compromise; bold, new initiatives harming entrenched bureaucratic interests will be less likely. This new group of bureaucrats, including those working in foreign affairs, has participated actively both in the policy-making process and in the protection of bureaucratic interests.

The participation of bureaucrats in the policy-making process is primarily reflected in day-to-day affairs. Foreign affairs bureaucrats may play an active role within their own jurisdictions. In the Chinese Embassy to the United States, for example, diplomats have improved their efficiency by focusing their attention on key institutions of US foreign policy, including not only the executive branch, but also the American legislature. In the mid-1980s, the Chinese embassy in Washington established a division of congressional affairs to conduct extensive research and diplomatic activities.[19] This has allowed foreign affairs bureaucrats opportunities to make policy suggestions to the top and has thus enhanced their influence in the policy-making process.

The National People's Congress (NPC) offers another example of increased bureaucratic participation in the policy-making process. In China, Party staff members, the government, and the Congress are all regarded as government employees; they are all part of the central bureaucracy. The NPC Foreign Affairs Committee is largely staffed by retired high-ranking diplomats; it too can be considered a part of the bureaucratic establishment. Although the NPC has long been regarded as a rubber-stamping body, since the 1980s it has increased its influence.

An interesting episode regarding the issue of Hong Kong took place in May 1984, several months before the signing of the historic Sino-British agreement on Hong Kong's return to China in 1997. On the morning of 20 May 1984, Deng Xiaoping made an unplanned statement to some Hong Kong and Macau reporters and the delegates to the NPC. Deng made it clear that only he, himself, the premier, the foreign minister, the director of the State Council's Hong Kong and Macau Affairs Office, and the director of the Hong Kong Branch of Xinhua could speak officially about Beijing's Hong Kong policy. Any other officials' statements should be considered 'invalid and unofficial'. Deng's angry remarks were aimed at two NPC vice-chairmen, Geng Biao and Huang Hua, who had served as defence minister and foreign minister, respectively, before serving on the NPC. Geng had openly suggested that China would not deploy any troops in Hong Kong; and Huang had said that Hong Kong could be represented in the Chinese mission to the United Nations.[20] Although the two senior NPC leaders' statements were refuted by the paramount leader, who emphasized that the People's Liberation Army would be stationed in Hong Kong after 1997, the fact that they could express a different view at all is a significant indicator of the NPC's potential role.

In his study of the NPC's potential influence upon China's policy-making process, Kevin O'Brien (1990: 793–794) argues that the NPC is 'neither a classic conservative legislature, nor a dynamic base for mobilization that propels social groups into the political process'. O'Brien believes that semi-retired elites, regional leaders, and mass representatives express minority opinions and exert a moderating influence, largely by 'highlighting adverse public opinions and by insisting on procedural regularity and a systematic approach to problems'. In foreign policy as well as in domestic politics, the NPC may eventually become a place for bargaining and compromise. Several examples from the latter part of the Deng reform era have proven this argument. One recent example is the NPC's annual meeting in March 1995, where the two candidates for vice-premiership, Jiang Chunyun and Wu Bangguo, received only 64 per cent and 86 per cent of votes respectively (rather than the usual rubber-stamp approval votes) — an unprecedented, low record at the national level. Furthermore, NPC vice-chairman Tian Jiyun, a former Politburo member and vice-premier, openly advocated more rambunctious debates and multi-candidate elections in parliament to fill cabinet slots.[21]

One can, indeed, hear more calls in recent years for the enhancement of the NPC's power. Victor Sit, a NPC deputy from Hong Kong, for example, proposed in May 1995 that the NPC should be reformed further along the following lines:

- it should become a full-time institution;
- restructure its organization to become a real organ of power;
- formalize relationships between the NPC, the administration, and the Party; and
- improve the election system and establish regular and efficient links between the representatives and the voters.[22]

Broadening Policy Agendas

Participation in the policy-making process seems certain to increase as the number of issues on the policy agenda increases, especially in cases where these issues do not involve major strategic or political decisions. As China has opened to the outside world, foreign policy decisions have became more complex and wide ranging. This is particularly noticeable in the areas of foreign economic and cultural exchange, and military policy and arms sales, issues which involve a larger number of participants, and thus a greater variety of interests in the policy-making process than is usual. These players tend to enjoy greater autonomy than did those who participated in the vertical authoritarianism system.

Economic and Trade Policies

In the era of modernization, economic development is a top priority, and as a result, China has become increasingly involved in the global markets. China's exports and imports as a percentage of gross national product (GNP), for example, increased from 4.7 per cent and 5.2 per cent respectively in 1978 to 17.2 per cent and 14.8 per cent respectively in 1990.[23]

Table 4.1 shows that the total volume of China's foreign trade has increased significantly under Deng. The speed of growth has accelerated drastically since the beginning of Deng's Opening and Reform policy in 1978. One can see this growth more clearly from Figure 4.1. Although still 'a shallow integration with the world economy', as Susan Shirk (1994: 86) points out, 'China was able to achieve rapid economic reform'. It is believed that as long as China sticks to its goal of modernization, its economy will continue to move in the direction of further integration with the world outside its borders.

The increase in foreign economic activities has involved more participants from various governmental agencies in the decision-making process. In addition to the Ministry of Foreign Affairs, for example, government institutions such as the Ministry of Foreign Economic Relations and Trade, and the National Planning Commission have played prominent roles in China's external economic relations. Other ministries related to economic development have also increased their dealings with foreign countries. One good example in this regard is the unprecedented expansion in the number of Chinese foreign trading companies. In the era of Mao, there were only a few such companies, but by the early 1990s, there were well over 1,000 trading entities at the national level. Even though one cannot regard this devolution of power and proliferation of traders as a fundamental liberalization of the foreign trade system, it does represent increasing bureaucratic interests in China's foreign economic relations (M. Ross, 1994: 448).

Military Policy and Arms Sales

China's military policy in the Deng era, especially arms sales, has drawn international attention. As Paul Godwin (1992: 200–201) has argued, China's military strategy in the 1990s is to be 'more capable of responding to a variety of potential conflicts around China's periphery'. Although Beijing believes that China's strategy for national defence in the twenty-first century 'should be based on fighting major wars and fighting nuclear wars', adequate preparation for local and limited wars is also a primary concern.

It became increasingly clear to Beijing in the 1980s that rather than preparing for a nuclear war with the Soviet Union, China must be able to fight local and limited wars. So between 1985 and 1988, China reduced its military regions to seven from eleven and reorganized the army. It then formed crack units and a rapid-reaction force. Furthermore, the Gulf War of 1991, with its dazzling display of high-tech

Table 4.1: China's Foreign Trade 1950–1992 (in billions of yuan)

Year	Export	Import	Total
1950	2.02	2.13	4.15
1951	2.42	3.53	5.95
1952	2.71	3.75	6.46
1953	3.48	4.61	8.09
1954	4.00	4.47	8.47
1955	4.87	6.61	10.98
1956	5.57	5.30	10.87
1957	5.45	5.00	10.45
1958	6.70	6.17	12.87
1959	7.81	7.12	14.93
1960	6.33	6.51	12.84
1961	4.77	4.30	9.07
1962	4.71	3.38	8.09
1963	5.00	3.57	8.57
1964	5.54	4.21	9.75
1965	6.31	5.53	11.84
1966	6.60	6.11	12.71
1967	5.88	5.34	11.21
1968	5.76	5.09	10.85
1969	5.98	4.72	10.70
1970	5.68	5.61	11.29
1971	6.85	5.24	12.09
1972	8.29	6.40	14.69
1973	11.69	10.36	22.05
1974	13.94	15.28	29.22
1975	14.30	14.74	29.04
1976	13.48	12.93	26.41
1977	13.97	13.28	27.25
1978	16.76	18.74	35.50
1979	21.17	24.29	45.46
1980	27.12	29.88	57.00
1981	36.76	36.77	73.53
1982	41.38	35.75	77.13
1983	43.83	42.18	86.01
1984	58.05	62.05	120.10
1985	80.89	125.78	206.67
1986	108.21	149.83	285.04
1987	147.00	161.42	308.42
1988	176.67	205.53	382.20

Table 4.1: (cont.)

Year	Export	Import	Total
1989	195.60	219.99	415.59
1990	298.58	257.43	556.01
1991	383.06	339.87	722.93
1992	444.02	421.06	865.08

Source: Compiled from *International Financial Statistics Yearbook, 1993* (Washington: IMF, 1993); *Chinese Statistical Yearbook 1992* (Beijing: Statistical Bureau of the PRC, 1992)

weaponry, stunned the People's Liberation Army (PLA).[24] As a consequence, the modernization of military equipment has become a top priority for the PLA.

For a long period China provided arms free of charge to its Asian friends and neighbours, mostly to North Korea, North Vietnam, and Pakistan. This policy was changed in 1979 after China adopted the Opening and Reform policy under Deng. Since then the PLA has quickly become a major arms supplier to the world. In the period 1987 to 1991, for example, China bypassed Britain and became the fourth largest seller in the arms trade, behind the United States, the former Soviet Union, and France.

Since the early 1980s and well into the 1990s, Chinese PLA units established a vast, military-backed empire with thousands of businesses. The most notables are the PLA General Staff Department's Poly Group Corp., the PLA General Logistics Department's Xinxing Corp., and the Kaili Ltd., run by the PLA General Political Department, together with the businesses run by the air force, the navy, and the Commission of National Defence Technology and Industry. These business groups are running everything from airlines to pig farms and 'generating revenue that may equal the entire defence budget'.[25]

This rapid development has both a long-term and a short-term goal. In the long term it will provide a basis for China on which to build political influence in regional and global affairs. In the short run, however, these arms sales are valued for their ability to generate foreign exchange for the PLA's modernization drive.[26]

Profit seeking by selling arms abroad is a direct result of domestic political and economic changes. The Chinese military experienced significant budget cuts throughout most of the 1980s. In 1979, China spent 17.5 per cent of its total budget on defence; by 1987, this had been

Figure 4.1 China's Foreign Trade (1950–1992)

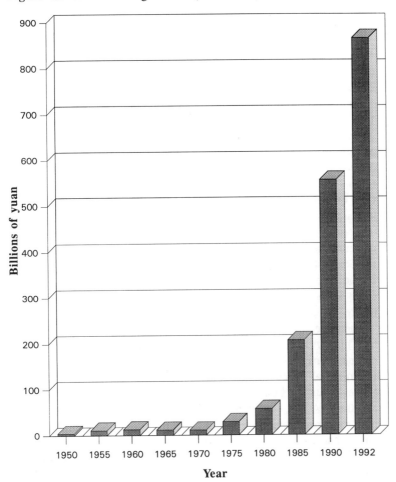

94   INTERPRETING CHINESE FOREIGN POLICY

reduced to 8.2 per cent.[27] The major cut took place in 1980 and 1981, when actual military expenditures were reduced by 13 per cent in each year. These military cuts continued until 1989. The reduction in this period can be seen from Table 4.2 and Figure 4.2.

One can also see from Table 4.2 that the trend of military budget cuts was halted in 1989 when Beijing faced domestic turmoil. The post-Tiananmen government significantly increased its defence budget from 1989 to 1991. Although defence outlay grew from Rmb 16.8 billion in 1981 to Rmb 37.2 billion in 1991, the increases were easily swallowed up by inflation. According to a 1993 estimation, the military's purchasing power has fallen by one quarter since the late 1970s.[28] China's 1995 defence budget rose to Rmb 63.1 billion (US$7.5 billion) from Rmb 58 billion in 1994 and Rmb 43 billion in 1993. Chinese foreign minister Qian Qichen defended China's position at the ASEAN Regional Forum in Bangkok in July 1994 by stressing that 'the main purpose for this increase . . . is to offset the impact of the reduction of the purchasing power of the money'. He further compared China's 1994 military budget (US$6.7 billion) with Japan's US$30 billion and America's US$200 billion defence budget, stating, 'If you make such comparisons, you come to the conclusion that China's military forces are defensive in nature.'[29]

There are, however, some serious doubts about the figures published by China. According to estimates made by a number of international organizations or foreign government agencies, such as the Stockholm International Peace Research Institute, the International Institute for Strategic Studies (London), the Arms Control and Disarmament Agency, and the CIA and Pentagon of the United States, China's actual 1995 military expenditures vary from US$10 billion to US$50 billion, much larger than the Chinese official accounts.[30] In addition, having experienced the sweet taste of profit-making, the PLA was not about to stop its arms sales activities. Since 1989 the PLA has continued to sell arms.

The military's autonomy in external relations has its limitations, however. Although the PLA traditionally has had an enormous influence over political issues, it is in no position to challenge the authority of the Chinese Communist Party.[31] The removal of the brothers Yang Shangkun and Yang Baibing from leading military positions, a result of the 14th Party Congress of October 1992, was widely believed to be a demonstration of the long-standing principle of 'the Party commands the gun'.[32]

It is only natural that there are differing opinions among various institutions. The most noteworthy one is the difference between the

Table 4.2: Chinese Military Expenditure, 1950–1993

Year	Military Expenses (billions of yuan)	Growth Rate (%)
1950	2.8	
1951	5.3	89
1952	5.8	9
1953	7.5	29
1954	5.8	−23
1955	6.5	12
1956	6.1	−6
1957	5.5	−10
1958	5.0	−9
1959	5.8	16
1960	5.8	0
1961	5.0	−14
1962	5.7	14
1963	6.6	16
1964	7.3	11
1965	8.7	19
1966	10.1	16
1967	8.3	−18
1968	9.4	13
1969	12.6	34
1970	14.5	15
1971	16.9	17
1972	15.9	−6
1973	14.5	−9
1974	13.3	−8
1975	14.2	7
1976	13.4	−6
1977	14.9	11
1978	16.8	13
1979	22.3	33
1980	19.3	−13
1981	16.8	−13
1982	17.6	5
1983	17.7	1
1984	18.1	2
1985	19.1	6
1986	20.1	5
1987	21.0	4

Table 4.2: (cont.)

Year	Military Expenses (billions of yuan)	Growth Rate (%)
1988	21.8	4
1989	25.2	16
1990	29.0	15
1991	37.2	28
1992	37.8	2
1993	43.3	1

Source: *Sipri Yearbook 1991, World Armaments and Disarmament* (Oxford: Oxford University Press, 1991); *Chinese Statistical Yearbook 1992* (Beijing: Statistical Bureau of the PRC, 1992), *Chinese Statistical Abstract 1994* [Zhongguo Tongi Zhaiyao] (Beijing Statistical Bureau of the PRC, 1994)

Ministry of Foreign Affairs and the PLA over controversial arms transactions such as nuclear and missile sales. Table 4.3 is a summary of China's nuclear sales and transfers for the past forty some years.

Conflicting issues between the Ministry of Foreign Affairs and the PLA, such as the question of missile and nuclear sales, are referred to a special group supervized by the highest leadership of the Party, which coordinates various interests and acts as an arbitrator. Beginning in the late 1980s the Ministry of Foreign Affairs was allowed to send representatives to participate in the group's discussion of arms sales. Once a decision is made by this elite group, all subordinate groups normally adhere to it.

In the late 1980s, after a series of high-level negotiations between China and the United States, Beijing agreed that it would not sell Silkworm missiles to the Middle East. In general, the PLA has cooperated with this policy, although it has tested the policy's limits by inquiring about possible buyers without actually signing contracts.[33] In February 1991, the Ministry of Foreign Affairs formally denied allegations that China was continuing to sell arms to Iraq during the Persian Gulf War,[34] and in June 1991 Beijing agreed to participate in a US-sponsored conference to establish guidelines limiting the sale of arms and nuclear-related technology to the Middle East.[35] The PLA's foreign affairs working conference was held in July 1991, directly following the State Council's foreign affairs working conference.[36] Beijing has made concerted efforts to coordinate foreign policy and international activities among key institutions.

Figure 4.2 Chinese Military Expenditure (1950–1993)

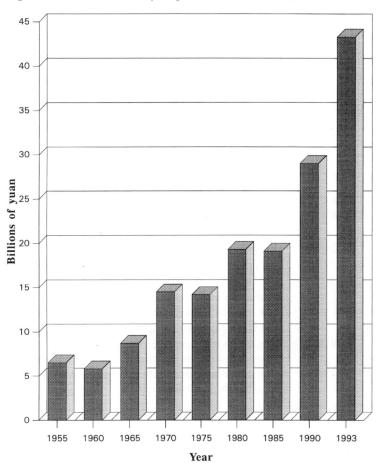

Table 4.3: China's Nuclear Sales and Transfers (1950s–February 1992)

Recipient & Time Period	Nature of Transaction
1. Algeria 1983–91	Under a secret agreement, supplied a nuclear reactor large enough to make weapons-grade plutonium.
2. Argentina 1981–85	Sold at least 60 metric tons of heavy water to run reactors capable of making plutonium, uranium concentrate (possibly 45 tons), low-enriched uranium hexafluoride, and about 12kg of 20-per cent-enriched uranium as fuel for research reactors.
3. Brazil 1984	Sold uranium enriched to 3 per cent, 7 per cent, and 20 per cent in three shipments totalling 200kg.
4. India 1982–87	Sold at least 130 tons of heavy water through Alfred Hempel, a West German broker.
5. Iran 1985–90	Under a secret cooperation agreement, trained several Iranian nuclear technicians in China, and may have supplied technology for reactor construction. May have contracted to sell a research reactor.
6. Iraq 1989–90	Helped Iraq manufacture special magnets for stabilizing ultra-high-speed centrifuges for enriching uranium. Agreed, in violation of UN trade embargo, to sell 7 tons of lithium hydride, which can be used in the manufacture of nuclear weapons.
7. North Korea 1950s–60s	Trained North Korean scientists in nuclear technology.
8. Pakistan 1983–89	Supplied a reliable bomb design, enabling Pakistan to make a warhead weighing less than 400lb. Reportedly supplied enough highly enriched uranium for two atomic bombs. Aided Pakistan's efforts to enrich uranium at its Kahuta plant. Sold tritium gas capable of boosting the yield of fission bombs. Provided special magnets for centrifuges at the Kahuta plant, which produces nuclear test for Pakistan in 1989 at its Lop Nor testing ground. Agreed to supply a 300-mega-watt nuclear power station despite an international nuclear supply embargo.
9. South Africa 1981	Sold 30 tons of 2.7-per cent and 30 tons of 3-per cent-enriched uranium through Alfred Hempel.
10. Syria 1992	Syria indicated intent to import small research reactor from China.

Source: *Christian Science Monitor*, 10 March 1992, p. 3; See S. Kim (1994a: 148)

A more recent development in the area of arms and diplomacy was the meeting between Chinese Foreign Minister Qian Qichen and his US counterpart, Warren Christopher in Washington in October 1994. They jointly stated that they would work together to promote the earliest possible achievement of an international convention banning the production of fissile materials for nuclear weapons. The two sides also signed an agreement on missile technology, under which China for the first time promised that it will not export ground-to-ground missiles inherently capable of reaching a range of at least 300 kilometres with a payload of at least 500 kilograms. These accords reportedly were reached after the US first lifted its sanctions on hi-tech exports.[37] A further development in military diplomacy occurred in November 1995, when, in response to the international call for transparency in military affairs, and to assuage the concerns of neighbouring countries over the alleged 'China Threat', the Chinese State Council, issued a *Defense White Paper*, revealing in detail China's military budget and arms control related matters.[38]

Human Rights

Though there has been a gradual relaxation of control over people's political and social lives and some progress in Beijing's respect for human rights under Deng, China is still widely regarded as lagging far behind international standards. Beijing has insisted that the issue of human rights is not only related to political rights, but also to economic and social rights, which are related to China's economic development and cultural and historical background.[39] China's beliefs are echoed by most of its Asian neighbours. At Asia's first regional human rights conference, held in Bangkok in March 1993, many government representatives indicated that they shared a vision of human rights that places economic growth and community development ahead of individual freedoms; the 30-point Bangkok Declaration placed great emphasis on non-interference in the internal affairs of states.[40] This vision stands in contrast to the standard position of many Western governments, which believe that all countries should be held to the same standards of human rights protection, regardless of their level of economic development.

After the Tiananmen Incident, there was a downturn in Sino-American bilateral relations, largely prompted by Washington's concern over China's human rights record and treatment of the political dissidents and their supporters. The Ministry of Foreign Affairs, however, has worked hard within its jurisdiction to improve relations with the United

States.[41] It was the Ministry of Foreign Affairs that hosted the December 1990 visit of Richard Schifter, the US assistant secretary of state for human rights, during which he held 16 hours of talks with his Chinese counterparts and submitted a list of 150 political prisoners about whom the US was particularly concerned.[42]

The Ministry of Foreign Affairs also arranged meetings with a broad range of high-level US government officials from ministries or agencies of public security, justice, minority nationality affairs, birth control and family planning, religious affairs, and the Supreme Court. The discussions were quite broad and frank.[43] The Schifter visit was regarded as a compromise by Chinese authorities; Beijing has always insisted that human rights issues are internal affairs and had repeatedly refused to discuss its human rights record with foreign governments. One should note, however, that these talk were largely symbolic and produced little notable result.

As time passed, the United States somewhat softened its tough position toward China. Three months after the Clinton administration overtly delinked Beijing's human-rights performance from its MFN trading status in May 1994, US Commerce Secretary Ron Brown took his visit to Beijing. In contrast to previous US missions, which enquired about published lists naming hundreds of detainees, the new post-MFN approach seemed to be discreet remonstrances in closed-door 'mutual engagement' sessions. Brown assured American businessmen at an American Chamber of Commerce breakfast in Beijing that 'the administration would no longer let politics put them at a disadvantage to foreign competitors in China'.[44]

Nevertheless, pressures from outside, in the long run, may help to bring gradual improvement to human-rights conditions within China. Some efforts are less heavy-handed than others. In December 1994, for example, the Brussels-based International Confederation of Free Trade Unions, aiming to improve the working conditions of China's 300 million workers, asked foreign companies doing business in China to do their part to promote change in workers' working conditions from the inside. Some companies, such as the American jeans manufacturer Levi Strauss and footwear producers Nike and Reebok, were already pursuing a 'code of practice' under which their contractors and suppliers in China must meet certain environmental, health, safety, and wage requirements.[45] While this may not initially amount to getting China to do anything about its own labour practices, a number of Western firms, by volunteering to police themselves, are attempting to set an example for Chinese management. The trend may develop. In the summer of 1995, the Clinton

Table 4.4: Chinese Students and Scholars in the United States (1979–1987) (number of new arrivals)

Year	No. of Students	No. of Scholars	Total
1979	668	631	1299
1980	2674	1232	3906
1981	3021	2036	5057
1982	2103	1694	3797
1983	2575	1861	4436
1984	3460	2188	5648
1985	5508	3049	8557
1986	8107	N/A	8107
1987	8507	N/A	8507
Total	36623	12691	49314

Source: Leo A. Orleans (1988), *Chinese Students in America: Policies, Issues and Numbers*

administration called upon American companies operating in China to avoid using child or prison labour and to protect the environment.[46] Although these principles are voluntary, the US government has made it clear that it would encourage and perhaps provide 'awards for those companies that practice these principles the most effectively' (Lord, 1995: 249). As China further integrates into world economy and international affairs, China's internal behaviour norms, including the human-rights issue, will inevitably be affected by external influences.[47]

Cultural and Educational Exchange

Cultural and educational exchanges with foreign countries have increased tremendously since Deng's ascension to power. Institutions in the field of international cultural and educational exchange, such as the Academy of Sciences, the Academy of Social Sciences, the National Commission of Education, and the National Commission of Sciences and Technology, have all broadened their external activities since China started its Open Door policy in the late 1970s.

China began to send students to the United States in the late 1970s, shortly after relations between the two countries were normalized. This flow continued and grew as shown at Table 4.4.

By 1990, mainland Chinese students became the largest contingent of foreign students studying in the United States, bypassing students from Taiwan.[48] In 1993, for example, more than 45,000 students from

China and 37,000 from Taiwan were studying in the United States. They represented the largest and third-largest numbers of foreign students in the country, respectively.[49] In addition to students, China has also annually sent large numbers of scholars abroad. In 1993, there were 130,000 Chinese students and scholars studying in foreign countries — about 100,000 of them in the United States.[50]

There also has been an influx of foreign students and scholars to China since the late 1970s. Although the total number still remains small when compared with the number of Chinese students abroad, it has increased rapidly. The total number of foreign students in China reached 6,000 in 1988 (up from 1,800 in 1982), about one quarter of which were from Africa. While invitations to African students to attend Chinese universities were offered with the idea of promoting international exchange and mutual understanding, racial conflicts did occasionally occur between Chinese and African students in the 1980s, often inciting campus riots. Incidents of this kind were reported in several large cities such as Nanjing and Tianjin, causing complaints from some African students of racial discrimination (Sautman, 1994).

The number of foreign students in China increased rapidly in the early part of the 1990s — from 12,000 in 1992, to 26,000 in 1994. Students from 138 countries, recruited by some 200 Chinese universities and colleges nationwide, were studying in more than 800 specialties.[51]

Today, China sends a large number of students and scholars to study abroad, primarily in capitalist countries such as the United States, Japan, Canada, Great Britain, Germany, France, and Australia. In addition, Beijing has also sent thousands more Chinese officials to these countries on short-term visits to learn about Western societies and institutions. In the case of the United States, for example, scientific and technological exchange programmes linked virtually every American cabinet department with its Chinese counterpart. And several American corporations conducted educational programmes for Chinese officials and managers as a way of developing business opportunities in China (Harding, 1994: 379). One may notice that there is also a sizeable body of Chinese students in the post-communist Russia.

The impact of sending students to the West has been mixed. Wendy Friedman (1994: 176–177) has summarized some of the effects:

- exposure to international standards of scholarship has driven up Chinese standards of scholarship;
- students have brought back valuable knowledge which is not available in China;

- many students have chosen to remain abroad (the brain drain phenomenon);[52] and
- Chinese students' economic and political expectations have been raised by their exposure to Western societies.

To the Beijing government, it is obvious that the first two consequences are welcome and that the third and fourth results are undesirable. According to a 1993 figure, for example, of the 200,000 Chinese students who had left since the early 1980s, only 70,000 had returned to China.[53] But in overall terms, China has greatly benefitted from the cultural and educational exchanges.

Beijing attempted to formulate new policies for China's overseas students. A national working conference on overseas students was held in Beijing in November 1995. State Counsellor Li Guixian stated a '12-character policy' to guide the country's practice for sending students abroad:

- *zhichi liuxue* — [continue] to support sending students abroad [to obtain well-trained advanced personnel];
- *guli huiguo* — encourage overseas students to return to China; and
- *laiqu ziyou* — allow overseas students to move in and out of China freely.

Li also emphasized that China should fully utilize 'the two teams of overseas students' — those who have returned to China and those who have remained abroad — to promote China's modernization course.[54]

Greater Representation of Local Interests

Under horizontal authoritarianism, the relationship between the central government and local elites has become much closer, and local interests have started to play a role in foreign relations, particularly in foreign economic relations. Under vertical authoritarianism, central authorities controlled virtually all aspects of local activities — political, economic, and social. The activities of local elites were controlled by a wide range of mechanisms: control of the appointment and dismissal of major provincial officials, such as first Party secretaries, governors, and military commanders; control of mobile military forces, notably the field armies; control of the propaganda apparatus; and control of key economic resources, such as metals and transportation.[55]

Whereas vertical authoritarianism tends to favour the central government, horizontal authoritarianism may favour the province. In China it took place in two ways: the inclusion of more diversified interests as inputs in the policy-making process, and the process of decentralization. Throughout the period of reform prior to the summer of 1989, a gradual loosening of the constraints on local authorities occurred. There are now many open areas, in particular coastal cities or provinces such as Guangdong, Fujian, Shandong, Jiangsu, Zhejiang, Liaoning, Shanghai, and Tianjin, as well as the five Special Economic Zones of Hainan, Shenzhen, Zhuhai, Xiamen, and Shantou. Local governments in these areas have a high degree of authority in terms of local economic activities and external economic relations. The central government permits these local governments to retain a portion of the foreign exchange they earn to encourage exports and local economic development. With greater access to foreign currency, provinces such as Guangdong and Fujian can enjoy autonomy in conducting external economic activities. Some China specialists believe that in these cases the relationship between the centre and the provinces has become interdependent (Lieberthal and Oksenberg, 1988: 352).

The struggle to retain and strengthen local power has not stopped in the 1990s. There are frequent reports of local resistance to central government efforts to tighten control over local economic and external activities. In some cases provincial governors have worked together to oppose recentralization of certain economic policies. One of the most notable examples in this regard is Ye Xuanping, the governor of Guangdong province. At a meeting of provincial leaders held in November 1990, Ye strongly articulated provincial opposition to the fiscal recentralization plan proposed by the central authority, and demanded continued financial autonomy. Other provincial leaders followed his lead and 'presented a unified front against the center', which postponed the original plan (Shirk, 1993: 194–195). This incident indicates 'the striking new power of local governments to shape decisions by the central government' (Montinola, Qian, and Weingast, 1995: 69).

Increasingly, regional leaders have aspired to challenge Beijing's dominance and to hijack the central polity, redefining it to their own advantage. One problem is the gradual decline of the central financial power. During the first 15 years of reform (1979–94), the overall state revenue, as a proportion of GDP declined from 26 per cent to just under 12 per cent, barely a third of the proportion in major developed countries. In his budget speech in March 1995, Finance Minister Liu Zhongli reconfirmed the tax reforms begun in the previous year. But success has been limited. As Susan Shirk put it, 'central leaders have talked tough about fiscal reapportionment'. Ex-premier Zhao Ziyang in 1987, his succcessor Li Peng in 1989, President Jiang Zemin in 1993, and economics tsar Zhu Rongji in 1994 — all vowed to rein in spendthrift provinces, only to back down later. According to Shirk's observation, regional power-brokers form one of the biggest and most powerful blocs in what she calls the 'selectorate' — 'the elite Party stratum that will decide who does what in the post-Deng redistribution of power'.[56]

In a study of China's economic development strategy and its implications for Chinese foreign policy, Barry Naughton (1994) suggests that different regional developments may bring different foreign policy preferences. According to Naughton, there is a 'tripartite China': 'the rapidly growing South Coast with its international contacts handled by overseas Chinese' mainly from Hong Kong, Taiwan, South-East Asia, and North America; 'the Communist Core in the North and Northeast growing at a moderate and managed rate' that favours close ties with Korea, Japan, and Russia; and a 'deep interior left out of the growth process to date'.

Local interests can also be heard more loudly at the National People's Congress (NPC). In the March 1995 NPC annual convention, 33 per cent of the deputies voted against a new central bank law. Support for the law was the lowest, proportionally, of any central-government prepared document in memory. The NPC delegates made what *The Youth Daily* called a 'great and exciting discovery' that their voices can be used as an effective vehicle for advocating local interests.[57]

Provincial power has also been strengthened by the fact that more provincial governors or first Party secretaries have been promoted to central leadership positions. For example, before becoming premier of the State Council and Party general secretary, Zhao Ziyang has served as a provincial boss in Guangdong, Inner Mongolia, and Sichuan. The post-Tiananmen general secretary, Jiang Zemin, was previously first secretary of Shanghai. Four of the seven members of the Party's Standing Committee, elected at the 14th Party Congress in October 1992, were first Party secretaries or governors. In the spring of 1995, Party secretaries of Shandong and Shanghai, Jiang Chunyun, and Wu Bangguo, were promoted to become vice premiers. These promotions have inevitably increased the influence of local interests and strengthened the ties between the centre and the local levels.

After the Tiananmen Incident, the United States suspended official bilateral exchanges. Few high-level Chinese officials were invited to visit the United States. However, in July 1990, a Chinese mayoral delegation paid an official visit to the United States to 'enhance mutual understanding and improve bilateral relations'.[58] This delegation was headed by Zhu Rongji, then mayor of Shanghai (he was promoted to vice premier in spring 1991 and became a member of the Party's Standing Committee in the autumn of 1992), the highest official to visit the United States since the Tiananmen Incident. Zhu conducted extensive diplomatic activities, meeting with National Security Advisor Brent Scowcroft, State Department Deputy Secretary Lawrence Eagleburger, and Speaker of the US House of Representatives Thomas Foley.[59] These activities further confirmed the more visible participation of provincial officials in foreign relations.

Despite these advances, local authorities are not autonomous. The participation of local elites is usually limited to local affairs and can be further limited by the central government at any time. On 1 January 1991, for instance, Beijing removed export subsidies, a measure designed to diminish the growing independence of regional governments.[60]

The Increasing Importance of Think Tanks

Intellectuals and think tanks are assuming an increasingly important role in foreign policy making. Under Mao, numerous anti-intellectuals campaigns were conducted, such as the Anti-Rightist Campaign of 1957 and the Cultural Revolution of 1966 to 1976. These massive and often ruthless political campaigns effectively silenced the voices of the intellectuals.

Since the early 1980s, however, foreign affairs think tanks have expanded in number and in the scope of their participation. The State Council, for example, runs its own Center for International Studies. Each ministry with a foreign policy agenda, such as the Ministry of Foreign Affairs, the Ministry of National Security, and the Ministry of Foreign Economic Relations and Trade, has its own research institute. Several internationally oriented research institutions at the Academy of Social Sciences concentrate not only on world political and economic relations, but also on international regional studies. Major universities in Beijing, such as Beijing University and the People's University, also house research institutions.

Most of the work of these research institutions is of two kinds: research into international affairs and the preparation of background reports; and analysis of foreign policy issues and the formulation of proposals for action. They have institutional or private internal channels to various levels of authority, and their opinions may differ from official lines. In this way, think tanks and intellectuals have played an advisory role in the foreign policy-making process. From 1978 to 1985, for example, there were debates about Soviet socialism among intellectuals as well as among government bureaucrats.[61] These debates fostered the internal preparations necessary for Beijing to normalize its relations with Moscow by the end of the 1980s.

Nevertheless, the political influence of Chinese intellectuals upon foreign policy issues has remained weak. Think tanks have a fairly high degree of freedom to conduct internal discussions on a variety of issues, but it is difficult, if not impossible, for research institutes to voice dissenting points of view openly. A scholar who is allowed to discuss foreign policy issues in public is expected to explain and justify the official line. For example, in the mid-1980s Deng Xiaoping repeatedly stated that large-scale world war was not imminent because the forces for peace in the world had grown, and therefore it was justifiable to accord defence a low priority in the budget. In an interview with foreign reporters in Beijing, Huan Xiang, an expert in foreign affairs and director of the State Council's Centre for International Studies, commented: 'Deng Xiaoping's peace thoughts are based on China's economic development and the political and economic reforms. . . . The basic things that China relies on in order to safeguard peace are political and economic reforms and development. I think that this is Deng's thought.'[62]

This is a typical explanation of the top leader's thoughts and justification of a policy. Intellectuals have not yet become an independent entity in China's political life. They have gained more freedom to discuss policy issues internally, but externally or publicly they must support official lines. This is an important characteristic of horizontal authoritarianism.[63]

General Political and Economic Conditions

The dynamics of general political and economic changes in China have always had a direct impact on Beijing's foreign policy. The change in Beijing's attitude toward foreign loans in the era of Deng is a good example in this regard. Always sensitive to issues of national sovereignty and foreign intervention, Beijing became suspicious of foreign loans following the Communist victory in 1949.[64] The prevention of foreign intervention and influence was a high priority of Chinese leaders at that time. As late as 1977, the Chinese leadership insisted that China should not allow any foreign interests or jointly managed companies to develop domestic resources or accept foreign credits. According to a *Renmin Ribao* editorial in 1977: 'We never permit the use of foreign capital to develop our domestic resources as the Soviet revisionists do, never run undertakings in concert with other countries and also never accept foreign loans. China has neither domestic nor external debts.'[65]

Japan was the first major industrialized country to broach the issue of foreign loans to China. Following the normalization of Sino-Japanese relations in 1972, Tokyo raised the issue of government loans as a form of economic cooperation on several occasions. These overtures were unequivocally rejected by Beijing.[66]

This rigid stance began to change, however, after 1978, when Beijing began its Opening and Reform policy, raising economic development and modernization to its highest priority. Beijing gradually realized that foreign loans were a necessary means of obtaining cheap capital, which China needed for economic development. Hotly sought-after foreign capital, advanced technology, and markets of industrialized countries such as the United States, Japan, and members of the European Community have become increasingly attractive to China's decision-makers.

Foreign government 'soft loans' proved to be useful as fiscal crises repeatedly threatened China's key projects. In 1979, Japan became the first non-communist government to offer government loans to China. Other Western countries, such as Belgium and Denmark, and international organizations, including the World Bank, quickly followed suit.

The growing importance of loans from Japan and other industrialized countries was made clear in a public statement by Deng Xiaoping in 1988 in which he described the loans as 'extremely significant'.[67] Deng made the statement when he received Prime Minister Noboru Takeshita, who had just pledged a third governmental loan package of 810 billion yen (US$5.4 billion) to China.[68] After the Tiananmen Incident of June 1989, Japan followed the lead of the United States and other Western countries and froze governmental loans to China. A year later, Japanese Prime Minister Toshiki Kaifu announced that Japan would resume its package of government loans to China at the economic summit of seven major industrialized nations.[69] Chinese Premier Li Peng immediately indicated that Beijing would 'actively cooperate' with Tokyo in implementing the loan projects.[70] Deng and Li's remarks clearly reflected the changing priorities in China's foreign policy orientation. (Chapter 6 will provide a detailed case-study on Japan's official development assistance to China.)

The Power of the People

Another characteristic of horizontal authoritarianism that affects foreign policy-making is the role played by the popular mood. This mood was affected by what Brantly Womack (1987: 479–481) called the 'shift in the relationship of Party to people between the revolutionary and post-revolutionary stages'. Because of the society's authoritarian nature, the expression of popular political demands in China is different from that in democratic societies, where institutionalized, articulated means of expressing these demands exist, such as popular elections, opinion surveys, interest groups, and lobbying activities. In China, two unofficial forms of political participation have developed in recent years: open demonstrations, such as the ones that took place during the spring and summer of 1989, and passive resistance. This development is a direct result of the political turmoil of the Cultural Revolution, and it represents a gradual change in China's political culture. Both forms of participation are effective in communicating popular demand to the authorities.

Passive resistance was widely adopted after the military crackdown of 1989. As a *Far Eastern Economic Review* article commented a year after the Tiananmen Incident:

There is a conspiracy . . . perhaps strongest in Peking [Beijing] but extending throughout China. . . . It is a conspiracy of silence, the sum of thousands of individual decisions not to inform on friends, neighbours or colleagues. This spontaneous mass refusal has stymied attempts to mount a full-scale investigation and purge of participants in last year's disturbances.[71]

Many political discussions organized by the authorities for the purpose of 'purifying thinking' turned into occasions for people to criticize the Party for its inept leadership and clumsy handling of the demonstrations.[72] A dramatic example of passive resistance took place in an official, controlled election for the city's People's Congress in Beijing in December 1990. In the Haidian district, where most of the city's universities are concentrated, 300 people voted for disgraced Party chief Zhao Ziyang, although Zhao's name was not on the ballot and the only choices on the ballot were carefully screened Communist Party loyalists.[73]

To maintain Communist rule and domestic stability, the Beijing leadership must take this kind of political demand into consideration. Although international pressure plays a part in eliciting concessions from the Beijing leadership — such as the release of several hundred political prisoners and the permission granted to top dissident Fang Lizhi to go abroad in 1990, and the early release of Wang Dan, the most wanted student leader, in spring 1993 — such actions also represent a response to domestic demands that Beijing display a 'gentler' image toward its own people.

The Effect of Change

Under vertical authoritarianism, characterized by one-person domination, foreign policy tends to appear in a formulaic manner and is concerned with ideology. Early studies of the Mao era emphasized the revolutionary nature of Chinese foreign policy. By contrast, under horizontal authoritarianism, more players and more diverse issues are involved in the process of foreign policy-making. There is more collective decision-making. With more interests and players involved, Chinese foreign policy appears less rigid and more pragmatic. In recent years, a number of foreign analysts have noted the 'growing flexibility ... that has characterized China's foreign relations' (Harding, 1987: 243), an agility that 'can leave the more cautious and ponderous American (and Soviet) decision-making process a step or two behind' (Pye, 1988: 106).

The development of horizontal participation in foreign relations has its limitations, however. In China, every governmental institution or agency is controlled by the CCP. To be promoted to positions of higher authority, officials must rise through the ranks of the bureaucratic hierarchy. As a result, an individual seeking greater autonomy may be placing his or her political career in jeopardy. The risk is greater if strategic or political issues are involved. Even today, sensitive and strategically important issues such as China's relations with major powers are handled by a small group of top leaders. And the influence of the Party chief, in this case Jiang Zemin, who is also president of the PRC, often overshadows other leaders. There are five leading groups directly under the Party's Politburo over different policy areas: foreign affairs, finance and economics, ideology and propaganda, Taiwan affairs, and legal and political affairs. Up until mid-1996, Jiang has held the head position for the first four leading groups, in addition to his chairmanship of the powerful Central Military Committee. Jiang did not have the head position for foreign affairs until March 1995, when he replaced Premier Li Peng for the position (Li then, together with Foreign Minister Qian Qichen, became vice head for the policy-setting organ).[74] Any major decisions regarding Taiwan, for example, were made by Deng and his associates in the 1980s and then by Jiang Zemin and his colleagues in the early and middle of the 1990s, based upon Deng's guiding principles.

Horizontal authoritarianism is a progressive political development, a gradual departure from the regime of one-person domination. Similar developments have occurred in Taiwan and South Korea, where horizontal authoritarianism was a step between vertical authoritarianism and the ongoing process of political democratization characterized by parliamentary politics.

Since 1978 to the present (with the exception of the Tiananmen Incident of 1989 and aftermath which lasted for about two years) China has been moving in the same direction toward horizontal authoritarianism as South Korea and Taiwan did in the previous decades. It differs, however, from their experience in important respects: its basic economic structure, especially regarding private enterprise, is still less developed; the degree of external political influence, particularly from the West, is more restricted; and the quality of top leadership in terms of educational level and awareness of democracy and political development is generally lower. Therefore, one cannot predict with any certainty that China will automatically follow in the footsteps of other East Asian societies.[75] With the survival of the current Communist regime open to question, China faces a long period of uncertainty in its domestic politics; this inevitably brings a degree of uncertainty to Chinese external behaviour.

Notes

1 See his classical work *The Prince and the Discourses*, Niccolo Machiavelli (1950).
2 'China's Important Role in World Affairs', *Beijing Review* (15–21 October 1990): 11–12. Qian states that a stable political situation and growing economy 'creates favourable conditions for diplomatic work'.
3 The idea of fragmented politics was first discussed in Kenneth Lieberthal and Michael Oksenberg (1988), and was later elaborated on in Lieberthal and David Lampton (1992) and Lieberthal (1995).
4 See D. Barnett (1985: 7).
5 This judgment is widely shared among scholars and analysts. See, for example, Michel Oksenberg (1991: 4).
6 Also see Frederick Teiwes (1984).
7 For a full account of China's reassessment of the two superpowers in the early 1980s, see Carol Hamrin (1983).
8 For an excellent analysis and summary of the factionalism model of Chinese politics, see Lowell Dittmer and Yu-Shan Wu (1995).
9 Robert Delfs, 'Thought Control, Conservatives behind Chen Yun in Reform Struggle', *Far Eastern Economic Review* (8 November 1990): 19–20.
10 *World Journal*, 19 June 1991, p. 10; *World Journal*, 27 July 1991, p. 10.
11 See David Shambaugh (1992: 257–259).
12 Carl Goldstein, 'Death Watch: Is Deng's Frail Health a Boon to Conservatives?', *Far Eastern Economic Review* (24 February 1994): 17–18.
13 'Yuanlao xiaoshi youli yu disandai lingdao?' [Is the Passing Away of Senior Statesmen Conducive to the Third Generation of Leadership?], *Yazhou Zhoukan* [The International Chinese Newsweekly] (23 April 1995): 20–23.
14 While emphasizing that Jiang Zemin was the core of the third generation of collective leadership, Deng claimed that 'the core of our first generation of collective leadership was Chairman Mao' and 'I am the core of the second generation'. See Deng Xiaoping, 'Urgent Tasks of China's Third Generation of Collective Leadership', 16 June 1989 (Deng, 1994: 300–302).
15 Willy Wo-lap Lam, 'President All But Unassailable in Battle for Post-Deng Power', *South China Morning Post*, 15 November 1994, p. 1.
16 Willy Wo-lap Lam, 'Jiang's Faction Pushes Agenda', *South China Morning Post*, 16 December 1994, p. 11.
17 Tai Ming Cheung, 'Policy in Paralysis: Deng's Cameo Fails to Tilt the Delicate Balancing Act', *Far Eastern Economic Review* (10 January 1991): 10–11.
18 For analyses of the changes in Chinese bureaucracy, see Hong Yung Lee (1991); and Martin K. Whyte (1989).
19 Zhao Xixin, Minister in the Chinese Embassy to the United States, interview with the author, Washington, DC, 8 February 1991.
20 For a detailed recollection of this episode, see Xu Jiatun (1993: 106–111), his memoirs. Also see Andy Ho, 'Tracking Down China's Official Line', *South China Morning Post*, 27 October 1994, p. 23.
21 Lincoln Kaye, 'Vital Signs', *Far Eastern Economic Review* (30 March 1995): 14–15.
22 Victor Sit, 'The Power of Change', *South China Morning Post*, 27 May 1995.
23 See K. C. Yeh (1992: 528).

24 Nayan Chanda, 'Fear of the Dragon', *Far Eastern Economic Review* (13 April 1995): 24–26.
25 For detailed accounts of the PLA's massive business activities and their relations to China's arms sales, see the cover story 'PLA, Inc., China's Military Launches Profit Offensive', by Tai Ming Cheung, *Far Eastern Economic Review* (14 October 1993): 64–71.
26 See John Calabrese (1990: 873).
27 See Eberhard Sandschneider (1990: 113–124).
28 Tai Ming Cheung, 'Serve the People', *Far Eastern Economic Review* (14 October 1993): 66.
29 Nayan Chanda, 'Gentle Giant: China Seeks to Calm Southeast Asia's Fears', *Far Eastern Economic Review* (4 August 1994): 15–16.
30 Nayan Chanda, 'Fear of the Dragon', *Far Eastern Economic Review* (13 April 1995): 24–6.
31 For the PLA's role in China's political life, see Ellis Joffe (1987); Gerald Segal and William T. Tow (eds.) (1984); and Hsiao-shik Cheng (1990).
32 For a detailed account, see Tai Ming Cheung, 'Back to the Front: Deng Seeks to Depoliticize the PLA', *Far Eastern Economic Review* (29 October 1992): 15–16.
33 Douglas Paal, Director of Asian Affairs of the US National Security Council under the Bush administration, interview with the author, Washington, DC, 5 February 1991; and Kent Wiedemann, Director of the Office of Chinese and Mongolian Affairs of the US State Department, interview with the author, Washington, DC, 25 February 1991.
34 *Renmin Ribao* (People's Daily), 2 February 1991, p. 1.
35 Tai Ming Cheung, 'Missile Refrain', *Far Eastern Economic Review* (27 June 1991): 12–13.
36 *Renmin Ribao*, 1 August 1991, p. 1.
37 Nigel Holloway, 'Goodwill Proliferates', *Far Eastern Economic Review* (20 October 1994): 20.
38 'Fanji "zhongguo weixielun"', [Dismissing Concerns of a 'China Threat'], *Yazhou Zhoukan* [The International Chinese Newsweekly] (3 December 1995): 30–32. For a detailed and comprehensive research on China's arms control policy, see A. I. Johnston (1996).
39 See James Hsiung (ed.) (1986), *Human Rights in East Asia*, and Andrew Nathan (1986), 'Sources of Chinese Rights Thinking'.
40 Gordon Fairclough, 'Standing Firm: Asia Sticks to Its View of Human Rights', *Far Eastern Economic Review* (15 April 1993): 22.
41 Douglas Paal, interview with the author.
42 Susumo Awanohara and Tai Ming Cheung, 'Abusive Treatment: China Hedges Response to US Human Rights Pressure', *Far Eastern Economic Review* (3 January 1991): 8–9.
43 Kent Wiedemann, Director of the Office of Chinese and Mongolian Affairs of the US State Department, who participated in this visit, interview with the author.
44 Lincoln Kaye, 'Commerce Kowtow: Human-Rights Concerns Lost in Rush of US Deals', *Far Eastern Economic Review* (8 September 1994): 16–18.
45 Shada Islam, 'Pressure on Beijing: Foreign Firms Urged to Insist on Workers' Rights', *Far Eastern Economic Review* (29 December 1994, and 5 January 1995): 16.
46 'United States: China Business Code', *Far Eastern Economic Review* (8 June 1995): 57.
47 For further detailed analysis of the human right issue in Chinese foreign policy, see Andrew Nathan (1994), 'Human Rights in Chinese Foreign Policy'.
48 For a detailed account of educational exchange between China and the United States, see Joyce K. Kallgren and Denis Fred Simon (eds.) (1987); Leo A. Orleans (1988); and Changgui Chen and David Zweig (1994).

49   Mahlon Meyer, 'Class Politics: Taiwanese, Chinese Students Don't Mix, Even on US Campuses', *Far Eastern Economic Review* (1 December 1994): 56–58.
50   The Xinhua General Overseas News Service, 1 July 1993.
51   Xinhua News Agency, 19 April 1995.
52   For a detailed analysis of China's brain drain, one may refer to Changgui Chen and David Zweig (1994).
53   The Xinhua General Overseas New Service, 1 July 1993.
54   *Renmin Ribao* [People's Daily] (Overseas Edition), 16 November 1995, p. 3.
55   For an excellent analysis, see Kenneth Lieberthal and Michel Oksenberg (1988: 339–53).
56   Lincoln Kaye, 'The Grip Slips', *Far Eastern Economic Review* (11 May 1995): 18–20.
57   Lincoln Kaye, 'Vital Signs', *Far Eastern Economic Review* (30 March 1995): 14–15.
58   'Quarterly Chronicle and Documentation', *The China Quarterly*, 124 (December 1990): 780.
59   Kent Wiedemann, Director of the Office of Chinese and Mongolian Affairs of the US State Department, interview with the author.
60   Elizabeth Cheng, 'Power to the Center: China Removes Export Subsidies to Curb Regional Privileges', *Far Eastern Economic Review* (24 January 1991): 34–35.
61   For a detailed account, see Gilbert Rozman (1987).
62   Huan Xiang, interview with foreign reporters in Beijing, 21 June 1985, in *Wen Wei Po*, 22 June 1985, pp. 1–2, in Foreign Broadcast Information Service, *FBIS Daily Report China*, 24 June 1985; quoted in Carol Lee Hamrin (1990: 141).
63   For further readings on the relationship between intellectuals and the State in China, see Merle Goldman (ed.) (1987).
64   One exception was the government loans of US$1.5 billion received from the Soviet Union and East European socialist countries from 1953 to 1960.
65   *Renmin Ribao*, 2 January 1977, p. 1.
66   See Chae-jin Lee (1984: 113).
67   *Japan Times*, 27 August 1988, p. 1.
68   Ibid.
69   *Japan Times*, 12 July 1990, p. 1.
70   *Renmin Ribao*, 26 July 1990, p. 1.
71   *Far Eastern Economic Review* (31 May 1990): 17.
72   For details, see Hong Shi (1990: 1210), 'China's Political Development after Tiananmen: Tranquillity by Default'.
73   *Far Eastern Economic Review* (24 January 1991): 9.
74   Willy Wo-Lap Lam, 'Jiang's Power Continues to Grow', *South China Morning Post*, 17 March 1995, p. 1.
75   For an excellent collective work featuring a comparison of democratization in East Asia (China, Japan, Korea, Hong Kong, and Taiwan), see Edward Friedman (1994).

5   Power/Regime Macrostructure and Strategy and Tactics: From Rigidity toward Flexibility

This chapter analyses the *power/regime macrostructure* and its effect on the behaviour patterns and style of Chinese foreign policy. In most Chinese foreign policy decision-making cases there are two overriding factors: first, the *dynamics of power and authority* in Chinese politics; and second, the issue of *regime legitimacy*. The previous chapter has already provided some vivid pictures of power politics as they are played out in foreign policy, including aspects of the relationship between Mao Zedong and Zhou Enlai in the era of Mao, and the two different power centres represented by Deng Xiaoping and Chen Yun, respectively, in the Deng era. It is clear from these examples that power politics and regime legitimacy, in both international and domestic arenas, can have a direct impact on Chinese foreign policy.

This chapter will examine further micro-level behaviours such as foreign policy strategies and tactics. In order to identify behaviour patterns, it is important to analyse the choices and preferences that decision-makers face and ask why they would select a certain policy among a variety of choices. In his discussion of the micro-macro linkage, James Coleman (1987: 168) suggested that at the micro level 'each individual has a preference order, and this preference order leads to a vote. The micro-to-macro transition occurs through counting of votes and application of a decision rule to produce a macro-level election outcome.' There are, obviously, no voting actions per se in the Chinese foreign policy-making process, yet one can still study the convergence between elements at the micro and macro levels through an inquiry of the power politics macrostructure. The decision-makers' choices are often influenced by changes in the elements at the macro level over time, which cause them to apply different strategies and tactics. Therefore, understanding strategies and tactics at the micro level and their linkage to elements at the macro level are crucial to comprehending a country's external behaviour.

In the process of analysing the power/regime macrostructure, this chapter conducts a broad investigation of Beijing's characteristic foreign policy strategies and tactics. As Anthony Giddens (1984) points out, the basic domain of the study of social sciences 'is neither the experience of the individual actor, nor the existence of any form of societal totality, but social practices ordered across time and space'. The examination of the issue of strategy and tactics has made it possible for researchers to conduct research focusing on historical, social, and ideological changes, thereby avoiding static analyses.

In conducting this investigation, we will first briefly review the origins and usages of two Chinese concepts — *yuanzexing* (adherence to principle) and *linghuoxing* (flexibility) — and then looks, in turn, at foreign policy issues and at Beijing's negotiating style. Understanding Chinese behaviour regarding certain *issues* (the first category under discussion) requires distinguishing between *essential principles* and *rhetorical principles* and between high priorities and low priorities. The second category — leadership style — has become a noteworthy topic of study within foreign policy studies.[1] For the purpose of interpreting Chinese foreign policy, it calls for an examination of Beijing's use of official and unofficial arrangements, of formal and informal channels, and of intervention by top leaders. Both categories will be illustrated by a variety of case studies involving both major powers and minor states.

The Impact of Ideology and Traditional Thinking

Thomas Robinson (1994: 558–563) has argued that there were three domestic determinants of Chinese foreign policy during the era of Mao — the primacy of politics, the weight of the past, and ideology — that, when combined, can explain 'most of the direction, timing, and specifics of Beijing's international orientation under Mao'.

'We have two parents', emphasized Mao Zedong, 'Kuomintang society and the October Revolution.'[2] By 'the October Revolution' Mao was, of course, referring to the influence of Marxist–Leninism brought to China by the victory of the 1917 Russian Bolshevik revolutionaries. By 'Kuomintang society' he meant 'the ideas, attitudes, and institutions that developed not only during two decades of Kuomintang rule, but throughout China's long history' (Schram, 1989: 134). The intrigues in China's traditional thinking, particularly the ancient imperial courts, are thought to have been a far more powerful influence on Mao's deeper thinking than Marxism–Leninism.[3] For example, one of the ancient principles for diplomacy is *yuanjiao jingong*, an admonition to 'negotiate with faraway countries while fighting those that are near'. Mao precisely cited this principle when he first raised the possibility of improving relations with the United States just after the Sino–Soviet border clash in 1969 (Z. Li, 1994: 514). China's top military commanders shared Mao's idea of *yuanjiao jingong*, Mao found, when he privately consulted Marshals Chen Yi, Ye Jianying, Xu Xiangqian, and Nie Rongzhen on foreign and defence policies in the spring 1969 (Gong, 1992: 41).

The combination of ideology and traditional thinking is one of the major bases upon which the Beijing leadership has conducted foreign policy. The influences of Marxism and cultural tradition[4] have extended to foreign, as well as to domestic policy and policy-making, and are evident in the strategies and tactics Beijing characteristically employs in the pursuit of the PRC's foreign policy goals. These influences are apparent in one of the consistent and distinctive behaviour patterns of Chinese foreign policy — a duality of rigidity and flexibility based on the concepts of *yuanzexing* and *linghuoxing*.

Yuanzexing *and* Linghuoxing

When one examines Chinese government documents, one notices the frequent appearance of two terms: *yuanzexing*, meaning 'principle' or 'principled'; and *linghuoxing*, meaning 'flexibility'. Zhou Enlai, the designated PRC premier and foreign minister, drafted a CCP Central Committee document entitled 'Instructions on the Work of Foreign Affairs', which was issued in January 1949, nine months before the establishment of the People's Republic. The instructions emphasized that, 'with regard to foreign affairs, we should properly master *yuanzexing* and *linghuoxing*, so that we can be firm with our stance and yet be flexible' (P. Li, 1994: 306). When used with regard to external affairs, *yuanzexing* refers to a set of principles[5] that include national interests, sovereignty, and China's socialist road; by contrast, *linghuoxing* recognizes the necessity for flexibility and compromise in the international arena.

Influenced by the dialectical philosophy of Marx, the Chinese Communists believed that the world was essentially dichotomous — composed of two opposing forces (positive and negative) that confront one another.[6] They recognized that the capitalist class used both militant and peaceful means to govern the proletariat class. To overthrow capitalism, they believed, revolutionaries must adhere to basic principles, yet be flexible enough to take advantage of opportunities as they arise. A good revolutionary must be prepared to apply different strategies to promote social development, depending on the situation or the circumstances. Mao Zedong proposed the strategy of *yuanzexing* and *linghuoxing* as early as the 1930s; like a classic Chinese coin, a true revolutionary should be square inside, yet round outside, meaning staying firm inside (to stick to principle) and flexible outside.[7] In their examination of Mao's revolutionary strategy and international behaviour, Tang Tsou and Morton Halperin (1965: 80) argued that, 'Mao followed a pattern of action and adopted a set of principles' that helped him 'achieve political gain from a position of military weakness'.

Mao and his colleagues developed this thinking in both domestic and foreign policies. Mao developed dual, or 'two-legged' strategies for China's socialist economic construction, for example, emphasizing not only industry, but also agriculture, focusing not only on coastal development but also on inland development, in order to create a more balanced economic policy. In dealing with 'foreign imperialist and reactionary forces', Mao used 'revolutionary dual strategies to oppose anti-revolutionary dual strategies'. In 1946, Mao described the United States as having 'dual characteristics': due to the inevitability of its long-term strategic decline, the United States was ultimately a 'paper tiger'; however, due to its military and technological superiority, in the short term the United States must be treated as an 'iron tiger'.[8]

Mao's strategy of *yuanzexing* and *linghuoxing* drew not only on Marxist philosophy, but also on traditional Chinese thinking. The traditional Chinese belief of *zhongxueweiti, xixueweiyong*, for instance, advocates using Chinese values as principles and using Western values for technical and practical purposes.[9] The ancient Chinese military strategist Sun Zi (Sun Tzu) claimed that 'the art of war is ambiguity' and reaction to a situation depends on the circumstances and viewpoints of the leaders. Based on the combination of Marxism and Chinese tradition, Mao held the unchallengeable leading position within the PRC's foreign policy hierarchy, not only in the institutional sense, but also in the moral and legitimate sense.

An examination of any individual event reveals a mixture of rigidity and flexibility in Beijing's behaviour patterns and policy choices. Beijing is rigid in terms of sticking to basic principles, but may be flexible in practical and technical matters; yet these two conditions may change as the situation changes (as later examples will show). Chinese leaders use the combination of principled and flexible behaviour to achieve maximum advantage for regime preservation; power politics, therefore, can be considered a key factor behind this type of foreign policy behaviour.

Let us now examine some concrete circumstances to analyse Beijing's behaviour patterns.

Top Leaders' Power Politics

In China, as in most other countries, important foreign policy decisions are made directly by the top leadership. However, in the PRC the extreme degree of control and involvement of the leadership is particulary noteworthy. Mao Zedong was 'totally dominant' and made almost all of the important decisions; Deng Xiaoping is regarded as having 'played a pivotal role' among the political elite.[10] Bureaucrats in the foreign affairs and foreign trade ministries are responsible for negotiations and implementation and may appear flexible over less important or lower priority issues, but they have little room to manœuvre on important issues because China's foreign policy-making system is highly central-ized and hierarchical. Even though there has been a move since the late 1970s 'from individual to collective decision-making' (Barnett, 1985: 16), and 'from vertical to horizontal authoritarianism' (see Chapter 4), this process is still far from being institutionalized.

Consequently, changes in foreign policy correspond closely to the preferences of top leaders and changes in Chinese leadership. Let us take the drastic changes of China's policy toward the United States and Soviet Union in the 1960s and 1970s as an example. The break-up with the Soviet Union and the rapprochement with the United States during this period was primarily due the changing international environments explained in Chapter 3. But this change was also closely connected with Mao Zedong's deep-rooted personal preference. In order to see clearly the link between personal preference at the micro level and the power structure at the macro level behind Chinese foreign policy issues, we need to look more closely at Mao's own foreign policy preferences.

According to the recollections of Mao's personal physician Li Zhisui, Mao's many private conversations revealed his true feelings about the United States, which he held even during the period of icy relations between the two countries during the 1950s and 1960s. Mao's personal admiration towards the United States is reflected by the following statements:

- During the war against Japan, the United States sent a military mis-sion to Yan'an, 'and we all got along very well'.
- Unlike Russia, 'the United States never occupied Chinese territory'.
- Mao expressed his deep-rooted admiration for the technology, dy-namism, and science of the United States and the West when he said,

'The United States has trained many skilled technicians for China', and 'I like having American- or British-trained people working for me.'
* Mao worried about China's cultural stagnation and thought Western ideas would reinvigorate China, thereby creating 'something new that was neither Chinese nor Western but a hybrid' (Z. Li, 1994: 68, 101, 102, 124, 180, and 514).

Mao's conversations during this period also revealed his displeasure with the Soviet Union and its leaders, including both Stalin and, in particular, Khrushchev (Z. Li, 1994: 114–119). Mao's personal preference was also reflected in his interest in studying foreign languages. As early as 1955, while there were still massive campaigns in China to 'learn from our Soviet Big Brothers', Mao intimated that 'some people think I should learn Russian, but I don't want to. I'd rather learn English' (Z. Li, 1994: 68).

The fact that Mao began to express his dislike of the Soviet Union from as early as the late 1950s has been further confirmed by some recently disclosed materials from China. In a collection entitled *Jianguo Yilai Mao Zedong Wengao* [The Scripts of Mao Zedong since 1949] (1993), there is a 'speech outline' written by Mao in 1959.[11] In this outline, Mao listed a number of mistakes committed by the Soviet Union that damaged Sino-Soviet relations from 1945 to 1959. In addition to some well-known incidents (such as Stalin's doubt about the nature of the Chinese revolution in the late 1940s, and the Soviet support of India during the Sino-Indian border disputes of the late 1950s and early 1960s), the most interesting accusation was the alleged Soviet involvement in China's domestic power politics — in the incident of Gao Gang and Rao Sushi of 1953 to 1954,[12] and the famous Lushan Conference of 1959.[13] These two incidents represented the most severe internal challenges to the leadership of Mao and his associates up to that point. It is not surprising to see that Mao was not able to tolerate any external support of these internal threats.

One hypothesis is that Mao's personal preferences played little role in policy toward the United States or the Soviet Union when external conditions did not allow (as during the Korean War); his leanings were often outweighed by other concerns such as national interests and survival and national security (He, 1994). At least as early as April 1949, Mao clearly raised the possibility of establishing formal diplomatic relations between the PRC and the United States.[14] Due to the international and domestic circumstances at that time, however, this consideration did not work out.

Nevertheless, this personal preference would help to redirect China's foreign policy when conditions were ripe. The combination of a change of international environment (macro level) and Mao's personal preferences (micro level) made it possible for China to change its policy toward the United States in the early 1970s. In other words, even during periods of outward hostility toward the United States (such as the 'lean to one side' policy and the Korean War), Mao was always aware that the United States was a potential alternative to the Soviet Union toward which to turn for help.

During the early part of Cultural Revolution, a group of ultra-leftist leaders, including Defence Minister Lin Biao and Mao's wife Jiang Qing (head of the Gang of Four), vigorously advocated a strategy of promoting world revolution.[15] With this faction holding the upper hand, China carried out a radical and rigid foreign policy and maintained few contacts with the outside: only Albania and a few African countries were considered to be friends of China. This self-imposed isolation caused China to lose diplomatic flexibility. Furthermore, there were differences within China's top leadership — notably between Lin Biao and Zhou Enlai — on major foreign policy issues. As Lowell Dittmer has pointed out, a more conciliatory and flexible policy towards the United States, Japan, and other Western Bloc countries (recommended by moderates) was 'less compatible with Lin's bureaucratic interests than any conceivable alternative, as it tended to favour the modern urban industrial sector and shore up the moderate forces of arch-rival Zhou Enlai' (Dittmer, 1978: 113–114). It is clear, therefore, that individuals' different policy preferences within the top leadership are an important key to understanding Chinese foreign policy.

In the late 1960s and early 1970s, Mao Zedong and Zhou Enlai were facing the domestic chaos of the Cultural Revolution and a changing international environment marked by the 1969 Sino-Soviet border clashes. These events led Mao and Zhou to seek open relations with the Western Bloc powers, especially the United States and Japan.

In 1971, Lin Biao, Mao's heir apparent, was alleged to have conducted an unsuccessful coup and was killed soon after under suspicious circumstances in an airplane crash. After Lin's death, Zhou and his more moderate faction gained day-to-day control of foreign affairs from the radicals, led by Jiang Qing. Chinese foreign policy under Zhou was much more moderate than it had been under Lin Biao and Jiang Qing. Due to the apparent decline of Mao's health at that time and his deep disappointment over Lin's betrayal, Mao allowed Zhou to exert greater influence over Chinese foreign policy.

Many foreign observers of China have learned that different power centres or governmental agencies may have different policy orientations. On some occasions, foreign officials dealing with China have even tried to take advantage of this phenomenon. For example, it was known in 1994 that there was a rivalry relationship between the two top Chinese agencies in charge of Hong Kong affairs: the State Council's Hong Kong and Macau Affairs Office and the Xinhua News Agency in Hong Kong, China's *de facto* representative in Hong Kong. The former, under its director Lu Ping, was perceived to be more moderate and sympathetic towards the Colony than the latter, which was headed by Zhou Nan, a veteran diplomat and a hardliner. The British Hong Kong government thought that by manipulating the rivalry between these two agencies it could win some support from Beijing for its policies. In late 1994, when the government proposed an ambitious old-age pension scheme, it first provided Lu Ping's office with a copy of its proposal, but left Xinhua in the dark. In this case, however, the tactic was unsuccessful. Both Lu and Zhou stood united in their objection to the plan.[16]

In some instances, foreign policy issues can be used directly to serve the purpose of internal power politics. One good example in this regard is the decision by Party General Secretary Hu Yaobang to invite 3,000 Japanese youths to China in 1983. The highly touted visit of 3,000 Japanese youths took place in October 1984, and aroused considerable resentment among young Chinese as well as the old guard Party leadership over what they perceived as a 'waste of money' and Hu Yaobang's immature working style. This personal foreign affairs decision by Hu was reportedly criticised by top CCP leaders and was one of the causes leading to his eventual downfall three and half years later. On 16 January 1987, at an enlarged meeting of the Politburo, influential Party elder Bo Yibo, among others, presented a list of specific charges against Hu, which became Central Document No. 3 of 1987. Among other charges (see note 17), the document precisely criticized Hu for 'making unauthorized statements and taking unauthorized actions regarding foreign policy, such as inviting 3,000 young Japanese to visit China' (Goldman, 1994: 208–210).[17] At this meeting, Hu was forced to make a 'self-criticism' and to resign from the top Party position.

The interplay of power politics and foreign policy was also reflected in the realm of information gathering. One such example concerned Hong Kong. For many years, Liao Chengzhi, a CCP Politburo member, was in charge of Hong Kong affairs within the highest leadership in Beijing. Although a well-respected politician and a veteran statesman in international affairs, Liao was criticized by several other Politburo members, such as Xi Zhongxun, for trying to 'monopolize information' about Hong Kong (Xu, 1993: 12–16). To 'correct' this problem, the Party secretary general, Hu Yaobang, and Politburo member Wan Li in early 1983 opened up a secret information channel — they sent Qiao Zonghuai (son of former Chinese foreign minister Qiao Guanhua) to the Chinese University of Hong Kong, under the guise of 'visiting scholar', to collect information about Hong Kong's political development and to report directly to Hu and Wan. After the sudden death of Liao Chengzhi several months later, this channel become unnecessary and was closed. Qiao was transferred to the Hong Kong Xinhua News Agency, the PRC's representative agency in Hong Kong, and later was promoted to become the Agency's deputy head (Xu, 1993: 12–16).

A distinctive characteristic of the Chinese negotiation style has been, and will continue to be, intervention by the top leadership in negotiations at which the top leadership is not actually present. Chinese policy can become more flexible or more rigid as the result of an intervention, depending on the prevailing domestic politics as well as the personalities of the leaders. Here again, we can see interactions between the micro and macro levels. Two cases illustrate this style of policy-making: Mao's intervention in the Nagasaki flag incident resulted in a rigid policy; Zhou's intervention in the Sino-Japanese aviation negotiations resulted in a flexible policy (Whiting, 1989: 187).

In 1958, the fourth Sino-Japanese unofficial trade agreement was abruptly suspended as a result of the Nagasaki Flag Incident of May 1958, when two Japanese youths pulled down a Chinese flag at a stamp show in a Nagasaki department store. The flag incident, together with Prime Minister Nobusuke Kishi's official trip to Taiwan, where he was alleged to have encouraged Chiang Kai-shek to realize Taiwan's goal of retaking the Mainland, led Mao to believe that the Kishi government was hostile toward China, and that the flag incident was a Tokyo–Taipei plot. To 'maintain the dignity of an independent sovereign state and to protect its rights', the Chinese government felt it had no choice but to suspend trade relations with Japan.[18] Mao Zedong, himself, reported made this drastic decision, despite internal reservations from moderate elements in the central leadership and in the governmental bureaucracy who would have preferred to adopt a more mild measure that could preserve basic trading channels between the two countries.[19] Mao's inflexibility reflected his radical approach (stemming from his own brand of Marxism) to China's foreign relations at that time.

During the process of normalization with Japan in 1972, Premier

Zhou Enlai was responsible for the daily operation of Chinese foreign policy; he was in charge of virtually every detail of Sino-Japanese negotiations and the preparation of bilateral documents, such as joint statements, communiques, treaties, and agreements (including economic agreements). During this period, the central bureaucracy was governed by the rule of *yishi yibao:* 'one matter, one report' (each and every foreign policy matter had to be reported to the top leaders).[20] According to Toshio Oishi, deputy leader of the Japanese delegation for negotiating the trade agreement in Tokyo, the Chinese delegation stopped several times during negotiations to telephone Beijing and wait for instructions. Oishi says, 'I was told that they had to wait for instructions from Premier Zhou himself.'[21] Lin Liande, then director of the Japan Division of the Chinese Foreign Trade Ministry, recalls that the premier was in charge of every detail of the negotiations, and read and corrected negotiation drafts.[22]

On several occasions when bilateral negotiations reached an impasse, top Chinese leaders intervened to break the deadlock.[23] This was the case with an aviation agreement in the summer of 1973. Japan and China could not reach a compromise over the conditions (the name, the flag, and landing airport) under which Taiwan's airline would be allowed to fly to Japan. The Chinese delegation, in Tokyo to conduct negotiations for the trade agreement, stalled the start of talks.[24] The Japanese government, under pressure both domestically (from the LDP's conservative wing) and externally (from the Taiwan authorities and their lobbyists), deliberated over whether to make further concessions.

The situation remained unresolved until foreign minister Masayoshi Ohira's visit to Beijing in January 1974. Ohira had two goals: to sign the trade agreement; and to seek a breakthrough on the aviation agreement. The first mission — a purely ceremonial task — was accomplished with great fanfare. Ohira was received by both Mao and Zhou, and his picture appeared on the front page of *Renmin Ribao*, China's leading official newspaper.[25] As for the second goal, both sides were unwilling to make concessions. On the last day of his visit, Ohira had a talk with his Chinese counterpart Ji Pengfei. During the conversation, a Chinese official walked into the conference room and asked Ji to receive a telephone call. Twenty minutes later Ji proposed new terms that were very similar to the Japanese proposals. Within two hours, the two foreign ministers reached a compromise on the aviation agreement. Premier Zhou had called and made the breakthrough.[26]

Under an authoritarian government a top leader's personal style may become a unique characteristic of national diplomacy. Mao was known

to use personal tactics to achieve diplomatic ends. According to his personal physician, Mao's actions were sometimes dramatic (Z. Li, 1994;
105–106, 568). At least four times during the 1960s and early 1970s,
for example, Mao feigned serious, terminal illness in front of important
visitors from the Soviet Union, the United States, France, and Japan,
respectively, to test these countries' reactions. These visitors and Mao's
performance are as follows:

- The Soviet ambassador to China (1963) — Mao was 'covering himself with a terry-cloth blanket, feigning lethargy and pain, pretending
  to have great difficulty talking';
- American journalist Edgar Snow, whom Mao believed to be a CIA
  agent and a conduit of information to the highest levels of the American government (1965) — Mao told Snow he 'was going soon to
  meet God';
- French minister of culture Andre Malraux (1965) — Mao told the
  visitor he 'did not have long to live'; and
- Japanese Prime Minister Kakuei Tanaka (1972) — Mao told Tanaka
  that he 'could not live much longer'.

All of these performances were actually Mao's unique game for
testing foreign reactions to China and to his possible death.

It can also be instructive to pay close attention to a foreign-policy
decision-maker's past experiences, particularly those experiences that
relate to the foreign countries in question, for that may affect a leader's
personal preference. One should be careful, however, about looking for
and drawing connections — it is difficult to second-guess the minds of
policy-makers and best to rely on the associations and connections that
they, themselves have made.

One example was Deng Xiaoping's strong reaction to the economic
sanctions that Western nations imposed on China after the Tiananmen
Incident in 1989. Deng made the following critical remark:

I am a Chinese, and I am familiar with the history of foreign aggression against
China. When I heard that the seven Western countries, at their summit meeting,
had decided to impose sanctions on China, my immediate association was [the
period of foreign intervention in] 1900, when the allied forces of the eight
powers invaded China. Six of these same seven countries, excluding Canada,
together with czarist Russia and Austria, constituted the eight powers that formed
the allied forces in those days.[27]

Someone like Deng, who was born in 1904, must have had many
bitter memories of the humiliations that China suffered beginning with
the late Qing Dynasty. This was particularly true for Deng, due to his

early politicization during his school days and while he was in Paris as a teenager, at a time when these memories were fresh in the minds of the Chinese people as a whole. The youthful Deng's experiences and memories were coloured by the nationalist sentiment of the day.

One such humiliation (now infamous), was the sign placed in the municipal parks of foreign-administered Shanghai during the early twentieth century, which allegedly read: 'Chinese and Dogs Not Admitted'.[28] In the semi-official biography of Deng Xiaoping by his daughter Deng Maomao (1993), there are many recollections of the younger Deng's personal observations of China's suffering at the hands of Western powers. Deng's post-1949 experience as one of China's top leaders in charge of both domestic and foreign affairs — in particular China's confrontations with the United States in the 1950s and 1960s and with the Soviet Union in the 1960s and 1970s — further enhanced his belief (obtained from his early politicization) that foreign powers aimed to humiliate and take advantage of China.

The combination of these experiences prompted Deng to make the following tough statement toward Western sanctions in 1990:

One special feature of China's development is that it has proceeded under international sanctions for most of the forty years since the founding of the People's Republic. If there is nothing else we're good at, we're good at withstanding sanctions. . . . China will never accept interference by other countries in its internal affairs.[29]

Deng reiterated the claim when he told former US President Richard Nixon on his visit to China after the Tiananmen Incident: 'Don't ever expect China to beg the United States to lift the sanctions. If they lasted a hundred years, the Chinese would not do that.' Deng further explained, 'If China had no self-respect, it could not maintain its independence for long and would lose its national dignity.' Then, Deng made a point from the perspective of China's domestic politics: 'If any Chinese leader made a mistake in this regard, the Chinese people would never forgive him, and he would surely fall.' The conclusion therefore was that 'too much is at stake' to capitulate to foreign pressure on the principle of non-interference.[30]

Essential Principles and Rhetorical Principles

Now, let us further analyse the concepts of *linghuoxing* and *yuanzexing*. The principles involved in the application of *yuanzexing* to foreign policy and diplomatic relations may belong to one of two types: *essential* and *rhetorical*. Essential principles express China's vital and enduring national interests, including its defence and assertion of its sovereignty; Beijing's adherence to these principles are consistently firm. Rhetorical principles are formulated in respect of highly sensitive, but less substantial issues. These issues often serve as secondary goals that lie outside the immediate scope of policy objectives and often disappear or are resolved once the essential principles are met. When referring to principles, Chinese leaders mean what they say; these issues are regarded as high priorities.

Principles and priorities in Beijing's policy shift depending on how Beijing assesses its own regime survival both internationally and domestically. Domestic power politics is a critical consideration, for foreign policy issues often can be used as weapons for the internal power struggle. The status of a principle also depends on a given situation; the degree of flexibility shown by the government corresponds to the priority of the issue.

Since its establishment in 1949, the Beijing government has insisted that whenever the PRC establishes diplomatic relations with another nation, that nation must explicitly recognize that there is only one China, that Taiwan is a part of China, and that Beijing is the sole representative of China. When the PRC opens diplomatic relations with another country, that country must cut off relations with Taiwan. Conversely, when Taiwan sets up relations with another country, Beijing severs its relations with that country to avoid a 'two Chinas' situation. This principle has been consistently upheld because it is crucial to regime legitimacy in both the international community and domestically.

The issues of sovereignty and regime legitimacy clearly fall within the category of essential principles. When Beijing perceives that such principles are being threatened, it will appear tough, even threatening the use of military force. This might be the case if Taiwan were to announce its independence.

As long as essential principles are preserved, Beijing may show flexibility, rendering some of its other principles rhetorical. When the PRC is dealing with foreign countries over the issue of Taiwan, it is rigid in political, official relations, but flexible in unofficial matters, such as trade and cultural ties. All major powers, including the United States, Japan, and Germany, as well as countries in North-East and South-East Asia have maintained unofficial offices in Taipei without provoking strong reactions from Beijing. Even Russia (and some former Soviet states) and Vietnam began quietly to develop unofficial links with Taiwan in the early 1990s.

The role of essential and rhetorical principles is also illustrated by Beijing's processes of normalizing relations with major nations, which can be illuminated by the following examples of the former Soviet Union, the United States, and France.

After the rapid decline of relations in the 1960s with its former ally, Beijing adopted a hostile policy toward Moscow. The deterioration of bilateral relations was highlighted by the border military conflict in 1969. China began to call the Soviet Union a 'social imperialist' and 'hegemonic', and worked hard to organize a global united front to oppose 'Soviet military expansion'.

From the late 1970s to the mid-1980s, Soviet leaders repeatedly asked the PRC for a normalization of relations. The PRC submitted three conditions on issues which constituted major external threats to the Beijing regime at that time, for normalizing relations with Moscow:

- a reduction in the number of Soviet troops on the Sino-Soviet and Sino-Mongolian borders;
- the withdrawal of Soviet troops from Afghanistan;
- an end to Moscow's support of the Vietnamese invasion of Cambodia.

Only after Moscow met all of these conditions did Beijing agree to normalize bilateral relations, a change that was marked by the Deng–Gorbachev summit in May 1989.

Taiwan was the major obstacle to the establishment of formal diplomatic relations between the United States and China after Nixon's visit to Beijing in 1972. In 1975, President Gerald Ford visited Beijing to negotiate bilateral relations with Chinese leaders. Deng Xiaoping, then vice premier, laid out the policy of '*duanjiao, feiyue, chejun*', three principles for the normalization of Sino-American relations:

- *Duanjiao*: the United States must cut off official relations with Taiwan;
- *Feiyue*: the United States must abrogate the mutual defence treaty with Taiwan;
- *Chejun*: US troops must withdraw from Taiwan.

After President Jimmy Carter entered the White House in 1977, Secretary of State Cyrus Vance was sent to China, where Deng Xiaoping reiterated these three principles.[31] The normalization of Sino-American relations in January 1979 was achieved only after the Carter Administration demonstrated a willingness to meet China's three conditions concerning its relationship with Taiwan. (Thereafter, it should be noted, Carter and the US Congress moved quickly to pass the 'Taiwan Relations

Act' to preserve unofficial relations with Taiwan.) Since then, Chinese leaders have repeatedly stated that the issue of Taiwan is one of the most crucial and sensitive problems in the Sino-US relationship. Chinese President Jiang Zemin, for example, reiterated this point when he met US President Bill Clinton in October 1995 during the United Nations convention in New York.[32]

While China was thus uncompromisingly rigid in its dealings with the United States over its major principles on the issue of Taiwan, it did make some compromises in the negotiations towards achieving the three conditions. For instance, China's original explanation for the second condition of normalization — *feiyue* — was that the United States should abrogate the mutual defence treaty with Taiwan prior to the official establishment of diplomatic relations between China and the United States in January 1979. However, the US side insisted that the treaty should not be repealed before its expiration date of 31 December 1979 — a year later than the Chinese demanded. Considering the difficulties the Americans had, the Chinese side eventually accepted the US suggestion. The US–Taiwan defence treaty, therefore, was not abolished until a year after the Sino-US rapprochement (Gong, 1992: 318).

China also showed flexibility in its negotiations for the establishment of relations with France. In 1964, when France decided to establish formal diplomatic relations with the PRC, Beijing demanded that France cut off relations with Taiwan. During the negotiation process, France proposed that it set up relations with Beijing first, and then allow Taipei to terminate relations with France. Beijing agreed, as it was certain that Taiwan would have no alternative but to do so (at that time Taipei refused to consider 'dual recognition' as it does now). When Paris announced the opening of official diplomatic relations with Beijing, Taipei did sever its relations with France.[33] Technically, there was a short period of 'dual recognition' of both the PRC and Taiwan, because the French government preferred to let Taipei take the initial step in cutting the diplomatic relationship. There was an interesting, related episode: in order to make sure that Taipei would cut its official ties with Paris, Beijing asked a pro-Taiwan newspaper in Hong Kong, through a secret channel, to publish an editorial urging Taiwan's President Chiang Kai-shek immediately to sever ties with France for the sake of *minzu zhengqi* (national justice). Chiang later told the paper that he fully agreed with the suggestion, and did, ironically, what Beijing had hoped.[34] In this way, China focused on its essential principle — establishing diplomatic relations with France — while being flexible on tactical issues.

A similar practice was adopted three decades later. In September 1991, China established official diplomatic relations with Latvia, newly independent from the former Soviet Union. But in April 1992, Latvia allowed a Taiwanese consulate to open. The PRC government immediately withdrew its diplomats from Latvia's capital Riga, making clear that it would not return its diplomats to Riga 'until Latvia recognizes Beijing as the sole and legal government of China and until the Taiwanese consulate is closed'. But Beijing, none the less, continued to maintain diplomatic ties with Riga and to communicate with the Latvian Foreign Ministry on a range of issues. This practice made Latvia, for a short period of time, the only country to have diplomatic relations with both Beijing and Taipei at the same time.[35] This unusual circumstance lasted for about two years until July 1994 when Latvia signed a joint statement with the PRC, cutting off diplomatic ties with Taiwan, thereby normalizing bilateral relations between the two countries. From Beijing's perspective, this practice was to 'leave enough room for diplomatic manœuvring', and to 'prevent the "Latvia phenomenon" from spreading' (Qu, 1994: 21–22). This case can also serve as a good example to illuminate the combination of 'adherence to principle' and 'flexibility' in Chinese foreign policy.

Essential principles are core conditions that are directly linked to China's national interests and sovereignty. As we have established in this chapter, Beijing's stance on essential principles is consistently firm. China's external security (as with the former Soviet Union) and the issue of diplomatic recognition of Taiwan (as with the United States) are essential principles related to regime survival and legitimacy. Rhetorical principles refer to highly sensitive, but less substantial issues, such as the technical issues involved in the Chinese–French negotiations. Rhetorical principles usually serve secondary goals that may differ from immediate policy objectives, and may disappear or be resolved when the primary goals are achieved.

High Priorities and Low Priorities

Like every country, China has both high priorities and low priorities in its foreign policy. The Chinese often apply *yuanzexing* to high-priority issues and *linghuoxing* to low-priority issues.

Beijing and Washington's negotiations over US arms sales to Taiwan in 1982 provide one example of this. The PRC insisted that the United States specify a date on which it would end arms sales. Washington was willing to set a limit on both the quality and the quantity of future sales, but it was unwilling to set a date for the termination of sales. Beijing accepted Washington's proposal on 15 August 1982, four days before the final date upon which the Reagan administration could notify the US Congress of the extension of the agreement with Taiwan on the joint production of F-5E aircraft. As one China-watcher points out, Beijing recognized at the last minute that 'it could either choose to accept the communique without a clear cut-off date or allow American arms sales to Taiwan without any quality and quantity limitations'.[36] In this case, the high priority was an agreement with Washington to limit arms sales to Taiwan; specific conditions, such as a clear cut-off date, became low priority. Beijing was willing to make concessions over low-priority issues, while maintaining a firm stance on high-priority ones.

Another example is the 1973 to 1974 Sino-Japanese negotiations for the first post-normalization trade agreement. Because China had long opposed the technology export restrictions imposed by the Coordinating Committee of the Consultative Group (COCOM)[37] and demanded full most-favoured-nation (MFN) treatment from Japan, Japan anticipated tough negotiations over the trade agreement. Members of the Japanese delegation agreed on two principles before meeting with the Chinese: the agreement should be reached as soon as possible and Japan had to uphold the COCOM restrictions because Japan–US relations were the cornerstone of Japanese foreign policy. During these internal discussions, Japanese bureaucrats saw four possible outcomes from the negotiations:

- 'Full MFN treatment', meaning the immediate abolishment of the COCOM restrictions;
- 'MFN *except* COCOM', meaning that COCOM restrictions would be clearly indicated;
- 'MFN with specific definitions without mention of COCOM', meaning that the agreement would sound like full MFN treatment, but both sides would understand that the MFN treatment could not go beyond the specific definitions. This outcome would allow the Japanese government to avoid violating the COCOM restrictions;
- Failure to reach an agreement.[38]

During the negotiations, the Chinese delegation raised the issue of COCOM when the MFN clause was discussed. The Chinese argued that Japan's export control was discriminatory against China, and because friendly relations were being established between the two countries, Japan should abolish those restrictions.[39] The Japanese maintained that all goals could be accomplished except those that involved 'multinational agreements', meaning COCOM. After several rounds of negotiation, it became clear that the Chinese would not insist on an immediate abolition of the COCOM restrictions.

Actually, the Chinese had anticipated this difficulty before they came to Tokyo, and were prepared not to delay or disrupt the trade agreement, which was the delegation's first priority.[40] The surprising, compromising attitude of the Chinese delegation allowed the rest of the negotiations to proceed smoothly. The agreement expanding bilateral trade between China and Japan was signed in Beijing in January 1974.

Yet another of flexibility is the evolution of the PRC's policy toward Taiwan's membership in international economic organizations (IEOs) within the context of Beijing's priority concern over regime legitimacy. The IEOs include such organizations as the United Nations Development Programmeme (UNDP), the International Monetary Fund (IMF), the World Bank, General Agreement on Tariffs and Trade (GATT), which has become the World Trade Organization (WTO), and the Asian Development Bank (ADB). These organizations are the principal multilateral institutions which provide coherence and stability to the international monetary, financial, and commercial systems. They have therefore been a major factor in establishing and maintaining the conditions that have made possible the relatively free flow internationally of goods and capital that has contributed to international economic growth (Jacobsen and Oksenberg, 1990: 1).

As discussed earlier, in 1971 the United Nations voted to admit Beijing as the sole representative of China, as a result of which the PRC gained not only UN membership, but also a permanent seat on the UN Security Council. For the next twenty plus years, Beijing began to participate actively in international economic organizations, including the World Bank, the IMF, and the ADB. At the same time, Taiwan's relationship with IEOs has been complicated severely by the changing status of Beijing and its policy toward Taipei.

There are many factors that are influential in determining Taiwan's relations with international economic organizations, such as the changing dynamics of international relations, Beijing's Taiwan policy and its relationship with Taipei, and Taiwan's internal conditions and Taipei's degree of its flexibility. But the most decisive factors since the 1970s have been the Beijing–Taipei rivalry and Beijing's concern for regime legitimacy.[41]

Taiwan's participation in international economic organizations such as the IMF, the World Bank, and GATT, has been closely linked to the issue of the UN membership, since most of these organizations are affiliated with the United Nations. The PRC was approved for UN membership in October 1971; at the same time, Taiwan was expelled from the international organization. Harold Jacobson and Michel Oksenberg (1990) have made a detailed study on Beijing's participation in IEOs and its relationship with Taipei. According to this study, prior to the early 1970s the PRC, due to its lack of UN membership, was excluded from the World Bank, the IMF, and the GATT. Taiwan was represented in most of these organizations. However, Beijing made consistent efforts to change its status. As early as 1950, the issue of Chinese representation on the IMF board of directors was raised by Czechoslovakia and Poland, Beijing's East European allies. On one other occasion, Czechoslovakia, supported by Yugoslavia and India, also proposed a resolution that would have excluded the Taiwan-designated Chinese governors, executive directors, and their alternates from the IMF and the World Bank. This resolution was defeated by a hand vote after the Philippines suggested that this issue was actually a political issue and it should be solved by the United Nations. Although the issue was raised again during the later years, the vote remained the same.[42]

China was a founding member of the GATT. In 1950, however, the Nationalist government withdrew from the organization after its flight to Taiwan and in the aftermath of the chaos of the civil war. Later on, in 1965, Taiwan requested, and was granted observer status in the GATT. This observer status was terminated in 1971 when Beijing obtained its UN membership. At that time, the PRC was not actively pursuing GATT membership because of domestic difficulties (stemming from the Cultural Revolution). Instead, Beijing asked its permanent mission to the UN office in Geneva to monitor GATT activities.

Taiwan's status within the World Bank and the IMF was primarily damaged by the loss of its UN membership. Taiwan's presence in the Fund and the Bank had been reduced by its own actions. Taiwan had lost the right to appoint executive directors in 1960 because of the decline in the relative size of its quota and subscription.[43] After Beijing entered the United Nations in 1971, Taiwan had tremendous difficulty in maintaining its status in these organizations. From 1972 on, Taiwan was not represented on the executive board of either institution. In fact, in November 1973 World Bank President Robert McNamara sent a telegram to the PRC stating that Beijing's application to join the World Bank would be welcomed (Jacobson and Oksenberg, 1990: 63–64). This gesture was perhaps influenced by the significant progress in PRC–US relations marked by the Shanghai Communique of February 1972 and the exchange of liaison offices in Beijing and Washington in February 1973.[44]

Due to internal political chaos and ideological considerations at that time, Beijing decided not to join the World Bank and the IMF. The socialist system and Mao's principle of self-reliance in world affairs, for example, were cited as some key considerations. The PRC's decision to participate in the IMF and the World Bank came in early 1979 under the new leadership in Beijing headed by Deng Xiaoping. After more than a year of prolonged negotiations, the PRC was allowed to represent China in the Fund and the Bank in 1980. One basic condition from the Beijing side for membership was that Taiwan must be excluded from these international organizations. Subsequently, Taipei departed from the IMF and World Bank.[45]

From Beijing's perspective, the issue of GATT membership is somewhat different from membership in the World Bank and the IMF. Beijing understands that full participation in the GATT would give China certain privileges in international trade. But, on the other hand, decision-makers in Beijing also realize that there would be some 'disadvantages' related to the protection of China's domestic industries and market: first, Beijing, in turn, 'would have to make concessions by opening its markets to GATT members'; second it 'would have to submit its trade regime to international scrutiny and surveillance; and finally, the PRC would have to undertake measures to liberalize its trade regime' (Jacobson and Oksenberg, 1990: 83). All these considerations delayed Beijing's application to the GATT.

In 1983, the PRC was granted observer status in the GATT, and in 1986 it formally applied for full GATT membership. Since then there have been prolonged negotiations between Beijing and the GATT, now known as the 'World Trade Organization' (WTO), which have lasted well into the mid-1990s.

Taiwan's status with the GATT has often been tied with Beijing's application. In 1987 Taipei moved to contact the GATT secretariat, asking about the possibility of Taiwan's association with the GATT. In 1991 the Bush administration decided to support Taiwan's GATT membership. The GATT established a 'Taiwan Working Group' for this matter the following year (Feeney, 1994: 245).

Taipei's application for GATT membership seems politically less controversial than the issue of UN membership. Article XXXIII of the General Agreement stipulates that territories that have autonomy in customs matters are allowed to have separate representation. In fact, Hong Kong became a contracting party of the GATT in 1986, with a promise from the GATT council that Hong Kong could retain its separate status after the PRC acquired sovereignty over the territory (Jacobson and Oksenberg, 1990: 101–102).

The Asian Development Bank (ADB) is a different example. Although there were confrontations between Beijing and Taipei over ADB membership, both sides showed a certain degree of flexibility on various occasions. Taiwan was a founding member of the ADB in 1966. In 1983, the PRC officially applied for membership on the condition that Taiwan be expelled. Most members, such as the United States and Japan, opposed Taiwan's ouster.

Subsequently, there was a PRC–ADB understanding in 1985 that Taiwan would have to use a new name — 'Taipei,China' — to continue its membership. Taipei strongly opposed the move and refused to attend ADB meetings for the next two years. Under the leadership of Lee Teng-hui, Taiwan returned to the ADB meeting in 1988 in Manila, although an 'Under Protest' sign was used to cover the nameplate on the table (Taipei's protest against the fact that it was not allowed to participate under its official name, 'The Republic of China'). Furthermore, Taipei sent an official delegation to Beijing the next year to attend the ADB annual meeting. All these developments have reflected a certain degree of flexibility on the part of both Beijing and Taipei.[46]

To understand the PRC's policy toward the United Nations and the international economic organizations, it is important to examine the priorities of Chinese foreign policy. As mentioned eariler in this chapter, any issue that is tied to Beijing's concern for regime legitimacy, both internally and externally, is considered a top priority on the foreign policy agenda. Taiwan's membership with the United Nations is one of those issues that Beijing believes it has no choice but to oppose to the end. No political leaders in Beijing can afford to let a 'two-Chinas' situation officially occur without a fight. Then, what about IEOs, which are, after all, only economic organizations? It is clear now that Beijing has regarded UN-related IEOs such as the World Bank and the International Monetary Fund to be politically significant, and therefore Beijing is less flexible on the question of Taiwan membership, which it considers to be threatening; whereas non-UN related IEOs such as the GATT (or WTO) and ADB are less politically oriented, therefore Beijing may appear flexible.

Official Arrangements and Unofficial Arrangements

China is believed to be slow and inflexible in making official arrangements with other countries. At the same time, however, Beijing may show great flexibility in making unofficial arrangements to solve politically difficult issues. Sadako Ogata, a well-known Japanese scholar of international affairs, has noted that the long period of unofficial relations between China and Japan produced 'an ample supply of those [Japanese] who were in contact with Beijing and who frequently competed with each other for recognition [to serve as informal channels for normalization]'.[47] Unofficial arrangements are likely to be handled through informal channels, which not only convey important information and messages to and from top Chinese leaders, but also serve as the foundations upon which formal and official arrangements can later be built.

For example, before moving to full diplomatic relations with Japan, Singapore, South Korea, Israel, and the United States, the PRC first made unofficial arrangements with each. In the case of the United States, Washington and Beijing agreed to set up liaison offices in one another's capitals in 1973, one year after Nixon's visit to China, but six years before official diplomatic relations finally were established.

The detailed process of initiating unofficial arrangements prior to the establishment of formal diplomatic ties is well illustrated by the case of Japan. During the 1950s, when the Cold War dominated the international environment, China was aligned with the Soviet Union, and Japan's foreign policy was largely under control of the United States. There was little opportunity for China and Japan to have any official bilateral exchange in either the political or the economic fields. Despite the US influence on Japanese policy, however, the Japanese perceived China in a different light than did the United States.[48] Japan's Ministry of Foreign Affairs (MOFA) gradually developed a policy known as *seikei bunri*: to differentiate economic activities from political ones. Under *seikei bunri*, any Japanese, except government officials, could visit China without obtaining a permit from MOFA.[49]

Beijing's official response to *seikei bunri* was tough. Premier Zhou Enlai openly repudiated it, claiming that it was impossible to divide economic activities from political activities. He then presented three political principles to guide Sino-Japanese relations, which stated that Japan should not: (1) regard China as an enemy; (2) participate in any plot to create 'two Chinas'; and (3) obstruct the normalization of relations with China. These principles later became the criteria by which the Chinese chose Japanese companies, known as 'friendly firms' with which to do business. Though relatively small in size, these 300 'friendly firms' became the main channels for Sino-Japanese trade. Beijing's flexibility enabled the conclusion of unofficial trade agreements with Japan in 1952, 1953, 1955, and 1958.

In the early 1960s, the changing international environment, namely the Sino-Soviet split and the perceived security threat from the Soviet Union to both China and Japan, prompted Beijing and Tokyo to improve bilateral relations. Both countries were increasingly interested in establishing an institutionalized trade relationship. The result was the Memorandum Trade Agreement, concluded between the two countries in November 1962.

Despite the unofficial status of the Memorandum Trade Agreement, both sides treated as 'semi-official' the trade offices that the agreement established in Beijing and Tokyo. The signatory to the agreement for the Chinese side, Liao Chengzhi, while signing the agreement as chairman of the China–Japan Friendship Association, also held official posts in the Chinese government — he was a cabinet member as well as a member of the Party's central committee. The Japanese signatory, Tatsunosuke Takasaki, was a senior ruling Liberal Democratic Party (LDP) Diet member and a former minister of international trade and industry.

From the Chinese perspective, the Memorandum Trade Agreement was 'non-governmental' in name only, because in the socialist economic system the government at that time owned every trading company. For example, the China Council for Promoting International Trade, a counterpart to the Japanese trading companies, was under the jurisdiction of the Ministry of Foreign Trade. In addition, the Chinese representatives in the Tokyo trade office were mostly officials from the Ministry of Foreign Trade.

These unofficial contacts greatly facilitated Sino-Japanese bilateral exchanges. Pre-normalization unofficial trade between Japan and China developed rapidly. Using this arrangement, both countries showed great flexibility and gained significant economic benefits.

Beijing's willingness to make unofficial trade arrangements with Japan, however, did not mean that China would sacrifice its political principles. The Chinese government never gave up its three political conditions for normalization of Sino-Japanese relations: recognition of the People's Republic as the sole legal government of China; acceptance of Taiwan as an inalienable part of the territory of the People's Republic; and abrogation of Japan's peace treaty with the Taipei government.

Beijing's inflexibility on these conditions was displayed in its treatment of the Japanese news media. An agreement continuing the exchange of reporters between Japan and China was concluded in the 1968 negotiations on memorandum trade. According to this agreement, if a Japanese newspaper did not sign a pledge to abide by the three political principles, it would not be permitted to send a correspondent to China. Japanese reporters who 'violated' these principles were expelled from China (*Mainichi, Sankei, Yomiuri,* and *Nishi Nippon*), denied re-entry into

China (*NHK*), or arrested on charges of espionage activities (*Nihon Keizai*). These strict rules and intense competition among the Japanese newspapers forced the Japanese press to practice self-restraint in editing and writing articles on China.[50]

By adopting different strategies toward official and unofficial arrangements, Zhou's conditions were used not only to promote bilateral trade through friendly Japanese firms, but also to create economic rapprochement prior to political rapprochement. In other words, Beijing used economic means to fulfill political goals. On most occasions, China took the initiative in trade relations, whereas the Japanese were generally reactive, due to Japan's deep concern over China's internal political instability and political pressure from Western powers, particularly from the United States. Unofficial trade arrangements enabled Tokyo to adopt a more pragmatic, and therefore more flexible, stance. As Chaejin Lee (1984: 11–12) has noted, the 'fact that associations acted as representatives of private companies and non-governmental organizations also made it easier than it otherwise would be for the Japanese to accept China's tough political demands'.

From the above exercises — distinguishing between essential and rhetorical principles, between high and low priorities, and between official and unofficial arrangements — we can see from actual cases the Chinese tactics of flexibility and rigidity in operation. As for the micro-macro model, we also can conclude that essential and rhetorical principles, for example (which are born of ideological, political, and nationalistic concerns) form part of the leaders' perceptions, which, in turn, affect the power/regime macrostructure. These concerns, as discussed in the above examples, determine the leaders' vision of alternatives and their choices of the country's external behaviour.

Formal Channels and Informal Channels

Like unofficial arrangements, informal channels are often used to solve politically difficult issues. These informal channels have proved particularly useful when Beijing is in a difficult position in the international arena. In the aftermath of the Tiananmen Incident, the summer of 1989, China faced world-wide condemnation which brought about economic sanctions by industrialized powers. Beijing, by utilizing many informal channels, worked hard to break the international isolation brought by economic sanctions. The first post-Tiananmen meeting between Foreign Minister Qian Qichen and heads of diplomatic missions abandoned formal ceremony and was held, instead, in a rather informal fashion. On 30 July 1989, Qian Qichen invited more than fifty ambassadors and their wives to a 'watermelon party' in a suburb of Beijing. At this party, Qian conducted many private conversations with a number of ambassadors, conveying both Beijing's official stance and the message that China would like to maintain friendly relations with these countries.[51]

The PRC also frequently used Hong Kong as a neutral place from which to set up informal channels for diplomatic purposes. Prior to the early 1990s, China did not have diplomatic relations with South Korea and Israel. Hong Kong became a convenient place for informal contact between China and these two countries. These informal contacts were mainly carried out through the consulates of South Korea and Israel in Hong Kong and the PRC's unofficial representative in Hong Kong, Xinhua News Agency. In addition to discussing political and economic relations, Beijing also asked the Xinhua News Agency to exchange messages and obtain information to help resolve unexpected incidents with these countries, such as the defection of a Chinese military airplane and the hijacking of a civilian Chinese airplane in the 1980s, both to South Korea (Xu, 1993: 351–352).

China's informal negotiating style can also be demonstrated by the process of Sino-Japanese rapprochement. Chinese leaders, Zhou Enlai in particular, showed great skill in communicating with the Japanese through informal channels in the 1960s and early 1970s, when there were no appropriate formal channels of communication between the two countries.

Sensing the changing mood of both the international environment (represented by US National Security Advisor Henry Kissinger's visit to Beijing and the subsequent acceptance of Beijing into the United Nations) and the domestic public, Japanese Prime Minister Eisaku Sato was desperate to open dialogue with Beijing in 1970 and 1971. He used a number of channels to pass important messages to Beijing and to arrange for high-level meetings between the two countries' leaders.[52] However, because of Sato's pro-Taiwan stance and 'unfriendly activities,' such as supporting anti-PRC resolutions in the United Nations, Premier Zhou rejected Sato's overtures and said that China would not consider negotiations 'as long as Sato was the leader of the Japanese government'.[53]

The rejection of Sato's efforts to establish formal channels did not mean that the doors to all channels were closed; on the contrary, Beijing set up informal channels to maintain the flow of information between the two countries. China sent its top 'Japan hands' as informal envoys to Japan on several occasions.

One such envoy, Wang Xiaoyun, visited Japan not in his official foreign ministry capacity but as deputy head of the Chinese Ping-Pong team that attended the 31st World Table Tennis Championship held in Nagoya in March and April 1971. In what became known as the 'first Wang whirlwind', Wang held a series of meetings with the LDP's anti-Sato leaders and with the leaders of opposition parties. The highlight of the visit was a meeting with leaders from Japan's top economic organizations, such as Keizai Doyukai, Keidanren, and Nikkeiren, which marked the first time Japanese business leaders had met with a high ranking Chinese official. After the meeting, the president of Doyukai, Kazutaka Kikawada, told the press that 'the improvement of Japan–China relations is a national issue for the 1970s'.[54]

Four months later, a follow-up visit — the 'second Wang whirlwind' — was made by Wang Guoquan on the occasion of the funeral of Kenzo Matsumura, a long-time pro-Beijing Liberal Democratic Party leader and active promoter of Sino-Japanese trade. Wang was vice-president of the China–Japan Friendship Association and a veteran Chinese diplomat. During his one-week stay, he contacted various political and economic leaders. The impact of this visit was particularly notable among business leaders. Some previously pro-Taiwan leaders, such as Shigeo Nagano, chairman of the board of Shin Nihon Seitetsu (Japan's largest steel company), announced the acceptance of Zhou's political conditions and called for improvement in Sino-Japanese relations.[55]

After the Tanaka administration was inaugurated in July 1972, both Japan and China accelerated the process of rapprochement. Many prominent political and business leaders wanted to confer with Chinese officials. A Chinese delegation led by Sun Pinghua visited Japan in August 1972 in the 'Sun whirlwind'. Sun's official position was deputy secretary-general of the China–Japan Friendship Association, but during his visit he was the head of the Shanghai Dance Drama Troupe. Sun conveyed an official message to Japan's foreign minister Masayoshi Ohira from China's foreign minister Ji Pengfei stating that, 'Premier Zhou Enlai welcomes and invites Prime Minister Kakuei Tanaka to visit China.'[56] Tanaka warmly received Sun and the Chinese dancers and accepted Zhou's invitation.

A second route of informal channels was through Japan's opposition parties. The two largest opposition parties, the Japan Socialist Party (JSP) and the Komeito–Clean Government Party (CGP), served as important informal channels in normalization, especially during 1971 and early 1972 when the process reached the final, delicate decision-making stages.

Beijing and the JSP had a long-established and cooperative relationship, and sought to form a 'grand coalition' to promote a mass normalization movement in Japan. In the summer of 1972, Beijing allowed the JSP to play a more direct role in normalization. Premier Zhou Enlai invited the former chairman of the JSP, Kozo Sasaki, who regarded himself as an informal 'communicator' between the newly elected prime minister Kakuei Tanaka and Zhou Enlai, to visit China. Before this visit, Sasaki met with Tanaka and Ohira. In Beijing, Sasaki gave the Chinese a detailed and frank assessment of Tanaka's China policy. He told Zhou that Tanaka and Ohira were sincere in accepting China's conditions regarding Taiwan. In return, Zhou stated that Tanaka's visit to Beijing would be welcomed.[57] Zhou also gave Sasaki personal assurances that Beijing would be flexible enough to make the Japanese comfortable in finalizing the normalization of relations between the two countries.[58] These messages were passed on to Tanaka and Ohira upon Sasaki's return to Tokyo.

Although it was broadly believed at the time that Sino-Japanese rapprochement would soon be realized, no one could forecast the method or the timing, as no preliminary discussions between China and Japan had taken place. No one in Tokyo knew for certain Beijing's position on the Japan–US Security Treaty and the Sato–Nixon Joint Communique.

For many years, the CGP did not have a clear-cut 'one-China' policy. Its adoption of such a policy in June 1971 was welcomed by the PRC, which invited the first official CGP mission, led by CGP chairman Yoshikatsu Takeiri, to visit Beijing, making it possible for the CGP to play a role in the rapprochement process.

Before his visit to Beijing, Takeiri discussed the China issue four times with prime minister Tanaka and foreign minister Ohira. After these discussions, Takeiri drew up a 21-point draft proposal based on his understanding of Tanaka's negotiating position.[59] This differed from the official Chinese stance on some issues, and did not mention the Japan–US Security Treaty.[60]

On July 25, only five days after Sasaki's visit, Takeiri presented the 21-point proposal to Zhou. During the next three days, Beijing leaders and Takeiri spent totally nine hours in discussions. Zhou bluntly asked, 'If we accept the draft proposal, will the Japanese government make a move?' Takeiri guaranteed the proposal by taking personal responsibility for Japan's positive response. That evening, he telephoned Tokyo to consult with Tanaka and Ohira, and received positive assurances.[61]

On the last day of Takeiri's stay in Beijing, Zhou presented Takeiri with the first Chinese draft of the Zhou–Tanaka joint communique.

Takeiri was amazed by the flexibility shown by the Chinese leader. Takeiri's notes from this meeting, labelled the 'Takeiri memo', were similar to the final communique and did not mention the Japan–US Security Treaty or the Sato–Nixon Joint Communique.[62] Tanaka received the Takeiri memo the day after Takeiri's return to Japan, and after two hours reviewing the memo, Tanaka told the CGP chairman that he would go to Beijing.[63] Formal diplomatic relations between Japan and China were established in late September 1972.

Beijing used informal channels as part of its 'people's diplomacy' toward Japan. Its goals were facilitating communications, enlarging Japan's pro-Beijing forces, and creating a 'China bandwagon' to apply pressure to the Japanese government through the cooperation of the Japanese people and various political forces. This strategy was especially effective with opposition parties and the business community. As Doak Barnett (1977: 126) has pointed out, while the Chinese involved themselves 'deeply in Japanese domestic politics', the Japanese since 1949 have had no direct impact on Chinese politics.

A Greater Realism

As this chapter has detailed, Chinese foreign policy can be both rigid and flexible depending upon how Beijing calculates its own interests in the changing international environment and the importance of this policy attached to the regime legitimacy. Furthermore, the dynamics of internal power politics have also proved to be key elements behind foreign policy considerations. Over the years, as Beijing has further consolidated its domestic control and international status, it appears more assertive in international affairs. The profound changes in China's macro-structure (symbolic, institutional, and power/regime), which we have analysed in this and previous chapters, have provided the conditions for the Beijing leadership gradually to move from rigidity toward flexibility in its foreign policy behaviour. But one has to remember that this is only a general trend; it does not predict flexibility or preclude rigidity in every circumstance. In practice, the duality of rigidity and flexibility remains a major characteristic of Chinese foreign policy behaviour. This is particularly true considering the uncertainty of the dynamics of power politics in China's political life.

An examination of Beijing's external behaviour patterns in terms of its strategy and tactics leads to the identification of two categories of principles in Chinese foreign policy: essential and rhetorical. As discussed at the beginning of this chapter, essential principles express

China's vital and enduring national interests, including sovereignty and regime legitimacy; Beijing's adherence to these principles is consistently firm. Rhetorical principles are formulated to deal with highly sensitive, but less substantial issues. These issues often serve secondary goals that lie outside the immediate scope of policy objectives.

Learning is also an important factor behind changes in China's external behaviour. Beijing has gradually realized, as Harvey Nelsen (1989: 263) points out, that at the strategic level the best deterrence is not belligerence, but being unyielding: 'Elevate issues to fixed principles and demands and then wait for the "correlation of forces" to change in China's favour. What cannot initially be gained from military conflict may later be won at the negotiating table.'

This foreign-policy behaviour pattern has enabled Beijing to establish a negotiating position for achieving maximum advantage. Before or upon entering negotiations, Beijing clearly states its principles, some rhetorical and thus 'negotiable' (*linghuoxing*), others essential and thus 'non-negotiable' (*yuanzexing*). However, the status of these principles may change, depending on timing, domestic conditions, and the international environment. For instance, non-negotiable principles may be converted to negotiable principles through the use of unofficial arrangements or informal channels.

The dual nature of Chinese principles prevents other countries from coercing China into unwilling concessions, while providing China with a bargaining tool. In this way, China takes a deductive approach to international behaviour, by first insisting on the clarification and codification of basic principles, and then 'allowing a most flexible application, even contravention, in practice to reach a desired agreement' (S. Kim, 1989b: 123). The Chinese ability to bargain involves the flexible interpretation of principles.

The combination of *yuanzexing* and *linghuoxing* in Chinese foreign policy reflects the influence of Marxist and Maoist thinking and of traditional Chinese attitudes to dealing with the outside world. The combination also reflects a 'greater realism' (Hamrin, 1986: 51) in pursuing maximum advantage in the international arena. This realism is the product of the interplay of international constraints and domestic considerations — centering on the issue of the PRC's regime survival. China's participation in a broader international arena and the process of internal political manoeuvring among the Chinese political elites is 'a continuing process of learning and adjustments' (Chan, 1989: 154).

Beijing has been able to set clear principles in advance to establish a negotiating position aimed at self-preservation and achieving the maximum advantage. Once principles are set, some conditions are negotiable and some are not. The non-negotiable principles (*yuanzexing*) are those that involve vital national interests such as regime legitimacy and the internal power politics. The negotiable principles are those regarded as low priorities or technical issues. Beijing's is a deductive approach to international behaviour: it insists on the clarification and codification of basic principles that allow a flexible application to reach a desired agreement.[64]

China's negotiating style, including official and unofficial arrangements, formal and informal channels, and the intervention of top leaders, deserves special attention. The PRC has often been slow and inflexible in making official arrangements with other countries and foreign entities. At the same time, however, Beijing has shown remarkable flexibility in making unofficial arrangements, usually through informal channels, to solve politically sensitive issues.

Power politics and top leaders' preferences at the micro level will remain an important variable in the formulation of Chinese foreign policy. Intervention by top leaders in the processes of negotiation will continue to play a crucial role in Beijing's external behaviour. However, the result of such intervention, which tends to be more pronounced during periods of stalemate and deadlock, is not predictable. In addition, as Arthur Lall (1968: 7) has noted, during negotiations Chinese diplomats retain their formation as a large group and do not break up into individual components. Unfortunately, this lack of individual initiative and discussion by junior and mid-level diplomats often inhibits any correction from below of misunderstandings that originate from above.

Notes

1 For a recent example of this type of examination, see James Goldgeier (1994).
2 Quoted from Stuart Schram (1989: 134).
3 This commonly held argument has been confirmed by the close observation of Mao's physician Li Zhisui. See Z. Li (1994: 124).
4 Many scholars have remarked on the important role that culture plays in politics. Samuel Huntington (1987: 22), for instance, noted that culture is 'a central independent variable' in explanations of different patterns of political development. Similarly, Lucian Pye (1991: 506) has emphasized the cultural element in the process of 'transitions toward democracy', asking such questions as 'what the cultural bases for democracy may be in the context of modernizing economies'.

In his study of the decision-making process, Fritz Gaenslen (1986: 101–102) emphasizes that even small cultural differences 'can matter a great deal in group decision-making', and urged scholars to 'try to document them'. Yet, as Raymond Cohen (1991: 153) has observed, culture has often appeared as 'the hidden dimension', — unseen, but exerting a pervasive influence on the behaviour of individuals, groups, and societies.
5 The word 'principles' has many meanings, of course. It is used here in the same sense that it is used by the PRC itself, as well as by scholars in the West, to refer to Beijing's external behaviour.
6 For a detailed discussion, see Suzanne Odgen (1989: 247).
7 See Bo Yibo (1989: 7).
8 See Mao Zedong, 'He meiguo jizhe anna luyisi sitelong de tanhua [A Talk with American Journalist Anna Louise Strong]', 6 August 1946 (Mao, 1994: 57–62). Mao's idea that 'imperialists are paper tigers' was reiterated and elaborated in 1958; See Mao Zedong 'Guanyu diguo zhuyi he yiqie fandongpai shibushi zhen laohu de wenti [On Whether Imperialists and Reactionaries are Real Tigers]', 1 December 1958 (Mao, 1994: 362–370).
9 For the *ti-yong* debate, see Joseph Leverson (1968: 59–69).
10 See Doak Barnett (1985: 2–9).
11 See Mao Zedong, 'Guanyu guoji xingshi de jianghua tigang [Speech Outline About the International Situation]' December 1959 (Mao, 1993: 599–603).
12 For details of the Gao-Rao Incident, see Frederick Tiewes (1990).
13 For details of the Lushan Conference, see Roderick MacFarquhar (1983); Jurgen Domes (1985); and Li Rui (1993).
14 See Mao Zedong, 'Ruguo meiying duanjue tong guomindang de guanxi ke kaolu he tamen jianli waijiao guanxi [We Could Consider Establishing Relations with the United States and Britain if They Would Cut Off Relations with the KMT]', 28 April 1949 (Mao, 1994: 83).
15 See, for example, Lin Biao (1965).
16 'Divide and Rule', *Far Eastern Economic Review* (1 December 1994): 12.
17 There were also, of course, more severe charges against Hu. These charges were detailed in Central Document No. 3 of 1987 and included opposing the campaigns against spiritual pollution and bourgeois liberalization, 'repudiating the left but not the right', tolerance of dissident intellectuals, failure to adhere to the Four Basic Principles (the socialist road, the dictatorship of the proletariat, the leadership of the Communist Party, and Marxism–Leninism and Mao Zedong Thought), and disobeying the collective decisions of the leadership on major issues.

18 'Why Was Sino-Japanese Trade Interrupted?' *Renmin Ribao* (People's Daily), 20 May 1958.
19 Liu Xiwen, former vice minister of the Foreign Trade Ministry of China, interview with the author, autumn 1986, Beijing.
20 Wu Xuewen, interview with the author, Fukuoka, 15 July 1986. Wu is one of a few 'Japan hands' in China, having received his education in Japan and served as a correspondent for China's Xinhua News Agency in Tokyo in the 1960s and 1970s.
21 Toshio Oishi, interview with the author, Tokyo, 6 March 1986.
22 Lin Liande, interview with the author, Beijing, 28 October 1986. Lin is one of a few Japan specialists in China. Before normalization he worked for the China Council for Promotion of International Trade dealing with Japan trade. After 1972, he was appointed as the first director of the Japan Division at the Ministry of Foreign Trade, and later was promoted to bureau chief. Lin retired in 1985 after being stationed for three years in Tokyo as China's Commercial Counsellor.
23 Liu Yanzhou, interview with the author, Tokyo, 12 April 1986. In 1964, Liu became one of the first Chinese journalists allowed to be stationed in Japan. He spent more than 15 years in Japan.
24 *Japan Times*, 31 August 1973.
25 *Renmin Ribao*, 6 January 1974.
26 Heishiro Ogawa, interview with the author, Tokyo, 8 March 1986. As the first Japanese ambassador to the PRC, Ogawa was a member of Ohira's delegation.
27 See Deng Xiaoping, 'We Are Working to Revitalize the Chinese Nation', 7 April 1990 (Deng, 1994: 344).
28 For a detailed study about this sign in Shanghai, see Robert Bickers and Jeffrey Wasserstrom (1995).
29 See Deng Xiaoping, 'China Will Never Allow Other Countries to Interfere in Its Internal Affairs', 11 July 1990 (Deng, 1994: 346).
30 See Deng Xiaoping, 'The United States Should Take the Initiative in Putting An End to the Strains in Sino-American Relations', 31 October 1989 (Deng, 1994: 321–322).
31 For details, see Han Nianlong (chief ed.) (1987: 225–231).
32 *Yazhou Zhoukan* [The International Chinese Newsweekly] (5 November 1995): 18–19.
33 See Han Nianlong (1987: 188–90).
34 Jin Raoru, 'Shuangchong chengren, dalu zao kai xianhe', [The Mainland Had Much Early Practice of Dual Recognition], *World Journal*, 10 January 1996, p. A10.
35 Jeffrey Lilley, 'Baltic Two-Step: Latvia Struggles to Maintain Ties with Both Chinas', *Far Eastern Economic Review* (13 January 1994): 27.
36 See Jaw-ling Joanne Chang (1991: 52).
37 The Coordinating Committee of the Consultative Group was created in 1949 by the United States, its European allies, and Japan to control the trade of strategic goods with the Communist bloc, headed by the Soviet Union. A similar committee specifically related to China was called the China Committee of the Consultative Group (CHINCOM) was established in September 1952 to enforce the control of exports to the PRC. Because these two committees were similar and often overlapped, COCOM is used here to refer to both trade organizations.
    With the end of the Cold War, the 17 COCOM nations agreed at in March 1994 to disband the 45-year-old Paris-based body. See *Japan Times* (Weekly International Edition), 5–11 September 1994, p. 3.
38 Toshio Oishi, interview with the author, Tokyo, 6 March 1986. Oishi was president of Japan Overseas Development Corporation at the time of interview.
39 Lin Liande, interview with the author, Beijing, 28 October 1986.
40 Ibid.
41 For general accounts of Beijing–Taipei–Washington relations centring on the Beijing–Taipei rivalry, see Martin Lasater (1984); June Dreyer (ed.) (1989); John Copper (1992).

42 For details, see Harold Jacobson and Michel Oksenberg (1990: 59–60).
43 Under the IMF's Articles of Agreement, member countries were assigned quotas; the size of a country's quota was based roughly on its share in international trade. Countries' voting rights were based upon their quotas. (See H. Jacobson and M. Oksenberg, 1990: 22).
44 For detailed accounts of these developments, see Martin Lasater (1984: 153–156).
45 See Harold Jacobson and Michel Oksenberg (1990: 77–78).
46 For details, see William Feeney (1994: 239–240).
47 See Sadako Ogata (1988: 103).
48 See Sadako Ogata (1965: 389). Ogata suggests that 'not many Japanese regard Communist China as a "Cold War" enemy, nor do they accept the "China = communism = enemy" equation that is so widely held in the United States.'
49 Heishiro Ogawa, the first Japanese Ambassador to Beijing, interview with the author, Tokyo, 8 March 1986.
50 See Osamu Miyoshi and Shinkichi Eto (1972).
51 Wang Li, 'Qian Qichen: xigua weijiao po zhicai' [Qian Qichen: Watermelon Diplomacy Breaks the Sanctions], Sing Tao Daily, 11 December 1994, p. c2.
52 Sato tried at least five channels, including the LDP's Secretary General Shigeru Hori, Japan's Consul General to Hong Kong Akira Okada, the Japan–China Memorandum Trade Office's Director Yaeji Watanabe, Tokyo Governor Ryokichi Minobe, and pro-Beijing LDP Diet member Seiichi Tagawa. For detailed accounts, see Quansheng Zhao (1993a), Part III; also see Seiichi Tagawa (1972: 24–25).
53 *Asahi Shimbun*, 11 November 1971.
54 *Asahi Shimbun,* 25 August 1971.
55 For an excellent account, see Sadako Ogata (1977: 195).
56 *Peking Review* (18 August 1972): 3.
57 *Asahi Shimbun*, 17 July 1972.
58 Zhou made the following personal assurances:

• China would be satisfied if Japan expressed a 'full understanding' — short of acceptance — of the three principles on the issue of Taiwan;
• China would accord the same protocol to Tanaka's visit as to Nixon's;
• an arrangement would be made for Tanaka's direct flight from Tokyo to Beijing;
• China understood the LDP's internal disputes over the question of Taiwan, and allowed Tanaka more time to deal with the issue of the Japan–Taiwan peace treaty; and
• China would take a flexible position on the issue of war reparations.

See Chae-Jin Lee (1976: 114).
59 See Jiji Tsushinsha Seijibu (1972: 27).
60 See Tadao Ishikawa (1974: 158–159).
61 See Japan–China Economic Association (1975: 5).
62 See Akihiko Tanaka (1985: 234–236).
63 See Japan–China Economic Association (1975: 5).
64 For a stimulating discussion, see Samuel Kim (1989b: 123).

6 Case Study: Japan's Official Development Assistance to China

To further advance the micro-macro linkage model of Chinese foreign policy, it is worthwhile to conduct an empirical summary. This chapter will present the case study of Japan's official development assistance (ODA) to China including government loans, grants, and technical aid. Studying China's interactions with Japan on a major foreign policy issue — in effect placing China in a concrete and comparative context — should not only advance our comprehension of Chinese foreign policy in the post-revolutionary era, but also demonstrate the applicability of the micro-macro linkage model to the study of foreign policy in general.

As an empirical exercise, this chapter uses Japan's ODA to China to illustrate further the characteristics of Chinese foreign policy elaborated in the previous chapters. Therefore, when reading this case study one may wish to bear in mind the theoretical approaches developed in the previous chapters. Table 6.1 provides an analytical guideline to study Chinese Policy towards Japan's ODA from the micro-macro linkage approach.

In addition to some familiar concepts discussed in previous chapters, one may notice in the 'micro process' part of Table 6.1 a concept that received less attention in earlier chapters — 'domestic win-sets'. This concept may aid in our comprehension of the micro-macro linkage model and its application to the study of international agreements. As mentioned earlier, this concept was put forth by Robert Putnam (1993) in his study on 'two-level games' — the idea being that the foreign policy-making process can be best understood as a two-level game, within which decision-makers are viewed as actors who play at both the politics of the international arena and the domestic environment. To further explain this external-internal-decision-makers synthesis, Putnam (1993: 438–439) has decomposed the international negotiation process into two stages:

Table 6.1: The Micro-Macro Linkage Model of Chinese Policy toward Japan's ODA

Macro Structures	Macrostructural Change	Micro Processes in Beijing
Symbolic Macrostructure	'Modernization' is set as national goal; China has further integrated into the world economy; pressures on China in human rights and other issues have also increased.	Changed from refusing to accept any loans to welcoming loans from abroad, as long as acceptance does not intervene in China's internal affairs.
Institutional Macrostructure	More institutional norms and mechanisms are conducive to the promotion of external economic activities.	Domestic win-sets for receiving Japanese loans have enlarged; diversified interests are perceived at the national and provincial levels.
Power/Regime Macrostructure	Reform-oriented leaders are in control, yet conservative forces are still influential; both groups emphasize national independence and interests.	More flexible in environmental and economic terms, but tough on the linkage between ODA and human rights issues and defence activities.

1. Bargaining between the negotiators, leading to a tentative agreement; call that Level I.
2. Separate discussions within each group of constituents about whether to ratify the agreement; call that Level II.

Based on this 'two-level games' idea, the concept of a *win-set* has been developed: 'for a given Level II constituency as the set of all possible Level I agreements that would "win" — that is, gain the necessary majority among the constituents.' One can argue further that larger win-sets make Level I agreement more likely.

According to Putnam (1993: 439–440), any successful agreement must fall within the domestic win-sets of each of the parties to the accord. Thus, agreement is possible only if those win-sets overlap; and the larger each win-set, the more likely they are to overlap. Conversely, the smaller the win-sets, the greater the risk that the negotiations will break down. To study 'two-level games', one needs to pay special attention to the impact of both international bargaining and the societal-institutional inputs on the choices of decision-makers. Before further discussing the application of the micro-macro linkage model to this case study, it is necessary to have an overview of Japan's ODA to China.

To get an overall picture of Japanese ODA to China, one needs to ask such questions as:

- Why did Japan decide in the late 1970s to deliver a major aid programme to China?
- What were the Japanese trying to do with their aid?
- Why after decades of isolationism did China decide to welcome foreign advisors and capital assistance from Japan?
- What was China's vision of how it could solidify its modernization aims by working with the Japanese donors?
- What problems did the resulting programme address, sequentially, and in what sense were its component parts the result of compromise among international and domestic forces in the two countries?
- How was this alignment of forces differentiated among different issue areas, such as stability versus the human right issues, infrastructure versus environment, or economic development versus defence budget?

In analysing these questions, this study is *sui generis*, in that it is not a straight case study comparing decision-making in Japan and China, nor is it a simple chronological policy history; rather, it is a series of actions that lay at the centre or confluence of international and domestic factors affecting two countries, and produced a fairly coherent succession of policies in East Asia from 1979 on. The following sections will try to answer the above questions first by looking at some basic factors influencing this aid, and then by separately examining the policy-making processes in China and Japan with regard to the aid issues.

An Overview of Japan's ODA to China

Since 1972 when China and Japan normalized their bilateral relationship, economic cooperation between the two countries has remained one of the most important factors in their development and in regional stability in the Asia-Pacific area. Chinese and Japanese policy-making in trade, foreign investment, joint ventures, technology transfer, and personnel exchanges has constituted a holistic set of policies deserving study in their own right. Exchanges between China and Japan are ushering in a major new period of Asian history.

Although the 1972 Sino-Japanese rapprochement and the 1978 Sino-Japanese Peace and Friendship Treaty laid foundations for the rapid development of bilateral relations, it was not until 1979 that China received any Japanese official development assistance (ODA). At that time, Beijing signed an agreement with Tokyo to receive a governmental loan. Since then, Japan has remained the largest ODA donor to China among the members of the Development Assistance Committee (DAC)[1] under the Organization for Economic Cooperation and Development (OECD); and China has ranked among the top list of the recipients of Japanese ODA. This is understandable, given that the United States was explicitly prohibited from extending ODA to China by the Foreign Assistance Act due to the fact that China was 'a member of the international communist movement'.[2] Yet, the US State Department and foreign aid agencies had consistently encouraged Japan to take the lead in the West's relations with China through foreign aid, with the strategic consideration that a moderate and open China would serve US interests (Orr, 1990: 73). China was a late-comer in joining Japan's list of aid recipients. Despite the late entry in 1979, Japanese aid to China grew substantially throughout the 1980s and well into the 1990s (see Table 6.2).

Japan is the largest ODA donor to China. During the period of 1979 to 1984, Japan's ODA to China accounted for 45 per cent of the total amount of the external aid that China received, including both bilateral aid (DAC members) and multilateral aid (international organizations). During the same period, the International Monetary Fund was the second largest aid donor (14 per cent) to China, with the United Nations agencies third (12 per cent), and West Germany fourth (9 per cent).[3] In terms of bilateral ODA to China in the 1980s and early 1990s, Japan remained the top donor among the DAC members. In 1990 and 1991, for example, Japan's shares of aid to China were more than half of the total bilateral ODA, and accounted for about one-third if the multilateral aid (from international organizations) is added (see Table 6.3).

China was also one of the largest recipients of Japanese aid. Traditionally, Indonesia was the top recipient of Japanese ODA. From 1982 to 1986, however, China became the first on Japan's ODA list. From 1987 to 1992 (except 1991), China ranked second, next to Indonesia.

From 1979 to 1995, there were three major packages of Japanese government loans to China, known as 'soft loans'. The first government-to-government loan was 350 billion yen (US$1.5 billion) for China's five-year plan (1979–84). This loan was pledged by Prime Minister Masayoshi Ohira in his visit to China in December 1979. Then, in March

Table 6.2: Japan's ODA Disbursements to China (US$ million)

Year	Grant Aid	Technical Assistance	Loan Aid	Total
1979	0.0	2.6	0.0	2.6
1980	0.0	3.4	0.9	4.3
1981	2.5	9.6	15.6	27.7
1982	25.1	13.5	330.2	368.8
1983	30.6	20.5	299.1	350.2
1984	14.3	27.2	347.9	389.4
1985	11.6	31.1	345.2	387.9
1986	25.7	61.2	410.1	497.0
1987	54.3	76.0	422.8	553.1
1988	52.0	102.7	519.0	673.7
1989	58.0	106.1	668.1	832.2
1990	37.8	163.5	521.7	723.0
1991	56.6	137.5	391.2	585.3
1992	72.1	187.3	791.2	1,050.6

Source: Gaimusho, *Wagakuni no seifu kaihatsu enjo* [Japan's Official Development Assistance], various volumes

Table 6.3: Share of DAC Countries in Total ODA Received by China (US$ million)

Year	Top Donor	Second Donor	Third Donor	Other Donors	Total Bilateral	Total Multilateral
1990	Japan	Germany	Austria			
	723.02	228.94	102.84	361.57	1,416.37	659.80
	(51.1%)	(16.2%)	(7.3%)	(25.5%)	(100%)	
1991	Japan	France	Germany			
	585.30	138.46	107.09	337.04	1,167.89	782.95
	(50.1%)	(11.9%)	(9.2%)	(28.8%)	(100%)	

Source: Gaimusho, *Wagakuni no seifu kaihatsu enjo* [Japan's Official Development Assistance], various volumes

of 1984 Prime Minister Yasuhiro Nakasone agreed to a 470-billion-yen (US$2.1 billion) package for the five-year period of 1985 to 1990. Prime Minister Noboru Takeshita, during his visit to Beijing in August 1988, promised a third loan package of 810 billion yen (US$5.4 billion at that time) covering 1990 to 1995. A more recent development in this regard is the agreement between the two countries in December 1994 for the fourth Japanese aid package to China — a yen loan of 580 billion yen (US$ 5.8 billion) covering the three-year period of 1996 to 1998.[4]

The large-scale bilateral economic exchanges and government aid from Japan has created economic interdependence between the two countries. Although trade with China in the late 1970s was less than 5 per cent of Japan's total trade, bilateral trade has increased rapidly since then. For years Japan, alternating with Hong Kong, was China's leading trade partner, accounting for approximately one-fourth of China's total foreign trade. Bilateral trade increased significantly at the beginning of the 1990s. In 1993, China emerged as Japan's second largest trading partner (only after the United States), having grown 30.9 per cent from the previous year.[5] Economic exchanges between China and Japan have far-reaching political and strategic implications. It is believed that Sino-Japanese relations will assume increasing importance in Asia as both the US presence and Soviet ambitions in the region fade in the post-Cold War era. As long as China pursues its goal of economic modernization and its political future remains uncertain, Japan's aid diplomacy will continue to play a crucial role in Sino-Japanese relations both economically and politically.

Detailed analysis suggests that the achievement of bilateral agreement over the issue of Japanese ODA to China was the product of quite different circumstances and considerations facing each government. The analyses will be conducted from two stages of the Japanese ODA to China: the *initial and mutually beneficial stage* (1979–88) — the first decade that China received ODA from Japan; the *crisis and bargaining stage* (1989–95) — Japan's decision to suspend and resume ODA to China after the Tiananmen Incident of 1989; and Tokyo's new ODA principles and Beijing's reaction. Furthermore, it will examine these two stages from both the Japanese and Chinese sides of the equation, making this a roughly comparative case study.

The Initial and Mutually Beneficial Stage (1979–88)

The first decade (1979–88) of Japan's ODA to China can be considered the 'initial and mutually beneficial' stage. The key issues during this period include Japan's decision to provide and China's decision to accept foreign aid in 1978. How have the international environments and domestic win-sets prompted decision-makers in the two countries to act on the ODA issues? Let us now examine the policy-making processes separately in China and Japan.

The Micro-Macro Linkage and Chinese Policy-making

As analysed in Table 6.1, the changes in the macrostructure of Chinese politics have had a profound impact on Beijing's policy toward foreign aid. To get a more comprehensive picture, we need first to understand the changes in China's symbolic macrostructure — lessons learned from China's interaction with external powers in China's modern history. Having experienced Western intervention beginning in the mid-nineteenth century with the Opium War (1839–42), China was sensitive to issues of national sovereignty and foreign intervention. This sensitivity led to two major types of reactions in China: first, anti-foreignism, represented by the mass-based Boxer Rebellion (1898–1901), which was extremely hostile toward a foreign political, military, and economic presence in China; and second, self-reliance, represented by the 'self-strengthening' movement of the late nineteenth century. The latter movement, led by intellectuals, called upon the Chinese people to oppose foreign aggression, but through the selective use of foreign ideas and goods. These reactions, as Margaret Pearson has written 'in various forms and degrees continue to manifest themselves' in the new era of the People's Republic.[6]

After the Communist victory in 1949, Beijing was suspicious about foreign loans and refused to pursue or accept them, with the exception of US$1.5 billion in government loans from the Soviet Union and East European socialist countries (lent from 1953 to 1960). Throughout the 1960s and most of the 1970s, China stuck firmly to Mao's idea of 'self-reliance' (*zili gengsheng*) rejecting economic cooperation with capitalist nations and isolating China from the capitalist world economy.

After the normalization of relations between China and Japan in 1972, Tokyo, on several occasions raised the issue of government loans as a form of economic cooperation, and was rejected unequivocally by Beijing (C. Lee, 1984: 113). As late as 1977, the Chinese leadership still insisted that China should not allow any foreign interests or jointly managed companies to develop domestic primary resources, and should not accept any foreign credits. A *Renmin Ribao* (People's Daily) editorial, for example, claimed that:

We never permit the use of foreign capital to develop our domestic resources as the Soviet revisionists do, never run undertakings in concert with other countries and also *never accept foreign loans*. China has neither domestic nor external debts.[7] (Author's italics.)

China's domestic and foreign policy changed drastically after late 1978 when Beijing began its Opening and Reform policy to promote modernization (the symbolic macrostructure). For the first time, China showed a willingness to accept foreign governmental aid, including loans and grants. In September 1978, in Beijing the two countries opened the first serious discussion on the possibility of Japan's ODA to China. The discussion took place between China's Liu Xiwen, vice-minister of foreign trade, and Japan's Yoshihiro Inayama, president of the Japan-China Economic Association. One month later, China's paramount leader Deng Xiaoping, during his Tokyo trip publicly confirmed China's intention to accept such loans.[8] Explanations for these major policy changes can be found in both the international and domestic environments.

Internationally, Beijing felt great pressure from the external environment. By the end of the 1970s, China was left far behind the four East Asian dragons (Taiwan, Hong Kong, Singapore, and South Korea), three of which were Chinese societies. All these economies were integrated closely with the world economy through various forms of economic interdependency, including the receipt of foreign loans. These successful examples also encouraged Beijing leaders to look abroad for foreign loans.

More importantly, decision-makers in Beijing first needed to obtain the necessary internal support for the striking change in China's attitude toward foreign loans. It was clearly necessary to make efforts to legitimize the change to enlarge the domestic win-sets for the anticipated policy shift. Despite the major shift in the symbolic macrostructure starting from the beginning of the Deng era in 1978 — from the priority of promoting world revolution, to an emphasis on China's modernization and global and regional stability — there was residual resistance, mostly from the conservative faction of power politics, to the acceptance of the foreign loans.

Let us look at the power/regime macrostructure behind China's policy toward foreign loans. Many of the political leaders within the Chinese decision-making body of the Party and the government at that time shared three concerns regarding foreign loans: first, they worried that capital flow from major powers (industrialized countries) might jeopardize China's sovereignty; second, that the opening up to the Western countries would bring in capitalist ideologies; and third, that borrowing foreign loans would end China's reputation as a 'no-debt' country and could damage the national image.[9]

To dispute these concerns, China's reform-minded decision-makers represented by Deng, and then Premier Zhao Ziyang, first emphasized the necessity of foreign loans to China's modernization. These leaders argued that the practice of foreign loans in the capitalist world was necessary to obtain cheap capital, which China badly needed for its economic development. Foreign loans and investment would offer China the following four items that could spur economic development: new sources of capital; advanced technology; advanced management skills; and access to international markets. In a detailed study of joint ventures in China, Margaret Pearson (1991: 51–56) has analysed major considerations behind China's Open Door policy. Reformers convincingly argued for the rationale of the Open Door policy: as long as the foreign loans and investment conformed to the state plan and remained subordinate to the domestic economy, it would not compromise China's sovereignty or essential independence. According to this school of thought, China was a fully independent and sovereign country that was not in danger of crumbing under pressure from outside, and China's socialist institutions would provide tools to control foreign loans and investment.[10]

The institutional macrostructure made it necessary to smooth domestic concerns at the institutional and bureaucratic level. Toward that end Chinese leaders repeatedly made statements emphasizing the issue of sovereignty and self-reliance. In September 1979, three month before the first loan package between China and Japan was signed, Vice Premier Gu Mu declared in his trip to Japan: 'We will accept loans from all friendly nations as long as China's sovereignty is not impaired and the conditions are appropriate.'[11] In late 1982, Premier Zhao Ziyang emphasized that 'the aim of our foreign economic and technical exchange is, of course, to raise our capacity for self-reliance'. Deng Xiaoping himself openly supported the point that the economic cooperation and joint ventures with foreign countries would enhance self-reliance in the long run.[12] In 1984 Deng further confirmed this point with a visiting Japanese delegation, stating, 'Our socialist economic base is so huge that it can absorb tens and hundreds of billions of dollars worth of foreign funds without being shaken.'[13]

The Chinese government made sure, right from the beginning of its acceptance of foreign aid, that China was in firm control of all major decisions, such as programme planning, project selection, development, and implementation. Based on this principle, China would carry extensive consultation and coordination with aid-giving countries, such as Japan.[14]

From the perspective of China's economic bureaucrats, there were also many incentives for obtaining Japanese ODA. First, Japanese government loans had comparative advantages. These government loans, known as 'soft loans', followed the international standard of providing longer payback periods and lower interest payment. That means the loans were repayable in thirty years at 3 (or a little more than 3) per cent interest with a ten-year grace period. Sometimes the interest rate was even lower. For example, in 1988 the Japanese government announced an interest reduction to approximately 2.6 per cent on yen loans to developing countries. China was one of the first countries to receive such a low interest rate.[15] In comparison, the conditions on loans that China might obtain from other channels were much tougher. The most notable are short-term private commercial loans and Export-Import Bank loans. For example, in May 1979, the Export-Import Bank of Japan agreed to a loan of US$2 billion with a fifteen year term at 6.25 per cent interest. Three months later, China obtained two commercial loans for a total of US$8 billion at a higher rate and with shorter payment periods (six months and four and a half years respectively) (Whiting, 1989: 121–122). The government loans clearly offered much better terms than the commercial and Export-Import Bank loans.

Second, although commercial loans were available, foreign government 'soft loans' proved more useful to successive Chinese demands for funds for large-scale infrastructural projects at both the national and provincial levels, such as railways, ports, and hydroelectric power plants. Indeed, there was a high concentration in Japanese loan aid, which accounted for 85 to 90 per cent of the first package of the total bilateral ODA. It would also meet Beijing's demand as fiscal crises repeatedly threatened China's key projects.

Third, as the first non-communist government to offer government loans to China, Japan played a leading role for other industrialized nations. Western countries such as Belgium and Denmark and international organizations, including the World Bank, quickly followed suit. A senior US official commented, 'Very clearly, China's most important international relationship is with Japan.'[16] Finally, Chinese economic bureaucrats gained valuable managerial skills and useful knowledge of obtaining entry into the international financial community through its experience with the Japanese loan agencies.[17]

These kinds of efforts made it possible to set up more institutional norms and mechanisms at the macrostructure level that would be con-ducive to the promotion of external economic activities. In the micro-process of decision-making, the enlarged domestic win-sets for receiving Japanese loans significantly enhanced the pro-reform leaders' position. Furthermore, Beijing could clearly perceive broad and diversified inter-est in Japanese aid at both the national and provincial levels.

Therefore, both international and domestic conditions favourably expanded China's domestic win-sets for receiving loans from Japan. This, in turn, further strengthened Beijing's bargaining power and flexibility in dealing with foreign loans. Under such international and domestic circumstances, Japan's available low-interest capital, advanced technology, and market became increasingly attractive to China's decision-makers.

The Micro-Macro Linkage and Japanese Policy-making

The interaction between macrostructure and 'micro-process' in Tokyo regarding Japanese ODA to China is a different case than that of China. The international conditions and domestic win-sets that Japan faced in the late 1970s were quite unlike the Chinese case. Let us examine in detail Japanese policy-making regarding ODA to China.

As with the case of China, to fully comprehend this policy decision we must first understand changes in the symbolic macrostructure and its effect on the micro-process in Japan. As early as 1961, Japan had become a member of the OECD's Development Assistance Committee (DAC), the world's donor club, which coordinates the donor countries that offer ODA, including government loans, grants, and technical aid to developing countries.[18] Since the mid-1960s, Japan has actively been involved in foreign aid programmes. Japan came a long way to replace the United States in the top donor position. In 1989, the appreciation of the yen gave Japan a push to become the world's number one donor. Due to economic and geo-political considerations, Tokyo continues to distribute the largest amount of Japanese aid to countries within the Asia region (71 per cent of Japan's total aid went to Asia in 1980, 68 per cent in 1985, and 65 per cent in 1992).[19] As discussed earlier, soon after the normalization of relations with China in 1972, Japan offered to provide ODA to China; but Beijing was not ready to accept outside aid from any country until late 1978. There were both international and domestic factors to explain Japan's enthusiasm for providing aid to China.

The amount of official development assistance a country can offer reflects its international status. As a DAC member, Japan was sensitive to its status within the group. Japan ranked fourth place in the club as early as 1968, and then contended for the second place with France (after the United States). Although Japan's total foreign aid spending rose rapidly, the per centage of ODA to GNP remained low. Prior to 1978, Japan spending on foreign aid remained at the level of around 0.25 per cent of GNP (for example, 0.23 for 1970, 0.25 for 1975, and 0.23 for 1978), far below a United Nations guideline of 0.7 per cent for industrialized countries. Japan's ranking was quite poor among the then 18 DAC members (Rix, 1980: 31–32). To keep its international standing, Japan was pressed to increase its aid spending. In July of 1978, Japanese Prime Minister Takeo Fukuda pledged to double Japan's ODA funds within three years. Thus, Japan viewed China as a new, appropriate recipient of this increased ODA budget. By convincing the DAC's Statistics Commission to include China on the DAC's list of 'less developed countries' (LDCs), Japan was able to include its ODA to China as part of its total ODA contribution.[20] Although still low, Japan's ODA as a percentage of GNP increased to the level of around 0.30 in the 1980s and 1990s. For example, the percentages were 0.32 for 1988, 0.32 for 1991, 0.30 for 1992 and 0.26 for 1993.[21] Japan's ODA in 1993 reached US$11.25 billion, or 20.5 per cent of the total ODA provided by DAC countries, placing Japan in the world's top aid donor position for the third consecutive year.[22]

Japan's economic competition with other industrialized powers was a major factor in the formulation of its aid policy toward China. Although Japan successfully cultivated the China market for several years, its leading position in this market was constantly challenged by other industrialized countries, making foreign aid an area of competition between Japan and the Western states. From the Japanese perspective, the ODA-supported, large-scale projects normally had 'high feasibility' status and received better publicity in the international community, and were therefore more desirable.

China's first loan request was for a package of eight infrastructure construction projects which included three hydro-electric power plants, three railroad lines, and two ports. When China began to explore loan possibilities for these projects in the summer of 1979, Tokyo was well aware of the competition from Western countries. For example, there were several private commercial loan offers from France (US$7 billion), Britain (US$5 billion), Sweden, and Canada. The Japanese also knew of US Vice President Walter Mondale's promise of US$2 billion Export–Import Bank credits to China when he visited Beijing in 1979. The

Japanese government understood these project loans would be a convenient and useful way to enhance Japan's long-range economic benefits; it would allow Japan, as Chae-jin Lee (1984: 116–119) pointed out, 'to establish a firm foothold in China's economic infrastructure, and induce a spillover effect to other areas of Sino-Japanese economic cooperation'.

From the first loan package (1979) Japan agreed to provide six (out of eight) construction projects earmarked for government loans. Tokyo selected railroad line and port projects from the Chinese request list, while two hydroelectric power plant projects were dropped. This selection clearly reflected Japan's economic interests. The two ports, Shijiusuo and Qinhuangdao, were important ports from which energy supplies (in particular coal) were exported to Japan. Two of the three railroad lines, the Yanzhou–Shijiusuo Railway and the Beijing–Qinhuangdao Railway, directly connected the two ports. Japan provided 62 per cent and 100 per cent of requested loan amounts respectively. The third railroad, the Hengyang–Guangzhou Railway, was irrelevant to Japan's energy supply route and thus received only 16 per cent of what China had asked. Tokyo rejected the two hydroelectric power plant projects (Longtan and Shuikou) because they were in conflict with Japan's economic interests. The Longtan Hydroelectric Power Plant would have had the capacity to supply electricity to a large aluminum refinery with an annual production capability of 600,000 tons, which was in conflict with Japanese joint-venture interests in aluminum production in Indonesia and Brazil.[23] These examples demonstrate that the actual selection from the requested projects reflected, as Greg Story (1987: 35) suggested, 'the needs of the donor rather than the recipient, that is, it followed Japanese rather than Chinese economic priorities'.

To Japan, China was important not only from an economic perspective, but also in strategic and political terms. As a *Beijing Review* article points out, 'by using its economic power, Japan seeks to become a political power'.[24] Despite Prime Minister Yasuhiro Nakasone's claim, during a Upper House hearing on ODA in the National Diet, that Japan would not bring strategic considerations into the distribution of Japanese foreign aid,[25] strategic considerations nevertheless clearly influence aid policies. Article 9 of Japan's postwar constitution renounces 'the right of belligerency'. Since Japan is precluded by its own constitution from wielding military power beyond its own borders, this leaves economic means, including ODA, as one of the prime ways available to the Japanese government to exercise international influence and to deal with its Asian neighbours, particularly China.[26]

Strategically, China's natural resources, in particular energy resources, were desirable for Japan. Japan was highly dependent on energy sources from the Middle East. After the oil shocks in the 1970s, however, Japan became aware that political instability in the Middle East could jeopardize assurance of that region's energy supply to Japan. Japan considered China — with its rich natural resources such as coal and oil and safer, cheaper, and closer sea routes — an ideal source from which to diversify its energy supply.

Japan was well aware of international sensitivity to Japan's aid diplomacy toward China. To soothe other countries' concerns, the Ministry of Foreign Affairs in September 1979 released the 'Ohira Three Principles' of aid policy to China. The three principles were aimed at:

- cooperation with the United States and other Western nations (primarily the EEC), to ease fears that Japan might move to monopolize the China market;
- balancing aid to China with aid to other Asian countries, especially ASEAN; and
- avoiding loans to China's defence-related industries.

The last principle was to deflect criticism from the Soviet Union, Vietnam, and South Korea.[27]

Since normalization, the Sino-Japanese relationship has experienced some political friction; the most notable discord surrounds the charge of Japan's 'revived militarism' (an issue that will be analysed in Chapter 7). In 1982, and again in 1985 to 1986, there were large anti-Japanese demonstrations in Beijing and other major Chinese cities inspired by China's sharp criticism of the Japanese government's revision of Japan's past war behaviour in school textbooks. During these controversies, Japan's political leaders pledged large-scale 'soft loans' to China. Although there was no direct connection between the sensitive textbook issue and the loans, the Japanese used government loans as goodwill gestures to cultivate political ties with the Chinese.

Japan's financial aid policy toward China provides an interesting example of interaction between the micro-process and the institutional macrostructure of our micro-macro linkage model. It is known that emotional ties toward China at the individual level also played a part in the formulation of Japanese aid policy. In public opinion polls taken in Japan for many years prior to 1989, China consistently was ranked second only to the United States as the most 'friendly' nation. Because of a shared culture and historical and geographical proximity, the Japanese emotion toward China was sometimes, as Swadesh De Roy suggests, 'above reason'.[28] There were also wide-spread feelings of regret among the Japanese, especially the older generation, about Japan's past war behaviour in China. Both of China's Nationalist and Communist Party leaders, Chiang Kai-shek in 1951 and Zhou Enlai in 1972, respectively, foreswore Japan's war reparations as goodwill gestures. Many Japanese felt that Japan could use government loans as surrogate reparations. As one experienced foreign banker in Hong Kong suggested, 'Financially these loans make no sense. Politically they are really disguised reparations.'[29] Although one could take issue with this statement, given that Tokyo has often selected projects for loans on the basis of potential economic benefits to Japan, as analysed earlier, it nevertheless reflects the political implications of Japanese aid to China.

To further promote the bilateral relationship and to increase mutual understanding at the public level, Japan concentrated most grants (not loans) toward humanitarian purposes and cultural exchanges. One of the most important projects was the China–Japan Friendship Hospital in Beijing, which cost 16.4 billion yen and accounted for 57 per cent of all grants to China in the 1980 to 1985 period. Other smaller projects during this period included:

- a Sino-Japanese youth exchange centre in Beijing (1985);[30]
- a rehabilitation centre in Beijing for the physically handicapped (1986) and water purification facilities in Changchun (1986);
- forest resources restoration (1988);
- an experimental fishery station in Hebei province (1988);
- a national library and a foreign language college in Beijing (1988);
- and preservation of the Dunhuang Mogao Cave on the historic Silk Road (1988).

The one-billion-yen grant in aid to the Mogao Cave was pledged by Prime Minister Noboru Takeshita when he visited China in 1988; he indicated that the grant was to 'appeal to the hearts of the Chinese people'.[31] Economic assistance to China also came in the form of technical and training support. In 1986, for example, of the ten thousand 'foreign experts' in China, about 40 per cent were Japanese; and a management training centre funded by the Japanese was opened in Tianjin that year.

Japan's aid diplomacy and the efforts to 'appeal to the hearts of the Chinese people' have been fruitful not only at the grass-roots level, but also at the level of individual decision-makers. American journalists noticed that despite problems surrounding the 'textbook controversy', the Japanese still maintained better access to top leaders in China than Western leaders and diplomats did. For example, in 1984 Chinese

Communist Party Secretary General Hu Yaobang invited visiting Japanese Prime Minister Yasuhiro Nakasone to a rare private family dinner.[32] (One may note, here, that this type of activity was not without repercussions. Hu paid a price for his affinity for invitations to Japanese when he was severely criticised in the context of later Beijing power politics.) In early 1985, Hu dined with Japanese Ambassador Yosuke Nakae three times in one week, whereas American Ambassador Arthur Hummel during his entire four-year posting met with Hu only once.

After signing the 1984 agreement transferring Hong Kong over to Chinese sovereignty in 1997, British Prime Minister Margaret Thatcher proudly announced that the Chinese officials agreed to receive a British trade delegation. But when the mission, including the ten top British industrialists, arrived in February 1985, they found themselves outdone by a 100-member delegation from the Japanese Chamber of Commerce. The Japanese delegation met with China's paramount leader Deng Xiaoping; the British did not. As a Western journalist concluded, 'no other country can compete with Japan for access in China'.[33]

In sum, the first decade (1979–88) of Japan's aid to China can be described as the initial and mutually beneficial stage. It is obvious that the decision-makers in Beijing and Tokyo faced quite different macrostructures and micro-processes with regard to the aid issue. These differences, however, did not prevent the two countries from engaging in extensive economic cooperation through the avenue of Japan's ODA programme. The fact that decision-makers in Beijing and Tokyo both perceived overlapping economic, political, and strategic interests between the two countries can provide a key explanation for the success of this policy.

The Crisis and Bargaining Stage (1989–1995)

The second stage of Japan's ODA to China began with the Tiananmen Incident of June 1989, the Chinese military crackdown on student-led demonstrations which left hundreds dead. This tragedy aroused worldwide protest and economic sanctions from Western industrialized countries. This international crisis inevitably shook Japan's ODA policy toward China, leading it to the stage of *crisis and bargaining*.

The Micro-Macro Linkage and Japanese Policy-making

With the drastic changes in macrostructure around China and Japan externally and internally after the Tiananmen Incident, Japan's initial reaction was cautious, yet clear. Both Prime Minister Sosuke Uno and top foreign affair officials either deplored Beijing's armed suppression or called it 'morally intolerable'. In the immediate post-Tiananmen period, because of a lack of clear direction, Japanese aid officials followed a 'case-by-case review' process for approving current loans and grants to China.[34]

Facing this changing international environment, Japan was under great international pressure. Although reluctant, Tokyo decided to join in the economic sanctions imposed on China by Western industrialized countries, putting a hold on its government loans. Japan was the only Asian country that went along with Western industrialized countries to impose economic sanctions against China for Beijing's military suppression of the student-led movement.[35] Yet, the Japanese government was cautious with the aid issue. Instead of calling it a 'sanction', Tokyo initially described the suspension of loan disbursements as necessary to protect Japanese aid officials in China due to the violent military action in Beijing.

One of the measures Japan adopted was to freeze its government loan of 810 billion yen, which had been scheduled for April 1990. Other measures included the suspension of high-level government contacts and several scheduled economic and cultural exchange meetings, including the inauguration of an investment-promotion organization for China and a Sino-Japanese meeting on high-technology transfer.

International pressure played a significant role in Japan's reaction toward the Tiananmen Incident. Tokyo was deeply concerned with its international obligations in terms of economic sanctions toward China. Many observers believed that if Japan did not take a tough stance on condemning China's military crackdown, Tokyo 'might find itself internationally isolated'.[36] This international pressure slowed Japan's process of lifting economic sanctions against China.

Despite a reluctance to extend the loans, the Japanese government also was cautious to avoid pushing China into further isolation. Immediately after the crackdown, chief spokesman for the Ministry of Foreign Affairs, Taizo Watanabe, emphasized that, 'What the government is taking into account most is the fact that relations between Japan and China are naturally different from those between the US and China', referring to the Japanese military's behaviour during World War II. He also warned that Japan must be cautious, for Beijing might launch a harsh attack against Tokyo's economic sanctions in order to distract domestic attention from the current unrest. This government view was also shared by many business leaders. For example, Bank of Japan Governor Satoshi

Sumita advocated a 'wait and see attitude' right after the Beijing crackdown.[37]

What the Japanese government awaited were clear signals from Western partners, notably the United States, that economic sanctions against China would be lifted. At that time the atmosphere in Washington was quite negative toward Beijing. Even though President George Bush extended China's most-favoured-nation (MFN) status, the US Congress was getting tougher in its policy toward China. The US lawmakers were determined to step up their efforts to limit World Bank loans to China by exercising their influence over the World Bank.[38] The Bush administration also held firm in its policy toward the loans. US National Security Adviser Brent Scowcroft told a key LDP leader, former Japanese foreign minister Hiroshi Mitsuzuka 'not to restore the credits too quickly'.[39] Under such circumstances, Japan appeared to be cautions in its own policy toward China.

Nevertheless, the United States had been ambivalent toward Japanese aid to China even before the Tiananmen Incident. On the one hand, the United States, itself, was explicitly prohibited from extending ODA to China by the Foreign Assistance Act, due to the fact that China was a communist country; and the Commerce Department viewed Japan's aid presence in China as suspiciously worrying regarding possible Japanese designs on the Chinese market. In addition, conservative lawmakers were also concerned about human rights violations in China, and felt that aid should not be extended to China. On the other hand, however, State Department and foreign aid agencies viewed this issue with the strategic consideration that Japan should take the lead in the West's relations with China through foreign aid to promote economic and political reforms in the PRC.

While refusing to implement new loans, Japan lifted its freeze on ongoing aid to China in August 1989 and was the first country to do so.[40] Since October 1989, the World Bank began to resume its lending to China for humanitarian aid including a US$30 million loan for earthquake relief (October 1989) and a US$60 million credit for agriculture projects (February 1990).[41] Following the World Bank lead, the Japanese foreign affairs ministry, for the first time after the Tiananmen Incident, decided to release a new grant aid of US$35 million in December 1989 for improving facilities at a Beijing television broadcasting station and a Shanghai hospital.[42]

Thereafter, Japan frequently reminded the United States and other Western countries that it was not in their interest to impose heavy sanctions on China. In other words, Japan's actions were heavily influenced by the general international environment; yet the concerns of the various Japanese government agencies played an important role in the gradual change of the symbolic macrostructure that had been conducive to the economic sanctions against China.

Japan also showed reluctance to openly criticize China in July 1989 at the Paris summit of seven major Western industrialized countries.[43] 'To isolate China will not be good for world peace and stability', Prime Minister Toshiki Kaifu claimed at a 1990 New Year's news conference.[44] The prospect of a wealthy Japan facing an isolated, chaotic China has long been a nightmare for Japanese decision-makers, and has prompted Japan's willingness to be a mediator between China and the Western world. A Japanese economic official put it this way, 'Japan should take one step ahead of other nations in improving its relations with China. Japan can help create a climate for other nations to improve their relations with Beijing.'[45]

Tokyo made its decision to resume loans to China one year after the Tiananmen Incident. At the Economic Summit of seven major industrialized nations held in July 1990 in Houston, Japanese Prime Minister Toshiki Kaifu announced that 'Japan will gradually resume' its third package of government loans to China valued at 810 billion yen, thereby ending its one-year economic sanctions against China.[46] This soft loan package to China is designed to last for five years, and about 15 per cent (120 billion yen, or US$0.8 billion) of the total amount is expected to be disbursed in the 1990 financial year.

Experienced observers of Asian affairs noted, as reported in the *Far Eastern Economic Review* that 'While other world leaders kept their distance . . . it was Japan which moved furthest and mostly quickly to restore friendly relations with Beijing in the aftermath of Tiananmen, and that it was Japanese Prime minister Toshiki Kaifu who undertook to act as the spokesman for China's interests at the Group of Seven meeting in Houston.'[47] Even though the United States and other Western economic powers did not immediately follow Japan's lead in changing their policies toward China, these countries did indicate their understanding of Japan's decision to lift sanctions.[48]

In terms of the domestic institutional macrostructure, the Japanese decision-makers faced strong reactions toward the Tiananmen Incident. Various political institutions frequently called for economic sanctions and this response to political repression in China received a wide range of political and public support. This support came not only from the ruling Liberal Democratic Party (LDP) and top government bureaucrats, but also from opposition parties. The LDP's Foreign Affairs Department

Chairman Koji Kakizawa openly called for economic sanctions, saying that Japan should make clear that it is a nation which respects the principles of democracy, freedom, and human rights. The Japan Communist Party (JCP) Secretariat Chief Mitsuhiro Kaneko asked to 'immediately halt economic assistance to China, because it is 'paid for by the sweat of the Japanese people's brows'. Japan's largest labour organization, the Japanese Private Sector Trade Union Confederation known as *Rengo* (with 5.4 million members), and the 4.5 million-strong General Council of Trade Union, announced that they would suspend exchanges with China to protest Beijing's action.[49]

Several of the opposition parties, however, also began to soften their stance and became active for Japan's aid diplomacy toward China. Whereas the Democratic Socialist Party (DSP) and the JCP remained uncompromised toward Beijing, the Japan Socialist Party (JSP) and the Clean Government Party (CGP) were ready to push for releasing the loans. Secretary General of the JSP Tsuruo Yamaguchi visited Beijing in mid-May 1990 and met with Jiang Zemin and Politburo Standing Committee member Song Ping; Yamaguchi promised that the JSP would continue to work hard to resume the third loan package.[50] At the end of May, Jiang Zemin and Li Peng met in Beijing with the visiting Clean Government Party delegation headed by its founder, Honorary President Daisaku Ikeda, with whom he discussed bilateral relations.[51] Equally important, Japan's business community began to complain that the hold on loans had 'seriously affected' exports to China and to advocate that government loans be resumed.[52]

To meet these domestic demands for resuming loans with China, the Japanese government pledged again to resume the loan package. Prime Minister Kaifu made the promise when he met with the Japan Socialist Party (JSP) Secretary General Tsuruo Yamaguchi before his eight-day visit to Beijing, and two months prior to the Houston summit of July 1990. Yamaguchi urged Kaifu to lift the freeze on the loan package. The prime minister told the JSP leader that there would be no problem in telling the Chinese leaders that 'Japan will certainly honor its promise' of loans totally 810 billion yen, but that there would be 'difficulties in resuming aid immediately'.[53]

Japan's dual-position toward the Tiananmen Incident clearly reflected pressures from different directions: notably the changing symbolic and institutional macrostructure. This complicated position was highlighted by a *Japan Times* editorial on the first anniversary of the Tiananmen Incident. As the editorial noted, Tokyo continued to condemn Beijing's repressive policy, while at the same time, it claimed that 'outsiders' one-sided perceptions of China have played an excessively great role in isolating China in the international community', and stated that, 'it is time to try to pave the way for China's full-fledged return to the international community'. It became increasingly clear to Tokyo that Japanese ODA to China not only possessed economic significance, but also was a crucial part of Japan's diplomacy toward China, directly affecting overall bilateral relations. The controversy forced the Kaifu government to search for a balance among various options, trying to confirm to both the West and China that Japan: (1) will continue to be in line with the West; and (2) will prevent pushing China into further isolation. Therefore, Japan needed to work on two diplomatic fronts — China and the West — in its post-Tiananmen policy toward China.

After the resumption of Japan's ODA to China in the summer 1990, bilateral relations between the two countries warmed up fairly quickly. Political, economic, and cultural contacts reached high levels. According to the evaluation of the Japanese foreign affairs ministry, Japan's aid programme to China was a 'total success,' in both political and economic terms.[54] With regard to the 1990 decision to resume loan aid to China, however, one may sense that the 'success' was more on the diplomatic front.

Influenced by the 1989 Tiananmen crisis, from the beginning of the 1990s Japan's ODA policy toward China began to change in response to the changing post-Cold War international order and more diverse domestic demands.

Prime Minister Toshiki Kaifu first announced the government's new ODA principles in April 1991 and this new emphasis was confirmed by Prime Minister Kiichi Miyazawa in January 1992. The new policy required that Japan's ODA be provided in accordance with the principles of the United Nations Charter (especially sovereign equality and non-intervention in domestic matters), and the following four principles:

(1) Environmental conservation and development should be pursued in tandem.
(2) Any use of ODA for military purposes or for aggravation of international conflicts should be avoided.
(3) Full attention should be paid to trends in recipient countries' military expenditures, their development and production of mass destruction weapons and missiles, their export and import of arms, so as to maintain and strengthen international peace and stability.
(4) Full attention should be paid to efforts by the recipient country to promote democratization, to introduce a market-oriented reforms,

and to enhance the security of basic human rights and freedoms of their citizens.[55]

This new emphasis on the environment, non-aggression, military openness, and human rights issues reflects a major shift in the symbolic macrostructure (changing perceptions) affecting Japan's ODA to China — that is, Japanese decision-makers held new interpretations of the political, economic, and security implications of the aid programmes to China. These principles have had far-reaching significance for Japan's ODA toward China in the 1990s and beyond.

Beginning in 1992, the two countries started a series of negotiations for the fourth Japanese aid package. The extensive protracted bargaining between China and Japan made it difficult to reach an agreement for the fourth package. While emphasizing that Japan would not push China on the human rights issue to the same extent as the United States did, Tokyo did tell Beijing that it would like to see China's military spending policy become 'more transparent.'[56] Japanese Prime Minister Morihiro Hosokawa, during his visit to Beijing in March of 1994, as the *Japan Times* noted, clearly 'urged China to make its military plans transparent for international relief.'[57]

Interestingly, the controversy in the aid negotiations between the two countries did not touch directly on the sensitive issues of human rights and military spending. Rather, the two sides concentrated on a seemingly technical issue — the length of the package. Japan's aid policy toward China underwent extensive review in 1993 and 1994. The Japanese government review focused on whether and how to change the previous preferential formula for Beijing, under which Tokyo had made an advance pledge of yen loans to cover a multi-year period.[58] In order to increase its control, Japan proposed that the previous pattern of five-year packages should be replaced by annual packages.[59] The Chinese side strongly opposed this proposal (which will be discussed later in detail).

From the Japanese perspective, there were four reasons for changing to yearly loan packages. First, China was then the only Japanese aid recipient enjoying such favourable treatment. All other recipients were given annual aid pledges. Second, there were increasing public concerns about the ODA budget among various circles in Japanese society. Third, it was normal practice and principle for the financial ministry to determine budget-related matters on an annual basis.[60]

And finally, there were considerable pressures from the Western powers, notably from the United States. According to Akio Suzuki, staff director of the Japan–China Economic Association, this change in loan periods reflected pressure from the United States. There had been frequent Japan–US consultations regarding Japan's China policy and Washington emphasized that Tokyo should take into account China's human rights when devising its ODA policy.[61] Changes in the symbolic and institutional macrostructure have definitely played a significant role in Japan's ODA policy-making. But one should not ignore the influence of the power/regime macrostructure, even though it may not be easy for outsiders to observe. An interesting explanation was that the politicians of the ruling party LDP had been firm supporters of the long-term arrangement for yen loans to China, whereas government bureaucracy was in favour of annual review. However, with the domestic chaos in Japanese politics in the early 1990s, particularly with the LDP's loss of power in the summer of 1993, the influence of politicians significantly declined. Thus, the proshort term arrangement voices became much stronger.[62] And Japanese aid policy became largely the result of coordination among governmental agencies, including the ministries of foreign affairs, finance, international trade and industry, and the agency of economic planning.[63] It is apparent in this case that the change in the power/regime macrostructure also played a notable role in Japan's new policy orientation.

The Micro-Macro Linkage and Chinese Policy-making

Like their counterparts in Tokyo, decision-makers in Beijing also had to deal with a changing macrostructure related to the serious challenges posed by the Tiananmen Incident. China first had to wrestle with a drastic change in the symbolic macrostructure. Beijing worked hard to restore its image and reputation in the international community, and to end the economic sanctions imposed by the industrialized countries led by the United States.

Alarmed by the worsening economic situation with the decline of foreign reserves, aid, and investment in the wake of Tiananmen, Chinese leaders worked hard to lift imposed economic sanctions. In this effort, China paid special attention to its top creditor and largest foreign trading partner, Japan. Fully aware of the subtle differences between Japan and the Western nations and the special role Tokyo could play, China tried specially to cultivate Japan's goodwill and solicit its understanding. Right before the Paris summit of July 1989, Chinese Premier

Li Peng praised Japan for its reluctance to further condemn China. After seeing Deng Xiaoping in Beijing in November 1989, Eishiro Saito, Chairman of the Federation of Economic Organization (*Keidanran*) confirmed that Deng and other Chinese leaders 'showed great expectation of Japan'.[64] During the same month, in his discussions about Western economic sanctions, Li Peng predicted that the sanctions would be lifted sooner or later; he said, 'Some will go first and others later. We'll wait and see which country will make the first move. The country which does so is brave and praiseworthy.'[65] The country, Li was referring to as making 'the first move', clearly was Japan.

But Tokyo did not immediately live up to Beijing's hope of softening its stance over the 810-billion-yen loan package, and only made a small grant (US$35 million) 'for humanitarian reasons' in December. By the end of 1989, Chinese Vice Premier Wu Xueqian showed his disappointment with Japan by criticizing Tokyo as standing behind Washington's policy of restricting high-level communications in the post-Tiananmen period; Wu was referring to the recent visit of US National Security Adviser Brent Scowcroft whom President George Bush had sent to Beijing.[66]

The Chinese side also made special efforts at the person-to-person level to lobby for Japan's release of loans. During a ten-day visit to Japan in January 1990, Zou Jiahua, Chairman of the Chinese State Planning Commission (the highest Chinese official to visit Japan since the Tiananmen Incident), conducted extensive diplomacy aimed at improving bilateral relations, and, in particular, at the government loan package. He held talks with Prime Minister Toshiki Kaifu and Foreign Minister Taro Nakayama, focusing on the 810-billion-yen loan issue. However, except for a goodwill gesture by Japan — plans to send an aid 'study' mission to China — there was no change toward 'an immediate extension of pledged loans to China'.[67] In a March 1990 statement, Chinese Foreign Minister Qian Qichen emphasized 'the historical background, geographical location and cultural heritage' between the two countries and called for 'better relations'.[68] Yet the annual bilateral subcabinet-level talks held shortly after Qian's statement did not lead to any progress in lifting Japan's economic sanctions.[69]

Nevertheless, Tokyo began to respond positively to Beijing's efforts after both Japan's domestic mood and international sentiment began to change gradually in 1990. Prominent political leaders either openly advocated lifting economic sanctions, or visited Beijing themselves to discuss with Chinese leaders problems between the two countries. In mid-April of 1990, LDP Secretary General Ichiro Ozawa asked Foreign

Minister Taro Nakayama to prepare for the release of loans, 'even if countries like the United States do not take a similar action'.[70] Michio Watanabe, head of one of the LDP's largest factions and former chairman of the LDP's Policy Affairs Research Council, visited China in early May and met with Party Secretary General Jiang Zemin and Premier Li Peng. Watanabe pledged to implement the loans as soon as possible, and told Li, 'I can say this clearly, after having conferred with other leaders in Japan.' Li thanked Japanese leaders for their efforts to have the loans made available, but also spoke of the harm that could come to Sino-Japanese relations 'if the loans are delayed too long'.

A few days after Watanabe's visit, 88-year-old ex-LDP Diet member Yoshimi Furui, a well-known China hand in Japan, visited Beijing and met with Li Peng. Li again emphasized that he did not want to see Sino-Japanese relations damaged [by the loan issue].'[71] Three months later, in July 1990, Japan decided to restore its governmental loans to China, becoming the first industrialized country to move forward in this direction.

Since then, Beijing sent clear signals to Tokyo that it would like to continue the pattern of Japanese ODA, and would like to work out the fourth package before the third one was set to expire in 1995. The domestic considerations behind Beijing's efforts were obvious. In government circles, Japanese ODA was widely regarded as very helpful in meeting China's demands for infrastructure items. Unlike some other Western countries that emphasized loans for 'soft construction', (for example, in support of social science research). Japanese loans were concentrated in 'hard construction' projects, such as providing capital and equipment for the transportation and energy sectors.[72] Chinese officials have praised loan aid from Japan, in comparison with aid from other countries, for its 'high level (the heads of the two countries, themselves, signed the agreements), generous amounts, greater number of loan items [projects], wide distribution, diversified fields, and obvious results'.[73] Technology assistance was also important to China's modernization drive. In 1993, almost 30 per cent of China's technology imports came from Japan. During his visit to Japan in February 1994, Vice Premier Zhu Rongji called upon the Japanese to 'give us more technology'.[74]

Nevertheless, Japan's new ODA guidelines brought some problems between the two countries. After China's June 1994 underground nuclear test, the Japanese government responded quickly and with displeasure. The head of the Foreign Ministry's Economic Cooperation Bureau Hiroshi Hirabayashi stated that, China's action 'will unfavourably affect the government's efforts to win public support and understanding for the provision of aid to China'.[75] On 7 October 1994, China conducted another nuclear test. Tokyo, 'in protest' against this action, immediately decided to defer sending a team to Beijing for talks on projects to be covered by the fourth yen loan. This mission, comprised of officials from the Ministry of International Trade and Industry, the Foreign Ministry, the Finance Ministry and the Economic Planning Agency, was due to leave on 16 October for two days of consultations.[76] This protest was not well received in Beijing. Nevertheless, the issue continued to plague the bilateral relationship. After China's new round of underground nuclear tests in May and August of 1995, Tokyo announced that as a response to the tests, Japan's aid to China in 1995 would be significantly cut by 93 per cent from 7.8 billion yen to about 0.5 billion yen (loans were not affected).[77] Chinese Premier Li Peng sharply criticized this action as 'economic blackmail'.[78]

During a meeting between Chinese President Jiang Zemin and Japanese Prime Minister Tomiichi Murayama in October 1995 in New York (both were there for a United Nations meeting), the two leaders exchanged tough messages over the aid issue. Murayama reiterated Tokyo's new stance that Japan would continue to reduce drastically economic aid to China until China put a complete stop to its nuclear tests; whereas Jiang made it clear that Beijing would oppose any attempt to use economic aid for political purposes.[79]

Japan's proposal for the annual pledge, rather than the previous multi-year pledge, also met strong resistance from China. Beijing worried that without a long-term arrangement, Japan might reduce its assistance to China.[80] More seriously, Tokyo might increase its bargaining leverage over other issues: ODA would become an avenue for the annual review of China's human right status, similar to Washington's practice with China's most-favoured-nation treatment status; and China would have to oppose any attempt to intervene in its 'internal affairs'. As for the emphasis on environmental issues, some Chinese officials believed that it was not practical, and that China had not yet reached the economic stage where it could be held to high environmental protection standards.[81]

Renmin Ribao (People's Daily), Beijing's policy mouthpiece, reflected this general line of thinking and openly supported the long-term loan arrangement rather than annual terms. It argued that Japan's five-year pledge of ODA to China had been in line with China's five-year plans for economic development, and were therefore conducive to the stable relationship between China and Japan.[82]

This controversy delayed agreement by the two countries on the fourth Japanese yen loan to China. Both Zhu Rongji's trip to Japan in February 1994 and Japanese Prime Minister Morihiro Hosokawa's trip to China in the following month could not produce a concrete agreement for the package, despite Hosokawa's claim that 'Japan will push forward its already promised loans'.[83]

The obstacles, however, did not stand long. A compromise finally was reached toward the end of 1994, and in December Japan and China signed an agreement on the fourth ODA package. This compromise agreement met neither China's demand for a five-year package, nor Japan's request for one-year programme; rather, it provided for a three-year (1996–98) loan package totalling 580 billion yen (US$5.8 billion).[84] The compromise actually followed a '3 plus 2' formula, dividing five years into two stages: the total amount for the first three years would be decided at the first stage, and the apportionment for the following two years would be discussed again at the second stage, making it resemble a five-year package (Nishimoto, 1995: 6).

At the macro level, one can clearly see overlapping perceptions of the economic and political benefits of aid cooperation on the part of policy-makers in both countries. Furthermore, at the micro level, one can also see strong bureaucratic interests sustaining the momentum of Japanese ODA to China. Since the early 1980s, the Chinese government established bureaucratic divisions charged specifically with handling foreign loans, under a number of government ministries with economic responsibilities, such as the Ministry of Foreign Trade and Economic Cooperation, Ministry of Finance, the National People's Bank, the National Planning Commission, and the National Commission of Science and Technology.[85] Japan's ODA programme also greatly aided provincial projects, and received high remarks from the bureaucrats at the local level as well. For example, local officials in Tianjin highly praised a project to update and expand telecommunication systems in Tianjin aided by the second and third yen loans.[86]

There were also well-established channels and mechanisms for coordination between China and Japan, including an annual bilateral, high-level conference on ODA projects, and monthly contacts between Chinese trade officials and Japanese Embassy economic officials. Therefore, information about changes and new intentions were exchanged well before formal negotiations. According to Long Yongtu, General Director of the International Trade and Economic Affairs Bureau of the Ministry of Foreign Trade and Economic Cooperation, there were 'no surprises' on the negotiation table between the two countries.[87] This can be regarded as a well-developed ODA regime sharing common interests between the bureau-cracies of China and Japan.

The ODA Relationship: Common Interests for Different Reasons

This case study demonstrates how the concept of micro-macro linkage enables us to conduct a more comprehensive study of policy-making in China and Japan. On most occasions during this 16-year period (1979–95) of Japanese ODA to China, decision-makers in Beijing and Tokyo faced different international and internal environments. At the initial stage China was compelled to open up to the outside world in order to achieved its national goal of economic modernization, whereas Japan aimed at increasing its international status and diversifying its supply of resources from the international market. The Tiananmen Incident of 1989 brought friction and controversy over Japan's governmental yen loan to China, when the two countries were facing different and opposing international pressures. China struggled hard to break up the economic sanctions imposed by industrialized countries; while Japan was under great pressure from the West, particularly the United States, to join and continue this sanction.

Despite these differing external and internal pressures, China and Japan were able to cooperate when their domestic win-sets featured overlapping interests. As discussed earlier, an international agreement can only be successful if it falls within the domestic win-sets of each of the parties to the accord. Thus, agreement is possible only if those win-sets overlap. If the overlap of the domestic win-sets is not big enough, there is a risk that the negotiations will break down. The consideration of economic benefits from this bilateral cooperation was a prevailing factor for both China and Japan. There are also institutional and bureaucratic interests within the two countries that seek to maintain the momentum and to continue to expand economic cooperation. China's domestic stability was another concern for the decision-makers in both Beijing and Tokyo; this prompted Japan to continue its large amount of aid to China. To apply Robert Putnam's concept, the policy-making processes in both China and Japan can be best understood as a two-level game, within which decision-makers play at both the politics of the international arena and the domestic environment.

In terms of China's foreign policy and its relations with Japan, one may conclude that the economic, political, and diplomatic interdependence between China and Japan will be a long-term phenomenon. Japan's

ODA to China has become an indispensable part of Sino-Japanese relations. The two stages of this massive economic cooperation between the two Asian powers may have significant policy and theoretical implications. From the Chinese perspective, Japan's aid programmes have provided large amounts of less expensive capital, and advanced technology for China's modernization drive, in particular, its large-scale infrastructure construction projects. In addition, it also has greatly enhanced China's position in the world economic system and the international markets.

As for Japan, it has not only ensured itself of a long-term supply of raw materials (energy in particular), but also broadly and deeply strengthened its position in the China market. The degree of Japan's involvement in China's economic affairs cannot be matched by any other country. The large-scale aid programmes have also enhanced Japan's international reputation as one of the world's top donors. The economic benefits are mutual. On the other hand, Japan has indeed increased its leverage in dealings with China. Aid diplomacy has enabled Japan fully to utilize its advantageous economic strength. The unexpected political turmoil in China — the Tiananmen Incident — and Japan's quick, yet cautious, reaction further demonstrates the importance of Japan's foreign aid to Tokyo's political and strategic goals. Aid diplomacy has served the function of promoting Japan's international status and smoothing relations with neighbouringing countries, in this case, China. This case also demonstrates that Japan has given priority to maintaining its role as a faithful partner to the West, and to the United States in particular. Even though Japan decided in July 1990 to gradually resume its government loan package, the fact that Japan imposed economic sanctions for more than a year demonstrates 'Tokyo's increasing efforts to translate economic clout into [political] influence and participation'.[88]

There are limitations on Japan's economic and political influence to China. Loans bring debts which can become a serious problem. As pointed out earlier, China has already encountered difficulties at some stages in its foreign debts repayment schedule. These difficulties may be transferred onto Chinese domestic politics. Japan could again be blamed for an 'economic invasion' as it was during the Chinese students demonstrations in the mid-1980s. Although economic sanctions have political leverage, they may also produce a backlash. It may stimulate nationalist feelings in China, creating a new-round of anti-Japanese sentiment.

There is also equally important significance in the PRC's regional

and global diplomatic calculations. To Beijing, Japan was its most understanding and closest partner among the industrialized countries. Japan's
ODA to China enabled Beijing to act more assertively when facing
possible Western economic sanctions over political issues. The annual
debate and review in the United States linking China's human rights
re-cord to most-favoured-nation (MFN) treatment was regarded as a
hostile challenge to the Beijing regime. One of the reasons for what is
considered a failure on the part of the US to link MFN to human rights
was that Japan and the European Union countries by and large were not
likely to follow the US lead in this regard. In other words, the close
economic ties between China and Japan, and Japan's ODA in particular,
enhanced China's bargaining power in the international arena.

Notes

1   The DAC has 21 members, including all the European donors, plus Japan, Australia, Canada, and the United States. According to the DAC criteria, ODA can consist of capital grant assistance, technical cooperation, capital subscriptions, governments loans, or contributions to United Nations agencies and international financial institutions.
2   US Congress, *Legislation on Foreign Relations Through 1985*, 1, p. 171.
3   See Tasuku Okubo, *China and Japan: Financial Aspects*, Tokyo: Sophia University, 1986, p. 5.
4   Charles Smith, 'Eager to Please: Tokyo Sets Aside Own Rules in China Aid Package', *Far Eastern Economic Review* (26 January 1995): 25–26.
5   'China Emerges as Japan's 2nd Largest Trading Partner in 1993', *The Japan Times* (Weekly International Edition), 31 January–6 February 1994, p. 1.
6   For a detailed analysis of the impact of historical legacy upon China's Open Door policy, see Margaret Pearson (1991: 38–51).
7   *Renmin Ribao* (People's Daily), 2 January 1977, p. 1.
8   *Beijing Review* (25 October 1978): 15–17.
9   Long Yongtu, General Director of the International Trade and Economic Affairs Bureau of the Ministry of Foreign Trade and Economic Cooperation of China, interview with the author, 4 January 1994, Beijing.
10 For a more general background of the evolution of ideological change in China, see Yan Sun (1994).
11 *Beijing Review* (14 September 1979): 4–5.
12 *China Daily*, 13 October 1984, p. 1.
13 See Deng Xiaoping, 'Building a Socialism with a Specifically Chinese Character', 30 June 1984 (Deng, 1994: 72).
14 Sun Yongfu, Deputy Director, the Planning Division of the International Exchange Center of the Ministry of Foreign Trade and Economic Cooperation, interview with the author, Cambridge, Massachusetts, 19 March 1994.
15 *Bangkok Post*, 21 July 1988, p. 28.
16 Amanda Bennett, 'Japan Excels in Relations with China, A Fact that Washington Finds Useful', *Wall Street Journal*, 13 April 1984.
17 Yu Zhensheng, Deputy Chief of the Fifth (Japan) Division of the Foreign Financing Administration Bureau of the Ministry of Foreign Trade and Economic Cooperation of China, interview with the author, 7 January 1994, Beijing.
18 See Philip Trezise, 'U.S.-Japan Economic Issue', in The Atlantic Council of the United States (ed.), *The United States and Japan*, Lanham and New York: University Press of America, 1990, p. 35.
19 See Robert Orr, 'The Rising Sun: What Makes Japan Give?', *The International Economy* (September/October 1989): 81; and Gaimusho (1993), *Wagakuni no seifu kaihatsu enjo* [Japan's Official Development Assistance].
20 See Chae-Jin Lee (1984: 120–121).
21 Gaimusho, *Wagakuni no seifu kaihatsu enjo* [Japan's Official Development Assistance], various volumes; and *Japan Economic Institute Report*, 1B (5 January 1990): 13.
22 'Tokyo Once Again Top Aid Donor', *The Japan Times* (Weekly International Edition), 4–10 July 1994, p. 2.

23 *Asahi Shimbun*, 1 December 1979; Chae-Jin Lee (1984:121).
24 Chu Qimen, 'Tokyo Seeks More Political Clout', *Beijing Review* (18–24 June 1990): 17.
25 *Asahi Evening News*, 31 January 1985, p. 1.
26 Masaji Takahashi, Japanese Consul General in Honolulu, interview with the author, 17 July 1990, Honolulu.
27 *Asahi Shimbun*, 3, 4, and 9 September 1979; also see Greg Story (1987: 34); and Chae-Jin Lee (1984: 118–119).
28 Swadesh De Roy, 'Japan's Image of China', *Daily Yomiuri*, 14 January 1985.
29 Quoted from Allen Whiting (1989: 123), *China Eyes Japan*.
30 *Japan Times*, 14 October 1985.
31 *Japan Times*, 7 May (p. 7) and 25 August (p. 1) 1988.
32 Amanda Bennett, 'Japan Excels in Relations with China'.
33 Jim Mann, 'China and Japan: How They Buried Centuries of Hate', *International Herald Tribune*, 6 May 1985, p. 6.
34 *New York Times*, 7 June 1989, p. A8.
35 *Journal of Commerce*, 30 November 1989, p. 5A.
36 *Japan Times*, 6 June (p. 12) and 7 June (p. 10) 1989.
37 *Japan Times*, 6 June (p. 12), 7 June (p. 10) 1989; and 10 January (p. 1) 1990.
38 Susumu Awanohara, 'No More Favors: U.S. Lawmakers Expected to Maintain Anti-China Stand', *Far Eastern Economic Review* (7 June 1990): 56–57.
39 Henry Cutter, 'Politicians Prepare to Restore China Aid', *Japan Times* (Weekly International Edition), 28 May–3 June 1990, p. 1.
40 Steven Weisman, 'Foreign Aid Isn't Easy for Japan', *New York Times*, 20 August 1989, p. 3E.
41 *Sing Tao International*, 11 May 1990, p. 15.
42 *China Daily*, 6 December 1989, p. 1. Also see *Japan Times*, 29 November 1989, p. 3.
43 *Japan Times*, 5 July (p. 1), and 15 December (p. 1) 1989.
44 *New York Times*, 15 January 1990, p. 5.
45 *Japan Times*, 9 November 1989, p. 12.
46 *Japan Times*, 12 July 1990, p. 1.
47 *Far Eastern Economic Review* (23 August 1990): 32.
48 *Far Eastern Economic Review* (19 July 1990): 57–58.
49 *Japan Times*, 8 June (p. 1), 25 June (p. 1), 27 June (p. 3), and 1 July (p. 3) 1989.
50 *Renmin Ribao*, 19 May (p. 1), and 21 May (p. 1) 1990.
51 *China Daily*, 1 June 1990, p. 1.
52 *Japan Times*, 3 May 1990, p. 7.
53 *Japan Times*, 11 May 1990, p. 1.
54 Takashi Nagai and Tetsuro Taniuchi, Director and staff of the Evaluation Division of the Foreign Affairs Ministry, interview with the author, 21 December 1993, Tokyo.
55 Ministry of Foreign Affairs, *Japan's ODA 1992*, Tokyo: Association for Promotion of International Cooperation, 1993.
56 Yoshio Nomoto, Director of the China and Mongolia Division of the Foreign Affairs Ministry, interview with the author, 17 December 1993, Tokyo.
57 'Hosokawa Renews Pledges to Beijing', *Japan Times* (Weekly International Edition), 28 March–3 April 1994, pp. 1, 5.
58 Hisane Masaki, 'Aid Policy toward China Comes under Review', *The Japan Times* (Weekly International Edition), 22–28 November 1993, p. 3.
59 Michihiko Kunihiro, Japanese Ambassador to China, interview with the author, 19 December 1993, Tokyo; Reichiro Takahashi, Deputy Director of the Technical Cooperation Division of the Foreign Affairs Ministry, interview with the author, 16 December 1993, Tokyo.

60 Masato Kitera, Director of the Grant Aid Division of the Foreign Affairs Ministry, and Kaoru Shimazaki, Deputy Director, Loan Aid Division of the Foreign Affairs Ministry, interview with the author, 21 December 1993, Tokyo.

61 Akio Suzuki, staff director of the Japan–China Economic Association, interview with the author, 20 December 1993, Tokyo.

62 Nobuo Maruyama, Director of the Economic Cooperation Department of the Institute of Developing Economics, interview with the author, 17 December 1993, Tokyo.

63 Michio Kanda, Director, Takumi Ueshima and Jitsuo Takasugi, staff members, Planning Department of the Japan International Cooperation Agency, interview with the author, 22 December 1993, Tokyo.

64 *Japan Times*, 4 July (p. 1), and 14 November (p. 1) 1989.

65 'Li Peng on Domestic and World Issues', *Beijing Review*, 32, 49 (4–10 December 1989): 12–14.

66 *Japan Times*, 30 December 1989, p. 1.

67 *Japan Times*, 24 January 1990, p. 1.

68 'Foreign Minister Qian Meets the Press', *Beijing Review*, 33, 15 (9–15 April 1990): 17.

69 *Korea Herald*, 28 March 1990, p. 1.

70 *Japan Times*, 17 April 1990, p. 1.

71 *Renmin Ribao*, 4 May (p. 1), 5 May (p. 1), and 14 May (p. 1) 1990. Also Henry Cutter, 'Politicians Prepare to Restore China Aid'.

72 Huang Xueqi, Division Director of the International Trade and Economic Affairs Department of the Chinese Foreign Trade Ministry, interview with the author, 25 December 1993, Beijing.

73 Yang Lianghua, 'Excellent Cooperation Mechanisms', *Renmin Ribao* (Overseas Edition), 15 November 1993, p. 2.

74 'Zhu: China Needs Japan's Technology', *China Daily*, 28 February 1994, p. 1.

75 'Beijing Warned Nuke Test May Affect Aid', *The Japan Times* (Weekly International Edition), 20–26 June 1994, p. 2.

76 'Loan Team to Beijing Protests Nuclear Test', *The Japan Times* (Weekly International Edition), 24–30 October 1994, p. 2.

77 'Japan: Aid to China Cut', *Far Eastern Economic Review* (1 June 1995): 13; and 'Ri jian jingyuan kangyi beijing heshi' [Japan Reduces Economic Aid To Protest Beijing's Nuclear Test], *Yazhou Zhoukan* [The International Chinese Newsweekly] (10 September 1995): 62.

78 'Minzu zhuyi gaozhang yu beijing de qiangying waijiao', [The Rise Of Nationalism And Beijing's Tough Diplomacy], *Yazhou Zhoukan* [The International Chinese Newsweekly] (1 October 1995): 8.

79 *Yazhou Zhoukan* [The International Chinese Newsweekly] (5 November 1995): 18–19.

80 Huang Xueqi, Division Director of the International Trade and Economic Affairs Department of the Chinese Foreign Trade Ministry, interview with the author, 25 December 1993, Beijing.

81 Yu Zhensheng, Deputy Chief of the Fifth (Japan) Division of the Foreign Financing Administration Bureau of the Ministry of Foreign Trade and Economic Cooperation of China, interview with the author, 7 January 1994, Beijing.

82 Yang Lianghua, 'Excellent Cooperation Mechanisms'.

83 'Hosokawa Renews Pledges to Beijing', *Japan Times* (Weekly International Edition), 28 March–3 April 1994, pp. 1, 5.

84 Charles Smith, 'Eager to Please: Tokyo Sets Aside Own Rules in China Aid Package', *Far Eastern Economic Review* (26 January 1995): 25–26.

85 Sun Yongfu, Deputy Director, the Planing Division of the International Exchange Center of the Ministry of Foreign Trade and Economic Cooperation, interview with the author, Cambridge, Massachusetts, 19 March 1994.

86 Yu Chuanmei, Department Chief, the Department of International Finance and Foreign Economy of the Tianjin Commission of Foreign Economic Relations and Trade, and Yu Xiuru, Director Engineer of the Tianjin Post and Telecommunication Administration, interview with the author, 11 January 1994, Tianjin, China.
87 Long Yongtu, General Director of the International Trade and Economic Affairs Bureau of the Ministry of Foreign Trade and Economic Cooperation of China, interview with the author, 4 January 1994, Beijing.
88 'Japan's New Gospel: Kaifu Signals Tokyo's Desire for Influence in Asia', *Far Eastern Economic Review* (17 May 1990): 13.

PART III

CONCLUSIONS: CHINESE FOREIGN POLICY IN THE POST-COLD WAR ERA

7 Modernization, Nationalism, and Regionalism

Three key words, *modernization*, *nationalism*, and *regionalism*, can be used to illuminate the basic trends of Chinese foreign policy in the post-Cold War era. Modernization, China's concentration on economic growth, has served as a basic guideline for China's internal and external activities. Nationalism[1] has emerged as a leading ideological current behind China's drive toward modernization. In the post-Cold War era, nationalistic sentiment appears particularly strong among Chinese intellectuals and government officials as well as other circles of Chinese society. Regionalism[2] emphasizes that, despite its global aspirations, the PRC has remained a power within Asia. Beijing has confined China's international political, economic, and military activities primarily to the Asia-Pacific region.

This chapter examines these three trends as they are manifest in China's foreign relations in the Asia-Pacific area, namely Japan, the Korean Peninsula, South-East Asia, Russia, and the United States, as well as the issue of Taiwan. The purpose here is not to provide comprehensive pictures of China's bilateral relations with the selected countries; but rather to use these cases to demonstrate the influences that act upon Chinese foreign policy and to illuminate Beijing's external behaviour patterns and policy choices. To elaborate these points, some historical background will also be discussed. This exercise will demonstrate how to apply the micro-macro linkage model (by examining different factors at the micro and macro levels in actual specific incidents) to explain shifts in Chinese foreign policy.

Although people now regard the PRC more as a regional rather than global power,[3] no one doubts that it remains a major player in East and South-East Asian regional affairs. From Beijing's perspective, the combined area of East and South-East Asia has remained one of the most important areas of consideration for Chinese foreign policy, not only in the military and political dimensions, but also in the economic dimension, which has direct implications for China's modernization drive.

From Table 7.1, one can see that China's regional trading partners, ranked by size, in 1994 were: Asia (US$142.2 billion), Europe (US$43.8 billion), North America (US$38.6 billion), Latin America (US$4.7 billion), Oceania (US$4.6 billion), and Africa (US$2.6 billion). It is clear that China's foreign trade with Asian countries is more than that of the countries outside of Asia combined. East and South-East Asia, as shown in Figure 7.1, constituted the main bulk of the trading activities, accounting for 55 per cent of China's foreign trade; and trade within 'Greater China'[4] — with Taiwan, Hong Kong, and Macau — has also ranked prominently.[5]

Empirical case studies of Chinese foreign policy in the areas of East and South-East Asia, which can be considered China's priority region, are quite meaningful to the study of China's foreign policy as whole.

In addition to economic and trade relations, security issues within the Asia-Pacific region are another factor of paramount concern to Beijing. Of immediate concern are China's territorial disputes over Xisha (Paracel) and Nansha (Spratly) Islands with Vietnam and several Association of South-East Asian Nations (ASEAN) states. The arms race in East Asia is a notable and potentially worrying trend affecting security issues in the region. According to a Pentagon study released in early 1995, Asia will become the world's biggest importer of arms by the end of the decade. Between 1994 and 2000, East Asia will account for 30 per cent of global demand for arms, and South Asia will count for five per cent. It estimated that the Asian market as a whole will be worth US$76 billion to US$87 billion over the six-year period. Taiwan is expected to be Asia's largest buyer, followed by Japan and South Korea.[6] Facing this situation, the United States has decided to maintain its troop strength in East Asia steady at about 100,000 men, rather than to reduce their numbers as previously planned.[7]

In order to get more detailed pictures of China's economic and security interests in the Asia-Pacific, let us look at China's most important bilateral relations in the region.

Japan: China's Most Important Asian Partner

Chinese foreign policy toward Japan, now China's most important neighbour/partner in Asia, has been greatly influenced by the changes of symbolic macrostructure, namely Beijing's changing perception and interpretation of Japan. From the victory of the Communists in 1949 to

Table 7.1: China's Major Trading Partners, 1994 (Unit: US$1 million)

Region and Selected Countries	Export	Import	Total Value (US$1 million)
Asia	73446.70	68765.15	142211.85
Japan	21573.12	26320.77	49893.89
Within Greater China	35273.16	23673.45	58946.67
Hong Kong	32364.51	9456.62	41821.16
Macau	666.50	132.00	798.50
Taiwan	2242.15	14084.83	16326.98
Korea (North)	424.52	199.22	623.74
Korea (South)	4402.30	7318.34	11720.65
ASEAN	6379.01	6829.85	13208.85
Brunei	16.26	0	16.26
Indonesia	1051.70	1588.37	2640.07
Malaysia	1117.66	1622.67	2740.32
Philippines	475.69	272.40	748.09
Singapore	2558.42	2482.02	5040.44
Thailand	1159.28	864.39	2023.67
Burma	369.11	143.28	512.39
Cambodia	35.27	1.00	36.27
Laos	35.97	4.38	40.36
Vietnam	341.66	149.19	532.82
Africa	1749.05	893.98	2643.03
Europe	18803.98	25040.20	43844.19
EEC	14580.23	16938.76	31518.99
United Kingdom	2414.00	1769.90	4183.91
Germany	4761.45	7136.73	11898.23
France	1424.36	1939.01	3363.37
Italy	1590.66	3068.06	4658.72
Former USSR	1946.55	4662.58	6609.13
Russia	1581.14	3495.75	5076.89
Latin America	2454.75	2247.38	4702.13
North America	22860.16	15801.30	38661.46
Canada	1396.94	1830.75	3227.69
USA	21461.48	13970.42	35431.90
Oceania	1723.84	2915.61	4639.45
Australia	1487.87	2451.81	3939.68

Source: *China's Latest Economic Statistics*, February 1995, pp. 19–23

Figure 7.1 China's Foreign Trade (1994)

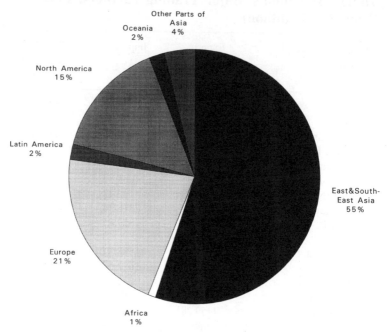

the early 1970s, Chinese policy toward Japan was strongly influenced by the Cold War. During this period, China regarded Japan as a 'running dog of American imperialism'. Since China began to normalize its relations with Japan in 1972, this view has changed substantially and much progress has been made in developing diplomatic relations. Today, China uses quite different phrases to describe Japan, phrases such as 'good neighbour' and 'good friend', despite sporadic problems between the two countries, which will be discussed below.

This new perception of Japan is also reflected in economic matters. Since the normalization of relations between the two countries in 1972, bilateral trade has been flourishing. Japan has been a major source of capital, technology, and manufactured imports to China. In 1993, for example, Japan was China's foremost foreign trading partner. Sino-Japanese trade was about one-third higher than the size of Sino-US trade in terms of total value. Japan has a large share of Chinese markets in virtually every field except aircraft technology, which is dominated by the US Companies. Since the beginning of the 1990s, Japanese direct investment in China has also picked up momentum. In the first six months of the 1994 fiscal year (April to September), for example, China was the second largest destination for Japan's overseas direct investment. It reached US$1.14 billion, a 63.5 per cent increase from the same period the year before, next only to that in the United States (US$6.60 billion), and it exceeded Japanese direct investment in Britain (US$1.08 billion).[8]

Understandably, the increase in Sino-Japanese economic relations has also brought some problems. In much of the 1980s, for example, China criticized Japanese protectionism against Chinese goods, while Japan claimed that China should better control its imports of consumer goods, such as imported passenger cars, which could be easily controlled by the Chinese government. In the area of technology transfer, China was pressing Japan to increase its export of high technology, while Japan was restrained by its membership in the Coordinating Committee of the Consultative Group (COCOM), as mentioned in Chapter 5 (see Note 37 in Chapter 5), until it disbanded in 1994.[9]

China's institutional macrostructure was also a source of influence on the perception of Japan. With their strong desire for modernization, the Chinese were seeking models for their own economic and political development and see Japan, which was closer culturally and socially to China than was Europe or the United States, as a prototype that would permit more rapid Chinese economic development and satisfy popular demands for democratization.

The political development of post-war Japan prior to 1993 created a situation in which one large party — the Liberal Democratic Party (LDP) — functioned as the ruling party, and several minor parties served as the opposition. This phenomenon of one-party domination has set an example as a transitional stage for political development in several other East Asian societies, such as South Korea (where the Democratic Liberal Party was dominant) and Taiwan (where the Kuomintang controlled the government). The Japan model, therefore, may be referred to as an East Asian transitional model for democratic development. Beijing is aware that this model offers a way for the Communists to maintain their rule in China while allowing opposition forces to exist. Japan's so-called '1955 political system',[10] which was fundamentally democratic in nature and thus likely to meet the growing demand for democracy, seems flexible enough to meet various social demands and yet stable enough to meet the requirements of high-speed economic development with little political and social turmoil. As such, although it has not found favour among China's leadership in the Deng era, the 'East Asian transitional model' may prove attractive to the next generation of China's political leaders as a transitional step towards democracy.

China's interests in Japan have become more diversified as it has also increased its bilateral cultural and social exchanges with Japan. For instance, in 1992 there were approximately 50,000 Chinese students in Japan. While many of them were pursuing advanced studies, about one-half were so-called 'language students' who work and earn money in Japan under the premise of studying the language.[11] An increase in such bilateral exchanges will have a direct impact on the direction of China's political and economic development.

The issue of 'Japanese militarism' is another important subject that reflects Beijing's changing interpretation of Tokyo's intentions towards China. This issue also, on some occasions, involved the dynamics of China's domestic mood and its power politics (the power/regime macrostructure). Due to the bitter memory of Japan's invasion of China during World War II, China's fears of Japanese militarism are sincere and enduring. However, Beijing has shown itself prepared either to play down or to emphasize those fears, depending upon it's changing policy agenda.

In the 1960s and early 1970s, Beijing's concern about Japanese militarism was primarily motivated by international–diplomatic considerations. After the 1969 Sato–Nixon joint communique, which stated that 'the maintenance of peace and security in the Taiwan area was also a most important factor for the security of Japan',[12] Zhou Enlai accused Eisaku Sato's government of increased militarism and of pursuing Japan's wartime goal of a 'Greater East Asia Co-prosperity Sphere'.[13] During a visit to North Korea in the spring of 1970, Zhou argued vigorously that 'Japanese militarism has revived and has become a dangerous force of aggression in Asia.'[14]

However, in response to the international environment, which was marked by competition and hostility between the United States and the Soviet Union, Mao Zedong eventually came to view Japan and Western Europe as intermediate zones between the 'revolutionary forces' of the Third World countries and the two 'reactionary' superpowers. China sought to cultivate friendly relations with Japan and Western European countries. Beijing's need for economic development also prompted it to seek closer relations with Tokyo and to reduce the Chinese media's criticism of 'Japanese militarism' through its political control of all the news media in China. Such criticism disappeared completely after Kakuei Tanaka became Japanese prime minister in 1972. At that time, China launched a new campaign calling for 'Sino-Japanese friendship' and 'normalization of relations', believing that the transition from Sato to Tanaka presented China with the best opportunity to conduct direct contacts with the Japanese government. By the late 1970s, China was actively seeking an international coalition to counter Soviet expansionism, and had not only ceased opposition to Japan's rearmament, but was actually seeking closer defence relations with Japan (Newby, 1988: 70).

By the beginning of the 1980s, Beijing's concern about Japanese militarism was rooted chiefly in China's domestic development, namely the rising nationalism of Chinese intellectuals and other circles of Chinese society, an ideological current strengthened by the drive toward modernization. In 1982, the issue of militarism reappeared as a result of the 'textbook controversy'. Japan's Ministry of Education was sharply criticized by liberal and left-wing domestic forces and Japan's Asian neighbours (including China, Thailand, Hong Kong, and North and South Korea) for revising the description of Japan's wartime behaviour in school textbooks. Rather than stating that Japan had 'invaded' China and other parts of Asia, the Japanese Ministry of Education changed the wording to 'entered', a policy which provoked protests throughout East and South-East Asia. Beijing launched a full-scale campaign attacking Japan's militaristic tendencies. The campaign continued until Tokyo promised to review the disputed terminology prior to Prime Minister Zenko Suzuki's visit to Beijing to mark the tenth anniversary of normalized relations. Suzuki reportedly spent a considerable amount of his time in Beijing reassuring the Chinese leaders of Japan's position.

The textbook controversy resurfaced in 1985 and 1986, when new editions of the textbooks with similar sanitized descriptions of Japan's actions in World War II were published. The problem was further exacerbated by Prime Minister Nakasone's official visit to the Yasukuni Shrine to honor Japanese killed in World War II. The shrine contains the remains not only of Japanese soldiers but also of a number of Japanese war criminals, including General Hideki Tojo, the commander-in-chief of the Japanese army in China during the war. Following Nakasone's visit, China's news media launched a new wave of criticism against Japanese militarism, triggering student demonstrations in Beijing, Shanghai, and other major Chinese cities, and giving expression to popular nationalistic sentiment.

China's response to Japan's 'militarism' is an example of a shift from the predominant influence of the symbolic macrostructure to that of the power/regime macrostructure. As a result, Beijing's concern shifted from external to internal considerations. In the early 1970s, the primary purpose of criticizing Japan's 'revived militarism' was to challenge Prime Minister Sato's conservative position in the hopes that a pro-Beijing leader would replace Sato, thereby accelerating Sino-Japanese rapprochement. Once normalization was realized, however, Japan was viewed as a friendly country and the issue of militarism at the symbolic macrostructure in bilateral relations became much less important.

In the 1980s, the main concerns behind the issue of 'Japanese militarism', sparked by the textbook controversy, shifted to domestic factors. Among the Chinese people, this controversy aroused nationalistic feelings. For the Beijing government, the affair offered an opportunity both to promote nationalism at home and to pressure Japan to make political and economic concessions. There was, for example, an indirect link between the militarism issue and the Sino-Japanese trade imbalance, expressed by Chinese student demonstrators in such slogans as 'Down with the Japanese economic invasion!'

The issue of Japan policy was also a factor in Beijing's power politics. The 1986 student demonstrations were patriotic in nature and initially corresponded with Beijing's official line. But these demonstrations also provided students with an opportunity to express their dissatisfaction with the corruption of the Chinese leadership and the slow pace of economic and political reforms. This dissatisfaction eventually led to student unrest in a dozen or so Chinese cities and triggered a new power struggle in Beijing. The result of this round of struggle for power was the downfall in January 1987 of Party General Secretary Hu Yaobang, who suffered many criticisms, one of which was his mishandling of Japan-related issues. This foreign policy issue was therefore also used as a powerful weapon for the power struggle in domestic politics (see also Chapter 5, note 17).

After the power struggle settled, Beijing became concerned about the domestic consequences of its anti-Japanese campaign and felt the need to mend its relations with Tokyo. Consequently, the issue of militarism was dropped for the time being; instead the government used propaganda to effect a gradual change in popular perceptions of Japan (Whiting, 1989: 193–6), which corresponded with a change in overall relations between the two countries.

With sufficient provocation and an appropriate domestic environment, however, the militarism issue could reappear. A more recent concern about Japan's militarism came in summer 1994. A Chinese navy-sponsored magazine *Xiandai Jianchuan* (Modern Naval Vessels) published an article warning that Japan's navy was no longer exclusively defence-oriented and the country's capability to project military power must be monitored carefully. Citing Japan's dispatches of forces abroad for UN peacekeeping operations, and minesweepers for operations in the Persian Gulf area, the article further suggested that 'Japan is probing world opinion regarding its embarkation on a new militaristic path.'[15]

In the APEC summit meeting held in November 1994 in Jakarta, Chinese President Jiang Zemin had a 45-minute meeting with Japanese Prime Minister Tomiichi Murayama. Jiang made a clear warning to Japan with his statements that: 'Militarism sometimes comes to the surface inside Japan' (referring to the repeated gaffes by Japanese ministers as they attempted to whitewash Japan's wartime history); and 'Japan must reflect on its history and it is important that you educate your youth on this.'[16] On the other hand, Japan has also felt uneasy about China's military development. In October 1994, Japanese Defence Agency chief Tokuichiro Tamazawa told US Defence Secretary William Perry that Japan is 'anxious about [the increase in] the transparency' of China's defence budget.[17]

The negotiations for the 1978 Sino-Japanese Peace Treaty is a good example to illuminate how macrostructural changes affected Beijing's diplomatic strategies and tactics at the micro level and vice versa. The normalization of relations between China and Japan in 1972 was propelled by the changing international environment, most notably the beginnings of Sino-US rapprochement marked by the 1972 visit of President Richard Nixon to Beijing. China and Japan agreed to begin talks for a peace treaty in September 1974, but agreement was not reached on the treaty until 1978. Two issues precluded an earlier agreement: China's insistence on an 'anti-hegemony clause' in the treaty and a dispute over the islands the Chinese call 'Diaoyu' and the Japanese know as 'Senkaku'.

Diaoyu, a cluster of unpopulated rocky islands located between Taiwan and the Ryukyu Islands, has long been a point of dispute between Beijing and Tokyo, both of which claim ownership of the islands, which are reported to lie in an area possessing significant oil deposits.

In the 1970s, the dispute triggered anti-Japanese demonstrations in Taiwan. The controversy further intensified in April 1978 when more than 100 Chinese fishing boats sailed around the islands. At that time it appeared that the dispute, if not rapidly resolved, could jeopardize negotiations for a Sino-Japanese peace treaty. Before the disagreement worsened, a Chinese vice foreign minister stated that 'both sides have agreed to handle the territorial problem by separating it from the negotiations for the proposed treaty'. In his 1978 visit to Japan, Deng

Xiaoping deflected queries about the islands by suggesting that the issue could be 'handled better by the next generation' (Whiting, 1989: 68–9). The dispute was shelved and did not feature in the negotiations for the peace treaty.

Zhou Enlai first raised the condition that the anti-hegemony principle form the bedrock of future Sino-Japanese relations in January 1975 (Park, 1976: 477). Chinese polemics against the Soviet Union as a 'major hegemonistic power' left little doubt as to the target of an anti-hegemony clause. Japan, however, was strongly opposed to such a clause, claiming that it symbolically identified the Soviet Union as an expansionist power and that Japanese acceptance could be construed as alignment with China against the Soviet Union. Beijing was unwilling to concede, and reluctantly Tokyo agreed to include the clause in the peace treaty. Beijing then agreed to insert an additional clause stipulating that 'relations with any third nation [i.e. the Soviet Union] would not be affected by the treaty'.[18] In this indirect way, Beijing succeeded in bringing Japan into the anti-Soviet united front together with the United States and Western Europe, strengthening the recently created, new structure of world politics in the late 1970s — a structure that favoured China's concerns for security and modernization.

Clearly, the Beijing leadership assigned different priorities to the anti-hegemony clause and the dispute with Japan over the islands. For Beijing, the anti-hegemony clause was metaphorical of its attempts to establish an international united front against Soviet expansionism — perhaps its major preoccupation at the time — and thus the inclusion of such a clause was not a demand to be bartered away. By contrast, the Diaoyu dispute was perceived by Beijing as having no immediate importance — and certainly not worth interrupting the peace treaty process for — and thus the Beijing leadership showed flexibility on this issue. The different priority accorded the two issues was further demonstrated by Beijing's threat that if Japan did not agree to the anti-hegemony clause, the Diaoyu Islands would become an endless territorial dispute.[19] This example shows how the Diaoyu issue was used to further a higher priority goal. At the same time, Beijing was careful not to abandon its claim to the island, which was, and still is, occupied by the Japanese. In fact, in 1992, China intensified its claim when the National People's Congress passed the Law of the People's Republic of China on its Territorial Waters and Contiguous Areas. This stipulated that China's territorial sovereignty included the Diaoyu Islands, among others (S. Kim, 1994a: 150–151). In addition, Beijing repeatedly called for

Sino-Japanese joint development of the disputed area (Tian, 1993: 631–632). The issue remains a source of tension between the two countries.

Beijing's keen concern over regime legitimacy in the international community can be found in the disputes around the issue of Taiwan in Sino-Japanese relations. Even though Japan issued a number of official statements in 1972 declaring Taiwan to be Chinese territory, Taiwan continued to remain a potentially volatile issue between China and Japan. Not least because Japan ruled Taiwan as a colony for so long, some Japanese were keen to pursue a special relationship with Taiwan, and would, therefore, have preferred the status quo of separation in the Taiwan Straits. Such opinions irritated the Chinese government, which viewed any suggestion of 'two Chinas' or 'one China, one Taiwan' as an impermissible assault on China's territorial integrity. Despite its pursuit of closer relations with Japan, China was inflexible on the Taiwan issue. For instance, there was a continuing controversy surrounding a student dormitory in Kyoto called 'Guanghua Hostel' (*Kokaruo* in Japanese). Both Beijing and Taipei claimed ownership of this dormitory on Japanese soil, and Japan was caught in the middle. For Tokyo, this was a legal dispute that had to be resolved in the courts and in which the government should not intervene. For Beijing, the issue concerned its national sovereignty and was considered a test of Japan's professed belief about the status of Taiwan.[20]

The unhappy episode between the two countries was brought to a head during the Asian Games in Hiroshima in October 1994, when Taiwan's vice-premier Hsu Li-teh was invited to attend the Games. This, coupled with Taiwan's President Lee Teng-hui's failed attempt to visit Japan at the same time brought about strong protests from Beijing.[21] At one point, Beijing even considered boycotting the Asian Games because of the Taiwan problem.[22] During the next month's APEC forum meeting in Jakarta, Japanese Prime Minister Tomiichi Murayama in his meeting with Chinese President Jiang Zemin, attempted to ease strained ties with Beijing by reiterating that Tokyo does not support the development of 'two Chinas'. 'Frankly speaking,' Jiang told Murayama, 'opposition [against Japan] appeared among the Chinese people following Hsu's attendance at the Asian Games. But the Chinese government has been coping with the problem with restraint.'[23] Nevertheless, after President Bill Clinton allowed Lee Teng-hui in the summer of 1995 to visit his *alma mater* Cornell University in the United States, there was speculation that Japan may eventually open the way for Lee to visit Japan under the name of visiting his *alma mater* Kyoto University.[24]

Whatever the case, the Taiwan issue will more than likely remain a sour point in Sino-Japanese relations.

When one looks at the future directions of Chinese foreign policy toward Japan, one should pay close attention to the macrostructure within which the two countries must function. Despite such contentious issues as Japanese militarism, the fact that Japan is China's foremost trading partner and that China's markets will become increasingly important to Japan will ensure that Sino-Japanese relations remain close. It is widely recognized that the most important bilateral relationship in East Asian regional affairs is that between China and Japan.

This relationship, of course, is of great interest to the United States. During the last 100 years, the triangular relationship between China, Japan, and the United States has been unstable, with alliances and allegiances often shifting. Today, none of the three nations is forced to choose between the other two as friend or enemy and the three countries share many common interests. The United States and Japan see China as a basis for stability and prosperity in East Asia, and both have supported China's modernization drive since the 1970s. China no longer opposes the US–Japanese military security agreement, and both the United States and China support Japan's demand for the return of the disputed northern islands occupied by Russia since the end of World War II, and would like to see Japan's security guaranteed.

None the less, differences do exist. Japan fears China's continued nuclear testing and development of capabitilities and the apparent growth of PLA-controlled capital. China continues to view Japan as highly nationalistic and is therefore sensitive about the rearming of Japan; in contrast, the United States views Japan as an essentially democratic and pacifist nation. Cooperation will be necessary to maintain stability among the three countries. Considering the changing directions of the symbolic macrostructure among these countries, policies such as human rights and high-technology transfers to China may require further coordination between Japan and the United States, and China and the United States may need to consult more closely on the subject of Japan's rearmament and the regional security issues in general.

The Korean Peninsula: The Balance Between North and South

The two major themes of modernization and regionalism have played a leading role in China's shift in policy toward the Korean Peninsula.

This can also be explained from the perspective of the changing symbolic macrostructure. In the 1950s, the PRC, inspired by its perceived threat of invasion by Western imperialists, participated in the Korean war and provided substantial military support to the North Koreans in its war with the South. Strategic and political calculations most definitely dominated the PRC's Korea policy in this period. Beijing also learned lessons from the Korean war which proved very costly for China in terms of casualties, the political implications for China's foreign policy, and the evolution of East Asian international relations.

With the changing international and domestic environments, Beijing made substantial adjustment to its Korea policy. Despite its openly stated alignment with Pyongyang, China long ago (since the complete withdrawal of its military forces from the North in 1958) ceased to support a North Korean military attack on the South. Since the opening of the Deng era, Beijing has consistently expressed interest in avoiding another major military conflict; it has, therefore, a particular interest in the creation and maintenance of a peaceful and stable situation on the Korean Peninsula which would lead to the peaceful unification of North and South Korea. Beijing hailed the talks that took place in September 1990 between North Korean Prime Minister Yon Hyoung Muk and South Korean Premier Kang Yong Hun as 'a good beginning' that 'will help alleviate tensions and promote the process of Korean reunification'.[25] Beijing has also encouraged both Pyongyang and Seoul to create a nuclear-free Korean Peninsula,[26] a move that would be in line with China's national interests.

There have been sporadic quarrels between Beijing and Pyongyang during the past several decades; the nadir occurred in 1969, the peak of China's chaotic Cultural Revolution, when Chinese and North Korean forces clashed along their border.[27] The PRC nevertheless managed to maintain a workable relationship with North Korea. High-level bilateral visits took place virtually every year. Political developments in China and Eastern Europe since the late 1980s brought Beijing and Pyongyang closer together. Kim Il Sung was one of the few world leaders who openly supported Deng Xiaoping's military suppression of student demonstrations in Tiananmen Square 1989.

From the 1960s to the mid-1980s, Pyongyang was able to play the 'Beijing card' against the 'Moscow card', effectively preventing China from moving closer to Seoul. As the international situation changed, especially after the Soviet Union and Eastern European countries established diplomatic relations with South Korea, the PRC gained more freedom and confidence in expanding its relations with South Korea. In fact, in the post-Cold War era, beginning with the late 1980s, Beijing has had strong incentives to develop relations with Seoul, because a closer relationship might increase China's leverage in dealing with the Korean problem and with East Asia as a whole. As one US official in Washington suggests, 'Having good relations with both [Koreas] puts China in the best possible situation' in world politics as well as regional affairs.[28]

Several events that took place in the year 1990 were described in a *Beijing Review* article as indicative of South Korea's shedding 'the cloak of the Cold War'. These events were the establishment of diplomatic relations between South Korea and the Soviet Union; three meetings between the prime ministers of North and South Korea; and the decision by China and South Korea to set up non-governmental trade offices in each other's capitals. These developments are seen as part of the 'realignment of relations among Asian nations.'[29]

The changes in institutional macrostructure and power/regime macrostructure have also played a major role in the evolution of China's policy toward Korea, a policy that was significantly altered in September 1992, when China finally agreed to establish official diplomatic relations with South Korea. It had taken more than two years for Beijing to follow Moscow's lead in establishing relations with Seoul.

Beijing's need for North Korean support for the survival of the Chinese Communist regime after the Tiananmen Incident became a potential obstacle to establishing relations with South Korea. Beijing and Pyongyang were isolated at that time, both from the other remaining socialist countries and from the international community at large, and relied on each other for moral support. The collapse of Soviet Communism and the development of political democratization and pluralization in the former Soviet Union and Eastern Europe caused alarm in Beijing. In some countries, local communist parties formally relinquished their monopoly of political power; in others, their power simply collapsed. Beijing's leaders were pleased to announce to the Chinese people that Kim Il Sung firmly supported the 1989 military crackdown against the student demonstrations that was ordered by Deng Xiaoping. This political and moral support was highlighted when Kim Il Sung paid his 29th visit to China in October 1991.[30]

Furthermore, these mutual moral supports between the two countries translated into personal relations at the micro level. The Chinese attachment to North Korea throughout the 1980s was underpinned by personal ties and sympathies. Leaders such as Deng Xiaoping, Chen Yun, Yang Shangkun, Li Xiannian, Peng Zhen, Wang Zhen, and Bo Yibo held leading positions during the 1950s, and were personally involved to varying degrees in the Korean War. Their contemporaries in North Korea, headed by Kim Il Sung, also retained power. This decades-long friendship was sustained and enhanced through frequent, mutual public or private visits.

In the aftermath of the Tiananmen Incident, the struggle for succession to political authority from the aging leadership became the predominant concern of the Chinese Communist Party. This struggle had a profoundly deadening effect on all aspects of Chinese domestic and foreign policy, rendering the formulation of new initiatives and imaginative policy virtually impossible. It was much more difficult for the Beijing leadership at that time to break or downplay its ties with North Korea than it was for Gorbachev, who shared with Kim Il Sung neither age nor personal ties.

On the other hand, however, China had long since shifted its domestic priorities from political campaigning to economic modernization. Economic development was one of Beijing's primary incentives for normalizing relations with South Korea. China's modernization programmes cannot be realized without extensive external support and exchanges from industrialized countries that can provide advanced technology, capital, markets, and managerial skills. South Korea was an obvious nearby supplier of these sources, and the addition of Korean suppliers to those from Japan and the West, would help to diversify China's sources.

South Korea has become increasingly important as a trading partner for China. In 1993, Sino-South Korean trade reached US$8.2 billion, far exceeding trade with North Korea of US$899.6 million. In his November 1995 state visit to South Korea, President Jiang Zemin re-emphasized the importance of China's ties with South Korea, and projected that bilateral trade in 1995 would reach the level of US$15 billion.[31]

As a newly industrialized country and a close neighbour, South Korea is also able to provide China with valuable experience and lessons in terms of economic development strategy, especially in 'export-led' industrialization. South Korean businessmen began to conduct direct investment and joint ventures in China, most notably in Shandong province. In April 1994, for example, South Korean Technology Minister Kim Si Joong announced that conglomerates, including Samsung and Hanjin (the owner of Korean Air), would help China produce mid-sized commercial airplanes.[32]

The first official step toward enhancing bilateral relations was an agreement to set up trade offices in each other's capitals in October 1990. South Korea quickly appointed a former assistant foreign minister as the head representative of its trade office, and both offices formally opened in the spring of 1991. This led to the normalization of relationship between the two countries the following year.

Yet, China has had to balance its actions between the two Koreas to meet various demands from both external and internal fronts. It appears to be in China's best interest to maintain a warm relationship simultaneously with North and South Korea. Beijing is believed to have a certain degree of influence over Pyongyang in terms of North Korea's policy toward Seoul. In May of 1991, for example, North Korea announced a dramatic reversal of its 'one Korea' policy, saying that it would seek separate United Nations membership, a move which South Korea had been demanding. This policy shift was reportedly based on Kim Il Sung's idea of a 'federal system', that is, 'one nation, one country, two systems and two governments', which is supported by the PRC.[33] Beijing is reported to have played a key role in Pyongyang's sudden shift,[34] engaging in much behind-the-scenes manœuvring. In late 1990, Beijing made it clear to Pyongyang that China would not commit itself to meeting North Korea's demand for a veto of any South Korean application to join the United Nations.[35] In April and May of the following year, Beijing and Pyongyang held frequent consultations on the UN membership issue, including a visit by Chinese Premier Li Peng to North Korea in early May.[36] Immediately after North Korea's announcement to seek separate UN membership, Li Peng commented that this move was 'an interim measure before the unification', and would be 'welcomed by the international community, including China'.[37] The two Koreas now have separate UN memberships, a major step toward peaceful settlement in the Korea Peninsula.[38]

China's balancing act between its policies toward both countries, is also reflected in the controversial issue of nuclear development in North Korea. In the spring of 1994, the International Atomic Energy Agency (IAEA) under the United Nations unearthed fresh evidence of North Korea's clandestine nuclear programme. IAEA director Hans Blix called the Yongbyon facility, which Pyongyang described as a radiochemical laboratory, 'the most proliferation-sensitive facility' of North Korea's seven nuclear installations. Thereafter, Pyongyang was under tremendous pressure from Washington and Seoul (in addition to the threat of possible economic sanctions from the international community) to open further its nuclear installations for international inspection.[39] On one hand, while admitting that China did not have accurate information regarding North Korea's nuclear weapons development programme,[40] Beijing opposed economic sanctions on Pyongyang. In meeting with South Korean President Kim Young Sam and Foreign Minister Han

Sung Joo during their 26–30 March visit to Beijing, Chinese leaders made clear that China would oppose any economic sanctions on North Korea, and would even be reluctant to go along with a resolution from the United Nations Security Council. Rather, Beijing said it would like to have more time to 'work its persuasion on Pyongyang before any UN sanctions are imposed', and demanded that the Security Council downgrade from a resolution to a non-binding 'statement' its plea for inspections of the North's nuclear installations. A vote on a resolution would require China to go on record with either a veto or an abstention. A statement requires no vote.[41]

On the other hand, Beijing, Washington, Tokyo, and Moscow have already reached a consensus on prohibiting the development of nuclear weapons in the Korean Peninsula, particularly in North Korea. Such cooperation serves not only China's security interests, but also its economic interests.

The death of Kim Il Sung in July 1994 and his replacement by his son Kim Jong Il did not change China's policy toward the Korean Peninsula. In his October–November 1994 visit to Seoul, Chinese Premier Li Peng assured South Korean President Kim Young Sam that China was positive toward the Geneva nuclear accord signed between North Korea and the United States in September.[42] Soon after, Chinese President Jiang Zemin also expressed 'strong support' for the nuclear deal to US President Bill Clinton when the two met at the APEC summit in Jarkata.[43] At the same time, Beijing indicated that it supported replacing the Panmunjom armistice with a permanent peace treaty — a position strongly supported by Pyongyang, but not Seoul. These actions further demonstrated that China was playing both sides of the Korean equation, and Beijing was in favour of resolving the North's nuclear issue but without hurting its interests in the North.[44]

As Beijing strengthened its ties with Seoul, there were signs in the mid-1990s that the Beijing–Pyongyang relationship appeared to be cooling. In July 1995, for example, a North Korean official told an American group visiting Pyongyang, members of a delegation of the New York-based Council on Foreign Relations, 'If you need to balance China's growing power, you should establish relations with us.'[45] (This comment is reminiscent of the balancing game North Korea played between China and the Soviet Union during the 1970s and 1980s.) Bilateral economic exchanges also were reduced. According to an unpublished study by the American Enterprise Institute's Nicholas Eberstadt and three other scholars, China's food exports to North Korea dropped from US$149 million in 1993 to US$55 million in 1994, and its coal and oil exports fell from US$264 million to US$194 million.[46] It will be interesting for East Asian specialists to watch the changing dynamics of this triangular relationship among Beijing, Seoul, and Pyongyang as the twenty-first century approaches.

The future of Korea — specifically, the North–South conflict and the issue of Korean unification — is closely connected with China. As Jiang Zemin emphasized when he met Kim Il Sung in October 1991: 'China is concerned about the situation on the Korean Peninsula, since detente and stability in this region have a direct bearing on the overall situation in North-East Asia.'[47] The Chinese interest in Korean unification is also accentuated by the involvement of the United States, Japan, and Russia.[48]

There will also, inevitably, be problems between the two countries; their differing political systems and levels of economic development are sure to contribute to the friction. The ground for cooperation will, however, be much greater than that for conflict. Each side, for instance, may regard the other as a counterweight to the increasing economic and military strength of Japan. This possibility was further confirmed by the fact that during Jiang Zemin's visit to Seoul in November 1995, the Chinese president and South Korea's Kim Young Sam jointly condemned Japan's past militarism.

The Issue of Taiwan: A Top Priority

As discussed in earlier chapters, the Taiwan issue is an utmost priority in Beijing's foreign policy,[49] reflecting a deeply rooted nationalism among China's political leaders as well as its people. For Beijing, the Taiwan question is inextricably linked to issues of national sovereignty and regime legitimacy. The PRC's policy toward Taiwan is also closely tied with its interpretation of the domestic and international situation. By applying the micro-macro linkage model, one may arrive at a better understanding of the evolution of Beijing's policy toward Taiwan (see Table 7.2).

For most of the Mao era, the PRC's sense of vulnerability produced a determined assertion of its claims to Taiwan. During the 1950s and 1960s, the PRC was isolated by the West and excluded from major international organizations such as the United Nations. With the US Seventh Fleet stationed in the Taiwan Straits, Beijing viewed the United States as a major threat. Japan, which had occupied Taiwan for 50 years prior to 1945 and was firmly allied with the United States in the post-World War II era, was also considered a potential aggressor. These

Table 7.2: The Micro-Macro Linkage Model of the PRC's Taiwan Policy (1949-present)

Macro Structures	Macrostructural Change	Micro Processes in Beijing
Symbolic Macrostructure	The PRC's international status and domestic control have been enhanced; tendency toward *taidu* (independence) has increased in Taiwan.	Changed from 'liberation of Taiwan by force' to 'peaceful unification' and 'one country–two systems'; yet alarmed by *taidu*.
Institutional Macrostructure	Decision-making institutions are significantly affected by nationwide economic and political reforms.	Perceives much more diversified interests in PRC's Taiwan policy, affected by intertwined economic, political, and cultural exchanges across the Taiwan Straits.
Power/Regime Macrostructure	Power politics and regime legitimacy are less influenced by communist ideology, but more by regime survival and the rising nationalism.	More flexible in conducting bilateral negotiations and the conditions for eventual unification, yet standing firm in opposing 'two Chinas' and *taidu*; refusing to give up military means as an option.

concerns were the foundation for Beijing's uncompromising policy regarding Taiwan during the first three decades of the PRC's existence, a policy that left no room for concessions where the issues of sovereignty and regime legitimacy were involved. Prior to 1979, Beijing attached great importance to the restoration of Taiwan as a province of China, and insisted on the slogan of 'Liberate Taiwan'.

Since 1979, the PRC has experienced fundamental changes both domestically and internationally. Beijing's primary emphasis has gradually but surely shifted from revolution to modernization as explained in Chapter 3. These changes, and Beijing's establishment of official relations with the United States in 1979, have enabled the PRC to gain international recognition. All the major capitals of the world now recognize Beijing as the legitimate ruler of China and officially consider Taiwan to be a part of China. About 180 countries have established relations with the PRC; fewer than thirty small countries maintain relations with Taiwan (see Table 3.2).

International recognition has, in turn, changed Beijing's interpretation of the outside world. Beijing tends much less to perceive outside powers as threats than it did in the 1950s and 1960s, when China was isolated from the international community. It has new confidence in dealing with Taiwan, and, as a result, its attitude toward Taiwan has become much more conciliatory, with the Maoist slogan of 'Liberate Taiwan' giving way to Deng's proposals for 'peaceful unification' and 'one country-two systems'. This change of policy, corresponding to the initials from Taipei under the leadership of Chiang Ching-kuo and Lee Teng-hui, has brought unprecedented bilateral economic and cultural exchanges across the Taiwan Straits. This relatively peaceful environment, however, would change if there is a major policy shift in Taiwan. For Beijing, the most unwelcome scenario for the future of Taiwan would be a move by Taiwan to become a legally independent state — *taidu* in Chinese — which would force Beijing to discontinue its peace overture. Such a prospect appalls the leadership of the PRC, who, like the Chinese people as a whole, are deeply ingrained with Chinese nationalism. This possible development has been heightened by the PLA's missile tests and military exercises in the summer of 1995 and spring of 1996, in an attempt to warn Taiwan away from independence.

Beijing's obsession with protecting national sovereignty and regime legitimacy can be best demonstrated by an examination of the case of the Taiwan independence movement that has become popular among some sectors of the Taiwanese society, particularly within the leading opposition Democratic Progressive Party (DPP).

Since the early 1990s, Taiwan has worked hard to lobby for membership in the United Nations. At the 28-member General Committee of the United Nation's 49th General Assembly in late September 1994, there was a debate, instigated by several small pro-Taiwan states, on whether to establish an *ad hoc* committee to analyse 'the exceptional situation of Taiwan's status and recommend a solution at the 50th session'.[50] Beijing clearly opposed this move. Only seven delegations addressed the General Committee in favour of Taiwan (the draft was originally sponsored by 14 countries outside of the committee); the proposal then was defeated without a vote. Thus, another round of Taiwan-launched UN campaign was lost.[51] Nevertheless, this kind of campaigning by Taipei and resistence from Beijing is expected to continue for as long as the phenomenon of Beijing–Taipei rivalry exists in the international community.

Beijing's sensitivity toward regime legitimacy was further demonstrated by its strong reaction to the development of *taidu* activities on the island in the early 1990s.[52] The PRC was alarmed by Taiwan's diplomatic efforts to promoting itself within international community, such as:

- President Lee Teng-hui's nine-day diplomatic tour in early 1994 to Indonesia, the Philippines, and Thailand, in the name of a 'golfing holiday';[53]
- the Taiwan president's May 1994 visit to Nicaragua, Costa Rica, South Africa, and Swaziland — four of the 29 countries that officially recognize Taiwan;[54] and
- President Lee's April 1995 'private visits' to the United Arab Emirates and Jordan; and[55]
- Taiwan Premier Lien Chan's June 1994 secret visit to Mexico after an official visit to Central America.[56]

Soon after, Beijing began openly to criticizing Lee's '*taidu* tendency'. A series of articles in the *Renmin Ribao* (People's Daily) and in pro-Beijing newspapers in Hong Kong charged the native Taiwanese leader with discriminating against Chinese Mainlanders in his government and obstructing unification. 'Lee Teng-hui should rein in the horse at the edge of the precipice before committing a serious blunder', the *People's Daily* warned.[57]

The most direct challenge to Beijing was Lee's 'private visit' to the United States in June of 1995. The PRC demonsrated its anger with bitter propaganda attacks against Lee, as well as missile exercises in the East China Sea in July and August. The first test was in a target area 150 kilometers north of Taipei. The following day, Taiwan's stock market dropped 229 points, or 4.2 per cent.[58] To put more pressure on Taiwan, Beijing launched another round of missile tests and military exercises in March 1996, right before the Island's March 23 presidential election. The guided ballistic missiles were tested within 30 miles of Taiwan, and the war games were conducted only 11 miles from one of the Taiwan-controlled off-shore Islands.[59] This was seen as, according Thomas Friedman of *The New York Times*, an action designed to 'terrify Taiwan away from any thoughts of independence — without actually going to war.'[60] Beijing's reaction produced considerable impact on Taiwan's domestic politics and its future directions in the international arena.[61]

The December 1995 parliament election in Taiwan demonstrated this impact. It was believed that the PRC's pre-election bluster helped

Taiwan's New Party, which tended to go softer on ties with the Mainland, to triple its seats from seven to twenty-one; at the same time, the ruling KMT reduced its majority (from ninety-six to eighty-five) in the legislature to a water-thin three seats. There are, of course, many other reasons for the shift in votes, such as the New Party's middle-class image and the KMT's problems with corruption (known as *heijin zhengzhi*, or 'black money politics').[62]

The PRC's Taiwan policy has been further complicated by the internal dynamics of China's power politics. Few, if any political leaders in Beijing could afford to be labelled a *lishi zuiren* (a person condemned by history) for taking action that would permanently split the nation; such an appellation would be a lethal blow to any leader engaged in Beijing's continuing power struggles.

Out of fear of *taidu*, Beijing has consistently refused to pledge not to use force against Taiwan. Jiang Zemin, the secretary general of the CCP, stated in December 1992 that 'The PRC will adopt resolute measures if Taiwan declares *taidu*.'[63] The pursuit of *taidu* would, in other words, involve the risk of war. The Taiwan people have taken the possibilities of war seriously. A best-selling book entitled *August 1995: China's Violent Invasion of Taiwan* — a fictional account of a Mainland invasion of the island upon the latter's declaration of independence — sold 60,000 copies in less than two months in the summer of 1994, a further indication of the sensitivity of the issue.[64] Indeed, after the death of Chiang Ching-kuo in 1988, Beijing has seen an increasing likelihood of *taidu*. Based on this analysis, Deng Xiaoping suggested that among the two methods for China's unification — peaceful and military means — the latter is the more likely outcome for which Beijing would need to prepare; and the time for military action is when Taiwan openly declares independence.[65]

To Beijing's advantage, international conditions make *taidu* unlikely to occur in the near future. Ever since the PRC entered the United Nations in 1971, general opinion in the international community towards *taidu* has been unfavourable, mainly out of fear of the undesirable, possible consequences of war in the region. No major power in today's world would want to support openly a declaration of Taiwan's independence at the expense of breaking relations with the PRC and triggering an international crisis.

None the less, despite the unpropitious international environment, Beijing remains acutely sensitive to the issue of *taidu*. As long as Taiwan maintains *de facto* separation from the Mainland, political forces within and outside the island will continue to demand *taidu*. This tendency will be enhanced if further political turmoil occurs on the Mainland akin to the Tiananmen Incident. Under such circumstances, public opinion in the international community might take a more sympathetic attitude toward Taiwan.

There have been other changes at the macrostructure level. In particularly, Beijing's new Opening and Reform policy since 1978 has contributed to the significant changes in the PRC's Taiwan policy. This change occurred in 1979, when Beijing changed its Taiwan policy by advocating three links (trade, transportation, and postal services) and four exchanges (between relatives and tourists, academic groups, cultural groups, and sports representatives). In turn, the increased and intertwined economic, political and cultural exchanges across the Taiwan Straits has brought much more diversified interest and considerations into Beijing's policy-making process.

Bilateral relations gained further momentum in October 1987, when the Taiwan authorities reversed their long-standing 'Three No's' policy (no contact, no negotiations, and no compromise) and began allowing their citizens to visit the Mainland. A year later, specific groups from the Mainland were allowed to visit the island. Bilateral contacts have since increased dramatically.

In 1988, more than 430,000 from Taiwan visited the Mainland, and of those more than 40 per cent were not 'Mainlanders' but 'Taiwanese' who did not necessarily have Mainland relatives. Some 3,100 people from the Mainland visited Taiwan in 1989. In the same year, the number of visitors from Taiwan reached 500,000, a number that reached 1.5 million in 1992 and 1993 respectively, as shown in Table 7.3, and continued to increase to about 2.8 million in 1994.[66]

In terms of accumulated number, between 1987 and 1992 there were more than 4.2 million visits by the people of Taiwan to the Mainland, and about 40,000 visits by Mainland people to Taiwan.

Taipei's decision to open direct telephone and mail links with the Mainland resulted in a dramatic growth in contacts, with more than 10 million letters being exchanged in 1988. In 1989, Taiwanese authorities allowed their newspaper and television reporters to be based on the Mainland. Amid great publicity, an official twelve-member delegation headed by Taiwan's finance minister, Shirley Kuo, visited Beijing in early May 1989 to attend the Asian Development Bank meeting. Many important political, economic, and academic figures from Taiwan followed Kuo's lead in the years after.

The total value of bilateral trade, mostly through Hong Kong, has also increased dramatically, from US$78 million in 1979 to US$12.9

Table 7.3: Traffic Between Taiwan and China (1988–1994)

Year	Two-way Trade (Hong Kong/China*) US$ million	Visitors (from Taiwan to China)
1988	7501	430766
1989	9226	530534
1990	10003	925768
1991	14377	995714
1992	17945	1511990
1993	21215	1541628
1994	13665 (through July)	580000 (through June)

*Indirect trade through Hong Kong

Source: Taiwan Government; Quoted from Julian Baum, 'Ready When You Are', *Far Eastern Economic Review* (15 September 1994): 63

billion in 1993 (see Table 7.1). If one adds Taiwan's trade with Hong Kong, the figure in 1993 reached US$21.2 billion (see Table 7.3). The Mainland became Taiwan's third largest export market in 1993, after only the United States and Hong Kong.[67] Direct and indirect Taiwanese investment on the Mainland has also increased rapidly, despite the political turmoil of 1989. For example, more than 4,600 businessmen from Taiwan attended the Guangzhou Trade Fair in 1990 to conduct trade and investment negotiations with their Mainland partners. In 1992, Taiwan businessmen invested US$2.5 billion in the Mainland, and this figure reached US$15 billion by the middle of 1994. China has become the number one investment place for Taiwan, far exceeding Taiwan's investment Malaysia, Thailand, Indonesia, Vietnam, and the Philippines (ranked after China by amount).[68] Beijing hopes that these sorts of economic and person-to-person contacts will eventually preclude Taiwan's independence and lead to national unification.

One encouraging sign came from the Taiwan side toward the end of 1994, when Vincent Siew, former chairman of the Council of Economic Planning and Development, was appointed head of the Mainland Affairs Council. During his one-year chairmanship, Siew, who had a reputation for flexibility and an orientation toward economics, proposed setting up 'offshore centres' to process trade with the PRC. These would probably be located inside the port districts of Kaohsiung and Taichung.

Premier Lien Chan also gave his blessing by stating, 'In the current stage, trade should play a primary role in the government's Mainland policy.' Although up to early 1996 there had been no definite plans made, it appeared that with a strong push from Taiwan's business community, Taipei was prepared to open direct trade with the Mainland.[69]

When looking toward future developments, one may conclude that the Taiwan issue will remain a top priority in Chinese politics and foreign policy. Beijing believes that the longer the separation between the Mainland and Taiwan continues, the stronger will grow Taiwan's tendency toward independence. It appears necessary, therefore, for Beijing to reassess the symbolic macrostructure of the Taiwan issue and to understand the political reality of a unified China. Today's Taiwan is far different from the Taiwan that was ruled by Chiang Kai-shek and Chiang Ching-Kuo. Taiwanese society is fundamentally pluralistic; the KMT, although still the ruling party, no longer has a monopoly of power. The pluralistic nature of Taiwanese politics was further demonstrated by the December 1994 election in Taiwan, where the KMT maintained its Taiwan provincial governorship, but lost the Taipei mayorship to the DPP. The incumbent KMT Mayor Huang Ta-chou had to settle for third place in the race, after not only the DPP's Chen Shui-bian, but also Jaw Shau-kang, representing the youngest opposition party — the New Party.[70]

The decline of the KMT's influence was further demonstrated, as mentioned earlier, by the December 1995 parliamentary election. The ruling KMT's split was speeded by the decision by two of its vice chairmen — Lin Yang-kang and Hau Pei-tsun — to register their candidacy for president and vice president for the March 1996 presidential elections, to fight against the KMT's official candidates Lee Teng-hui and Lien Chan.[71] Lin and Hau were consequently expelled from the ruling party, but were warmly welcomed by the New Party. Even though Li Teng-hui was re-elected president in March 1996, a three-party structure — KMT, DPP, and the New Party — was firmly established in Taiwan politics.

Taiwan is unlikely to return to China under a political system of one-party domination; although Beijing believes it has already made a major concession in allowing Taiwan to maintain a capitalist political and economic system, a capitalist system also usually means a multiparty system. In the long run, if Beijing does not want to see an independent Taiwan, it may have to prepare for a more pluralistic society, in which the Communist Party may have to relinquish its monopoly of political power.[72]

The changing international and domestic situation will force Taipei to choose between several possibilities. Its reluctance to talk with Beijing in the 1980s was viewed — not only on the Mainland but also in Taiwan — as reflecting indecision rather than valid apprehension.[73] In a March 1991 interview, a high-ranking official at the Taiwan Foreign Affairs Ministry emphasized the importance of mutual understanding and the need for a *junzi xieding* (gentleman's agreement) between the two sides, in which Beijing's decision to allow Taiwan to participate in the international community will not lead to independence.[74] This kind of agreement requires mutual trust, and to develop that trust the two sides must sit down and talk.

The talks between the PRC's Wang Daohan and Taiwan's Koo Chenfu in April 1993 in Singapore were widely hailed as 'the first formal meeting' since the end of the civil war in 1949. In addition to their 'non-official' positions as heads of agencies designated to handle bilateral affairs, the men are close confidants of Jiang Zemin and Lee Tenghui, respectively. These talks were regarded as 'a first step toward unification or, more modestly, the most promising attempt yet to alleviate tensions which have kept Taiwan isolated and under siege for most of the past 45 years.'[75] A year later in August 1994, Wang's deputy Tang Shubei, vice chairman of Beijing's Association for Relations Across the Taiwan Straits, conducted negotiations with his Taiwan counterparts in Taipei, the highest ranking PRC official to visit to Taiwan since 1949. The two sides reached tentative agreement on terms for repatriating illegal immigrant and hijackers and settling fishing disputes.[76] There were also reports that Jiang Zemin's and Lee Teng-hui's personal envoys secretly met in Hong Kong, Macau, or Beijing.[77] One may expect that more bilateral talks, whether through open or secret channels, will follow. This micro-level interchange may prove significant to future changes in cross-Straits relations at the macro level.

South-East Asia: The Change of Perception

Beijing's drive for modernization and its desire for regional stability has significantly affected the transformation of China's relations with the nations of South-East Asia. This transformation exemplifies the macrostructural shift from an ideologically rigid, isolationist policy under Mao to the less doctrinaire, more pragmatic, and cooperative approach favoured by Deng. Indeed, whereas for Mao isolationism was desirable, for Deng the very threat of international isolation was sufficient to inspire a rapid improvement in China's relations with its South-East Asian neighbours.

South-East Asia is comprised of the seven countries of the ASEAN (Brunei, Indonesia, Malaysia, the Philippines, Thailand, Singapore, and Vietnam, which became a formal member in July of 1995), Cambodia, Laos, and Burma. Cambodia and Laos have achieved observer status, and Burma expressed interest in becoming an observer in 1996. These three observer countries eventually will join the team in the near future, making ASEAN a ten-member organization covering all of South-East Asia.[78] This direction was confirmed further when all of the ten nations' top leaders attended the meeting for the first time at the Fifth ASEAN Summit, held in Bangkok in December 1995.[79] In the 1950s and 1960s, China dismissed the members of ASEAN as mere 'running dogs of US imperialism'. Although Beijing changed its view of the nature of ASEAN in the 1970s, its relations with South-East Asian countries did not improve immediately. Indonesia, for example, which broke relations with China in 1964 after a failed coup attempt by the Indonesian Communist Party, remained suspicious of Beijing for more than two decades, until 1990 when it formally normalized relations with China. In addition, the anti-communist Singaporean government for about four decades did not establish diplomatic relations with the PRC.

China's relations with the countries of Indochina have likewise been far from smooth. Until the early 1970s, the PRC enjoyed a 'comrade-plus-brother' type of relationship with Vietnam, fighting first against France (the early 1950s) and then against the United States (the 1960s and early 1970s). But after the Vietnamese Communists defeated the South and achieved national unification, Sino-Vietnamese relations worsened rapidly, primarily due to Vietnam's occupation of Cambodia and the territorial disputes along the border and in the South China Sea. To break Vietnam's ambition of dominating the entire Indochina area (as mentioned in Chapter 3), China launched a punitive war against Vietnam in 1979.

One major problem between China and some of the South-East Asian countries in the mid-1990s is that a number of disputes remain unresolved, notably the territorial claims over some of the South China Sea islands (disputes with Vietnam, the Philippines, Malaysia, and Brunei). The main bulk of the dispute areas are Xisha (Paracel) and Nansha (Spratly) Islands. Within the Nansha area for example, most of the disputing parties occupied several islands, which are claimed by Beijing (as well as Taipei) as Chinese territory.[80] From a Chinese account, the PRC actually controlled eight islands in the Nansha area, with Taiwan controlling only one, the Philippines nine, Malaysia nine, and Vietnam twenty-seven. Brunei had claims, but did not actually control any islands (F. Sun, 1994: 14–15). The South China Sea is also important to international shipping — about one-fourth of the world's shipping passes through this area (Gallagher, 1994: 171), and most of Japan's oil imports are transported on this sea route.[81]

With regard to the sovereignty issue in this area, China, up until 1995, had conducted major military actions: in January 1974, the Chinese army and navy took Xisha from South Vietnam; in March 1988, the Chinese navy took six atolls in the Nansha archipelago from Vietnam; and in February 1995, China moved further south and planted its flag on Meiji (Mischief) Reef, which the Philippines claimed (and Beijing disputed) was part of its Kalayaan group of islands. The PRC has repeatedly called for bilateral negotiations for the joint economic development of the Nansha area, but so far has received no positive responses from the contending nations. China's most recent action in the Meiji Reef area rung alarm in several South-East Asian capitals.[82] Philippine President Fidel Ramos, for example, immediately protested China's move onto Mischief Reef and then announced the creation of a taskforce that would strengthen its territorial claim in the Nansha area.[83] In March, the Philippine navy removed Chinese markers on several reefs and atolls and detained four Chinese fishing vessels in the area.[84] These actions were criticized by Beijing. In August 1995, the two countries reached an agreement that the dispute should not be resolved through military means and that both sides should observe the international ocean laws issued by the United Nations.[85]

In addition to the sovereignty issue, there also are strong economic motivations behind Beijing's actions. Potential oil production holds the key in this regard. A 1995 official *China Youth* report gives an idea of how China regards the region as promising. According to the report, the Spratlys are the key to controlling 10 billion tons of oil, or more than one-eighth of China's proven reserves of about 78 billion tons. The paper claimed that the South China Sea was destined to become a 'second Middle East'.[86]

A number of studies have been conducted to analyse Beijing's policy choices for dealing with the South China Sea disputes. By applying a formal model approach, for example, Samuel Wu and Bruce de Mesquita (1994) have conducted a study on the likelihood that China would use military forces over the dispute in the South China Sea. They conclude that, since reformers in the PRC will have a much better chance to implement their agenda, 'policies that emphasize a stable international environment are expected to prevail in the near future'. Therefore, China is 'unlikely to engage in any significant uses of force' to pursue its agenda in the South China Sea 'over the next few years'. (Wu and de Mesquita, 1994: 398–9) On the other hand, however, one cannot over-look the driving force of nationalism that fuels China's territorial claims. While Beijing may try its best to avoid a major war in the area, it may also conduct limited military actions, or 'local war', to enhance its positions in the area.[87] As a *Far Eastern Economic Review* editorial suggested, China, itself, may not 'know exactly what it wants to do — but wants to ensure it has the capability to do so when it finally does decide. That is not an unreasonable position for a great power, as China is destined to be.'[88]

In other words, the connections between the macrostructrure and the micro process in terms of future foreign policy direction are still unclear. One may only hope that the Chinese government may become more transparent in security matters that will reduce its neighbours suspicions.

China's relationship with South-East Asia began to improve steadily from the early 1980s; the turning point was the Tiananmen Incident of 1989. As discussed earlier, because of the diplomatic and economic sanctions imposed by Western nations, Beijing faced isolation from the international community. The collapse of the Soviet and East European communist regimes, leaving China the largest remaining communist regime, further exacerbated Beijing's international position of aliena-tion. Beijing was forced to adjust its foreign policy to face the chal-lenges of the post-Cold War era.

One of China's new initiatives was an Asia-oriented foreign policy. In the wake of the Tiananmen Incident, Beijing accomplished four concrete steps in this direction in the early 1990s. First, in August 1990 Beijing normalized relations with Indonesia. Second, two months later, China established diplomatic relations with Singapore. Third, Beijing has been actively involved in the UN peacekeeping forces in Cambodia since 1990. And fourth, Beijing normalized relations with Hanoi in 1991, leading to a visit to Vietnam by Premier Li Peng in December 1992, at the end of which Li announced 'We have much more common points than disputes.'[89] By the end of 1994, there were three rounds of talks between Beijing and Hanoi on disputes over their common 1,130-kilometre land border. Some progress was reportedly made during these talks.[90] This improvement in the relationship was highlighted by the visit of President and Party Secretary General Jiang Zemin to Singapore and Malaysia in November 1994, on the way to Indonesia to attend the APEC meeting. On the way back home, Jiang paid an official visit to

Vietnam, the first such visit for the past several decades. At the end of the visit, China and Vietnam agreed to form an expert group to negotiate settlement of their maritime disputes over the South China Sea Islands. Chinese foreign minister Qian Qichen also stressed that both countries felt they should shelve their disputes and concentrate on their countries' economic development.[91]

The improvement of relations between China and its South-East Asian neighbours in the first half of the 1990s has produced both positive and negative impacts in terms of regional international relations. Since the beginning of the 1990s, for example, trade between Burma and southern China, with Yunnan province in particular, has been flourishing as never before. Bilateral trade reached US$490 million in 1993. There has been also simultaneous growth in military ties between Rangoon and Beijing, which significantly enhanced relations between the two countries.

The development of further military cooperation between China and Burma worried South-East Asian neighbours, who were alarmed by the massive Chinese shipments to Burma's army, air force, and particularly the Burmese navy. Indonesian military sources, for example, say they consider that granting China military access to Burmese bases would present a threat to the Straits of Malacca, a major waterway for South-East Asia's sea-borne trade. Although Beijing denied it intended to project its influence into South-East Asia, many regional governments feared China was using Burma to expand its military and political reach.[92] The visit of Chinese Premier Li Peng to Burma in December 1994, aiming to enhance the so-called *baobo qingyi*, or 'brotherly relationship' between the two countries, marked the first such high-level visit since 1981.[93]

The boom in Sino-Burmese relations also brought some unintended consequences: a surge in logging, opium production, and illegal Chinese emigration. The Mekong River has become the leading conduit out of China for illegal migrants to the West. 'Snakeheads', the merchants of migration, charged about Rmb 220,000 (US$26,000) in 1994 for passage overseas. At the same time, thousands of Chinese, most of whom were engaged in commercial activities, were content to stay in Burma.[94] These developments have created social, as well as international problems. Sometime down the road, Beijing will have to deal seriously with these problems. Indeed, one of the major issues discussed during Li Peng's 1994 visit was how to cooperate to repress drug smuggling along the Sino-Burmese border.[95]

China's chief concern for South-East Asia is stability. The normalization of relations with Vietnam in November 1991 following the Vietnamese withdrawal from Cambodia has presented an opportunity for

Beijing to exercise its influence in the area. At the same time, China continues to work with the ASEAN states to promote economic prosperity and regional stability. Vietnam's inclusion in ASEAN in 1995 has been regarded as a counter to China's weight, reshaping the balance of power and political and strategic relations in East and South-East Asia. Vietnam's armed forces of more than 850,000 armed men has remained much bigger than those of Thailand and Indonesia (300,000 soldiers each), which had the biggest ASEAN forces.[96]

In the future, Beijing will likely continue to cooperate in the international arena, particularly with regional nations, in the post-Cold War era. A larger regional coordinating organization may be necessary to prevent military and political crises and to coordinate economic activities in East and South-East Asia. The PRC, along with Taiwan and Hong Kong, would be expected to play an active role in such an organization, as would North Korea, South Korea, Japan, and the ASEAN states. The participation of the United States and Russia would also be helpful and would ensure that their interests are not be jeopardized. Malaysian Prime Minister Datuk Seri Mahaghir Mohamad suggested a new East Asian trading bloc when he met with visiting Japanese Prime Minister Toshiki Kaifu in January 1991.[97] Among existing organizations, the Asia-Pacific Economic Cooperation (APEC) group, which includes the PRC, Taiwan, Hong Kong, South Korea, Japan, Australia, Canada, New Zealand, the United States, and the ASEAN countries, seems to be a particularly promising instrument for enhancing trade between the nations of the region.

Changing Relations with Russia

China's policy toward Russia has been closely linked with Beijing's changing perception (the symbolic macrostructure) of the power of Soviet/Russia. The collapse of the Soviet empire and communist ideology profoundly influenced China's domestic and foreign policies. The fear of 'spiritual pollution' from the republics of the former Soviet Union and Eastern Europe was at least as great as that from the West,[98] and prompted Beijing to recall Chinese students from Russia and most parts of Eastern Europe. China was even afraid of 'spiritual pollution' from democratizing Mongolia. During negotiations for a transport treaty between the two countries in 1991, Beijing insisted that cross-border travel be limited to residents of the border areas, whereas Ulan Batur favoured no such restrictions, hoping for more tourism across the border.[99] Indeed, after the 1992 departure of Russian troops, Beijing's concern about Mongolia is more on the ideological side, rather than about security. One observer says the Chinese view Mongolia as a 'dagger in China's heart, before as a Soviet satellite, and now as a newly democratized country right on China's doorstep'.[100]

Faced with dramatic changes in the former Soviet Union and Eastern Europe, Beijing drew grim conclusions about how to defend socialism in China. An internal Chinese Communist Party document outlined five lessons learned from the failed Soviet coup of August 1991:

• Proletarian dictatorship should be maintained.
• No multi-party system should be allowed.
• State-owned enterprises and the state-controlled sector should be the basis of the economy.
• The Party must command the army.
• The campaign against 'bourgeois liberalism' should be stepped up.[101]

At the same time, the decline of the Soviet threat has presented new possibilities in China's security thinking, particularly in the Asia-Pacific area. If China and Russia continue to follow a pragmatic line, they may further improve their bilateral relations. Indeed, following three summits — Mikhail Gorbachev's visit to Beijing in 1989, Jiang Zemin's visit to Moscow in 1991, and Boris Yeltsin's visit to China in 1992 — bilateral relations have significantly improved. As some Western observers pointed out as early as 1988, the Chinese 'have little to lose from inching toward Moscow in order to gain a bit more leverage'.[102]

Yeltsin's visit to Beijing produced meaningful results in Sino-Russian relations. By signing twenty-four joint statements, documents, and memoranda of understanding in areas including military and technological cooperation, space exploration, and nuclear energy development, China would be able to upgrade its military equipment significantly, while Russia would receive much needed food supplies.[103]

In September 1994, Chinese President Jiang Zemin paid another visit to Moscow. With a much more comfortable and stabilized bilateral relationship than the previous years, Jiang and Yeltsin signed a declaration confirming that China and Russia agreed not to aim nuclear missiles at each other, never to use force against each other, and to sharply limit the number of troops stationed along their border. An equally important result of the visit was the economic agreement signed by the two leaders. Yeltsin told Jiang, 'We pay much attention to studying the experience of economic reforms in China', referring to China's successful reform policies and remarkable economic growth over the past decade. Less than a year later, Jiang paid another visit to Moscow in May of 1995, to participate in celebrations marking the end of World War II in Europe; and Chinese Foreign Minister Qian Qichen declared that 'There are no problems in bilateral relations.'[104] Indeed, bilateral economic relations between the two countries had developed rapidly. China became Russia's second largest trading partner after Germany. The total trade volume reached US$7.68 billion in 1993, doubled in the last three years.[105] China's institutional macrostructure was also conducive to the rapid development of bilateral relations. The Chinese military establishment, for example, welcomed further exchanges with Russians.

Russia has now become a new source of advanced military equipment in the PLA's efforts to upgrade. In November 1994, for example, China signed a US$1 billion deal with Russia to buy four Kilo-class patrol submarines, a major upgrade for the Chinese navy.[106] One other development along the Sino-Russian border is the ongoing Tumen River development project, a UNDP (United Nations Development Programme) supported plan to develop an international trading region in the border area linking China, Russia, and North Korea. China is especially interested in this project because it would allow direct access to the Sea of Japan through the Tumen River.[107]

Although better relations with Russia (and the other republics that have replaced the Soviet Union) would facilitate China's modernization drive, it was impossible, as Chinese Premier Li Peng noted, for the Chinese to return to the 'old days' of the 1950s. Li also stressed that a Sino-Soviet political rapprochement would not jeopardize China's ties with the United States.[108] In other words, China's rapprochement with the former Soviet Union would not lead China to abandon its cooperation with the United States and Japan. To the contrary, the powers may find more reasons to cooperate than to confront each other. In the early 1990s, for example, Beijing, Washington, Tokyo, and Moscow reached a consensus on prohibiting the development of nuclear weapons on the Korean Peninsula, particularly in North Korea. Such desire for cooperation demonstrates Beijing's need to bring all the major powers together, including Russia and the United States, to maintain stability in the Asia-Pacific region.

One should not, however, ignore potential problems between the two countries. One problem has been the exodus of illegal Chinese immigrants to the Russian Far East and Siberia. According to Russian newspaper reports in 1995, since the beginning of the 1990s, two to five million Chinese have moved to Russia. These people at the micro level were motivated by their individual calculations for profit-taking

advantange of the gradual thaw of Sino-Russian relations and the relaxation of the border. This threatens to become, at the macro level, a
major bone of contention between Moscow and Beijing, since the
Russians may feel uneasy about a sizeable Chinese community within
their territory.[109]

There has also been Russian criticism about the sale of sophisticated
weaponry to China. Alexei Voskressenski, deputy director of the
Moscow-based Russia–China Centre, forcefully called for paying close
attention to the 'long-term consequences of these deals, given Chinese
pressures in the Russian Far East'. He warned of 'an authoritarian
neighbour with an economy roughly the size of America that might one
day see in the Russian Far East a solution to its demographic pressures'.
Voskressenski even suggested that Russia should further strengthen ties
with Taiwan 'to counterbalance the growing presence of China in the
Russian Far East'.[110] His call, however, did not go too far in Moscow
at the time.

One thing we may learn from the past history of relations between
the two neighbouring giants is: a pattern of shifting and uncertainty.
Beijing and Moscow are still in the process of adjusting their policies
toward each other. The future development of Sino-Russian relations
toward the end of the century will largely depend upon the changing
dynamics at both the macro and micro levels in each country.

Sino-US Relations: A Zig-Zag Pattern

Any discussion about China's regional-oriented foreign policy, and the
nationalism behind that policy, would be incomplete without analysis
of relations with the United States, given the immense impact of the
superpower's impact on this region. This brief discussion, however,
only concentrates on the more recent developments, without further
detailing historical legacies, some of which have been discussed in the
previous chapters.[111]

Chinese foreign policy toward the United States can also be analysed
from the micro-macro linkage perspective. One sees clearly the impact
of the dynamics of symbolic macrostructure on the evolution of relations between China and the United States. The most recent major
downturn in Sino-American relations took place after the Tiananmen
Incident of 1989, when the two sides regarded each other as the major
ideological threat. This downturn has serious implications for all three
major fields of bilateral relations: political, economic, and strategic.

Beginning from the early 1990s there was a gradual warming of the brisk relationship between Beijing and Washington. In late 1991, the Beijing leadership indicated that it attached great importance to its relations with Washington, and was pleased to host US Secretary of State James Baker, calling his visit 'a success,'[112] despite the serious disagreements over a variety of issues, such as human rights concerns, voiced during his stay. China also regarded the United States, with Japan and the European Community, as its major source of advanced technology, capital, and markets. President Bill Clinton, although he criticized the PRC on such issues as human rights and unfair trading practice during his presidential campaign, made a critical decision in 1994 to delink the human rights issue from the renewal of China's most-favoured-nation (MFN) status to China, thereby removing a major obstacle to improve bilateral relations.[113]

On the other hand, as long as the future of Taiwan remains unsettled, the potential for Sino-American conflict will continue. As Deng Xiaoping once pointed out to a visiting head of an Asian country, 'The question of Taiwan is the main obstacle to better relations between China and the United States, and it might even develop into a crisis between the two nations.'[114]

To make things worse, the Republican victory in the US congressional elections in November 1994 produced what one specialist called the 'most pro-democracy, pro-Taiwan, pro-Tibet, anti-Chinese Communist Party and anti-People's Liberation Army' Congress in recent memory.[115] Senator Jesse Helms, the new chairman of the powerful Senate Foreign Relations Committee, for example, reportedly claimed that, 'Given the choice of Chinas, I would take Taiwan every time.' And Helms' counterpart in the House Foreign Affairs Committee Benjamin Gilman, a long-time supporter of Tibet's exiled leader, the Dalai Lama, was the sponsor of a bill declaring Tibet an occupied country.[116] Gilman also stated in the summer of 1995 that 'If the people of Taiwan want to join the United Nations as an independent nation, then they should be allowed to do so'.[117] These claims have antagonized Beijing. To make things worse, House Speaker Newt Gingrigh in July called for the United States to re-establish diplomatic ties with Taiwan.[118] All these sentiments have demonstrated the micro elements at work in the overall Sino-American relationship.

The most visible challenge to Beijing was President Bill Clinton's decision to allow Lee Teng-hui to pay a 'private visit' to the United States in June of 1995. To be sure, Clinton's decision was made under enormous pressure from the US Congress, which earlier passed a resolution in favour of granting Lee a visa to the US; the resolution passed by a vote of 97 to 1 in the Senate and 360 to 0 in the House of Re-presentatives.[119] Beijing was particularly angry that it had taken as a matter of faith US Secretary of State Warren Christopher's early vow that Washington would not permit Lee's visit.[120] This presents a classical example of conflicting elements in the policy-making process — con-gressional action versus state department promise — producing consid-erable impact on the macro-level structure. This phenomenon will certainly continue to be a detrimental factor in future Sino-US relations.

As mentioned earlier, in order to show its anger over Lee Teng-hui's alleged independence tendency, the PRC conducted a series of military exercises and missile tests around the island in the summer of 1995 and spring of 1996. In March 1996, Washington reacted strongly by send-ing two aircraft carrier groups — *Independence* and *Nimitz* — to the waters near Taiwan; they were the 'largest US force in the region in the recent past.'[121] Beijing's reaction was even angrier, pushing its war games even closer to Taiwan. 'The Chinese felt compelled to react, tit for tat,' Paul Godwin of the National Defense University in Washing-ton commented, 'They couldn't be seen as backing down to what they view as hegemonic politics.'[122] Clearly, there will always remain the potential danger of military clash and escalation around the issue of Taiwan between China and the United States.

There were also economic problems. The first incident in Sino-US relations at the beginning of 1995 was the threat of trade wars caused by the clash over intellectual property rights.[123] China and the United States reached an agreement in February of 1995, right before US sanc-tions on more than US$1 billion in Chinese-made imports were to take effect. The understanding was that China would close 7 of 29 factories that copied and distributed pirated computer software and audio and video compact discs, and that Washington would soften its opposition to China's entry into the new World Trade Organization (WTO), the metamorphosed the GATT. In March, US Trade Representative Mickey Kantor indicated that his country would back China's bid to join WTO, and soften its stance on China's status as a 'developing country', mean-ing that it may obtain certain trade concessions.[124] But in June of 1995, US trade negotiators and manufacturers were alarmed again by the report that the Chinese government had allowed all but one of the seven compact disc factories it closed for piracy violations to reopen.[125] All these developments indicate that economic frictions will remain a major bone of contention between Beijing and Washington.

In order to better prepare China for entrance to the WTO, President Jiang Zemin made an announcement at the Osaka APEC summit in

November 1995 that, starting from next year, China would reduce 30 per cent of import tariffs on more than 4,000 items.[126] Starting 1 April 1996, China cut its average import tariffs to 23 per cent, down from the previous average of about 39.5 per cent.[127] Up through early 1996, China was still in the process of negotiating its WTO membership with major economic powerhouses, such as the United States, the European Union, and Japan. One may expect that clashes between the United States and China in the political, economic, and cultural dimensions will continue.

The general picture of Sino-American relations can be explained by the micro-macro linkage model. From the perspective of the symbolic macrostructure, the two countries' national interests are not fundamentally in conflict. Indeed, the strategic foundation that brought the two countries together in 1972 is still largely in place. Beijing has always attached great importance to its relations with the United States. With the end of the Cold War and the collapse of the Soviet power in the early 1990s, Deng Xiaoping issued a sixteen-character instruction to guide China's policy toward the United States:

- *zengjia xinren* (to increase mutual trust);
- *jianshao mafan* (to reduce trouble);
- *zengjia hezuo* (to enhance cooperation);
- *bugao duikang* (to avoid confrontation).[128]

With this guidance, Beijing has attempted (arguably with success) to keep a low profile and to avoid open confrontation with the United States through the first half of the 1990s.

Washington also has consistently recognized the importance of Beijing's cooperation on East and South-East Asian regional affairs, such as Korean unification and the Cambodian peace settlement.[129] The international competition for the China market is also a major consideration in US foreign policy toward China. One such example is the aircraft industry. There has been 'air-traffic congestion at the ground level in Beijing' (as a *Far Eastern Economic Review* article termed it) as the world's three main aircraft manufacturers — Boeing and McDonnell Douglas of the United States, and the European consortium Airbus Industries — compete for the China market. This market represents a potential US$66 billion over the period of twenty years after 1994.[130] American companies, such as Boeing and McDonnell, do not wish to see the loss of business opportunities due to political factors. After all, many other Western countries have put economics ahead of politics when dealing with China. One fresh memory for the Americans was the

French government's decision in early 1994 to cut off future arms sales to Taiwan and to mend fences with Beijing, so that France could tap into China's booming economy.[131] France had suffered economic and political retaliation from Beijing over its previous sale of military jets to Taiwan[132]. The last-minute settlement between Beijing and Washington over the copyright protection disputes in February 1995, averting a major trade war worth more than US$2 billion seemed to demonstrate the importance each capital attached to the other.[133] This kind of consideration, inspired by economic (as well as strategic) factors, will continue to play important roles in Sino-US relations for the years to come.

In sum, modernization, nationalism, and regionalism — general trends in Chinese foreign policy in the post-Cold War era — are evident and seem likely to continue into the post-Deng era. The Beijing leadership's interpretation of internal conditions and the external environment will continue to play an important role in Chinese foreign policy. For example, if Washington is perceived as a threat to China instead of a good partner, or if Moscow's departure from Marxism–Leninism is perceived as jeopardizing the legitimacy of Beijing's rule, China will likely reduce its relations with the United States or Russia, even at the expense of economic loss.

Notes

1 China's nationalism has long been a focus of Chinese foreign policy studies. For some excellent examples in this regard, see Allen Whiting (1995); James Townsend (1992); and Michel Oksenberg (1986/7), 'China's Confident Nationalism'.
2 'Regionalism' used here should not be confused with central–local relations in China's domestic politics.
3 See, for example, John Copper (1980: 132) in which China is described as 'a second-ranking power'.
4 There are different definitions for the concept of 'Greater China'. In a broad way, it refers to, as Harry Harding has put it, the 'rapidly increasing interaction among Chinese societies around the world as the political and administrative barriers to their intercourse fall'. In a more narrow sense, it focuses 'exclusively on Hong Kong, Macau, Taiwan and mainland China'. See Harry Harding (1993: 660–664). For example, *Business Week* [(10 October, 1988): 54–55] referred to 'Greater China' as the 'prospective result of the three-way economic integration of Hong Kong, Taiwan and the Mainland'.
5 One should note that China's trade with Hong Kong is largely a function of re-export to other countries, including North America and Europe.
6 'Defence', *Far Eastern Economic Review* (9 March 1995): 13.
7 Ibid.
8 'Direct Investment in China Soars', *The Japan Times* (Weekly International Edition), 12–18 December 1994, p. 12.
9 *The Japan Times* (Weekly International Edition), 5–11 September 1994, p. 3.
10 The 1955 political system refers to the long-time (1955–93) one-party (LDP) domination in Japan. The original idea was first raised by Junnosoke Masumi in his '*Seiji taisei*', published in *Shiso* in June 1964. It was later elaborated in his *Postwar Politics in Japan* (1985: 329–342).
11 *Renmin Ribao* (People's Daily), 27 November 1992, p. 4.
12 See *Department of State Bulletin* (15 December 1969): 555–558.
13 *Peking Review* (5 December 1969): 11.
14 *Peking Review* (10 April 1970): 5.
15 Quoted from 'China Snipes at "Offensive" Maritime SDF', *The Japan Times* (Weekly International Edition), 13–19 June 1994, p. 3.
16 Simon Beck, 'Jiang Presses Leaders Over One-China Policy', *South China Morning Post*, 15 November 1994, p. 13.
17 'Tokyo Ready to Talk Defense with Beijing', *The Japan Times* (Weekly International Edition), 31 October–6 November 1994, p. 2.
18 For detailed accounts of the negotiations for the Sino-Japanese Peace Treaty, see Robert Bedeski (1983).
19 For details of Beijing's concerns over the Diaoyu (or Senkaku Islands) see Daniel Tretiak (1978).
20 The Guanghua Hostel, built in Kyoto in 1931, was purchased by the Taiwan government and used to house Chinese students. In 1962, it was formally registered under the ownership of the Taiwan government. After the normalization of relations between Beijing and Tokyo, the PRC began demanding ownership of the building. In 1977, the Kyoto District Court recognized that the PRC had succeeded to ownership when Taiwan lost Japanese recognition. But in 1982, the Osaka High Court

overruled and ordered the Kyoto court to reexamine the case, causing the court to
reverse its earlier decision in 1986 and to declare in favour of the Taiwan authorities.
Beijing protested. In 1987, the Osaka High Court sustained the Kyoto decision in
favour of Taiwan. The issue has remained controversial ever since. For further
details, see Allen Whiting (1989: 152–157).

21 Julian Baum, 'Regrets Only', *Far Eastern Economic Review* (22 September 1994):
14–16; and Lincoln Kaye, 'Lip Service: China–Taiwan War of Words Heats Up',
Far Eastern Economic Review (20 October 1994): 20.

22 'China May Boycott the Asian Games', *The Japan Times* (Weekly International
Edition), 12–18 September 1994, p. 2.

23 'Tokyo Sticks to One-China Policy Line', *The Japan Times* (Weekly International
Edition), 21–27 November 1994, p. 5. Also see Simon Beck, 'Jiang Presses Leaders
Over One-China Policy'.

24 'Kang na er xia yi zhan shi jingdu [Kyoto Will be the Next Stop after Cornell]',
Yazhou Zhoukan [International Chinese Newsweekly] (4 June 1995): 28.

25 'Korea's First High-Level Talks', *Beijing Review*, 33, 39 (24–30 September 1990): 15.

26 Xu Baokang, 'A Good Foundation for Solving the Nuclear Problem in the Korean
Peninsula', *Renmin Ribao*, 2 December 1991, p. 6.

27 Nayan Chanda, 'Lesser Evil', *Far Eastern Economic Review* (21 December 1995):
17–18.

28 Nayan Chanda, 'Chinese Welcome North Korea's Kim, But Relations are Subtly
Changing', *The Asian Wall Street Journal Weekly*, 21 October 1991, pp. 24 and 26.

29 Hu Xueze and Bing Jinhu, 'World Situation Unstable Despite Detente', *Beijing
Review*, 34, 2 (14–20 January 1991): 27–31.

30 Lincoln Kaye, 'Friend in Need', *Far Eastern Economic Review* (17 October 1991):
14–15.

31 *Renmin Ribao*, 16 November 1995, p. 1.

32 'South Korea: Aircraft for China', *Far Eastern Economic Review* (21 April 1994): 83.

33 'China Backs DPRK Reunification Efforts', *Beijing Review*, 34, 20 (20–26 May
1991): 8–9.

34 Damon Darlin, 'North Korea Reverses Position on UN, Seeks Admission Separately
From South', *The Asian Wall Street Journal Weekly*, 3 June 1991, pp. 18 and 23.

35 Ted Morello, 'Veto Vanishes: Thaw Clears Way to (United Nations) Membership
for Koreas', *Far Eastern Economic Review* (5 December 1990): 15.

36 *World Journal*, 12 April 1991, p. 1.

37 'Li Peng on Domestic and World Issues', *Beijing Review*, 34, 26 (1–7 July 1991):
24–29.

38 This 'interim' concept with regard to UN membership stands in sharp contrast to
Beijing's firm opposition to Taiwan's UN membership for fear of the creation of
'two China's'. See next section for a detailed analysis.

39 Nayan Chanda, 'Seal of Disapproval', *Far Eastern Economic Review* (31 March
1994): 14–15.

40 'South Korea: Information Gap', *Far Eastern Economic Review* (21 April 1994): 13.

41 'Making Haste Slowly: Seoul, Tokyo, Play up to Beijing on North Korean Issue',
Far Eastern Economic Review (7 April 1994): 16. For a detailed analysis of China's
assessment of North Korea, see Banning Garrett and Bonnie Glaser (1995).

42 Shim Jae Hoon, 'Sitting on the Fence', *Far Eastern Economic Review* (10 November
1994): 15.

43 'Beijing Backs North Korea Pact', *South China Morning Post* , 15 November 1994,
p. 1.

44 Shim Jae Hoon, 'Sitting on the Fence', *Far Eastern Economic Review* (10 November
1994): 15.

45 Nayan Chanda, 'Lesser Evil', *Far Eastern Economic Review* (21 December 1995):
17–18.

46 Ibid.

47 'North Korea Leader Pays 39th China Visit', *Beijing Review*, 34, 41 (14–20 October 1991): 7.

48 Some scholars believe that from the security perspective, China would not want to see a united Korea. Chalmers Johnson (1995: 67), for example, argues that Beijing 'prefers a structurally divided Korea that is unable to play its full role as a buffer between China, Russia, and Japan, thereby giving China a determining influence on the peninsula'.

49 Although both Beijing and Taipei have officially regarded the status of Taiwan and the question of its reunification with the Mainland as domestic issues, the issue of Taiwan clearly has international implications, given the long period of separation and the involvement of the major powers.

50 Ted Morello, 'Hearing Problems: Taiwan's UN Feeler Quashed by Beijing', *Far Eastern Economic Review* (6 October 1994): 29.

51 At the 1993 General Assembly of the United Nations, seven countries sponsored the draft item in favour of Taiwan. They were all Central American nations: Belize, Costa Rica, El Salvador, Guatemala, Honduras, Nicaragua, and Panama. Of these countries, only Nicaragua remained a sponsor in 1994.

52 See 'The *Taidu* Reactionary Trend Must be Stopped', *Renmin Ribao*, 7 September 1991, p. 1.

53 Julian Baum, John McBeth, and Rodney Tasker, 'In His Private Capacity: President Lee Scores Points in Holiday Diplomacy', *Far Eastern Economic Review* (24 February 1994): 18–19.

54 Julian Baum, 'Fast Friends: Lee's Tour Staves off International Isolation', *Far Eastern Economic Review* (9 June 1994): 18.

55 A planned visit to Israel was cancelled due to protests from Beijing. See 'Taiwan: Presidential Progress', *Far Eastern Economic Review* (13 April 1995): 13.

56 'Taiwan: Secret Visit', *Far Eastern Economic Review* (16 June 1994): 13.

57 Julian Baum, 'Dire Straits: Beijing Frets Over a More Independent Taiwan', *Far Eastern Economic Review* (21 July 1994): 19–20.

58 Julian Baum, 'Lee's Challenge', *Far Eastern Economic Review* (September 14, 1995): 20–21.

59 'China Tells US to Stay Out of Strait', compiled from reports by *The New York Times*, *The Los Angeles Times*, and The Associated Press, see the *Virginian Pilot* (18 March 1996): A1 and A5.

60 Thomas Friedman, 'Chinese Leadership Will Not Go Over the Brink, Right?', *The New York Times* (14 March 1996).

61 This impression was based on the author's field research in Taiwan in August 1995, during the period of the PRC's missile exercises in the East China Sea. The author interviewed people from different sides of Taiwanese politics, including (but not limited to) Chang King-yuh, Minister of State and later Chairman of the Mainland Affairs Council; Chang Hsiao-yen, Minister of State and Chairman of the Overseas Chinese Commission; Chiang Wego, President of the Society for Strategic Studies and brother of the late President Chiang Ching-kuo; Huang Yaoyu, Director General of the Department of Mainland Affairs of the KMT; Kao Koong-lian, Vice Chairman of the Mainland Affairs Council; Chiao Jen-Ho, Secretary General of the Straits Exchange Foundation; Wang Chian-Hsuan, Chairman of the New Party; Chang Chung-ya, Deputy Director of the Department of Foreign Affairs of the Democratic Progressive Party (DPP); and Hsieh Shu Yuan, Director of the Chinese Affairs Department of the DPP.

62 See Julian Baum, 'Politics is Local', *Far Eastern Economic Review* (30 November 1995): 14–15.

63 *Renmin Ribao*, 16 December 1992, p. 1.

64 Julian Baum, 'Fear of Falling: Prophet of Chinese Invasion Makes Many Nervous', *Far Eastern Economic Review* (13 October 1994): 24–26.

65 This strategy has been confirmed by the recollections of Xu Jiatun (1993: 561–562),

who was a former member of the CCP Central Committee, the highest ranking Chinese official exiled abroad.

66 *World Journal*, 21 November 1995, p. 1.

67 *Wen Wei Po*, 27 December 1994, p. 1.

68 Julian Baum, 'Not So Fast: Taiwanese Investment in China Slows as Costs Rise', *Far Eastern Economic Review* (28 July 1994): 77.

69 Julian Baum, 'China Bound: Odds Improve for Direct Trade Links', *Far Eastern Economic Review* (29 December 1994 and 5 January 1995): 15–16. For economic incentives for the improvement of cross-Straits relations, also see Yu-Shan Wu (1994), 'Mainland China's Economic Policy Toward Taiwan: Economic Needs or Unification Scheme?'.

70 Julian Baum, 'Split Ticket', *Far Eastern Economic Review* (15 December 1994): 14–16.

71 Juian Baum, 'One Party, Two Systems', *Far Eastern Economic Review* (30 November 1995): 18, 20.

72 According to one argument, unification with Taiwan could produce the unintended consequence of 'unification-led political pluralization'. Unification could serve as a catalyst for China's political pluralization, breaking the political monopoly of the ruling parties and integrating various social forces and social groups. For this speculative argument, see Quansheng Zhao (1989).

73 See John C. Kuan, 'An Analysis of KMT-CCP Cooperation and China Unification', a paper presented at the annual meeting of the American Political Science Association, 29 August–1 September 1991, Washington, DC.

74 Interview with the author, March 1991, Taipei.

75 Julian Baum, 'The Narrowing Strait: Taipei and Peking Prepare for Unofficial Talks', *Far Eastern Economic Review* (29 April 1993): 13.

76 Julian Baum 'Charm Offensive', *Far Eastern Economic Review* (18 August 1994): 14–15.

77 See the cover story 'Liang an mishi baoguang' [The Secret Envoys between the Taiwan Straits Are Revealed], *Yazhou Zhoukan* [The International Chinese Newsweekly] (30 April 1995): 22–25.

78 'Dongxie yingde guoji wutai de hecai' [ASEAN Receives Praise from the International Community], *Yazhou Zhoukan* [The International Chinese Newsweekly] (30 April 1995): 22–25.

79 Michael Vatikiotis and Rodney Tasker, 'Hang on Tight', *Far Eastern Economic Review* (11 January 1996): 81.

80 For a detailed historical study supporting the Chinese claims from the perspectives of Taipei (as well as Beijing), see Yang (1993), *Nanhai fengyun* [The International Conflicts in the South China Sea].

81 *The Economist* (4 July 1992): 32. For a detailed account of China's disputes in South China Sea with excellent maps, see Mark Valencia (1995), 'China and the South China Sea Disputes.'

82 For details, see Nayan Chanda, et al., 'Territorial Imperative', *Far Eastern Economic Review* (23 February 1995): 14–16. For the evolution of China's policy towards this area, see Jie Chen (1994).

83 'Ramos Sets Up Territory Taskforce', *South China Morning Post*, 23 February 1995, p. 11.

84 Rodney Tasker, 'A Line of the Sand', *Far Eastern Economic Review* (6 April 1995): 14–16.

85 'Zhongfei nansha zhengyi you zhuanji' [An Optimistic Change for the Sino-Philippines Disputes over the Nansha Islands], *Yazhou Zhoukan* [The International Chinese Newsweekly] (27 August 1995): 42–43.

86 Cited from Michael Richardson, 'China Scrambles for Oil', *International Herald Tribune*, 3–4 June 1995, p. 9.

87   For the idea of 'local war', see Lee Ngok (1991); and Guan Jixian (1993).
88   Editorial, 'The Spratlys Spat: Much Ado About China', *Far Eastern Economic Review* (13 April 1995): 5.
89   *Renmin Ribao*, 3 December 1992, p. 1.
90   Philippe Agret, 'Hanoi Beats the Drum to Solve Tense Border Disputes', *Eastern Express* (25 October 1994): p. 8.
91   'Vietnam: Spratly Negotiations', *Far Eastern Economic Review* (1 December 1994): 13.
92   Bertil Lintner, 'Enter the Dragon', *Far Eastern Economic Review* (22 December 1994): 22–24.
93   *Wen Wei Po*, 27 December 1994, p. 1.
94   Bertil Lintner and Chiang Saen, 'River of Dreams: Chinese Emigrants Pour Down the Mekong', *Far Eastern Economic Review* (22 December 1994): 26.
95   *Ta Kung Pao*, 28 December 1994, p. 7.
96   Saritdet Marukatat, 'Vietnam in ASEAN Will Counter China's Weight', *The Japan Times* (Weekly International Edition), 28 November–4 December 1994, p. 8.
97   Anthony Rowley, 'In the Bloc-Hole: Kaifu to Stall on East Asian Trade Group Plan', *Far Eastern Economic Review* (17 January 1991): 11–12.
98   For information about the changing relationship between China and Eastern Europe, see Alyson Bailes (1990).
99   'New Great Wall', *Far Eastern Economic Review* (7 November 1991): 8.
100 Bertill Lintner, 'Mongols Fear Hordes: China Seems Too Close for Comfort', *Far Eastern Economic Review* (18 May 1995): 30.
101 Nayan Chanda, 'This Week's Sino-Vietnamese Summit Crowns the Emergence of China as the Regional Power', *The Asian Wall Street Journal Weekly*, 4 November 1991, pp. 2, 20.
102 'Moscow, Meet Peking', *The Christian Science Monitor*, 30 September 1988.
103 *Renmin Ribao*, 19 December 1992, p. 1; also see 'Talks Open New Russia–China Era', *The Virginian-Pilot and the Ledger-Star*, 19 December 1992, p. A11.
104 Alexei Voskressenski, 'Russia's China Challenge', *Far Eastern Economic Review* (22 June 1995): 34.
105 Michael Specter, 'Russia and China Act to Cut Arms, Widen Ties', *The New York Times*, 4 September 1994, p. 8.
106 'China: Subs from Russia', *Far Eastern Economic Review* (23 February 1995): 13.
107 The author attended an international conference on the Tumen River development project at Hunchun and Yanji (both in Jilin province) and toured the area in August 1995.
108 *Renmin Ribao*, 19 September 1988; also see *The Christian Science Monitor*, 19 September 1988.
109 Alexei Voskressenski, 'Russia's China Challenge', *Far Eastern Economic Review* (22 June 1995): 34. For a detailed and balanced analysis, see James Moltz (1995). Moltz (1995: 521) states that there are no reliable estimates of the actual figures of Chinese in the Russian Far East area, and 'estimates vary from around 200,000 to over two million'.
110 Alexei Voskressenski, 'Russia's China Challenge'.
111 For detailed accounts of China's changing relationships with the United States and the Soviet Union from an historical perspective, see, for example, Gordon Chang (1990).
112 'Baker's China Mission Called a Success', *Beijing Review*, 34, 47 (25 November–1 December 1991): 7–8.
113 For detailed accounts of the controversy around the MFN treatment of China by the United States, see, for example, Qingshan Tan (1990); also David Lampton (1994).
114 See Deng Xiaoping, 'The Principles of Peaceful Coexistence Have A Potentially Wide Application', 31 October 1984 (Deng Xiaoping, 1994: 102).

115 Nayan Chanda, 'Storm Warning', *Far Eastern Economic Review* (1 December 1994): 14–15.
116 Ibid.
117 Nayan Chanda, 'Winds of Change', *Far Eastern Economic Review* (June 22 1995): 14–15.
118 Simon Reeve, 'Thanks But No Thanks', *Far Eastern Economic Review* (27 July 1995).
119 Nigel Holloway, et al., 'Shanghaied by Taiwan', *Far Eastern Economic Review* (1 June 1995): 14–15.
120 Matt Forney, 'Under Fire', *Far Eastern Economic Review* (31 August 1995): 38.
121 Dana Priest and Judith Havemann, '2nd Carrier Group Heads to Taiwan,' *The Washington Post*, March 11, 1996, p. 1.
122 'China Ratchets up Intimidation of Taiwan,' compiled from reports by The Associated Press, *The Los Angeles Times* and *The Washington Post*, see *The Virginia-Pilot*, March 16, 1996, p. A1 and p. A7.
123 Kari Huus, 'Back to Normal: US-China Trade War Looms Closer', *Far Eastern Economic Review* (19 January 1995): 52.
124 Rone Tempest, 'US Will Back China's Bid to Join WTO', *Los Angeles Times*, 14 March 1995, Section D, p. 2.
125 Richard Covington, 'Ignoring Copyright Pact, China Reopens Factories that Pirated U.S. Cds', *International Herald Tribune*, 2 June 1995, p. 1.
126 'Beijing yingxiang shijie jingji dachao' [Beijing is Ready for the Development of World Economy and Trade], *Yazhou Zhoukan* [The International Chinese Newsweekly] (3 December 1995): 22–24.
127 'China Duty Drop', *Far Eastern Economic Review* (11 January 1996): 81.
128 'Zhongmei zhijian shiqu zuihou de huxin' [The Last Mutual Trust is Lost Between China and the United States], *Yazhou Zhoukan* [The International Chinese Newsweekly] (18 June 1995): 7.
129 For the evolution of American foreign policy toward China, see Banning Garrett (1990).
130 Nury Vittachi and Michael Westlake 'Tribute Time: Western Aircraft Companies Woo China', *Far Eastern Economic Review* (25 August 1994): 42.
131 Lincoln Kaye, 'Learning to Bow', *Far Eastern Economic Review* (27 January 1994): 12–13.
132 In 1991, Taiwan arranged to purchase sixteen unarmed Lafayette-class frigates from France. Despite China's objection, France later agreed to sell sixty Mirage 2000–5s to augment Taiwan's air defence capabilities. China ordered the French consulate in Guangzhou closed and banned French companies from participating in the city's projected subway system. See Paul Godwin (1994: 182).
133 Lincoln Kaye, 'Trading Rights', *Far Eastern Economic Review* (9 March 1995): 16.

8   Policy Choices and New Research Agenda

This book's review and examination of China's foreign policy since the establishment of the PRC in 1949 has traced and illuminated China's transformation from a revolutionary power to a post-revolutionary state. We have examined the effect of this fundamental change on China's external behaviour patterns, the roots of these patterns in the international, domestic, and individual levels, and their effect on decision-makers' policy choices. By emphasizing the interactions between micro policy-making and the three dimensions of the macrostructure — *symbolic*, *institutional*, and *power/regime* — this book examines the link between different variables affecting Chinese foreign policy decision-makers' choices and alternatives. Such an approach provides an interdisciplinary framework for analysis and should facilitate a better understanding of Chinese foreign policy, its principal characteristics, and its future directions, as well as the policy-making process itself.

This approach, at the same time, recognizes the importance of each individual element, as well as the linkages among them. It argues that the interactions among the factors at the micro and macro levels are crucial for the formulation of Chinese foreign policy, and we need to apply the micro-macro linkage approach to examine and grasp the dynamics of the internal workings of Chinese foreign policy.

A nation's international behaviour patterns are based on the norms, values, and processes by and through which the country's decision-makers deal with domestic and international issues. Because behaviour patterns often affect a country's policy choices, those patterns have become an important research subject for scholars of international relations and comparative politics. In examining China's external behaviour patterns and policy choices, this study has also demonstrated that the micro-macro linkage approach is one of the most effective avenues for studying foreign policy and its formulation. As stated earlier, the challenge of the linkage approach is how to create theoretical concepts that translate or map variables at the individual level into variables characterizing social systems, and vice versa.

As the preceding chapters have illustrated, three pairs of phrases — *revolution* and *modernization, vertical authoritarianism* and *horizontal authoritarianism,* and *rigidity* and *flexibility* — are useful conceptual tools for understanding and interpreting the changing dynamics of Chinese foreign policy. Each of these concepts can be used to explain certain aspects of China's external behaviour patterns. A study of all three provides a complex picture of Chinese foreign policy since 1949.

For the past forty or so years, Beijing has exercised a distinctive combination of rigidity and flexibility in its external policy choices. Most, if not all countries exhibit flexibility and rigidity in their foreign policy behaviour. Foreign policy makers, as Robert Keohane (1984: 257) suggests, should maintain flexibility of action as much as possible to retain 'maximum room for manœuvre'. However, the dual character of Chinese foreign policy is more pronounced, in what Lucian Pye (1981: 28) calls 'the Chinese style of political rhetoric'. On the one hand, Beijing's policy may be viewed as being 'rigid and distorted,' or 'inflexible' and dangerously ideological (Hunt, 1984: 5). On the other hand, Chinese foreign policy has been described by Harry Harding (1987: 243) as encompassing 'growing flexibility and pragmatism'. Pye (1988: 106) believes that 'the very flexibility of Chinese pragmatism can at times raise problems, particularly in foreign relations, as the agility of Chinese leaders can leave the more cautious and ponderous American (and Soviet) decision-making processes a step or two behind'. This dual nature of rigidity and flexibility has been summarized as 'staying firm in principle but flexible in tactics' (S. Kim, 1989b: 123). The duality of Chinese foreign policy, as indicated in Chapter 5, can be best interpreted by the micro-macro linkage model. That is to focus on the changing dynamics of the three dimensions of macrostructure that decision-makers have to face.

Chinese Foreign Policy Choices

Although it is always risky to predict the character of a country's foreign policy and its choices, general trends in China's recent foreign policy — modernization, nationalism, and regionalism — are (as discussed in Chapter 7) evident and seem likely to continue into the post-Deng era.

When looking back at the previous chapters, one may reach several conclusions. First, changes in the symbolic macrostructure may have a decisive effect on the interpretation of the internal and external environments at the micro level, which, in turn, would bring about changes of foreign policy priorities. In other words, 'ideas serve as road maps' in foreign policy issues (Goldstein and Keohane, 1993: 12). As Bernhard Giesen (1987: 351) claims, 'Symbolic macrostructure can have explanatory emergence in relation to microsocial processes of interaction, whereas practical macrostructure cannot.' As we established in Part II, major orientational changes in the symbolic macrostructure are likely to bring about fundamental and strategic changes in Chinese foreign policy, such as the shift from a 'closed' policy under Mao to an 'open' one under Deng.

Secondly, tactical changes in Chinese foreign policy, such as the sale of arms, are likely to be governed by the dynamics of the institutional macrostructure, which has a direct influence on the rules and norms of political actions and mechanisms in the policy-making process. Furthermore, the institutional macrostructure is also influenced by changes at the symbolic macrostructural level. For example, the enlarged scope and degree of participation in the formulation of Chinese foreign policy, as discussed in Chapter 4, is not simply an institutional arrangement, but also reflects the changes of basic beliefs in China's political system.

Thirdly, concern for regime legitimacy and internal power politics may become a key element in concrete foreign policy issues. These considerations tend to affect, sometimes invisibly, foreign policy strategies, tactics, and behaviour patterns.

Finally, the intertwined picture of the three dimensions of the macro reality opens up the possibility of more alternatives and different channels through which decision-makers may consider their preferences and make choices. One of the primary tasks before foreign policy specialists is to discover and examine the opportunities and channels faced by decision-makers. At the same time, these available choices are situational and case contingent, thereby creating never-ending exercises in the study of a country's foreign policy.

Beijing's commitment to modernization will more than likely remain its first priority goal. Deng's policy of 'reform and openness' has not always progressed smoothly. Yet the Beijing leadership in the first half of the 1990s, centred around Jiang Zemin, seems confident that periods of slow economic growth, such as those caused by sanctions from the West and political instability following the 1989 Tiananmen Incident, are only temporary. In the early and mid-1990s, China was relatively stable politically and is prospering economically. According to the Asian Development Bank, China's economy grew 7 per cent in 1991 and 12 per cent in 1992, an 'exceptional strength' in the recessive world economy.[1] It seems most likely that 'Chinese economic growth until the turn of the century might even match the 9 per cent annual rate of expansion achieved in 1980–93' (Lardy, 1994: 18–22).[2] The confirmation of Deng's reform policy at the Communist Party's 14th National Congress in October 1992 and the National People's Congress meeting in the spring of 1995, were signals that Beijing would continue its Opening and Reform policy in the post-Deng era.

Given this apparent dedication to modernization, the only circumstance under which China might readopt a Maoist policy would be a drastic internal political shift toward radicalism akin to that of the Gang of Four. Such a shift would necessarily isolate China from the outside world and damage its modernization drive. However, a return to isolationism seems highly unlikely for a variety of reasons.

As discussed in Chapter 3, learning is one of the major catalysts of changes in foreign policy priorities. It is true that, in general, obstacles to learning are greater in closed systems, such as the former Soviet Union and China, than in open systems (Ziegler, 1993: 13).[3] But when considering the changes between the era of Mao and the era of Deng one has to take into account China's bitter experience during the ten-year Cultural Revolution (1966–76). The Cultural Revolution produced a consensus among the Chinese people as well as its leaders — never again! Radical revolutionary ideas no longer appeal to the majority of the people; instead, the drive toward a market economy now enjoys widespread support. In addition, the policy of reform and openness launched by Deng has gained a momentum of its own and has gradually transformed the Chinese policy-making structure from vertical to horizontal authoritarianism (as analysed in Chapter 4). Those forces that inspired Deng's policy continue to grow stronger. Chief among them are:

• the many supporters and beneficiaries of economic development and modernization efforts;
• the technocratic bureaucrats that are emerging among the elites;
• the passing away of the revolutionary generation;
• China's opening up to the outside world;
• and the enormous increase in the diversity and complexity of foreign-policy decisions.

Although the struggle to succeed Deng seems certain to be fierce (the removal of the brothers Yang Shangkun and Yang Baibing from top military positions at the 14th Party Congress in 1992 and the purge of the Beijing Party boss and Politburo member Chen Xitong in 1995 highlighted more in the power struggle), the transformation process from vertical to horizontal authoritarianism will continue, ensuring that political inputs and interests are considered in the formulation of Chinese foreign policy.

China's top foreign-policy priority is likely to remain, as Robert Sutter (1988: 206) has stated, 'the pragmatic quest for a stable environment needed for effective modernization and development'; or, as Donald Zagoria (1991: 11) has expressed the matter, China's foreign policy will 'continue to be subordinated by its powerful desire to modernize the Chinese economy and the need to maintain a peaceful international environment'. China's foreign policy will remain pragmatic, economically oriented, independent and yet generally disposed toward trying to get along in the international community.

However, even though the general direction of China's future development will be toward economic modernization and greater political participation, it will most likely follow a zig-zag pattern such as China has experienced in the past. A pragmatic and economically oriented foreign policy does not guarantee that China will not use military force to solve external conflicts. As we have established in previous chapters, regime legitimacy and its survival both externally and internally has always been a top priority in the PRC's policy-making calculations. Beijing, under a reform-minded leadership, did not hesitate to use military force to repress its own people in the Tiananmen Incident; military options cannot be ruled out just because of the prevalence of reform.

Internally, nationalism has been one of the driving forces behind China's modernization efforts. Some elite intellectuals who have strong nationalist voices, for example, have increased their influences among Beijing's leading circles.[4] Power politics within the ruling elites will more than likely remain a major factor for the decision-makers' calculations in formulating Chinese foreign policy. Therefore, highly sensitive issues, such as the issue of Taiwan (particulary its independence), the dispute over the South China Sea Islands with several South-East Asian countries, and the dispute with Japan over the Diaoyu (Senkaku) Islands, are potential areas for internal power struggles. These could lead to a variety of policy choices for the Beijing leadership including both diplomatic means and the use of military force.

Beijing's firm objection to *taidu* (independence for Taiwan) is a case in point. As discussed in previous chapters, no Chinese leader, conservative or reformers alike, could afford to be responsible for caving in on this issue and be cast as a *lishi zuiren*, or a 'person condemned by history'.

On this point, it is interesting to note a reflective analogy made by Deng Xiaoping over the issue of Hong Kong in 1982, two years before the Sino-British agreement of returning the Territory to China. According to the recollections of Xu Jiatun, the head of the Xinhua News Agency in Hong Kong until 1989, Deng's position on the issue of China's sovereignty over Hong Kong was uncompromising in his conversation with British Prime Minister Margaret Thatcher, (Xu, 1993: 84–87). He told Thatcher that China must bring Hong Kong back regardless whatever results the negotiations may produce. There was a clear implication from Deng's wording that China would use non-peaceful means to resolve the issue if necessary.

Deng claimed that, if China failed to recover Hong Kong in 1997, 'no Chinese leaders or government would be able to justify themselves for that failure before the Chinese people'. Deng further stressed, 'it would mean that the present Chinese government was just like the government of the late Qing Dynasty and that the present Chinese leaders were just like Li Hongzhang'.[5] The late Qing Dynasty was responsible for the failure and humiliation of Chinese foreign policy in modern China history beginning with the Opium War of 1839 to 1842. Li Hongzhang, a top military and administrative official during the late Qing Dynasty, was known among Chinese as a national traitor. Li presided over the signing of a number of unequal treaties with foreign powers. Under the terms of these treaties China relinquished sovereignty, ceded territory (such as ceding Taiwan to Japan), and paid indemnities.[6] The same charge could easily be applied to any political leader in Beijing who would let Taiwan go without an all-out fight, including the use of military force. No Chinese leader could afford politically to be identified as a 'contemporary Li Hongzhang'.[7] The sensationalist, best-selling thriller from Taiwan (as mentioned in Chapter 7) — which features a military takeover by mainland China once the Island declares its independence[8] — may not be as fanciful and groundless as it appears. As Deng repeatedly emphasized, 'we cannot rule out the use of force [with *taidu*] — that is something we must bear in mind, and so must the next generation.'[9] When facing the situation of *taidu*, as discussed in the previous chapters, the choices that decision-makers in Beijing may have are indeed quite limited.

On the other hand, Beijing is well aware that the political situation on Taiwan is more complex than before. In his visit to Taiwan in August 1994, Tang Shubei, the highest-ranking Beijing official to come to Taiwan, recalled a comment by paramount leader Deng Xiaoping that China's modernization must come before unification can be achieved.[10] This statement reflects two messages: First, Beijing realized that unification with Taiwan would be a prolonged process, and recognized the need to be patient. Second, the PRC intended to make every effort not to let the Taiwan issue hurt its modernization drive.

In fact, there have been increased calls on the Mainland for strengthening economic cooperation across the Taiwan Straits. The cooperation may even be extended to the security area, such as the South China Sea disputes between China and several South-East Asian countries. It is well known that Beijing and Taipei have held similar positions over the disputed territories. In February 1995, for example, officials in Hainan province openly called for joint efforts between the Mainland and Taiwan to recover and develop the South China Sea area. This suggestion was reported to the higher authorities in Beijing for further action.[11] In sum, the further integration of 'Greater China' (the PRC, Taiwan, Hong Kong, and Macau) will continue to be a prominent phenomenon in the Asia-Pacific region.[12]

Faced with the changing dynamics of the post-Cold War era, the PRC must address a number of issues concerning its present and future policies. Here, China's primary foreign policy goal is in line with its domestic priority — economic modernization. The central task for all PRC leaders, old and new alike, is to promote economic development and to control problems — such as the confusion over currency exchange rates in 1994, and inflation caused by an overheated economy in the early 1990s[13] — which have arisen as side-effects of economic reform. This will continue to be a basis for foreign policy decisions.

To combat uncertainty in its post-Tiananmen relations with the United States, Beijing has developed a multi-directional strategy, centred around regionalism, to prepare for any undesirable future developments. While trying hard to restore relations with the United States to the pre-1989 level, China has made manœuvres in three directions.

First, China has further expanded its influence in East and South-East Asian regional affairs, as discussed in Chapter 7, by cultivating relations with capitalist economies such as Japan, South Korea, the six ASEAN countries, Burma, as well as its relations within the other parts of Greater China — Taiwan, Hong Kong, and Macau.

Second, China has improved or enhanced its relations with the other two Asian socialist countries — Vietnam and North Korea, and the two former socialist neighbours — Russia and Mongolia. Within the same week in late November through early December in 1995, Jiang Zemin hosted the Vietnamese Party Secretary-General Do Muoi and Cuban President Fidel Castro in Beijing.[14] The PRC has also strengthened its footing in Central Asia. In May 1994, Li Peng made a swing through the central Asian former Soviet republics including Turkmenistan,

Uzbekistan, Kazakhstan, and Kyrgyzstan, further enhancing Beijing's position in this area.[15] Although it is unlikely at present, China may, if the domestic and international moods change, even set up an informal Asian-socialist alliance, consisting of China, North Korea, and Vietnam, to resist Western pressure for political and economic liberalization.

Finally, Beijing has continued to develop cooperative relations with industrialized countries (in addition to the United States) such as Japan and the Western European countries. As discussed in Chapters 6 and 7, China has always attached great importance to its relations with Japan. A stable Beijing–Tokyo relationship will serve as a key to regional stability in East Asia. Beijing has also managed to maintain cordial relations with the Europeans, particularly since the early 1990s. This was further demonstrated by the European Union Trade Commissioner Leon Brittan's visit to Beijing in November 1994, which showed a different attitude from the more hard-line American position in terms of such controversial issues as China's membership in the World Trade Organization.[16]

As the PRC's international status is gradually restored and strengthened in the wake of the Tiananmen Incident, Beijing's leadership will become more confident in world affairs, enabling China to exhibit more assertive behaviour. If the Chinese regime perceives itself as less threatened by foreign powers, particularly the United States, Russia, and Japan, it will become more cooperative in international affairs, and will behave more like an insider and a partner, than an outsider or challenger. As Harry Harding (1994: 399) argues, during the Maoist era Chinese cooperative relationships were both selective and volatile; whereas in the era of Deng, China has been willing to forge cooperative relationships with a much wider range of nations and international institutions. But if the world seems more threatening, considerations of national security and the issue of regime survival will take top priority in Chinese foreign policy, which may push Beijing to extreme directions.[17]

China will remain a regional power with global aspirations. Regionally it will concentrate its external activities in the Asia-Pacific area. In global matters, China will go along with the mainstream of world opinion while seeking to advance its own independent policy. Given the rapid decline of Soviet/Russian power, the collapse of communism, and the advent of a more cooperative relationship between Moscow and Washington, the extent to which China can pursue an independent course seems limited. In addition, with the potential ethnic unrest in the minority areas along the border regions, such as Tibet, Inner Mongolia, and Xinjiang, Beijing may have to pay close attention, not only to those areas, but also to bordering countries. Based on the concern over the spread of Islamic extremism in Xinjiang, for example, Beijing, from 1992 to 1995, closed the Karakorum Highway — the connection between Xinjiang and Pakistan which is near to Afghanistan and Tajikistan.[18]

The concept of an independent foreign policy is perhaps more useful for China with regard to the North–South divide; China would like to play a leading role in the Third World and will act more independently in its relationships with industrialized countries on behalf of Third World countries. As the only permanent Third World member of the UN Security Council, China may follow the policies of the major powers on some occasions, but may also act as a protector of Third World interests on some other occasions.

China's domestic mood is a crucial variable in its foreign policy. China's distinctive state–society relationship has, according to Lucian Pye (1992: 254–255), 'contributed to the peculiar rhythm of its politics'. The power struggles within the leading circle have produced 'not the Western pendulum swings between left and right, liberal and conservative, but an up-and-down motion of centralizing and decentralizing, of tightening and loosening the State's penetration of society'. This 'up-and-down' or 'tightening and loosening' motion is in line with the fact that major changes of leadership in China's domestic politics are likely to bring about orientational and strategic changes in Chinese foreign policy, such as the shift from a 'closed' policy under Mao to an 'open' one under Deng. Generally speaking, when the mood is 'down' or 'loosening', Beijing appears more flexible in its external actions, whereas in an 'up' or 'tightening' period, it appears more rigid. Each motion produces a different priority in Beijing's policy agenda.

The struggle for the transition of power prepared for the post-Deng era is looming large. Despite the speculation by some observers that the fate of the current Chinese top leader Jiang Zemin will be similar to that of Hua Guofeng (a transitional leader from 1976 to 1978 between the era of Mao and the era of Deng) Jiang has made every effort to secure his leading position.[19]

Some believe that the strengthening of Jiang's power base will be conducive to stable foreign and domestic policies in the post-Deng era. Yet, nobody can be assured exactly of what will happen after the death of Deng, since Chinese politics at both the institutional and individual levels is so uncertain and dynamic, and therefore unpredictable. It seems, however, that as long as the dust remains unsettled, a bold and imaginative alteration to the current foreign and domestic policies is unlikely, since individual leaders are still primarily concerned with avoiding a succession crisis in Chinese politics. This assessment is shared by many China watchers both inside and outside of the country. They have observed that, facing the forthcoming showdown for the post-Deng era, individual leaders engaged in Beijing politics have tended to appear tough toward such politically sensitive issues as the treatment of political dissidents. For example, just before US Secretary of State Warren Christopher's visit to Beijing in March 1994, Chinese authorities in Beijing and Shanghai grabbed a string of at least 13 high-profile political activists, including China's best-known dissidents Wei Jingsheng and Wang Dan. This action, however, was viewed by foreign observers as 'largely a result of domestic political struggle', not a diplomatic show.[20] With Wei Jingsheng's 're-arrest' and subsequent 14-year prison sentence in December 1995, Robin Munro of Human Rights Watch/ Asia commented that Beijing's purpose was to use this case to 'serve as an example [to the Chinese people]'.[21] It also reflected the Beijing leadership's lack of confidence in China's political stability.

The uncertainty of Beijing politics has made some already uncertain policy issues even more uncertain. The people of Hong Kong, for example, felt increasingly frustrated when 1994 passed with little progress on issues that must be resolved to allow the 'one country–two systems' approach adopted for capitalist Hong Kong when it reverts to socialist China on 1 July 1997.[22] In his May 1994 visit to Hong Kong, Lu Ping, the head of China's Hong Kong and Macau Affairs Office, made a blunt warning to those active in politics: if anyone attempts to use Hong Kong to influence Chinese politics, 'Hong Kong would be of negative value instead of positive value to China. This would be disastrous for Hong Kong.' In his comments on Lu's remarks, Cheung Man-kwong, a member of the Hong Kong Legislative Council (Legco), made a connection between China's Hong Kong policy and the power politics in Beijing by stating, 'Chinese leaders have turned ultra-conservative in all matters, Hong Kong included, because of the struggle over political succession.'[23]

The decline of communism, however, will enable Chinese foreign policy to become more flexible in many areas. At the same time, nationalism will continue to influence Chinese foreign policy and the protection of China's national integrity and national interests may make territory-related issues a factor in foreign policy disputes. Territorial disputes, such as that with Japan over the Diaoyu (Senkaku) Islands and those with Vietnam, Malaysia, and the Philippines over the South China Sea islands may become sources of international conflict.

Finally, Chinese foreign policy behaviour in general will continue to be a mixture of flexibility and rigidity, the balance varying according to the changing dynamics of power politics (the power/regime macro-structure), the Beijing leadership's perception of the fluctuating international and domestic environments (the symbolic macrostructure), and the increasing involvement of the bureaucratic and societal interests in foreign policy issues (the institutional macrostructure).

How Should Other Nations Deal with China?

What do China's external behaviour patterns and policy choices and its direction in the post-Cold War era mean for other countries? How can other nations deal more effectively with Beijing?

The first step in dealing with the PRC should be to examine the basis for each of its foreign policies. The micro-macro linkage approach developed in this book will prove helpful for comprehending the general background and basic orientation of Chinese foreign policy issues, and the role and affect of institutional changes, regime legitimacy and power politics.

One may, for example, ask such questions as: is a particular policy based on security-political considerations? Or is economic profit the primary motivation? Is the internal power struggle the true reason for an external policy? Different motivations in response to various macro-structures (symbolic, institutional, or power/regime) will present different sets of policy choices. For example, Beijing is usually more willing to show flexibility when dealing with economic issues — such as Taiwan's membership in the Asian Development Bank — than when political and nationalistic issues — such as the issue of *taidu* (Taiwan independence) — are at stake.

The advantage of the linkage model in more precisely interpreting Chinese foreign policy behaviour can be demonstrated by the case of China's 1958 massive bombardment of Jinmen (Quemoy). Jinmen and Mazu (Matsu), are the two small islands just off the coast of Fujian province still held by the KMT troops (see Chapter 3). One might think that Beijing's purpose was to take over Jinmen or even Taiwan. But if we examine deeper the micro-level of decision-making — the thinking of the top Chinese leaders, particularly Mao Zedong himself — we discover a different picture. According to some recently published recollections, there were at least four factors behind the military actions. First, Mao hoped to use the bombardment to challenge Khrushchev's bid to reduce tensions between the Soviet Union and the United States; this military action would reinforce the perception of a real strategic triangle and the recognition of China's crucial part in it. Mao believed that the islands (Jinmen and Mazu) 'are two batons that keep Khrushchev and Eisenhower dancing'.

Second, Mao's shelling of Jinmen was a dare to see how far the United States would go in defending Taiwan; Mao was even prepared at that time for the possibility that Americans might drop an atom bomb on Fujian province. Third, he used to his advantage the fact that the Taiwan issue served as an external pressure to help maintain the 'internal unity' of the top leadership in China's domestic politics. Mao was well aware, as he said, that 'once the pressure is off, internal disputes might break out'.

Fourth, rather than actually trying to retake the islands and thus settle the issue during that period, Mao preferred to keep the tension in play; he considered the two islands to be China's link to Taiwan and felt that without that link, it might be easier for Taiwan to go independent (Z. Li, 1994: 270–271, 262). Therefore, for Mao, the bombardment of Jinmen was not merely an action against Taiwan and a bilateral matter; it was one of his games within the domestic political arena and on the bigger board of world politics. The real motivations behind China's external behaviour, one may conclude, may be quite different from people have originally believed.

There were similar considerations behind Beijing's decision not to retake Hong Kong immediately after the Communist victory in 1949. Zhou Enlai had an internal talk in 1951 with the director of the Hong Kong branch of the Xinhua News Agency about the future of Hong Kong. During this discussion he argued that the decision not to recover Hong Kong was not based on the 'narrow thinking of territory and sovereignty principles'; rather it was based on the international, strategic consideration that 'it would be better to let Britain keep Hong Kong [for some time], so that we can fully utilize the differences between the United States and Britain [in terms of China policy] to enlarge our united front to fight against the diplomatic isolation and economic sanctions imposed on China by the Western camp led by the United States' (Xu, 1993: 472–475).

It often takes time for outside observers to comprehend the complicated pictures of internal and external considerations behind China's foreign policy decision. Patience and the use of informal channels, therefore, are two important elements when dealing with Beijing. The Chinese take a much longer-term view of the world than most countries. Thus Beijing believes it can afford to wait, and it often moves slowly and cautiously. Persistence and patience are valuable commodities in achieving fruitful negotiations. Informal contacts are helpful too. Negotiations conducted behind the scenes and informal channels and contacts are frequently more effective than open confrontation that may threaten the Chinese with an unacceptable loss of face or may appear to challenge China's sovereignty, both of which will result in inflexibility.

Caution should not be confused with inactivity. Moderate external pressure may make the Chinese leadership more sensitive both to inter-national criticism and to domestic demands. External pressure may also encourage Beijing to be more pragmatic and less rigid in its behaviour. The application of pressure, however, must be carefully calculated to correspond to China's domestic atmosphere. Should outside pressure become too strong and external criticism too harsh, the results may be counterproductive, arousing nationalism and anti-Western feelings in China. This could lead to a narrowing or even a closure of channels to the outside world.

The US decision to allow Taiwan's President Lee Teng-hui to visit the United States in June 1995, for example, was widely regarded as a newly initiated pressure on China, and (as discussed in the previous chapters) Beijing reacted swiftly and angrily. There were two different assessments regarding China's reaction.

One viewpoint, is reflected in the following words of a US diplomat: 'There is no change at all in the main relationship.' Or, as an American businessman assumed, 'It's just politics, the rhetoric of politics', and should be business as usual for the time to come.[24] James Lilley, the former US ambassador to Beijing and Taipei also did not believe Beijing's threat of 'grave consequences'; Lilley argued that previous warnings from Beijing had proved false, citing the examples of the sale of F-16s to Taiwan by President George Bush and the dispatch of a Clinton cabinet member to Taiwan.[25]

The other approach looked at the issue quite differently. A Hong Kong-based journal *Yazhou Zhoukan* argued that this incident might become the last straw of the foundation of mutual trust between the two countries, aggravating the already declining trend in bilateral relations beginning with the Tiananmen Incident of 1989. The journal further anticipated that the future development of the Asia-Pacific region would be marked by increased rivalry relationship between China and the United States.[26] Some American officials feared that Beijing's concerns that the US might abandon its One China policy could reach a boiling point — that over the next few years there could be military incidents in the Taiwan Straits. As former US Ambassador Chas Freeman, who most recently served as US assistant secretary of defence, put it: 'We face a year of living dangerously in this region'.[27] Freeman's concern was demonstrated by the military tensions in the Taiwan Straits in the spring of 1996.

Obviously, only history can judge which of the above arguments is closer to the reality. It is important to note that these two arguments have actually come from different perspectives. The former — that bilateral trade relations appeared to be 'business as usual' — came from a focus upon the institutional macrostructure. The latter — that mutual trust was lost, causing the two countries' basic interpretations of each other to change from 'constructive partner' to a threat to national interest and regime security — was based upon the symbolic macrostructure and the power/regime macrostructure. In other words, the loss of trust may indicate some fundamental damage to the foundation of Deng Xiaoping's sixteen-character guideline for China's US policy (introduced in the previous Chapter). No matter which argument one may believe, what is most important is that the interactions between the micro process in Beijing's policy-making and various dimensions of the macrostructure need to be fully understood.

An important policy paper (published by the Atlantic Council of the United States and the National Committee on United States–China Relations in early 1993) on Sino-American relations emphasized that when dealing with Beijing on such sensitive issues as human rights, the West should consider the stances of the majority of China's Asia-Pacific neighbours. These nations believe that 'different cultural and historical experiences, demographics, systems of governance, and stages of economic development' must be taken into account when dealing with China.[28] Considering cultural and historical factors, it will take time for China to develop a more sophisticated and reliable legal and governing system. This kind of consideration is likely to bring about an incremental, rather than a radical, approach in dealing with the PRC.

Alexander George (1991: 23) has suggested that policy-makers in every country must balance two objectives: 'protection of [their] interests and avoidance of measures that could trigger undesired escalation'. When dealing with China, a balanced policy is certainly the key to effective negotiations. With regard to Sino-American relations, Robert Scalapino (1991/92: 33) has argued, 'It is entirely appropriate for Washington to act in a pluralistic fashion, with private activities and official policies pursuing different emphases, and with maximum contact maintained at different levels.'

In the autumn of 1993, the Clinton Administration entered, according to US Assistant Secretary of State for East Asian and Pacific Affairs

Winston Lord (1995: 248), a stage of 'comprehensive engagement', meaning to 'engage the Chinese across a broad agenda of issues and at various levels, both work levels and high levels', including 'military-to-military talks'. Defence Secretary William Perry, for example, was deeply involved with what he called 'defense conversion' activities with the Chinese since then.[29] This 'maximum contact' or 'comprehensive engagement' between the two countries is important, not only for the advancement of bilateral relations but also for China's political development.

Given China's strategic importance in the Asia-Pacific area, and its huge population (one of every five human beings on earth lives in China), China's place in the world order 'is a matter of universal concern' (Halpern, 1965: 11). China's foreign policy will remain of vital importance to the rest of the world, especially to the United States, Japan, Russia, and the countries of the Asia-Pacific region. As Richard Nixon pointed out in 1989, 'with Japan already an economic superpower with the capability of becoming a military and political superpower, a strong, stable China . . . is essential to balance the power of Japan' in East Asia.[30] Bearing in mind the zig-zag pattern of Chinese foreign policy, one would hope to see in the future an open-minded China rather than an isolated China, a cooperative partner rather than a challenger to the international community. Because China will continue to be a key force in East Asia's stability and prosperity, a peaceful, constructive China will contribute directly to global stability and peace.

The Micro-Macro Linkage Approach and Research Agendas

Finally, let us return to the main approach applied in this book — the micro-macro linkage — to raise future research agendas for the study of Chinese foreign policy. Part I has discussed in detail the conceptual meaning of the linkage approach and its relation to the study of foreign policy. We should also pay attention to the structural aspect of the approach when attempting to apply it to our research. Here, it is important, to acknowledge again the limit of this study — that there is not yet sufficient empirical micro-level material to do a thorough application of this model, to fully cover the interactions between different levels with regard to foreign policy choices. In providing a theoretical framework, it is the author's hope that more research in this direction will be conducted.

In order to avoid the micro or macro extremes (such as emphases only on the international environment or on individual decision-makers) in social science studies, George Ritzer (1990: 357–364) has made the following integrative approaches (summarized by this author) which may become a foundation of future agendas for Chinese foreign-policy analysis:

- First, macro-oriented theorists should focus on micro-level issues and micro-oriented theorists should work at the macro levels;
- Second, more scholars who are not predisposed to one or another (micro or macro) levels of analysis should make efforts and contributions in this area of research, to help promote an inherently integrative, dialectical approach to analysis;
- And third, more analyses of the ongoing relationships between and among a greater variety of elements at both the micro and macro levels.

These suggestions may have at least two significant implications for the future research agenda for Chinese foreign policy studies. First, more precise research avenues for developing the micro-macro analytical line need to be discussed. And second, specific cases of Chinese foreign policy need to be laid out.

As Atul Kohli (1995: 46–47) has suggested (in his summary of the excellent symposium 'The Role of Theory in Comparative Politics'), there are two primary, yet contrasting concerns in the field of comparative politics: the problem-driven orientation that 'tends to relegate the role of theory mainly to that of a tool of empirical research; and the quest for causal generalizations which moves the role of theory 'to the forefront'. We need to bear these concerns in mind when applying the micro-macro linkage model to the analysis of foreign policy issues.

One may identify, from a combination of the above discussed approaches and this author's observations, at least the following research agendas for studying Chinese foreign policy by means of a micro-macro synthesis. (Several of these agendas, naturally, are the main themes of the previous chapters.)

In studying the ongoing relationships between the micro- and macro-levels, it is reasonable first to examine the effect of macro-level elements, such as the international and domestic environments, on China's foreign policy, and then turn attention to the effect of the micro-level factors such as the power politics that motivate the decision-makers. Domestic political, economic, and social structures, as Peter Gourevitch

(1978: 882) suggests, 'instead of being a cause of international politics', may become a 'consequence' of the changing international system. Two examples of efforts to examine the impact of foreign policy on domestic factors are Margaret Pearson's (1991) work on the impact of the Open Door policy on joint ventures and economic institutions in China, and Quansheng Zhao's (1989) study on the possible impact of the relationship between the PRC and Taiwan and the issue of unification on China's internal political development.

Issue-oriented research is another effective avenue for research. As discussed in Part I, the ranking of influential elements — international, domestic, or individual — that are most important to Chinese foreign policy may differ with each issue, and will depend on changes over time and location. One such effort in issue-oriented research is a collective study on China's quest for national identity (Dittmer and Kim, 1993). To examine the issue of national identity, this study adopted an interdisciplinary method, using historical, cultural, social, and anthropological perspectives, as well as political science approaches. In other words, this study has place China in a multi-dimensional picture around the major theme of national identity, thereby making a significant contribution to the toolbox for micro-macro research.

Another promising line of study is an approach which focuses on policy-making mechanisms and processes. Michael Mann's (1986) theory on macro-historical conflict, in which he advocates the importance of four dimensions of power (military/geopolitical, political, economic, and cultural/ideological) may be particularly useful in selecting various issues, as Chinese society has evolved toward a more pluralistic direction in the post-Mao era. One may also examine the links between domestic and international influences on China's foreign policy-making, and the effects of transnational developments (such as foreign direct investments) and institutions (such as the World Bank) on China's domestic institutions.

As illustrated in Chapter 6, one useful way to further our study of micro-macro integration in Chinese foreign policy is to conduct comparative analyses. Studies of other countries' foreign policy behaviours may provide examples for the study of Chinese foreign policy. One logical study would be a comparison of Chinese foreign policy-making and that of one or more socialist countries. One may look at research on the formulation of the former Soviet Union's foreign policy, and pay special attention to various analyses at either macro or micro levels.[31] Seweryn Bialer, in his analysis of the domestic roots of Soviet foreign policy (1981) discusses three dimensions: culture and ideology, politics and society, and economics. He then examines the Soviet Union in the context of Eastern Europe. One could adopt and further develop Bialer's way of research by including micro level analyses to survey Chinese foreign policy, and then make a comparisons with Soviet foreign policy. There are already comparative studies on Chinese and Soviet domestic political and economic reforms.[32] There have also been efforts to compare China with other countries; one example is a comparative study on China, Korea, Germany, and Vietnam around the theme of national unification and the 'politics of divided nations'. (See Zhao and Sutter, 1991).

The second part of the research agenda proposed here is to conduct theoretically informed case-contingent studies, namely empirical analysis applying the linkage approach. Graham Allison's (1971) study on the rational actor, organizational process, and bureaucratic politics using the Cuban missile crisis as a case study sets a brilliant example in this regard. Below are several examples of Chinese foreign policy issues that may be worth of our attention as case studies for research.

Foreign Policy and the Use of Military Force

As discussed in Chapter 3, the PRC has since 1949 used military forces seven times in the international arena, fighting against such opponents as the Americans, the Soviets, the Indians, and the Vietnamese. Although there are numerous studies on each of China's external wars, little research has been conducted along the analytical lines of micro-macro linkage. Let us take the studies on the Korean War as an example.

Allen Whiting (1960) conducted his pioneer work *China Crosses the Yalu: The Decision to Enter the Korean War* by applying the 'rational actor' model of the realist approach. Whiting argues that Beijing's decision to enter the war was based on the concern for national security that had been provoked by American rhetoric and actions, such as those of General Douglas MacArthur from Tokyo. This approach was praised as pathbreaking in advancing a new understanding of the PRC's foreign and crisis behaviour, and was followed by more recent works such as *Uncertain Partners: Stalin, Mao, and the Korean War* (Goncharov, Lewis, and Xue, 1994).[33] Nevertheless, some criticized the work for giving 'only secondary consideration' to 'the internal dynamic of policy formulation — the interaction of factions, organizational procedures, and bureaucratic politics' (Yu, 1994: 238–240). On the other hand, from the psychocultural perspective, the Korean war was seen by the Beijing leadership as a search not only for 'physical security', but also for 'psychological security' (Shih, 1990: 179–181). More important, according to this school of thought, were Beijing's efforts to search for a 'stable national self-image'. Thus, China's external military behaviour is interpreted as motivated by 'face-saving'. This approach can be criticized as overlooking the macro-level elements of both international and domestic environments.

Although the above-mentioned studies have laid good foundations for our understanding of the Korean War, each of them has only covered one part of the story. Fresh analyses applying the micro-macro linkage model may provide more comprehensive pictures of Beijing's decision to enter the Korean War, as well as other military and diplomatic actions. In each of these cases, one may analyse whether or not there were options other than military action facing the decision-makers at that time.

Bilateral Relations with Other Countries

The study of ongoing relationships among elements at different levels may lead to thorough analyses of China's relations with key international players, as opposed to its diplomatic relations in general. Most existing literature on China's relations with Russia, Japan, the United States, for example, tend to be studied exclusively from a single perspective (the Chinese perspective or its partner's perspective). A more challenging task is to study the relationship as a whole, giving equal attention to the domestic and international factors, as well as to individual decision-makers, which have faced the countries involved. Harry Harding's (1992) and Robert Ross' (1995) analyses on Sino-American relations are fine efforts in this direction.

Key Foreign Policy Decisions

Research on a number of key foreign policy decisions need to be conducted from both macro and micro levels. China's *yibiandao* policy — 'leaning toward one side,' meaning to favour the Soviet Union — raised by Mao in June 1949 (see Chapter 3), for example, profoundly limited Chinese foreign policy options for the next two decades. The conventional argument both within and outside of China has been that, given the international and domestic environments at that time, Beijing had no choice but to make an alliance with the Soviet Union.[34] One may challenge this proposition by analysing other possible options before the outbreak of the Korean War in June 1950.

Policies towards Taiwan and Hong Kong

Beijing's policies toward Taiwan and Hong Kong may also be analysed from the micro-macro linkage perspective. The issue of Hong Kong, for example, may fall right on the linkage line, being jointly a 'domestic' matter (reunification), a 'foreign' matter (PRC–Britain), and a matter of personal consideration for individual leaders (different outcomes may result in a positive or negative reputation in Chinese history: to be praised as a 'national hero', or to be condemned as a 'traitor').

Environmental Policy

China's environmental policy is an increasingly important, yet still largely neglected to which macro-micro linkage can be applied — a classic case of an important subject waiting to be defined and integrated into the synergistic study of Chinese foreign relations. Environmental policy can be seen, for example, as the triple intersection of Beijing's domestic power politics, China's external actions, and the global and regional international systems.[35] One may also study the formation of epistemic communities between China and its international partners on issues of mutual concern (such as the environmental issues), and their impact on China's domestic and foreign policy considerations.

Comparative Foreign Policies between the PRC and Taiwan

In addition to comparing China with other East Asian countries such as Japan (as was done in Chapter 6), one may also conduct comparative studies with other Chinese societies such as Taiwan. These comparisons are particularly useful when analysing the impact of traditional thinking and political culture on foreign policy issues.

Domestic Mood and Foreign Policy

There have been cycles in China's political atmosphere throughout the history of the People's Republic. As mentioned earlier, China's distinctive state–society relationship has contributed to the peculiar rhythm of its politics. The 'up-and-down' or 'tightening and loosening' motion is in line with the fact that changes in China's leadership are likely to bring about orientational and strategic changes in Chinese foreign policy, such as the shift from a 'closed' policy under Mao to an 'open' one under Deng. Within a given leadership, one may also see, although not always clearly, the correlation between domestic swings of 'tightening and loosening' and foreign policy issues. This causal relationship may best be demonstrated by the fact that under different domestic political atmospheres the Beijing authorities adopt different policies governing its citizens contacts with the outside world, such as overseas travel and study abroad. Research along this line, rather than concentrating on each level of the societal–institutional–individual synthesis, will help to develop a comprehensive analysis covering elements at different levels.

Individual Leaders and Foreign Policy Issues

As more empirical materials become available in the years to come, case studies on the involvement of individual leaders in major foreign policy issue will become more significant. Research could be conducted on the following topics:

- the impact of Mao Zedong's personal, successful military and revolutionary experience on revolution-oriented foreign policy during the era of Mao.[36]
- the relationship between Zhou Enlai's and Deng Xiaoping's earlier experiences of studying abroad (Japan and France for Zhou; and France and the Soviet Union for Deng) and their outward (and open) policies toward the outside world.

There are many more Chinese foreign policy issues that could serve as case studies for the micro-macro linkage approach. Examples include China's decision to open up to the outside world in 1978; the PRC's arms control policy (such as weapons acquisitions, deployment, and sales);[37] human right concerns and foreign policy; China's political and military advisors in other countries; and many more.

It is the author's hope that this fresh and analytical examination of the complex and sophisticated nature of Chinese foreign policy will foster a better understanding of how this policy is made and of how China is maneuvering the transition from revolutionary power to modern state within the international political and economic systems. Because China is such an important player in the drama of contemporary international relations, both Beijing and other capitals must genuinely comprehend the factors that influence Chinese external policy to sustain a stable and peaceful world order.[38]

To repeat the call of John Gaddis (1992/93), international relations theory in general needs to meet the profound changes brought by the post-Cold War era. The micro-macro linkage approach represents a fresh starting point, opening up new research agendas for the study of Chinese foreign policy. We do need this necessary and permanent change in the field. Without a more integrated approach to Chinese foreign policy, our understanding of what China has done, is doing, and will do in the future, will be at worst, prone to misinterpretation and error and at best, incomplete. This new focus on the intersection of macro and micro levels will likely endure as one of the most important conceptual guidelines for studying Chinese foreign policy for the time to come.

Notes

1 'Asian Economies Continue to be Star Performers', in *The Japan Times* (Weekly International Edition), 7–13 December 1992, p. 17.
2 Lardy's predictions are based on his analysis of following elements of Chinese economy: a strong agricultural foundation, high rates of saving and investment, effective human capital formation, relatively low income inequality, rapid demographic transition, rapid growth of manufacture exports, and high productivity growth.
3 Charles Ziegler (1993: 13) has explained why it is more difficult for learning to occur in closed systems: 'In closed systems central decision-makers are relatively isolated from lower level foreign policy organizations, and from factors in the domestic environment that might constrain their behavior. Closed systems also tend to buffer their populations from influences in the international environment which might introduce ideas challenging the structural basis of the system.'
4 Kari Huus, 'The Hard Edge', *Far Eastern Economic Review* (9 November 1995): 28. Huus observes, 'In China's elite intellectual circles, nationalism with a chauvinistic, authoritarian cast has been gaining credibility since the collapse of the Soviet Union exposed communism's clay feet. And the influence of these scholars, some say, is making itself felt within the halls of power'.
5 See Deng Xiaoping, 'Our Basic Position on the Question of Hong Kong — A Talk with British Prime Minister Margaret Thatcher', 24 September 1982 (Deng, 1994: 23–25).
6 Such treaties include the Sino-British Yantai Treaty, the Sino-French New Treaty, the Sino-Japanese Treaty of Shimonoseki, the Sino-Russian Pact, and the Peace Treaty of 1901 with eleven countries, including Great Britain, the United States, Russia, Germany, and Japan. See Deng (1994: 376, Note 13).
7 On the other hand, there are different assessments of Li Hongzhang and his role in modern Chinese history among some historians. One may see, for example, Samuel Chu and Kwang-Ching Liu (1994) eds., *Li Hung-Chang and China's Early Modernization*.
   For an interesting book review emphasizing the similarities between Li and Deng Xiaoping in terms of the drive for China's modernization, see Lynn Pan, 'The Ghost of Deng Xiaoping', *Far Eastern Economic Review* (8 December 1994): 46.
8 For details, see Julian Baum, 'Fear of Falling: Prophet of Chinese Invasion Makes Many Nervous', *Far Eastern Economic Review* (13 October 1994): 24–26.
9 See Deng Xiaoping, 'Speech at the Third Plenary Session of the Central Advisory Commission of the Communist Party of China', 22 October 1984 (Deng, 1994: 93).
10 Julian Baum 'Charm Offensive', *Far Eastern Economic Review* (18 August 1994): 14–15.
11 *Huanan Jingji Xinwen* [Economic News of South China], 24 February 1995.
12 Some scholars even argue that 'Greater China' may ultimately include the millions of overseas Chinese in the rest of Asia and the world; see Maria Chang (1995: 966), 'Greater China and the Chinese "Global Tribe"'. The distribution of overseas ethnic Chinese is as follows:

- Thailand: 6.58 million;
- Malaysia: 6.16 million;
- Indonesia: 5.05 million;

- Vietnam, Laos, and Cambodia: 2.46 million;
- Singapore: 2.36 million;
- North America: 2.32 million;
- Latin America: 0.8 million;
- The Philippines: 0.76 million;
- Europe: 0.62 million;
- Australia and New Zealand: 0.49 million;
- Japan and South Korea: 0.17 million;
- India and Pakistan: 0.12 million;
- Other places: 0.1 million

13   For China's economic problems, see Lincoln Kaye, 'Deafened by Decree: China's Currency and Tax Reforms Spread Confusion', *Far Eastern Economic Review* (13 January 1994): 80–81; and Carl Goldstein, 'Doctor's Orders: Beijing Tries Again to Cool China's Economy', *Far Eastern Economic Review* (17 February 1994): 44–45.

14   Matt Forney and Adam Schwarz, 'Socialist Realism', *Far Eastern Economic Review* (14 December 1995): 21; and *Renmin Ribao* (People's Daily), 28 November 1995, p. 1, and 1 December 1995, p. 1.

15   Ahmed Rashid, 'Chinese Challenge: Li Peng Visit Highlights Beijing's Growing Role in the Region', *Far Eastern Economic Review* (12 May 1994): 30.

16   Shada Islam, 'Friendly Signals: Europe Wants Its Own Pow-Wow with East Asia', *Far Eastern Economic Review* (17 November 1994): 30.

17   In his analyses of China's bilateral cooperative relationships, Harry Harding (1994) has divided them into three groups: 'China's links with wealthier and more powerful *benefactors* its strategic and economic ties to smaller and weaker *clients*, and its more equal, but less intense relationships with a larger number of foreign *partners*.'

18   Ahmed Rashad, 'Unwelcome Traffic', *Far Eastern Economic Review* (7 December 1995): 40.

19   Willy Wo-Lap Lam, 'Jiang's Power Continues to Grow', *South China Morning Post*, 17 March 1994, pp. 16–17.

20   For details, see Lincoln Kaye and Carl Goldstein, 'Bluff and Bluster', *Far Eastern Economic Review* (17 March 1994): 16–17.

21   Matt Forney, 'Getting Their Way: Beijing Grabs the Last Big Dissident', *Far Eastern Economic Review* (7 December 1995): 30–31.

22   'Free Trade: Key Asian Value', *Far Eastern Economic Review* (29 December 1994) and (4 January 1995): 28.

23   Louise de Rosario, 'Future Shock: Top Chinese Official Talks Tough in the Colony', *Far Eastern Economic Review* (19 May 1994): 24.

24   'US Visit Points to Better Ties', *South China Morning Post*, 13 June 1995, p. 8.

25   Nayan Chanda, 'Winds of Change', *Far Eastern Economic Review* (22 June 1995): 14–16.

26   'Zhongmei zhijian shiqu zuihou de huxin' [The Last Mutual Trust is Lost Between China and the United States], *Yazhou Zhoukan* [The International Chinese Newsweekly] (18 June 1995): 7.

27   Nayan Chanda, 'Winds of Change'.

28   See the Atlantic Council of the United States and the National Committee on United States–China Relations (1993), *United States and China: Relations at a Crossroads*, p. xvii.

29   Among the more controversial of these activities are military-related business transactions between the two countries. With William Perry's approval, for example, a Chicago-based American company transferred state-of-the-art communications technology to a Chinese company half-owned by the PLA. The high-tech items included a high-capacity fibre-optic system and high-speed or asynchroonous transfer mode (ATM) switches, which may help the Chinese military develop cutting-edge war-time command systems, combining the functions of command, control, communication,

computers and information, known as 'C⁴I'. For details, see Bruce Gilley, 'Peace Dividend', *Far Eastern Economic Review* (11 January 1996): 14–16.

30 'Advice from a Former President', *Time* (20 November 1989): 44–49.

31 One may see, for example, Morton Schwartz (1975); Erik Hoffmann and Frederic Fleron (eds.) (1980); Seweryn Bialer (1981); Richard Herrmann (1985); C. Ziegler (1993); and James Goldgeier (1994).

32 One fine effort in this regard is Minxin Pei's (1994).

33 In the book's concluding chapter, Goncharov, Lewis, and Xue (1993: 219) argue that 'their [Stalin and Mao's] private communications mostly carried a message of naked military-political interests and a priority for national security'. Other elements, such as ideology, 'played a secondary role'.

34 For a good analysis of the controversies surrounding China's *yibiandao* policy, see John Garver (1994: 39–43).

35 As perhaps the first step, a four-day conference entitled 'The Foreign Relations of China's Environmental Policy' was held in August 1991 in Racine, Wisconsin. Participants included environmental scientists, Chinese foreign policy specialists, and international relations theorists. A report based on the conference has been published by the American Enterprise Institute (1992). The author thanks Samuel Kim, who participated in this conference and brought this point to his attention.

36 For an excellent analysis in this regard, see Tang Tsou and Morton H. Halperin (1965), and Michael Hunt (1996).

37 Research in this regard has consistently been conducted by John Lewis. See, for example, Lewis and Xue (1988); and Lewis, Hua and Xue (1991); and Lewis and Xue (1994); see also A. I. Johnston (1996).

38 As Robert Keohane (1989: 152) suggests, 'Without altering the basic structure of anarchy, governments can make the world safer, or more dangerous, through the strategies they follow.'

Appendices

Appendix 1 The Chinese Communist Party Leadership

Year	Top Leader	Paramount Leader	Core Members
1945–56	Mao Zedong	Mao Zedong	Mao Zedong[a] Zhu De Liu Shaoqi Zhou Enlai Ren Bishi[c]
1956–66	Mao Zedong	Mao Zedong	Mao Zedong[a] Liu Shaoqi[b] Zhou Enlai[b] Zhu De[b] Chen Yun[b] Lin Biao[b] Deng Xiaoping[d]
1966–69	Mao Zedong	Mao Zedong	Mao Zedong[a] Lin Biao Zhou Enlai Tao Zhu Chen Boda Deng Xiaoping Kang Sheng Liu Shaoqi Zhu De Li Fuchun Chen Yun
1969–73	Mao Zedong	Mao Zedong	Mao Zedong[a] Lin Biao[b,e] Zhou Enlai Chen Boda Kang Sheng

Appendix 1 (cont.)

Year	Top Leader	Paramount Leader	Core Members
1973–76	Mao Zedong	Mao Zedong	Mao Zedong[a,f] Zhou Enlai[b,n] Wang Hongwen[b,g] Kang Sheng[b,l] Ye Jianying[b] Li Desheng[b,i] Zhu De[h,n] Zhang Chunqiao[h,g] Dong Biwu[h,l] Deng Xiaoping[i,b]
1977–82	Hua Guofeng	Deng Xiaoping	Hua Guofeng[a,f] Ye Jianying[b] Deng Xiaoping[b] Li Xiannian[b] Wang Dongxing[b,k] Chen Yun[b,j]
1982–87	Hu Yaobang	Deng Xiaoping	Hu Yaobang[d] Ye Jianying[o] Deng Xiaoping Zhao Ziyang Li Xiannian Chen Yun
1987–1992	Zhao Ziyang	Deng Xiaoping	Zhao Ziyang[d,m] Li Peng Qiao Shi Hu Qili[m] Yao Yilin
1992–	Jiang Zemin	Deng Yiaoping	Jiang Zemin[d] Li Peng Qiao Shi Li Ruihuan Zhu Rongji Liu Huaqing Hu Jintao

a: CC chairman
b: CC vice chairman
c: Ren Bishi died in 1950; Chen Yun took his place in the Secretariat.
d: General secretary
e: Lin Biao and Ye Qun died in a plane crash on September 1971 while fleeing the country.

Appendix 1 (cont.)

f: Mao Zedong died on 9 September 1976, and Hua Guofeng became chairman on 7 October 1976. He was replaced by Hu Yaobang at the Six Plenum (27–29) June 1981) of the Eleventh CC.
g: The Gang of Four was arrested on 6 October 1976.
h: These members were listed by stroke order.
i: Deng Xiaoping was reappointed to the Politburo in December 1973 and to the PSC as a vice-chairman at the Tenth CC's Second Plenum (8–10 January 1975), on the latter occasion apparently in place of Li Desheng, who reverted to full Politburo member.
j: Appointed at the Eleventh CC's Third Plenum (18–22 December 1978).
k: Dismissed at the Eleventh CC's Fifth Plenum.
l: Died in 1975
m: Dismissed at Thirteenth CC's Fourth Plenum, 23–24 June, 1989.
n: Died in 1976.
o: Resigned at the Twelfth CC's Fourth Plenum.

Source: Roderick MacFarquhar (ed.) (1993: 474–77)

Appendix 2 The PRC State Leadership

President	Premier	Foreign Minister
Mao Zedong[a] (1949–59)	Zhou Enlai[a,c] (1949–76)	Zhou Enlai (1949–58)
Liu Shaoqi[a,b] (1959–66)	Hua Guofeng[a,d] (1976–80)	Chen Yi (1958–72)
Li Xiannian[a] (1983–88)	Zhao Ziyang[a] (1980–88)	Ji Pengfei (1972–74)
Yang Shangkun[a] (1988–93)	Li Peng[a,e] (1988–)	Qiao Guanhua (1974–76)
Jiang Zemin[a] (1993–)		Huang Hua (1976–82)
		Wu Xueqian (1982–88)
		Qian Qichen (1988–)

a: Members of the Politburo at the time of appointment.
b: These office effectively disappeared early in the Cultural Revolution. Liu Shaoqi died in November 1969.
c: Zhou Enlai died on 8 January 1976, and Hua Guofeng became acting premier on 3 February. On 8 April, the *People's Daily* published the decision that he would no longer be 'acting', but now would be premier in his own right.
d: Hua Guofeng was replaced by Zhao Ziyang as premier at the third session (30 August– 10 September 1980) of the Fifth NPC.
e: Members of the PSC at the time of appointment.

Sources: Compiled from Roderick MacFarquhar, ed. (1993: 478–480)

References

Acheson, Dean (1971), *The Korean War*, New York: W. W. Norton.

Adelman, Jonathan R., and Chih-yu Shih (1993), *Symbolic War: The Chinese Use of Force, 1840–1980*, Taipei: Institute of International Relations, National Chengchi University.

Alexander, Bevis (1986), *Korea: The First War We Lost*, New York: Hippocrene Books.

Alexander, Jeffrey (1987), 'Action and Its Environments', in Jeffrey Alexander, Bernard Giesen, Richard Munch, and Neil Smelser (eds.), *The Micro-Macro Link*, Berkeley: University of California Press.

Alexander, Jeffrey, and Bernhard Giesen (1987), 'From Reduction to Linkage: The Long View of the Micro-Macro Link', in Jeffrey Alexander, Bernard Giesen, Richard Munch, and Neil Smelser (eds.), *The Micro-Macro Link*, Berkeley: University of California Press.

Allison, Graham (1971), *The Essence of Decision: Explaining the Cuban Missile Crisis*, Boston: Little, Brown.

Armstrong, J. D. (1977), *Revolutionary Diplomacy: Chinese Foreign Policy and the United Front Doctrine*, Berkeley: University of California Press.

Atlantic Council of the United States and the National Committee on United States–China Relations, The (1993), *United States and China: Relations at a Crossroads*, Washington, DC, and New York.

Bachman, David (1989) 'Domestic Sources of Chinese Foreign Policy', in Samuel Kim (ed.), *China and the World: New Directions in Chinese Foreign Relations*, Boulder, Colo.: Westview Press.

Bailes, Alyson J. (1990), 'China and Eastern Europe: A Judgement on the Socialist Community', *The Pacific Review*, 3 (3): 222–242.

Baker, James A. (1991/92), 'America in Asia: Emerging Architecture for a Pacific Community', *Foreign Affairs*, 70 (5) (Winter): 1–18.

Barnett, A. Doak (1977), *China and the Major Powers in East Asia*, Washington, DC: The Brookings Institution.

—— (1985), *The Making of Foreign Policy in China: Structure and Process*, Boulder, Colo.: Westview Press.

—— (1991), *After Deng, What? Will China Follow the USSR?*, Washington, DC: The Foreign Policy Institute, School of Advanced International Studies, The Johns Hopkins University.

—— (1993), *China's Far West: Four Decades of Change*, Boulder, Colo.: Westview Press.

Bedeski, Robert (1983), *The Fragile Entente, the 1978 Japan–China Peace Treaty in a Global Context*, Boulder, Colo.: Westview Press.

Behbehani, Hashim (1981), *China's Foreign Policy in the Arab World, 1955–75*, London and Boston: Melbourne and Henley.

Bialer, Seweryn, (ed.) (1981), *The Domestic Context of Soviet Foreign Policy*, Boulder, Colo.: Westview Press.

Bickers, Robert, and Jeffrey Wasserstrom (1995), 'Shanghai's "Dogs and Chinese Not

Allowed" Sign'; Legend, History, and Contemporary Symbol' *The China Quarterly*, 142 (June): 444–466.

Black, Cyril E., and Thomas P. Thornton (eds.) (1964), *Communism and Revolution*, Princeton: Princeton University Press.

Blumer, Herbert (1969), *Symbolic Interactionism*, Englewood Cliffs, NJ: Prentice-Hall.

Bo, Yibo (1989) *Lingxiu, yuanshuai, zhanyou* [Leaders, Marshals, and Friends], Beijing: Zhonggong zhongyang dangxiao chubanshe.

—— (1991), *Ruogan zhongda juece yu shijian de huigu* [Memoir: A Number of Important Decisions and Events], two volumes, Beijing: Zhonggong zhongyang dangxiao chubanshe.

Bobrow, Davis, Steve Chan, and John Kringen (1979), *Understanding Foreign Policy Decisions: The Chinese Case*, New York: The Free Press.

Bourdieu, Pierre (1977), *Outline of a Theory of Practice*, Cambridge: Cambridge University Press.

Breslauer, George W., and Philip E. Tellock (eds.) (1990), *Learning in US and Soviet Foreign Policy*, Boulder, Colo.: Westview Press.

Brzezinski, Zbigniew (1989), *The Grand Failure: The Birth and Death of Communism in the Twentieth Century*, New York: Scribner.

Brown, Harrison (ed.) (1982), *China Among the Nations of the Pacific*, Boulder, Colo.: Westview Press.

Burks, R. V. (1969), 'The Communist Polities of Eastern Europe', in James Rosenau, ed., *Linkage Politics: Essays on the Convergence of National and International Systems*, New York: The Free Press.

Burns, John P., and Stanley Rosen (eds.) (1986), *Policy Conflicts in Post-Mao China: A Documentary Survey, with Analysis*, Armonk, NY and London: M. E. Sharpe.

Calabrese, John (1990), 'From Flyswatters to Silkworms: The Evolution of China's Role in West Asia' *Asian Survey*, 30 (9) (September): 862–876.

Cameron, Effie, and Jeanne Skog (eds.) (1990), *State of the Pacific Basin, Economic, Political and Socio-Cultural Dimensions*, Kahului, Hawaii: Kapalua Pacific Center.

Central Committee of the Communist Party of China (1981), *Resolution on CPC History (1949–81)*, Beijing: Foreign Languages Press.

Chan, Gerald (1989), *China and International Organizations*, Hong Kong: Oxford University Press.

Chang, Gordon H. (1990), *Friends and Enemies: The United States, China and the Soviet Union, 1948–1972*, Stanford, Calif.: Stanford University Press.

Chang, Jaw-ling Joanne (1986), *United States-China Normalization: An Evaluation of Foreign Policy Decision Making*, Denver, Colo.: University of Denver and Occasional Papers/Reprint Series in Contemporary Asian Studies.

—— (1991), 'Negotiation of the 17 August 1982 US–PRC Arms Communique: Beijing's Negotiating Tactics', *The China Quarterly*, 125 (March): 33–54.

Chang, Maria Hsia (1995), 'Greater China and the Chinese "Global Tribe" ', *Asian Survey*, 35, (10) (October): 955–967.

Chang, Pao-min (1986), *The Sino-Vietnamese Territorial Dispute*, New York: Praeger.

Chang, Tsan-Kuo (1993), *The Press and China Policy: The Illusion of Sino-American Relations, 1950–1984*, Norwood, NJ: Ablex Publishing Corporation.

Chen, Changgui, and David Zweig (1994): *China's Brain Drain to America*, Berkeley: Institute of East Asian Studies, University of California, Berkeley.

Chen, Jian (1994), *China's Road to the Korean War*, New York: Columbia University Press.

—— (1995), 'China's Involvement in the Vietnam War, 1964–1969', *The China Quarterly*, 142 (June): 356–387.

Chen, Jie (1994), 'China's Spratlys Policy: With Special Reference to the Philippines and Malaysia'. *Asian Survey*, 34, (10) (October): 893–903.

Chen, King C. (1969), *Vietnam and China, 1938–1954*, Princeton: Princeton University Press.

——— (ed.) (1979), *China and the Three Worlds*, White Plains, New York: M. E. Sharpe.

Chen, Min (1992), *The Strategic Triangle and Regional Conflicts: Lessons from the Indochina Wars*, Boulder, Colo.: Lynne Rienner.

Chen, Qimao (1986), 'The Current Situation and Prospects for Asia and the Pacific', in Robert Scalapino and Chen Qimao (eds.), *Pacific–Asian Issues: American and Chinese Views*, Berkeley: Institute of East Asian Studies, University of California.

Chen, Xiaolu (1989), 'China's Policy toward the United States, 1949–1955', in Harry Harding and Yuan Ming (eds.), *Sino-American Relations, 1945–1955*, Wilmington, Delaware: Scholarly Resources Inc.

Cheng, Hsiao-shik (1990), *Party–Military Relations in the PRC and Taiwan*, Boulder, Colo.: Westview Press.

Cheng, Xiangjun (ed.) (1995), *Nü waijiaoguan* [Women Diplomats], Beijing: Renmin tiyu chubanshe.

Christensen, Thomas (1993), 'Domestic Mobilization and International Conflict: Sino-American Relations in the 1950s', Ph.D. dissertation, Department of Political Science, Columbia University.

Chu, Samuel, and Kwang-Ching Liu (eds.), (1994), *Li Hung-Chang and China's Early Modernization*, Armonk, New York: M. E. Sharpe.

Clapp, Priscilla, and Morton Halperin (eds.) (1974), *United States–Japanese Relations*, Cambridge: Harvard University Press.

Cohen, Abner (1976), *Two-Dimensional Man: An Essay on the Anthropology of Power and Symbolism in Complex Society*, Berkeley: University of California Press.

Cohen, Raymond (1991), *Negotiating Across Cultures: Communications Obstacles in International Diplomacy*, Washington, DC: United States Institute of Peace Press.

Cohen, Warren I. (1990), *America's Response to China*, New York: Columbia University Press.

Coleman, James (1987), 'Microfoundations and Macrosocial Behavior', in Jeffrey Alexander et al. (eds.), *The Micro-Macro Link*, Berkeley: University of California Press.

——— (1990), *Foundations of Social Theory*, Cambridge: The Belknap Press of Harvard University Press.

Collins, Randall (1990), 'Conflict Theory and the Advance of Macro-Historical Sociology', in George Ritzer (ed.), *Frontiers of Social Theory*, New York: Columbia University Press.

Connolly, William (ed.) (1984), *Legitimacy and the State*, New York: New York University Press.

Cook, Karen, Jodi O'Brien, and Peter Kollock (1990), 'Exchange Theory: A Blueprint for Structure and Press', in George Ritzer (ed.), *Frontiers of Social Theory*, New York: Columbia University Press.

Copper, John (1980), *China's Global Role*, Stanford, Calif.: Hoover Institution Press.

——— (1992), *China Diplomacy: The Washington–Taipei–Beijing Triangle*, Boulder, Colorado: Westview Press.

Crozier, Michel (1964), *The Bureaucratic Phenomenon*, Chicago: University of Chicago Press.

Cumings, Bruce (1989), 'The Political Economy of China's Turn Outward', in Samuel Kim (ed.), *China and the World*, Boulder, Colorado: Westview Press.

——— (1981 and 1990), *The Origins of the Korean War* (two volumes), Princeton: Princeton University Press.

Davis, Deborah, and Ezra F. Vogel (eds.) (1990), *Chinese Society on the Eve of Tiananmen: The Impact of Reform*, Cambridge: The Council on East Asian Studies, Harvard University.

Davis, Zachary (1995), 'China's Nonproliferation and Export Control', *Asian Survey* 35, no. 6 (June): 587–603.

Deane, Hugh (1990), *Good Deeds and Gunboats: Two Centuries of American–Chinese Encounters*, San Francisco: China Books and Periodicals.

Deng, Lifeng (1994), *Jianguo hou junshi xingdong quanlu* [The Complete Records of China's Military Actions Since 1949], Taiyuan: Shanxi renmin chubanshe.

Deng, Maomao (1993), *Wuo de fuqin Deng Xiaoping* [My Father Deng Xiaoping], Beijing: Zhongyang wenxian chubanshe.

Deng, Xiaoping (1984), *Selected Works of Deng Xiaoping (1975–1982)*, Beijing: Foreign Languages Press.

—— (1994), *Selected Works of Deng Xiaoping, Vol. 3 (1982–1992)*, Beijing: Foreign Languages Press.

Dernberger, Robert F., Kenneth J. DeWoskin, Steven M. Goldstein, Rhodes Murphey, and Martin K. Whyte (eds.) (1986), *The Chinese: Adapting the Past, Building the Future*, Ann Arbor: Center for Chinese Studies, University of Michigan.

Deutsch, Karl (1966), *The Nerves of Government*, New York: The Free Press.

Dittmer, Lowell (1978), *China's Continuous Revolutions*, Berkeley: University of California Press.

—— (1992), *Sino-Soviet Normalization and Its International Implication, 1945–1990*, Seattle: University of Washington Press.

Dittmer, Lowell, and Samuel Kim (eds.) (1993), *China's Quest for National Identity*, Ithaca, NY: Cornell University Press.

Dittmer, Lowell, and Yu-shan Wu (1995), 'The Modernization of Factionalism in Chinese Politics', *World Politics*, 47 (4) (July): 467–494.

Domes, Jurgen (1985), *Peng Te-Huai: The Man and the Image*, Stanford, Calif.: Stanford University Press.

Dorn, James, and Wang Xi (1990), *Economic Reform in China: Problems and Prospects*, Chicago: University of Chicago Press.

Dreyer, June Teufel, and Ilpyong J. Kim (eds.) (1989), *Chinese Defense and Foreign Policy*, New York: Paragon House.

Du Ping (1989), *Zai zhiyuanjun zongbu* [At the Headquarters of the Volunteers], Beijing: Jiefangjun chubanshe.

Easton, David (1965), *A Systems Analysis of Political Life*, New York: John Wiley & Sons.

Edwards, R. Randle, Louis Henkin, and Andrew J. Nathan (eds.) (1986), *Human Rights in Contemporary China*, New York: Columbia University Press.

Eisenstadt, S. N., and H. J. Helle (eds.) (1985), *Macro-Sociological Theory*, Vol. 1, London: Sage.

Elster, Jon (1993), *Political Psychology*, Cambridge: Cambridge University Press.

Eulau, Heinz (1986), *Politics, Self, and Society*, Cambridge: Harvard University Press.

Evans, Peter, Harold Jacobson, and Robert Putnam (eds.) (1993), *Double-Edged Diplomacy: International Bargaining and Domestic Politics*, Berkeley: University of California Press.

Fairbank, John King (1976), *The United States and China*, Cambridge: Harvard University Press.

Fan, K. (1972), *Mao Tse-tung and Lin Piao: Post-Revolutionary Writings*, Garden City, NY: Doubleday.

Fan, Mingfang (1992), *Gezhong yuanwei: zhongguo bianjiang zhu wenti* [Explanations: China's Border Problems], Xi'an: Shaanxi renmin jiaoyu chubanshe.

Feeney, William (1994), 'China and the Multilateral Economic Institutions', in *China and the World*, 3rd edn., Samuel Kim (ed.), Boulder, Colo.: Westview Press.

Fingar, Thomas (ed.) (1980), *China's Quest for Independence*, Boulder, Colo.: Westview Press.

Flathman, Richard (1980), *The Practice of Political Authority*, Chicago: University of Chicago Press.

Foot, Rosemary (1985), *The Wrong War: American Policy and the Dimensions of the Korean Conflict*, Ithaca, NY: Cornell University Press.

—— (1995), *The Practice of Power: US Relations with China Since 1949*, Oxford: Clarendon Press.

Friedman, Debra, and Michael Hechter (1990), 'The Comparative Advantages of Rational

Choices Theory', in George Ritzer (ed.), *Frontiers of Social Theory*, New York: Columbia University Press.

Friedman, Edward (1979), 'On Maoist Conceptualizations of the Capitalist World System', *The China Quarterly*, 80 (December): 806–837.

—— (ed.) (1994), *The Politics of Decentralization: Generalizing East Asian Experiences*, Boulder, Colo.: Westview.

Frieman, Wendy (1994), 'International Science and Technology and Chinese Foreign Policy', in Thomas Robinson and David Shambaugh (eds.), *Chinese Foreign Policy: Theory and Practice*, Oxford: Oxford University Press.

Funabashi, Yoichi, Michel Oksenberg, and Heinrich Weiss (1994), *An Emerging China in a World of Independence*, New York, Paris, and Tokyo: The Trilateral Commission.

Gaddis, John L. (1992/93), 'International Relations Theory and the End of the Cold War,' *International Security*, 17 (3): 5–58.

Gaenslen, Fritz (1986), 'Culture and Decision Making in China, Japan, Russia and the United States', *World Politics*, 39 (1) (October): 78–103.

Gallagher, Michael (1994), 'China's Illusory Threat to the South China Sea', *International Security*, 19 (1) (Summer): 169–194.

Gallicchio, Marc S. (1988), *The Cold War Begins in Asia: American East Asian Policy and the Fall of the Japanese Empire*, New York: Columbia University Press.

Garrett, Banning N. (1990), 'The Strategic Basis of Learning in US Policy Toward China, 1949–1988', in George W. Breslauer and Philip E. Tellock (eds.), *Learning in US and Soviet Foreign Policy*, Boulder, Colo.: Westview Press.

Garrett, Banning, and Bonnie Glaser (1995), 'Looking Across the Yalu: Chinese Assessments of North Korea', *Asian Survey*, 35 (6) (June): 528–545.

Garver, John (1982), *China's Decision for Rapprochement with the United States, 1968–1971*, Boulder, Colo.: Westview Press.

—— (1991), 'China–India Rivalry in Nepal: The Clash over Chinese Arms Sales', *Asian Survey*, 31 (10) (October): 956–975.

—— (1994), *Foreign Relations of the People's Republic of China*, Englewood Cliffs, NJ: Prentice Hall.

George, Alexander L. (1980), *Presidential Decisionmaking in Foreign Policy*, Boulder, Colo.: Westview Press.

—— (1991), *Avoiding War: Problems of Crisis Management*, Boulder, Colo.: Westview Press.

—— (1993), *Bridging the Gap Between Theory and Practice*, Washington, DC: US Institute of Peace Press.

Gerstain, Dean (1987), 'To Unpack Micro and Macro: Link Small with Large and Part with Whole', in Jeffrey Alexander et al. (eds.), *The Micro-Macro Link*, Berkeley: University of California Press.

Gibbons, Michael (1987), 'Introduction: the Politics of Interpretation', in Michael Gibbons (ed.), *Interpreting Politics*, New York: New York University Press.

Giddens, Anthony (1984), *The Constitution of Society: Outline of the Theory of Structuration*, Berkeley: University of California Press.

Giesen, Bernhard (1987), 'Beyond Reductionism: Four Models Relating Micro and Macro Levels', in Jeffrey Alexander et al. (eds.), *The Micro-Macro Link*, Berkeley: University of California Press.

Gilbert, Stephen P., and William M. Carpenter (eds.) (1989), *America and Island China: A Documentary History*, Lanham, Md.: University Press of America.

Gilks, Anne (1992), *The Breakdown of the Sino-Vietnamese Alliance, 1970–1979*, Berkeley: Institute of East Asian Studies, University of California.

Gill, R. Bates (1991), 'China Looks to Thailand: Exporting Arms, Exporting Influence', *Asian Survey*, 31 (6) (June): 526–539.

Godwin, Paul (1992), 'Chinese Military Strategy Revised: Local and Limited War', *The Annals of the American Academy of Political and Social Science*, 519 (January): 191–201.

—— (1994), 'Force and Diplomacy: Chinese Security Policy in the Post-Cold War Era', in Samuel Kim (ed.), *China and the World*, 3rd edn., Boulder, Colo.: Westview Press.

Goldgeier, James (1994), *Leadership Style and Soviet Foreign Policy*, Baltimore: The Johns Hopkins University Press.

Goldman Merle (ed.) (1987), *China's Intellectuals and the State: In Search of a New Relationship*, Cambridge: The Council on East Asian Studies, Harvard University.

—— (1994), *Sowing the Seeds of Democracy in China: Political Reform in the Deng Xiaoping Era*, Cambridge: Harvard University Press.

Goldstein, Judith, and Robert Keohane (eds.) (1993), *Ideas and Foreign Policy: Beliefs, Institutions, and Political Change*, Ithaca, NY, and London: Cornell University Press.

Goncharov, Sergei, John W. Lewis, and Xue Litai (1993), *Uncertain Partners: Stalin, Mao, and the Korean War*, Stanford, Calif.: Stanford University Press.

Gong, Li (1992), *Kuayue honggou: 1969–1979 zhongmei guanxi de yanbian* [Across the Wide Gap: the Evolution of Sino-US Relations, 1969–1979], Zhengzhou: Henan renmin chubanshe.

Goodman, David S. G. (1988), *Communism and Reform in East Asia*, Totowa, NJ, and London: Frank Cass and Company.

Gottlieb, Thomas (1977), *Chinese Foreign Policy Factionalism and the Origins of the Strategic Triangle*, Santa Monica, Calif.: The Rand Corporation.

Gourevitch, Peter (1978), 'The Second Image Reversed: The International Sources of Domestic Politics', *International Organization*, 32 (4) (Autumn): 881–911.

Griffith, William E. (1967), *Sino-Soviet Relations, 1964–1965*, Cambridge, Mass.: MIT Press.

Guan, Jixian (1993), *Gaojishu jubu zhanzheng zhanyi* [High-tech Local War], Beijing: Guofang daxue chubanshe.

Gurtov, Melvin (1967), *The First Vietnam Crisis: Chinese Communist Strategy and United States Involvement, 1953–1954*, New York: Columbia University Press.

Gurtov, Melvin, and Byong-Moo Hwang (1980), *China under Threat: The Politics of Strategy and Diplomacy*, Baltimore: The Johns Hopkins University Press.

Haggard, Stephen, and Bess Simmons (1987), 'Theories of International Regime', *International Organization*, 41 (3) (Summer): 513–17.

Halperin, Morton (1966), *The 1958 Taiwan Straits Crisis: A Documented History Rand Memorandum 4900 RM-ISA*, Santa Monica, Calif.: The Rand Corporation (unpublished).

Halpern, A. M. (ed.) (1965), *Policies Toward China: Views from Six Continents*, New York, Toronto, and London: McGraw-Hill.

Hamrin, Carol Lee (1983), 'China Reassesses the Superpowers', *Pacific Affairs*, 56 (2) (Summer): 209–230.

—— (1986), 'Domestic Components and China's Evolving Three Worlds Theory', in Lillian Harris and Robert Worden (eds.), *China and the Third World: Champion or Challenger?*, Dover, Mass.: Auburn House.

—— (1990), *China and the Challenge of the Future: Changing Political Patterns*, Boulder, Colo.: Westview Press.

—— (1994), 'Elite Politics and the Development of Chinese Foreign Relations', in Thomas Robinson and David Shambaugh (eds.), *Chinese Foreign Policy: Theory and Practice*, Oxford: Oxford University Press.

Han Nianlong (chief ed.) (1987), *Dangdai zhongguo waijiao* [Diplomacy of Contemporary China], Beijing: Zhongguo shehui kexue chubanshe.

Han, Huaizhi (1989), *Dangdai Zhongguo jundui de junshi gongzuo* [Contemporary Military Affairs of the Chinese Army], Beijing: Zhongguo shehui kexue chubanshe.

Harding, Harry (1983), 'Change and Continuity in Chinese Foreign Policy', *Problems of Communism*, 32 (March–April): 1–19.

—— (ed.) (1984), *China's Foreign Relations in the 1980s*, New Haven: Yale University Press.

—— (1987), *China's Second Revolution: Reform After Mao*, Washington, DC: The Brookings Institution.

—— (1988), *China and Northeast Asia*, Lanham, Md.: University Press of America.

—— (1992), *A Fragile Relationship: The United States and China since 1972*, Washington, DC: The Brookings Institution.

—— (1993), 'The Concept of "Greater China": Themes, Variations and Reservations', *The China Quarterly*, 136 (December): 660–686.

—— (1994) 'China's Co-operative Behaviour', in Thomas Robinson and David Shambaugh (eds.), *Chinese Foreign Policy: Theory and Practice*, Oxford: Oxford University Press.

Harris, Lillian Craig, and Robert L. Worden (eds.) (1986), *China and the Third World: Champion or Challenger?*, Dover, Mass.: Auburn House.

Hastings, Max (1987), *The Korean War*, New York: Simon & Schuster.

Hatch, Elvin (1973), *Theories of Man and Culture*, New York: Columbia University Press.

He, Di (1990), 'The Evolution of the People's Republic of China's Policy toward the Offshore Islands', in Warren Cohen and Akira Iriye (eds.), *The Great Powers in East Asia 1953–1960*, New York: Columbia University Press.

—— (1994), 'The Most Respected Enemy: Mao Zedong's Perception of the United States', *The China Quarterly*, 137 (March): 144–158.

He, Xiaolu (1985), *Yuanshuai waijiaojia* [Marshal and Diplomat], Beijing: Jiefangjun wenyi chubanshe.

Herrmann, Richard (1985), *Perceptions and Behavior in Soviet Foreign Policy*, Pittsburgh: University of Pittsburgh Press.

Hill, Christopher, and Margot Light (1985), 'Foreign Policy Analysis', in Margot Light and A. J. R. Groom (eds.), *International Relations: A Handbook of Current Theory*, London: Frances Pinter; and Boulder, Colo.: Lynne Rienner.

Hinton, Harold (1972), *China's Turbulent Quest*, Bloomington: Indiana University Press.

Ho, David Y. F. (1978), 'The Conception of Man in Mao Tse-tung Thought', *Psychiatry*, 1 (41) (November): 391–402.

Hoffmann, Erik, and Frederic Fleron (eds.) (1980), *The Conduct of Soviet Foreign Policy*, New York: Aldine Publishing Company.

Hong Shi (1990), 'China's Political Development after Tiananmen: Tranquillity by Default', *Asian Survey*, 30 (12) (December): 1206–1217.

Holsti, Ole R., and John D. Sullivan (1969), 'National–International Linkages: France and China As Nonconforming Alliance Members', in James Rosenau (ed.), *Linkage Politics: Essays on the Convergence of National and International Systems*, New York: The Free Press.

Hood, Steven (1992), *Dragons Entangled: Indochina and the China–Vietnam War*, Armonk, NY: M. E. Sharpe.

Hsiung, James C., and Samuel S. Kim (eds.) (1980), *China and the Global Community*, New York: Praeger Publishers.

Hsiung, James (ed.) (1986), *Human Rights in East Asia*, New York: Paragon.

Hu, Sheng (1955), *Imperialism and Chinese Politics*, Peking: Foreign Languages Press.

Huang, Jiashu (1994), *Taiwan neng duli ma?* [Can Taiwan Become Independent?], Haikou: Nanhai chuban gongsi.

Hudson, Valerie, with Christopher Vore (1995), 'Foreign Policy Analysis Yesterday, Today, and Tomorrow', *Mershon International Studies Review*, 39 (2) (October): 209–238.

Hunt, Michael (1984), 'Chinese Foreign Policy in Historical Perspective', in Harding, (ed.), *China's Foreign Relations in the 1980s*, New Haven, Conn.: Yale University Press.

—— (1996), *The Genesis of Chinese Communist Foreign Policy*, New York: Columbia University Press.

Hunt, Michael, and Odd Westad (1990), 'The Chinese Communist Party and International Affairs: A Field Report on New Historical Sources and Old Research Problems', *The China Quarterly*, 122 (June): 258–272.

Huntington, Samuel P. (1968), *Political Order in Changing Societies*, New Haven: Yale University Press.

—— (1987), 'The Goals of Development', in Myron Weiner and Samuel P. Huntington (eds.), *Understanding Political Development*, Boston: Little, Brown.

Ishikawa, Tadao (1974), 'The Normalization of Sino-Japanese Relations', in Priscilla Clapp and Morton Halperin (eds.), *United States–Japanese Relations*, Cambridge: Harvard University Press.

Jacobson, Harold K., and Michel Oksenberg (1990), *China's Participation in the IMF, the World Bank, and the GATT*, Ann Arbor, Mich.: The University of Michigan Press.

Janos, Andrew C. (1964), 'The Communist Theory of the State and Revolution', in Cyril E. Black and Thomas P. Thornton (eds.), *Communism and Revolution*, Princeton: Princeton University Press.

Japan–China Economic Association (1975), *Ni-chu keizai kyokao ho* [Bulletin of Japan–China Economic Association], Tokyo: Japan–China Economic Association.

Jervis, Robert (1976), *Perception and Misperception in International Politics*, Princeton: Princeton University Press.

Jetly, Nancy (1979), *India–China Relations 1947–1977*, Atlantic Highlands, NJ: Humanities Press.

Jiang, Arnold Xiangze (1988), *The United States and China*, Chicago: The University of Chicago Press.

Jiji Tsushinsha Seijibu (1972), *Dokyumento: Nitchu Fukko* [Documents: The Japan–China rapprochement], Tokyo: Jiji tsushinsha.

Joffe, Ellis (1987), *The Chinese Army After Mao*, Cambridge: Harvard University Press.

Johnson, Chalmers (ed.) (1970), *Change in Communist Systems*, Stanford, Calif.: Stanford University Press.

—— (1995), 'Korea and Our Asia Policy', *The National Interest*, 41 (Fall): 66–77.

Johnston, Alastair Iain (1995), *Cultural Realism: Strategic Culture and Grand Strategy in Chinese History*, Princeton: Princeton University Press.

—— (1996), 'Learning Versus Adaptation: Explaining Change in Chinese Arms Control Policy in the 1980s and 1990s', *China Journal*, no. 35 (January): 27–61.

Joseph, William, Christine P. W. Wong, and David Zweig (eds.) (1991), *New Perspectives on the Cultural Revolution*, Cambridge: The Council on East Asian Studies, Harvard University.

Kallgren, Joyce K., and Denis Fred Simon (eds.) (1987), *Educational Exchanges: Essays on the Sino-American Experience*, Berkeley: Institute of East Asian Studies, University of California.

Kallgren, Joyce K., Noordin Sopiee, and Soedjati Djiwandono (eds.) (1988), *ASEAN and China: An Evolving Relationship*, Berkeley: Institute of East Asian Studies, University of California.

Katzenstein, Peter (ed.) (1978), *Between Power and Plenty*, Madison: The University of Wisconsin Press.

Keith, Ronald (1989), *The Diplomacy of Zhou Enlai*, New York: St. Martin's.

Kelman, Herbert C. (1965) 'Social-Psychological Approaches to the Study of International Relations', in Herbert C. Kelman (ed.), *International Behavior: A Social-Psychological Analysis*, New York: Holt, Rinehart and Winston.

Keohane, Robert (1984), *After Hegemony: Cooperation and Discord in the World Political Economy*, Princeton: Princeton University Press.

—— (1989), *International Institutions and State Power: Essays in International Relations Theory*, Boulder, Colo.: Westview Press.

Keohane, Robert, and Joseph Nye (1977), *Power and Interdependence*, Boston: Little, Brown.

—— (1989), *Power and Interdependence*, 2nd edn., Boston: Scott, Foresman.

Kim, Ilpyong (ed.) (1987), *The Strategic Triangle: China, the United States and the Soviet Union*, New York: Paragon House.

Kim, Samuel S. (1977), *The Maoist Image of World Order*, Princeton: Center for International Studies, Princeton University.

—— (1979), *China, the United Nations, and the World Order*, Princeton: Princeton University Press.

—— (1989a), 'New Directions and Old Puzzles in Chinese Foreign Policy', in Samuel S. Kim (ed.), *China and the World: New Directions in Chinese Foreign Relations*, Boulder, Colo.: Westview Press.

—— (1989b), 'Reviving International Law in China's Foreign Relations', in June T. Dreyer (ed.), *Chinese Defense and Foreign Policy*, New York: Paragon House.

—— (1990), 'Chinese Foreign Policy after Tiananmen', *Current History* (September): 245–248, and 280–282.

—— (1991), *China In and Out of the Changing World Order*, Princeton: Center of International Studies, Princeton University.

—— (1992), 'Advancing the American Study of Chinese Foreign Policy', *China Exchange News*, 20 (3, 4) (Fall–Winter): 18–23.

—— (1994a), 'China and the World in Theory and Practice' and 'China and the Third World in the Changing World Order', in Samuel Kim (ed.), *China and the World*, 3rd edn., Boulder, Colo.: Westview Press.

—— (ed.) (1994b), *China and the World*, 3rd edn., Boulder, Colo.: Westview Press.

Kissinger, Henry (1969), 'Domestic Structure and Foreign Policy', in James Rosenau (ed.), *International Politics and Foreign Policy*, revised edn., New York: The Free Press.

Kleinberg, Robert (1990), *China's 'Opening' to the Outside World: The Experiment with Foreign Capitalism*, Boulder, Colo.: Westview Press.

Kohli, Atul, Peter Evans, Peter Katzenstein, Adam Przeworski, Susanne Rudolph, James Scott, and Theda Skocpol (1995), 'The Role of Theory in Comparative Politics: A Symposium', *World Politics*, 48 (1) (October): 1–49.

Kuan, John C. (1991), 'An Analysis of the KMT-CCP Cooperation and China Unification', paper presented at the annual meeting of the American Political Science Association, Washington, DC, 29 August–1 September.

Kuhn, Thomas, S. (1970), *The Structure of Scientific Revolution*, 2nd edn., Chicago: University of Chicago Press.

Lall, Arthur (1968), *How Communist China Negotiates*, New York: Columbia University Press.

Lampton, David M., and Catherine H. Keyser (eds.) (1988), *China's Global Presence: Economics, Politics, and Security*, Washington, DC: American Enterprise Institute in collaboration with the Institute of Southeast Asian Studies.

Lampton, David (1994), 'America's China Policy in the Age of the Finance Minister: Clinton Ends Linkage', *The China Quarterly*, 139 (September): 597–621.

Lardy, Nicholas (1994), *China in the World Economy*, Washington, DC: Institute for International Economics.

Laster, Martin (1984), *The Taiwan Issue in Sino-American Strategic Relations*, Boulder, Colorado: Westview Press.

Lee, Chae-Jin (1976), *Japan Faces China*, Baltimore: Johns Hopkins University Press.

—— (1984), *China and Japan: New Economic Diplomacy*, Stanford, Calif.: Hoover Institute Press.

Lee, Hong Yung (1991), *From Revolutionary Cadres to Party Technocrats in Socialist China*. Berkeley, Calif.: University of California Press.

Lee, Ngok (1991), 'The People's Liberation Army: Dynamics of Strategy and Politics', in Kuan Hsin-chi and Maurice Brosseau (eds.), *China Review*, Hong Kong: The Chinese University Press.

Leverson, Joseph (1968), *Confucian China and Its Modern Fate*, Berkeley: University of California Press.

Levine, Steven (1980), 'The Superpowers in Chinese Global Policy', in James Hsiung and Samuel Kim (eds.), *China and the Global Community*, New York: Praeger.

—— (1992), 'China and America: The Resilient Relationship', *Current History*, 91 (566) (September): 241–246.

Lewis, John, and Xue Litai (1988), *China Builds the Bomb*, Stanford, Calif.: Stanford University Press.
—— (1994), *China's Strategic Seapower: The Politics of Force Modernization in the Nuclea Age*, Stanford, Calif.: Stanford University Press.
Lewis, John, Hua Di, and Xue Litai (1991), 'Beijing's Defense Establishment: Solving the Arms-Export Enigma', *International Security*, 15 (4) (Spring): 87–109.
Li, Ping (1994), *Kaiguo zongli zhou enlai* [The Founding Premier Zhou Enlai], Beijing: Zhonggong zhongyang dangxiao chubanshe.
Li, Rui (1992), *Mao Zedong de zaonian yu wannian* [Mao Zedong's Early Years and Later Years], Guiyang: Guizhou renmin chubanshe.
—— (1993), *Lushan huiyi shilu* [The Record of the Lushan Conference], new edn., Hong Kong: Tiandi tushu [Cosmos Books].
Li, Zhisui (1994), *The Private Life of Chairman Mao: The Inside Story of the Man Who Made Modern China*, London: Chatto & Windus.
Liao, Kuang-sheng (1984), *Antiforeignism and Modernization in China, 1860–1980: Linkage Between Domestic Politics and Foreign Policy*, New York: St. Martin's Press.
Lieberthal, Kenneth (1984), 'Domestic Politics and Foreign Policy', in Harding (ed.), *China's Foreign Relations in the 1980s*, New Haven, Conn.: Yale University Press.
—— (1992), 'Introduction: The "Fragmented Authoritarianism" Model and Its Limitations', in Kenneth Lieberthal and David Lampton (eds.), *Bureaucracy, Politics, and Decision Making in Post-Mao China*, Berkeley, CA: University of California Press.
—— (1995), *Governing China*, New York: W. W. Norton.
Lieberthal, Kenneth, and Michel Oksenberg (1988), *Policy Making in China: Leaders, Structures, and Processes*, Princeton: Princeton University Press.
Lin, Biao (1965), *Renmin Zhanzheng Shengli Wansui* [Long Live the Victory of People's War], Beijing: Foreign Languages Press.
Lincoln, Edward (1993), *Japan's New Global Role*, Washington, DC: The Brookings Institution.
Little, Daniel (1989), *Understanding Peasant China: Case Studies in the Philosophy of Social Science*, New Haven and London: Yale University Press.
Liu, Xiao (1986), *Chushi sulian banian* [Eight Years as Ambassador to the Soviet Union], Beijing: Zhonggong dangshi ziliao chubanshe.
Loewenthal, Richard (1970), 'Development vs. Utopia in Communist Policy', in Chalmers Johnson (ed.), *Change in Communist Systems*, Stanford: Stanford University Press.
—— (1983), 'The Post-Revolutionary Phase in China and Russia', *Studies in Comparative Communism*, 16 (3) (Autumn): 191–203.
Lord, Winston (1995), 'A Sweet and Sour Relationship: An Interview with Winston Lord', *Current History* (September): 248–251.
Lukin, Alexander (1991), 'The Initial Soviet Reaction to the Events in China in 1989 and the Prospects for Sino-Soviet Relations', *The China Quarterly*, 125 (March): 119–136.
Macchiarola, Frank J., and Robert B. Oxnam (1991), *The China Challenge*, Boulder, Colo.: Westview Press.
MacFarquhar, Roderick (1983), *The Origins of the Cultural Revolution 2: The Great Leap Forward 1958–1960*, New York: Columbia University Press.
—— (ed.) (1993), *The Politics of China, 1949–1989*, Cambridge: Cambridge University Press.
Machiavelli, Niccolo (1950), *The Prince and the Discourses*, New York: Modern Library.
Madsen, Richard (1995), *China and the American Dream*, Berkeley, CA: University of California Press.
Malik, J. Mohan (1995), 'China–India Relations in the Post-Soviet Era: The Continuing Rivalry', *The China Quarterly*, 142 (June): 317–355.
Mancall, Mark (1984), *China at the Center: 300 Years of Foreign Policy*, New York: Free Press.

Mann, Michael (1986), *The Sources of Social Power*, Vol. 1, Cambridge: Cambridge University Press.

Mao, Tse-tung (Mao Zedong) (1961), *Selected Works of Mao Tse-tung*, Vol. 4, Beijing: Foreign Languages Press.

—— (1994), *Mao Zedong waijiao wenxun* [Selected Works of Mao Zedong on Foreign Policy], Beijing: Zhongyang wenxian chubanshe and shijie zhishi chubanshe.

Masumi, Junnosuke (1985), *Postwar Politics in Japan, 1945–1955*, Berkeley: Institute of East Asian Studies, University of California.

Maxwell, Neville (1970), *India's China War*, New York: Random House.

McKeown, Timothy (1986), 'The Limitations of "Structure" Theories of Commercial Policy', *International Organization*, 40 (1) (Winter): 43–64.

Medvedev, Roy (1986), *China and the Superpowers*, Oxford and New York: Basil Blackwell.

Meisner, Maurice (1977), *Mao's China: A History of the People's Republic*, New York: Free Press.

Merton, Robert, Ailsa Gray, Barbara Hockey, and Hanan Selvin (eds.) (1952), *Reader in Bureaucracy*, New York: The Free Press.

Miyushi, Osamu, and Shinkichi Eto (1972), *Chugoku hodo henko o truku* [Criticism on the Changing Report about China], Tokyo: Nisshin Hodo.

Moltz, James (1995), 'Regional Tensions in the Russo-Chinese Rapprochement', *Asian Survey*, 35 (6) (June): 511–527.

Montinola, Gabriella, Yingyi Qian, and Barry Weingast (1995), 'Federalism Chinese Style: The Political Basis for Economic Success in China', *World Politics*, 48 (1) (October): 50–81.

Morgenthau, Hans, and Kenneth Thompson (1985), *Politics Among Nations*, 6th edn., New York: Alfred Knopf.

Munch, Richard and Neil Smeleser (1987), 'Relating the Micro and Macro', in Jeffrey Alexander et al. (eds.), *The Micro-Macro Link*, Berkeley: University of California Press.

Nakamura, Robert, and Frank Smallwood (1980), *The Politics of Policy Implementation*, New York: St. Martin's.

Nathan, Andrew (1985), *Chinese Democracy*, Berkeley: University of California Press.

—— (1986), 'Sources of Chinese Rights Thinking', in R. Randle Edwards, Louis Henkin, and Andrew Nathan (eds.), *Human Rights in Contemporary China*, New York: Columbia University.

—— (1993), 'Is Chinese Culture Distinctive?', *The Journal of Asian Studies*, 52 (4) (November): 923–936.

—— (1994), 'Human Rights in Chinese Foreign Policy', *The China Quarterly*, 139 (September): 622–643.

Naughton, Barry (1994), 'The Foreign Policy Implications of China's Economic Development Strategy', in Thomas Robinson and David Shambaugh (eds.), *Chinese Foreign Policy: Theory and Practice*, Oxford: Oxford University Press.

Nee, Victor, and David Stark (1989), *Remaking the Economic Institutions of Socialism: China and Eastern Europe*, Stanford, Calif.: Stanford University Press.

Nelson, Harvey (1989), *Power and Insecurity: Beijing, Moscow and Washington, 1949–1988*, Boulder, Colo.: Lynne Rienner Publishers.

Nelsen, Harvey (1989), 'Continuity and Change in Chinese Strategic Deterrence', in June T. Dreyer and Lipyong J. Kim (eds.), *Chinese Defense and Foreign Policy*, New York: Paragon House.

Newby, Laura (1988), *Sino-Japanese Relations*, London and New York: Routledge.

Nishimoto, Takashi (1995), 'Riben dui zhongguo dalu de riyuan daikuan' [The Japanese Yen Loan to China], *Riben Zhanwang* [Japan Today], 39 (6) (June): 4–8.

Ng-Quinn, Michael (1983),'The Analytic Sense of Chinese Foreign Policy', *International Studies Quarterly*, 27 (2) (September): 203–224.

North, Robert C. (1978),*The Foreign Relations of China*, North Scituate, Mass.: Duxbury Press.

O'Brien, Kevin (1990), 'Is China's National People's Congress a Conservative Legislature?', *Asian Survey*, 30 (8) (August): 793–94.

Odell, John (1990), 'Understanding International Trade Policies and Emerging Successes', *World Politics*, 43 (1) (October): 139–167.

Odgen, Suzanne (1989), *China's Unresolved Issues: Politics, Development and Culture*, Englewood Cliffs, NJ: Prentice Hall.

Ogata, Sadako (1965), 'Japanese Attitudes Toward China', *Asian Survey*, 5 (8) (August): 389–398.

—— (1977), 'The Business Community and Japanese Foreign Policy: Normalization of Relations with the People's Republic of China', in Robert Scalapino (ed.), *The Foreign Policy of Modern Japan*, Berkeley: University of California Press.

—— (1988), *Normalization with China: A Comparative Study of US and Japanese Process*, Berkeley: Institute of East Asian Studies, University of California.

Oksenberg, Michel (1976), 'Mao's Policy Commitments, 1921–1976', *Problems of Communism* (November–December): 1–26.

—— (1986/87), 'China's Confident Nationalism', *Foreign Affairs*, 65, No. 3: 501–523.

—— (1991), 'The China Problem.' *Foreign Affairs*, 70 (3) (Summer): 1–16.

O'Leary, Greg (1980), *The Shaping of Chinese Foreign Policy*, New York: St. Martin's Press.

Olsen, Marvin, and Martin Marger (eds.) (1993), *Power in Modern Societies*, Boulder, Colo.: Westview.

Olson, Mancur (1990), 'The Logic of Collective Action in Soviet-Type Societies', *Journal of Soviet Nationalities*, 1 (2) (Summer): 8–27.

Orleans, Leo (1988), *Chinese Students in America: Policies, Issues and Numbers*, Washington DC: National Academy Press.

Orr, Robert (1990), *The Emergence of Japanese Foreign Aid Power*, New York: Columbia University Press.

Pareto, Vilfredo (1980), *Compendium of General Sociology*, Minneapolis: University of Minnesota Press.

Park, Yung (1976), 'The "Anti-Hegemony" Controversy in Sino-Japanese Relations', *Pacific Affairs*, 49 (3) (Fall): 476–490.

Parsons, Talcott (1937), *The Structure of Social Action*, New York: McGraw Hill.

—— (1982), *On Institutions and Social Evolution* (edited by Leon Mayhew), Chicago: University of Chicago Press.

Pearson, Margaret (1991), *Joint Ventures in the People's Republic of China*, Princeton: Princeton University Press.

Pei, Jianzhang (chief ed.) (1990), *Xinzhongguo weijiao fengyun* [The Diplomatic Activities of New China], Beijing: Shijie zhishi chubanshe.

Pei, Minxin (1994), *From Reform to Revolution: The Demise of Communism in China and the Soviet Union*, Cambridge: Harvard University Press.

Perkins, Dwight H. (1986), *China: Asia's Next Economic Giant?*, Seattle: University of Washington Press.

Pollack, Jonathan D. (1982), *The Sino-Soviet Rivalry and Chinese Security Debate*, Santa Monica, Calif.: The Rand Corporation.

—— (1984a), *The Lessons of Coalition Politics: Sino-American Security Relations*, Santa Monica, Calif.: The Rand Corporation.

—— (1984b), 'China and the Global Strategic Balance', in Harry Harding (ed.), *China's Foreign Relations in the 1980s*, New Haven: Yale University Press.

Polumbaum, Judy (1990/91), 'Dateline China: The People's Malaise', *Foreign Policy*, 81 (Winter): 163–181.

Putnam, Robert (1993), 'Diplomacy and Domestic Politics: The Logic of Two-Level Games', in Evans, Peter, Harold Jacobson, and Robert Putnam (eds.), *Double-Edged Diplomacy: International Bargaining and Domestic Politics*, Berkeley: University of California Press. It was originally published in *International Organization*, 42 (3) (Summer 1988).

Pye, Lucian (1961), 'The Non-Western Political Process', in James Rosenau (ed.), *International Politics and Foreign Policy*, New York: The Free Press.

—— (1975), 'The Confrontation between Discipline and Area Studies', in Lucian Pye, (ed.), *Political Science and Area Studies*, Bloomington: Indiana University Press.

—— (1977), 'Mao Tse-Tung's Leadership Style', *Political Science Quarterly*, 91 (summer).

—— (1981), *The Dynamics of Chinese Politics*, Cambridge, Mass.: Oelgeschlager, Gunn and Hain.

—— (1985), *Asian Power and Politics: The Cultural Dimensions of Authority*, Cambridge: The Belknap Press of Harvard University Press.

—— (1988), *The Mandarin and the Cadre: China's Political Cultures*, Ann Arbor: Center for Chinese Studies, The University of Michigan.

—— (1990), 'China: Erratic State, Frustrated Society', *Foreign Affairs* (Fall): 56–74.

—— (1991), 'Political Culture Revisited', *Political Psychology*, 12 (3) (September): 487–506 .

—— (1992), *The Spirit of Chinese Politics*, new edn., Cambridge: Harvard University Press.

Qian, Jiang (1987), *Pingpang waijiao shimo* [Ping Pong Diplomacy: The Beginning and End], Beijing: Dongfang chubanshe.

Qu, Xing (1994), 'Shilun dongou jubian he sulian jieti hou de zhongguo duiwai zhengce' [Chinese Foreign Policy After the Major Changes in Eastern Europe and the Disintegration of the Soviet Union], *Waijiao xueyuan xuebao* [Journal of Foreign Affairs College], 4: 16–22.

Quan, Yanchi (1989), *Mao Zedong yu heluxiaofu* [Mao Zedong and Khrushchev], Jilin: Changchun renmin chubanshe.

Quan, Yanchi, and Du Weidong (1990), *Gongheguo mishi* [China's Secret Envoys], Beijing: Guangming ribao chubanshe.

Rabinow, Paul, and William Sullivan (1979), *Interpretive Social Science: A Reader*, Berkeley: University of California Press.

Reardon-Anderson, James (1980), *Yenan and the Great Powers: The Origins of Chinese Communist Foreign Policy, 1944–1946*, New York: Columbia University Press.

Ritzer, George (1990), 'Micro-Macro Linkage in Sociological Theory: Applying a Metatheoretical Tool', in George Ritzer (ed.), *Frontiers of Social Theory*, New York: Columbia University Press.

Rix, Alan (1980), *Japan's Economic Aid*, New York: St. Martin's Press.

Roberts, Adam (1991) 'A New Age in International Relations?', *International Affairs*, 67 (3): 509–525.

Robinson, Thomas (1970), *The Sino-Soviet Border Dispute: Background, Development and the March 1969 Clashes*, Santa Monica, Calif.: Rand Corporation (Rand Rm-6171-PR).

—— (1994), 'Chinese Foreign Policy from the 1940s to the 1990s', in Thomas Robinson and David Shambaugh (eds.), *Chinese Foreign Policy: Theory and Practice*, Oxford: Oxford University Press.

Robinson, Thomas, and David Shambaugh (eds.) (1994), *Chinese Foreign Policy: Theory and Practice*, Oxford: Oxford University Press.

Rohrlich, Paul (1987), 'Economic, Cultural and Foreign Policy: The Cognitive Analysis of Economic Policy Making', *International Organization*, 41 (1) (Winter): 61–92.

Rong Zhi (1982), 'Two Views of Chinese Foreign Policy', *World Politics*, 34 (2) (January): 285–293.

Rosenau, James (1967), *Domestic Sources of Foreign Policy*, New York: The Free Press.

—— (ed.) (1969), *Linkage Politics: Essays on the Convergence of National and International Systems*, New York: The Free Press.

—— (1981), *The Study of Political Adaptation*, London: Frances Pinter.

—— (1990), *Turbulence in World Politics*, Princeton: Princeton University Press.

Ross, Madelyn (1994), 'China's International Economic Behaviour', in Thomas Robinson and David Shambaugh (eds.), *Chinese Foreign Policy: Theory and Practice*, Oxford: Oxford University Press.

Ross, Robert (1986), 'International Bargaining and Domestic Politics: U.S.–China Relations Since 1972', *World Politics*, 38 (2) (January): 255–287.

—— (1988), *The Indochina Tangle: China's Vietnam Policy, 1975–1979*, New York: Columbia University Press.

—— (1989), 'From Lin Biao to Deng Xiaoping: Elite Instability and China's US Policy', *The China Quarterly*, 118 (June): 263–299.

—— (1991), 'China Learns to Compromise: Change in US–China Relations, 1982–1984', *The China Quarterly*, 128 (December): 742–773.

—— (ed.) (1993), *China, the United States, and the Soviet Union*, Armonk, NY: M.E. Sharpe.

—— (1995), *Negotiating Cooperation: the United States and China: 1969–1989*, Stanford, Calif.: Stanford University Press.

Roth, Guenther, and Wolfgang Schluchter (1979), *Max Weber's Vision of History*, Berkeley: University of California Press.

Rozman, Gilbert (1985), *A Mirror for Socialism: Soviet Criticisms of China*, Princeton: Princeton University Press.

—— (1987), *The Chinese Debate about Soviet Socialism, 1978–1985*, Princeton: Princeton University Press.

—— (ed.) (1991), *The East Asian Region: Confucian Heritage and Its Modern Adaptation*, Princeton: Princeton University Press.

Salisbury, Harrison (1969), *War Between Russia and China*, New York: W. W. Norton.

Sandschneider, Eberhard (1990), 'The Chinese Army after Tiananmen', *Pacific Review*, 3 (2): 113–124.

Sautman, Barry (1994), 'Anti-Black Racism in Post-Mao China', *The China Quarterly*, 138 (June): 413–437.

Scalapino, Robert A., and Chen Qimao (eds.) (1986), *Pacific-Asian Issues: American and Chinese Views*, Berkeley: The Institute of East Asian Studies, University of California.

Scalapino, Robert A. (1987), *Major Power Relations in Northeast Asia*, Lanham, Md.: University Press of America.

—— (1989), *The Politics of Development: Perspectives on Twentieth-Century Asia*, Cambridge: Harvard University Press.

—— (1991/92), 'The United States and Asia: Future Prospects', *Foreign Affairs*, 70 (5) (Winter): 19–40.

Schaller, Michael (1979), *The United States and China in the Twentieth Century*, New York: Oxford University Press.

Schoenhals, Michael (1992), *Doing Things with Words in Chinese Politics*, Berkeley: Institute of East Asian Studies, University of California.

Schram, Stuart (1989), *The Thought of Mao Tse-Tung*, Cambridge and New York: Cambridge University Press.

Schwartz, Benjamin J. (1967), 'The Maoist Image of World Order', *International Affairs*, 11 (1): 92–102.

Schwartz, Morton (1975), *The Foreign Policy of the USSR: Domestic Factors*, Encino, Calif.: Dickenson Publishing Company.

Segal, Gerald, and William T. Tow (eds.) (1984), *Chinese Defense Policy*, Urbana and Chicago: University of Illinois Press.

Segal, Gerald (1994), 'China's Changing Shape', *Foreign Affairs*, 73 (3) (May/June): 43–58.

Senese, Donald J., and Diane D. Pikcunas (1989), *Can the Two Chinas Become One?*, Washington, DC: The Council for Social and Economic Studies.

Skinner, Quentin (ed.) (1985), *The Return of Grand Theory in the Human Sciences*, Cambridge: Cambridge University Press.

Shambaugh, David (1991), *Beautiful Imperialist: China Perceives America, 1972–1990*, Princeton: Princeton University Press.

—— (1992), 'Regaining Political Momentum: Deng Strikes Back', *Current History* (September): 257–259.

—— (1994), 'A Bibliographical Essay on New Sources for the Study of China's Foreign Relations and National Security', in Thomas Robinson and David Shambaugh (eds.), *Chinese Foreign Policy: Theory and Practice*, Oxford: Oxford University Press.

Shen, Zonghong, and Meng Zhaohui (chief eds.) (1990), *Zhongguo renmin zhiyuanjun kangmei yuanchao zhanshi* [History of the Chinese Volunteers' War Against the United States in Support of Korea], Beijing: Junshi kexue chubanshe.

Shichor, Yitzhak (1979), *The Middle East in China's Foreign Policy*, Cambridge: Cambridge University Press.

—— (1991), 'China and the Role of the United Nations in the Middle East: Revised Policy', *Asian Survey*, 31 (3) (March): 255–269.

Shih, Chih-yu (1990), *The Spirit of Chinese Foreign Policy: A Psychocultural View*, New York: St. Martin's Press.

—— (1993), *China's Just World: The Morality of Chinese Foreign Policy*, Boulder, Colo.: Lynne Rienner Publishers.

Shirk, Susan (1993), *The Political Logic of Economic Reform in China*, Berkeley: University of California Press.

—— (1994), *How China Opened Its Door*, Washington, DC: The Brookings Institution.

Simmons, Robert (1975), *The Strained Alliance: Peking, Pyongyang, Moscow and the Politics of the Korean War*, New York: Free Press.

Simon, Herbert (1985), 'Human Nature in Politics: The Dialogue of Psychology with Political Science', *American Political Science Review*, 79: 293–304.

Stinchcombe, Arthur (1987), *Constructing Social Theories*, Chicago: University of Chicago Press.

Stolper, Thomas (1985), *China, Taiwan, and the Offshore Islands*, Armonk, New York: M. E. Sharpe.

Story, Greg (1987), *Japan's Official Development Assistance to China*, Canberra, Australia: Research School of Pacific Studies, Australian National University.

Stuart, Douglas T., and William T. Tow (eds.) (1982), *China, the Soviet Union and the West: Strategic and Political Dimensions in the 1980s*, Boulder, Colo.: Westview Press.

Sun, Fusheng (1994), 'Zhanhou zhongguo yu dongnanya guojia guanxi de yanbian he fazhan' [The Evolution of Relations between China and South-East Asian Countries in the Post-War Era], *Waijiao xueyuan xuebao* [Journal of Foreign Affairs College], 37 (December): 9–15.

Sun, Yan (1994), *The Chinese Reassessment of Socialism, 1976–1992*, Princeton: Princeton University Press.

Suryadinata, Leo (1990), 'Indonesia-China Relations: A Recent Breakthrough', *Asian Survey*, 30 (7) (July): 682–696.

Susser, Bernard (1992), *Approaches to the Study of Politics*, New York: Macmillan.

Sutter, Robert (1983), *The China Quandary: Domestic Determinants of US China Policy, 1972–82*, Boulder, Colo.: Westview Press.

—— (1988), 'Implications of China's Modernization for East and Southeast Asian Security: The Year 2000', in David M. Lampton and Catherine H. Keyser (eds.), *China's Global Presence: Economics, Politics, and Security*, Washington, DC: American Enterprise Institute in collaboration with the Institute of Southeast Asian Studies.

Tagawa, Seiichi (1972), 'Hori kanjicho no seii o tou' [Questioning the Sincerity of Secretary General Hori], *Sekai* (March).

Tan, Qingshan (1990), 'The Politics of US Most-Favored-Nation Treatment to China: The Cases of 1979 and 1990', *Journal of Northeast Asian Studies*, 9 (1) (Spring): 41–59.

—— (1992), *The Making of US China Policy: From Normalization to the Post-Cold War Era*, Boulder, Colo.: Lynne Rienner.

Tanaka, Akihiko (1985), 'Bei-chu-so no aidade' [Surrounded by the US, China, and the USSR], in Akio Watanabe (ed.), *Sengo nihon no taigai seisaku* [Postwar Japanese foreign Policy], Tokyo: Yuhikaku.

Teiwes, Frederick C. (1974), 'Chinese Politics, 1949–1965: A Changing Mao', *Current Scene*, 12 (January and February): 1–15 and 1–18.

272   REFERENCES

—— (1984), *Leadership, Legitimacy, and Conflict in China: From a Charismatic Mao to the Politics of Succession*, Armonk, NY: M.E. Sharpe.

—— (1990), *Politics and Mao's Court: Gao Gang and Party Factionalism in the Early 1950s*, Armonk, NY: M.E. Sharpe.

Tian, Zengpei (ed.) (1993), *Gaige kaifang yilai de zhongguo waijiao* [Chinese Foreign Policy Since the Reform and Openness], Beijing: Shijie zhishi chubanshe.

Tow, William (ed.) (1991), *Building Sino-American Relations: An Analysis for the 1990s*, New York: Paragon.

—— (1994), 'China and the International Strategic System', in Thomas Robinson and David Shambaugh (eds.), *Chinese Foreign Policy: Theory and Practice*, Oxford: Oxford University Press.

Townsend, James (1999), 'Chinese Nationalism', *The Australian Journal of Chinese Affairs*, 27: 97–120.

Tretiak, Daniel (1978), 'The Sino-Japanese Treaty of 1978: The Senkakus Incident Prelude', *Asian Survey*, 18 (12) (December): 1235–1249.

Tsou, Tang, and Morton H. Halperin (1965), 'Mao Tse-Tung's Revolutionary Strategy and Peking's International Behavior', *American Political Science Review*, 59 (1) (March): 80–99.

Tsou, Tang (1986), *The Cultural Revolution and Post-Mao Reforms: A Historical Perspective*, Chicago: The University of Chicago Press.

—— (1994), *Ershi shiji zhongguo zhengzhi* [Twentieth Century Chinese Politics], Hong Kong: Oxford University Press.

Valencia, Mark (1995), *China and the South China Sea Disputes* (Adelphi Paper, no. 298), Oxford: Oxford University Press.

Van Ness, Peter (1970), *Revolution and Chinese Foreign Policy: Peking's Support for Wars of National Liberation*, Berkeley: University of California Press.

Verba, Sidney (1961), 'Assumptions of Rationality and Non-Rationality in Models of the International System', in Klaus Knorr and Sidney Verba (eds.), *The International System: Theoretical Essays*, Princeton: Princeton University Press.

Vertzberger, Yaacov (1984), *Misperceptions in Foreign Policymaking: The Sino-Indian Conflict, 1959–1962*, Boulder, Colo.: Westview.

Walder, Andrew G. (1986), *Communist Neo-Traditionalism: Work and Authority in Chinese Industry*, Berkeley: University of California Press.

Walsh, J. Richard (1988), *Change, Continuity and Commitment: China's Adaptive Foreign Policy*, Lanham, MD: University Press of America.

Waltz, Kenneth (1959), *Men, the State and War*, New York: Columbia University Press.

—— (1979), *Theory of International Politics*, Reading, Mass.: Addison-Wesley.

Wang, Bingnan (1985), *Zhong Mei Huitan jiunian huigu* [Review of the Nine-year-long Sino-American Ambassadorial Talks], Beijing: Shijie zhishi chubanshe.

Wang, Jisi (1994), 'International Relations Theory and the Study of Chinese Foreign Policy: A Chinese Perspective', in Thomas Robinson and David Shambaugh (eds.), *Chinese Foreign Policy: Theory and Practice*, Oxford: Oxford University Press.

Wang, Li (1993), *Xianchang lishi* [The Self-experienced History], Hong Kong: Oxford University Press.

Wedeman, Andrew Hall (1987), *The East Wind Subsides: Chinese Foreign Policy and the Origins of the Cultural Revolution*, Washington, DC: The Washington Institute Press.

Weiner, Myron, and Samuel P. Huntington (eds.) (1987), *Understanding Political Development*, Boston: Little, Brown.

Westad, Odd A. (1993), *Cold War and Revolution: Soviet–American Rivalry and the Origins of the Chinese Civil War*, New York: Columbia University Press.

Whiting, Allen S. (1960), *China Crosses the Yalu: The Decision to Enter the Korean War*, New York: The Macmillan Company.

—— (1972), 'The Use of Forces in Foreign Policy by the People's Republic of China',

The Annals of the American Academy of Political and Social Sciences, 402 (1972): 55–66.

—— (1975), *The Chinese Calculus of Deterrence: India and Indochina*, Ann Arbor: The University of Michigan Press.

—— (1977), 'Chinese Foreign Policy: A Workshop Report', SSRC Items 31 (March/June), quoted from James Hsiung, 'The Study of Chinese Foreign Policy: An Essay on Methodology', in James Hsiung and Samuel Kim (eds.), *China and the Global Community*, New York: Praeger, 1980.

—— (1979), *Chinese Domestic Politics and Foreign Policy in the 1970s*, Ann Arbor: Center for Chinese Studies, The University of Michigan.

—— (1989), *China Eyes Japan*, Berkeley: University of California Press.

—— (ed.) (1992), *China's Foreign Relations*, The Annals of the American Academy of Political and Social Science, 519, January.

—— (1995), 'Chinese Nationalism and Foreign Policy After Deng', *The China Quarterly*, 142 (June): 295–316.

Whyte, Martin K. (1989), 'Who Hates Bureaucracy? A Chinese Puzzle', in Victor Nee and David Stark (eds.), *Remaking the Economic Institutions of Socialism: China and Eastern Europe*, Stanford, Calif.: Stanford University Press.

Wich, Richard (1980), *Sino-Soviet Crisis Politics*, Cambridge, Massachusetts: Harvard University Press.

Wolfers, Arnold (1962), *Discord and Collaboration: Essays on International Politics*, Baltimore: The Johns Hopkins University Press.

Womack, Brantly (1987), 'The Party and the People: Revolutionary and Postrevolutionary Politics in China and Vietnam', *World Politics*, 39 (4) (July): 479–507.

Wu, Friedrich W. (1980), 'Explanatory Approaches to Chinese Foreign Policy: A Critique of the Western Literature', *Studies in Comparative Communism* (Spring): 41–62.

Wu, Samuel, and Bruce de Mesquita (1994), 'Assessing the Dispute in the South China Sea: A Model of China's Security Decision Making', *International Studies Quarterly*, 38 (3) (September): 379–403.

Wu, Xiuquan (1983), *Zai waijiaobu banian de jingli* [Eight Years at the Foreign Affairs Ministry], Beijing: Shijie zhishi chubanshe.

Wu, Xiuquan (1991), *Huiyi yu huainian* [Memoir], Beijing: Zhonggong zhongyang dangxiao chubanshe.

Wu, Yu-Shan (1994), 'Mainland China's Economic Policy Toward Taiwan: Economic Needs or Unification Scheme?', *Issues & Studies*, 30 (9) (September): 29–49.

Xie, Yixian (1993), *Waijiao zhihui yu moulue: xin zhongguo waijiao lilun he yuanze* [Diplomatic Wisdom and Strategy: The New China's Foreign Policy Theory and Principle], Zhengzhou: Henan renmin chubanshe.

Xu, Jiatun (1993), *Xu Jiatun huiyilu* [The Memoirs of Xu Jiatun], Hong Kong: Lianhebao.

Xu, Yan (1992), *Jinmen zhi zhan* [The Battle Over Quemoy], Beijing: Chinese Broadcast Television Publishing House.

—— (1993), *Zhongyin bianjie zhizhan lishi zhenxiang* [The True Historical Picture of the Border War between China and India], Hong Kong: Tiandi tushu (Cosmos Books).

Yahuda, Michael (1978), *China's Role in World Affairs*, London: Croom Helm.

—— (1983a), *Toward the End of Isolationism: China's Foreign Policy After Mao*, New York: St. Martin's.

—— (1983b), 'Perspectives on China's Foreign Policy', *The China Quarterly*, 95 (September): 534–540.

Yan, Xuetong (1994), 'Deng Xiaoping de guojia liyiguan' [Deng Xiaoping's View About National Interests], *Xiandai guoji guanxi* [Contemporary International Relations], 57 (July): 28–32.

Yang, Zhaoquan (1994), 'Zhongguo, chaoxian, hanguo guanyu zhongchao bianjie yange ji jiewu jiaoshe de yanjiu dongxiang' [Research on the Sino-Korean Border issues

Between China and North/South Korea], *Chinese Social Science Quarterly*, 8 (summer): 120–129.

Yang, Zuozhou (1993), *Nanhai fengyun* [The International Conflicts in the South China Sea], Taipei: Zhengzhong shuju.

Ye, Yumeng (1990), *Chubin chaoxian* [Send Troops to Korea], Beijing: Beijing shiyue wenyi chubanshe.

Yeh, K. C. (1992), 'Macroeconomic Issues in China in the 1990s', *The China Quarterly*, 131 (September): 501–544.

Yezhova, Galina, Viacheslav Lyubov, and Yuri Filatov (eds.) (1989), *USSR–China In the Changing World: Soviet Sinologists on the History and Prospects of Soviet–Chinese Relations*, Moscow: Novosti Press Agency Publishing House.

Yu, Bin (1994), 'The Study of Chinese Foreign Policy: Problems and Prospects', *World Politics*, 46 (2) (January): 235–261.

Yuan, Jie (1995), 'Nanwang de waijiao zhi lu' [The Unforgettable Diplomatic Missions], in Cheng Xiangjun (ed.), *Nü waijiaoguan* [Women Diplomats], Beijing: Renmin tiyu chubanshe.

Zagoria, Donald (1991), 'The End of the Cold War in Asia: Its Impact on China,' in Frank J. Macchiarola and Robert B. Oxnam (eds.), *The China Challenge*, New York: The Academy of Political Science.

Zelman, Walter (1967), *Chinese Intervention in the Korean War*, Berkeley: University of California Press.

Zhai, Qiang (1992), 'China and the Geneva Conference of 1954', *The China Quarterly*, 129 (March): 103–122.

Zhang, Zeshi (1988), *Wuo cong meijun jizhongying guilai* [I returned from the US Concentration Camp], Beijing: Zhongguo wenshi chubanshe.

Zhao, Quansheng (1989), 'One Country Two Systems and One Country Two Parties: PRC–Taiwan Unification and Its Political Implication', *The Pacific Review*, 2 (4): 312–319.

—— (1992), 'Domestic Factors of Chinese Foreign Policy: From Vertical to Horizontal Authoritarianism', *The Annals of the American Academy of Political and Social Science*, 519 (January): 159–176.

—— (1993a), *Japanese Policymaking — Informal Mechanisms and the Making of China Policy*, Westport, Conn: Praeger.

—— (1993b), 'Patterns and Choices of Chinese Foreign Policy', *Asian Affairs* 20 (1) (Spring): 1–5.

—— (1995), 'Achieving Maximum Advantage: Rigidity and Flexibility in Chinese Foreign Policy', *American Asian Review*, 13 (1) (Spring): 61–93.

Zhao, Quansheng, and Robert Sutter (eds.) (1991), *Politics of Divided Nations, China, Korea, Germany and Vietnam*, Baltimore: University of Maryland Law School.

Zhao, Ziyang (1987), 'Advance Along the Road of Socialism with Chinese Characteristics', in *Documents of the Thirteenth National Congress of the Communist Party of China*, Beijing: Foreign Languages Press.

Zhou, Enlai (1990), *Zhou Enlai waijiao wenxun* [Selected Works of Zhou Enlai on Foreign Policy], Beijing: Zhongyang wenxian chubanshe.

Zhu, Lin (1991), *Dashi furen huiyilu* [Memoirs of an Ambassador's Wife], Beijing: Shijie zhishi chubanshe.

Ziegler, Charles (1993), *Foreign Policy and East Asia: Learning and Adaptation in the Gorbachev Era*, Cambridge: Cambridge University Press.

Index

O'BRIEN, KEVIN, 88
Official Development Assistance (ODA),
32, 161, 175; from Japan to China,
148 passim; Japan's new ODA
principles, 168
Ogata, Sadako, 135
Ohira, Masayoshi, 124, 141, 151
Oksenberg, Michel, 5, 11, 13, 133
Olson, Mancur, 82
Olympic Games, 58, 154
Opium War, 46, 234
Organization for Economic Cooperation
and Development (OECD), 151
Ozawa, Ichiro, 171

PAAL, DOUGLAS, 113
Pakistan, 92, 98, 237
Pareto, Vilfredo, 22
Parsons, Talcott, 22
Partial nuclear test-ban agreement, 60
Pearson, Margaret, 154, 156, 245
Peng Dehuai, 83
Peng Zhen, 198
People's Liberation Army (PLA), 44, 96;
Defense White Paper, 99; military
budget, 93, 94; modernization of,
64, 217
People's University, 106
Perry, William, 193, 243
Persian Gulf War, 90, 96
Philippines, 45, 55, 205, 208, 211, 212
Ping-pong diplomacy, 83
Pollack, Jonathan, 12
Post-revolutionary state, 4
Power/regime macrostructure, 25, 115,
149, 170, 203, 239
Putnam, Robert, 19, 148, 175
Pye, Lucian, 13, 15, 230, 237

QIAN QICHEN: and ASEAN, 60, 94; and
economic development, 62; and
diplomacy, 79, 99, 138; and Japan,
171; power politics, 110; and Soviet
Union, 217; and Vietnam, 214; and
Zhou Enlai, 83
Qiao Guanghua, 29
Qiao Shi, 86
Qing Dynasty, 14, 125, 234

RADIO MOSCOW, 66
Ramos, Fidel, 212
Rao Sushi, 120
Reagan, Ronald, 131
Ritzer, George, 22–3, 244

Robinson, Thomas, 20, 116
Roh Tae Woo, 68
Romania, 55
Rosenau, James, 19, 20
Ross, Robert, 11, 12, 20, 247
Rozman, Gilbert, 11
Russia, 105, 125, 127, 215; see also
Sino-Russian relations

SAITO, EISHIRO, 171
Sanhe yishao (three reconciliations and
one reduction), 48
Sato, Eisaku, 139, 190, 192
Scalapino, Robert, 80, 242
Schifter, Richard, 100
School of realism, 9
Schram, Stuart, 116
Schwartz, Benjamin, 13
Scowcroft, Brent, 106
Segal, Gerald, 113 n31
Shambaugh, David, 11, 20
Shih, Chih-yu, 14
Shirk, Susan, 90, 104
Siew, Vincent, 208
Simon, Herbert, 28
Singapore, 136, 211, 213
Sino-ASEAN relations, 59–60, 161, 211;
disputes over South China Sea
Islands, 45, 61, 69, 186, 214, 235
Sino-British relations: concerning Hong
Kong's future, 64, 66, 88, 163, 240
Sino-French relations, 129
Sino-Indian relations: border war, 42–3
Sino-Japanese relations, 108, 137, 139,
151, 186; anti-hegemony, 192, 194;
cultural and social exchanges, 190;
Diaoyu (Senkaku), 69, 193–4;
economic relations, 188–9;
Guanghua Hostel, 195; Japanese
militarism, 161, 190–3; Memorandum Trade Agreement,
137; Sino-Japanese Peace Treaty
(1973), 193–4; 'textbook
controversy', 162, 191–2; three
political conditions, 136, 137;
see also Official Development
Assistance; Japan
Sino-Mongolian relations, 128
Sino-North Korea relations, 68, 197,
201; see also Korea
Sino-Russian relations, 216
Sino-South Korea relations, 68, 201;
economic relations, 197; see also
Korea

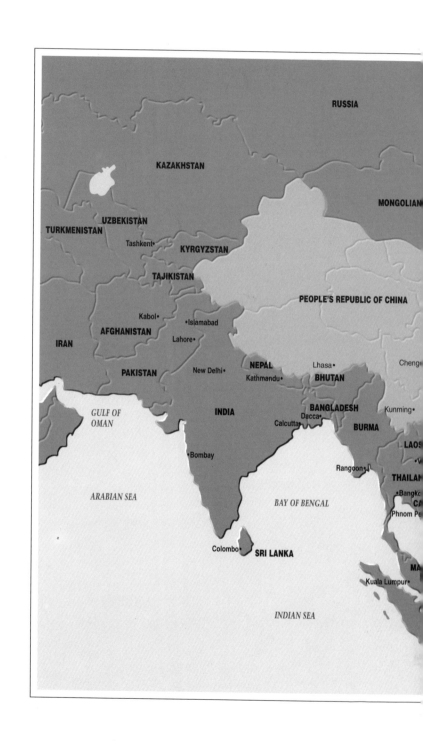